CW01622582

SOTHIS PRESS

Sothis Press aims to completely reimagine the public domain book with an emphasis on universal access to captivatingly designed print editions. We believe that technology will enable every single book ever published to be perpetually accessible in beautiful print form. Sothis is beauty in ubiquity.

www.sothis.press
1 Waterhouse Square, London, ECIN 2ST

Memorial De Sainte Helene

Journal of the Private Life and Conversations
of the Emperor Napoleon at
Saint Helena; Two Vols. In One

Emmanuel-Auguste-Dieudonné

SOTHIS PRESS

ISBN 978-1-0365-2626-9

Memorial De Sainte Helene
is in the public domain.

This edition is published by
 The company
is registered in England and Wales.
The Company Number is 14900389.

MEMORIAL DE SAINTE HELENE.

JOURNAL

OF THE

PRIVATE LIFE

AND

CONVERSATIONS

OF THE

EMPEROR NAPOLEON

AT SAINT HELENA.

BY

THE COUNT DE LAS CASES.

TWO VOLS. IN ONE.

LEXINGTON, K.

PRINTED BY THOMAS SMITH.

1823.

PREFACE.

Circumstances the most extraordinary have long kept me near the most extraordinary man of modern times. Admiration made me follow him without knowing him, and love attached me to him as soon as I did know him. The world is full of his glory, his deeds, and his monuments ; but no one knows the true shades of his character, his private qualities, or the natural disposition of his soul. This great void I undertake to fill up, and for such a task I possess advantages unexampled in history.

I collected and recorded, day by day, all that I saw of Napoleon, all that I heard him say during the period of eighteen months in which I was constantly about his person. In these conversations, which were full of confidence, and which seemed to pass, as it were, in another world, he could not fail to be portrayed by himself as if in a mirror, in every point of view, and under every aspect. Henceforth the world may freely study him : there can be no error in the materials.

The particulars here collected are, with regard to arrangement, in a state of great confusion ; they remain nearly in the order in which I noted them down at St. Helena. On recovering my manuscript, a short time ago, when it was restored to me by the

English Government, I at first intended to have arranged it in a new form and in a certain degree of connexion. But I was compelled to renounce this design: on the one hand, the state of my health prohibited application ; on the other, I felt myself controlled by time. I considered the speedy publication of my work as a sacred duty to the memory of him whose loss I deplore. I also hope it may afford pleasure to those who loved him, and force respect from those who were his enemies. Finally, I have a third and no less important object in this publication, namely, that it will afford an opportunity of defence to those who may find any thing stated in it of which they may imagine they have cause to complain : the public will judge, and history will speak, with greater certainty.

COUNT LAS CASES.

MY RESIDENCE

WITH

THE EMPEROR NAPOLEON

AT

ST. HELENA.

INTRODUCTION.

It is my intention to record daily all that the Emperor Napoleon did or said while I was about his person; but, before I commence my diary, I hope to be excused for offering a few preliminary remarks, which may be not altogether useless.

I never commenced the perusal of any historical work without first wishing to know the character of the author, his situation in society, and his political and domestic relations; in fact, all the important circumstances of his life; conceiving that nothing but a knowledge of these matters could furnish a key to his writings, or a safe ground of confidence in his statements. I therefore proceed to supply in my turn, that which I always sought for in others; and in presenting this diary, relate a few facts respecting my past life:

I was scarcely twenty-one years of age when the Revolution broke out, and had just been made a *Lieutenant de Vaisseau*, which corresponded with the rank of a field officer in the line; my family was at court, and I had been recently presented there myself. I was not rich; but my name and rank in life, together with my professional prospects, were likely, according to the calculating spirit of the times, to enable me to marry according to my wishes. It was at such a moment that our political troubles burst forth.

One of the principal vices in our system of admission to the service, was that of depriving us of the benefits of a solid and finished education. Withdrawn from school at the early age of fourteen, abandoned from that instant to ourselves, and launched, as it were, on a wide waste, how was it possible to attain the slightest notion of social organization, public rights, or the duties of civil life?

Thus, prompted by noble prejudice, rather than by a just sense of duty, above all led on by a natural fondness for generous resolves, I was amongst the first to hasten abroad and join our Princes; to save, as it was said, the Monarch from revolutionary fury, and to defend our hereditary rights, which we could not, it was asserted, yet abandon without shame. From the mode in which we had been educated, it required either a very strong head, or a very weak mind, to resist the torrent.

The emigration soon became general; this fatal measure is but too well known to Europe; nor can its folly, as a political blunder and a social crime, find any excuse in the present day, except in the unenlightened but upright character of most of those by whom it was undertaken.

Defeated on our own frontiers, discharged and disbanded by foreigners, rejected and proscribed by the laws of our country, numbers of us reached England, whose Ministers lost no time in landing on the shore of Quiberon. Being so fortunate as not to disembark, I had, after my return, time to reflect on the horrible alternative of fighting against our country under foreign banners; and, from this moment, my ideas, principles, and projects were either disconcerted or entirely changed.

Despairing of events, abandoning the world and my natural sphere, I devoted myself to study; and, under a borrowed name, went through a second course of education in attempting to assist that of others.

After a lapse of some years, the treaty of Amiens, and the amnesty offered by the First Consul, re-opened to us the gates of France. I had no longer any property there; the laws had disposed of my patrimony; but can any thing make us forget our native soil, or destroy the charm of breathing the air of our own country!

I hurried back, and was grateful for a pardon, rendered more acceptable, since I could say with pride I received it without having any motives of self-reproach. When monarchy was proclaimed soon after, my situation and sentiments were of the most singular description. I found myself a soldier, punished for a cause that had triumphed. Every day brought us back to our former ideas; all that had been dear to our principles and prejudices was renewed; and yet delicacy and honour rendered it a kind of duty in us to keep at a distance.

It was in vain that the new government loudly proclaimed the union of all parties; and equally so, that its chief had declared he would no longer recognize any but Frenchmen in France; in vain had old friends and former companions offered me the advantages of a new career to be chosen by myself. Unable to subdue the conflicting feelings which agitated my mind, I obstinately persevered in a system of self-denial; and devoting all my time to literature, I composed, under a feigned name, an historical work that re-established my fortune; after which, I passed five or six of the happiest years of my life.

Meanwhile, unprecedented events succeeded each other with extraordinary rapidity; they were of such a nature, and bore so peculiar a character, that it became impossible for any person whose heart possessed the least predilection for whatever was great or noble, to view them with indifference. The glory of our country was raised to a pitch unknown in the history of any other people; the administration of affairs was unexampled, not less by its energy than the consequences it produced; a simultaneous impulse, which was suddenly given to every species of industry, excited the emulation of all at the same moment; the army was unrivalled, striking terror abroad and creating a just pride at home.

Every day added to the number of our trophies, while numerous monuments proclaimed our exploits; the victories of Austerlitz, Jena, and Friedland; the treaties of Presburgh and Tilsit had constituted France the first of nations, and made her the arbitress of Europe. It was a signal honour to be a Frenchman; and yet all these exploits, labours, and prodigies, were the work of one man. For my own part, whatever might have been my former prepossessions and prejudices, I was now filled with admiration; and, as we all know, there is but one step from admiration to affection.

It was precisely at this period that the Emperor called some of the first families of France round his throne, causing it to be circulated amongst the rest, that he would consider those who remained aloof as bad Frenchmen. I did not hesitate for an instant; I have, said I to myself, fulfilled the obligation of my natural oath, that of my birth and education, to which I have continued faithful until its extinction. Our princes, too, were no longer thought of; we even doubted their existence. The solemnities of religion, the alliance of Kings, all Europe and the splendour of France, henceforth taught me that I had a new sovereign. Had those who preceded us, made so long a resistance to such powerful efforts, before rallying round the first of the Capets? I answered therefore for myself, that, happy in being thus enabled to obey a call which removed me with honour from the delicate situation in which I was placed, I freely and spontaneously transferred the zeal, loyalty, and attachment which I had constantly cherished for my old masters, to the new sovereign; the result of this step was my immediate admission at court.

In this state of things, I felt extremely anxious that my recent protestations should be ratified by deeds. The English had invaded Flushing and threatened Antwerp; I therefore hastened to assist in the defence of the latter place as a volunteer; and, on the subsequent evacuation of Flushing, my nomination to the office of chamberlain called me near the person of the Emperor. Being desirous of adding some more useful occupation to the duties of this honourable post, I solicited and obtained a seat in the Council of State. Hence followed several confidential missions: I was sent to Holland at the period of its union to the French Empire, in order to receive whatever related to the naval department; then to Illyria for the purpose of liquidating the public debt; and afterwards over half the Empire to superintend establishments of public beneficence. During our late misfortunes, I received some consoling proofs, that the inhabitants of the countries to which I had thus been sent, were not dissatisfied with my conduct.

Providence had however placed a limit to our prosperity. The catastrophe of Moscow, the disasters of Leipsic, and the siege of Paris, are well known. I commanded in that city one of the legions which acquired honours by its severe losses on the 31st of March. When the capitulation took place I gave up the command, feeling that other duties were to be performed near the person of my sovereign, but could not reach Fontainbleau in time:—the Emperor had abdicated, and was succeeded by the King.

My situation now became more singular than it had been twelve years before. The cause for which I had sacrificed my fortune, for which I remained so long in exile, and six years in a state of self-denial at home, was at length triumphant; but, nevertheless, the point of honour and other considerations were about to prevent my reaping any benefit from the event! What could be more capricious than my fate? Two revolutions had been effected in opposition to each other:—by the first I lost my patrimony; by the second I might have been deprived of life: neither one nor the other had been favourable to my fortune. Vulgar minds will only perceive an unfortunate tergiversation of opinions in this wayward destiny, while the lovers of intrigue will assert that I was twice a dupe: only the few will comprehend my motives, and do justice to my actions. Be this as it may, those early friends, whose esteem was not lessened by the line of conduct I had pursued, having now become all powerful, invited me to join them: it was impossible to obey the generous call; disgusted and disheartened, I resolved that my public life should terminate. Ought I to have exposed myself to the false judgment of those who were watching my proceedings? Could every body see what was passing in my mind.

Having now become a Frenchman even to enthusiasm, and unable to endure that national degradation of which I was a daily witness amidst foreign bayonets, I determined to endeavour to divert my thoughts at a distance from the scene of calamity. Having, therefore, gone to pass a few months in England, how altered did every thing appear there? On reflection, I found that it was myself who had undergone a great change.

I had scarcely returned, when Napoleon appeared on our coasts: he was transported to the capital as it were by magic, and this without battles, excesses, or effusion of blood. I thought I saw the stain brought on us by foreign hands effaced, and all our glory restored. Destiny had ordered otherwise!

No sooner did I hear of the Emperor's arrival, than I spontaneously repaired to attend on his person. I was present at the abdication; and, when the question of his removal was agitated, I requested permission to participate in his fate. Such had been till then the disinterestedness and simplicity, some will say folly, of my conduct, that, notwithstanding my daily intercourse as an officer of the household and member of his council, Napoleon scarcely knew me. "Do you know whither your offer may lead you?" said he, in his astonishment. "I have made no calculation about it," I replied. He accepted me, and I am at St. Helena.

I have now made myself known; the reader has my credentials in his hand: a host of contemporaries are living—it will be seen whether a single individual amongst them stands up to invalidate them: I therefore begin my task.

Return of the Emperor to the Elysée, after the Battle of Waterloo.

Tuesday, June 20th, 1815.—Heard of the Emperor's return to the Elysée Palace: placed myself in immediate attendance there. Found M M. Montalembert and Montholon there, brought by the same sentiment.

Napoleon had just lost a great battle; so that the safety of the nation thenceforth depended on the wisdom and zeal of the Chamber of Representatives. The Emperor, still covered with dust from the field of Waterloo, was on the point of hurrying into the midst of them, there to expose our dangers and resources, and to declare that his personal interests should never be a barrier to the happiness of France, thence to quit Paris immediately. It is said that several persons dissuaded him from this step, by leading him to apprehend an approaching ferment amongst the deputies.

It is as yet impossible to comprehend every report that circulates with regard to this fatal battle: some say there is manifest treason; others, a fatality, without example. Thirty thousand men under Grouchy lost their way and were too late, taking no part in the engagement; the army, victorious till the evening, was it is said suddenly seized with a panic towards eight o'clock, and became broken in an instant. It is another Crecy, another Azincourt, ———!* every one trembles and thinks all is lost!

The Abdication.

21st.—The best intentioned and most influential members of the national representation, have been tampered with all last evening and all last night by certain persons, who, if their word is to be taken produce authentic documents and demi-official papers guaranteeing the safety of France, by the mere abdication of the Emperor as they pretend.

The above opinion had become so strong this morning, that it seemed irresistible: the president of the assembly, the first men in the state, and the Emperor's particular friends, come to supplicate that he will save France by abdicating. Though by no means convinced, yet the Emperor answers with magnanimity:—he abdicates!

This circumstance causes the greatest bustle round the Elysée; the multitude rushes towards the gate, and testifies the deepest interest; numbers penetrate within the hall, while some even of the popular class scale the walls; some in tears, others in a state approaching to distraction,

* I had put in the text, *une veritable journee des Eperons*,† (a real day of spurs) and must not omit to state what led to its being expunged.

The Emperor who alone knew I kept a journal at St. Helena, one day expressed a wish that I should read a few pages to him: on coming to this expression, inadvertently thrown in, he suddenly exclaimed, "What have you done! Erase, erase, sir quickly! *Une journee des Eperons!* what a calumny! a day of spurs!" said he again, "ah! unfortunate army! brave men! you never fought better!" Then after a pause of a few moments, he added in a tone expressive of deep feeling:—"We had some great poltroons amongst us! May heaven forgive them! But as to France, will *she* ever surmount the effects of that ill-fated day!"

† In allusion to the battle of Guinegate, fought near Boulogne in 1513, between the army of Henry VIII and that of France. The French were completely routed on this occasion, and the celebrated Bayard taken prisoner while covering the retreat; this was so precipitate that the day was ever after styled *La journee des Eperons*, (or day of spurs,) because, as stated by contemporary historians, the French army made more use of their spurs than lances.—*Editor.*

crowd up to the Emperor, who is walking tranquilly in the garden, and make offers of every description. Napoleon alone is calm, constantly replying that they should in future apply this zeal and tenderness to the good of their country.

I presented the deputation of Representatives, in the course of the day: it came to thank the Emperor for his devotedness to the national interests.

The documents and state-papers, which have produced such a powerful sensation, and brought about the grand event of this day, are said to be official communications of M M. Fouché and Metternich, in which the latter guarantees Napoleon II. and the regency, in case of the abdication of the Emperor. These communications must have been long carried on unknown to Napoleon. M. Fouché must have a furious partiality for clandestine operations. It is well known that his first disgrace, which took place several years ago, arose from his having opened some negotiations with England of his own accord, without the Emperor's knowledge: he has in fact always shown the greatest obliquity in affairs of moment. Grant that his present mysterious acts do not prove fatal to our country!

Deputation of the Chamber of Peers—Caulaincourt—Fouché.

22d.—Went home to pass a few hours at my own house; in the course of this day the deputation of the Peers was presented: a portion of the Provisional Government was named in the evening. Caulaincourt and Fouché, who were of the number, happened to be with us in the antichamber: we complimented the first on his nomination, which was, indeed, only to congratulate ourselves on the public good: his reply was full of alarm. "We applaud the choice hitherto made," said we. "It is certain," observed Fouché with an air of levity, "that I am not suspected."—"If you had been," rudely rejoined the deputy Boulay de la Meurthe, who was also present, "be assured we should not have named you."

The Provisional Government presented to the Emperor.

23d and 24th.—The acclamations and interest without, continued at the Elysée. I presented the members of the Provisional Government to the Emperor, who, in dismissing them, directed the Duke Decrès to see them out. The Emperor's brothers, Joseph, Lucien, and Jerome, were introduced frequently through the day, and conversed with him for some time.

As usual, there was a great multitude of people collected round the palace in the evening: their numbers were constantly increasing. Their acclamations and the interest shown for the Emperor created considerable uneasiness amongst the different factions. The fermentation of the capital now became so great, that Napoleon determined to depart on the following day.

The Emperor quits the Elysée.

25th.—I accompanied the Emperor to Malmaison, and again requested permission to follow his future fortunes. My proposal seemed to create astonishment, for I was still only known to him by my employments; but he accepted the offer.

26th.—My wife came to see me; she had divined my intentions: it became a somewhat delicate task to avow them, and still more difficult to convince her of their propriety. "My dear friend," said I, "in following the dutiful dictates of my heart, it is consoling to reflect that your interests are not thereby prejudiced. If Napoleon II. is to govern us, I leave you strong claims to his protection; should heaven order it differently, I shall have secured you a glorious asylum, a name honoured with some esteem. At all events we shall meet again, at least in a better world." After tears and even reproaches, which could not but be gratifying, she consented to my departure, exacting a promise however, that I would allow her to join me without loss of time. From this moment, she manifested a courage and strength of mind, that would have animated myself in case of necessity.

The Minister of Marine comes to Malmaison.

27th.—I went to Paris for a short time, with the Minister of Marine, who came to Malmaison, on business respecting the frigates destined for the Emperor. He read me the instructions drawn out for the commanders, said his Majesty depended on my zeal, and intended taking me with him; adding, that he would take care of my family during my absence.

Napoleon II. is proclaimed by the Legislature.

Sent for my son to his school, having determined that he should accompany me. We prepared a small parcel of clothes and linen, then proceeded to Malmaison accompanied by my wife, who returned immediately. The road had now become rather unsafe owing to the approach of the enemy.

28th.—Being desirous to make some other arrangements before our departure, the Duchess de Rovigo took me and my son to Paris in her carriage. I found M M. de Vertillac and de Quitry at my house; these were the last friends I embraced; they were terrified. The agitation and uncertainty hourly increased in the capital, for the enemy was at the gates. On reaching Malmaison, we saw the bridge of Chatou in flames; guards were posted round the palace, and it became prudent to remain within the park walls. I went into the Emperor's room, and described how Paris had appeared to me; stating the general opinion that Fouché openly betrayed the national cause; and that the hopes of all patriots were, that his Majesty would this very night join the army, who loudly called for him. The Emperer listened to me with an air of deep thought, but made no reply, and withdrew soon after.

Napoleon quits Malmaison, and departs for Rochfort.

29th and 30th.—A cry of long live the Emperor! was continually heard on the great road to St. Germain: it proceeded from the troops who passed under the walls of Malmaison.

Towards noon General Becker came from Paris, sent by the Provisional Government; he told us with feelings of indignation, that he had received a commission to guard and watch Napoleon.*

* On my return to Europe chance threw the following documents in my way, relative to the above circumstance. I transcribe them here because I believe they are unknown to the public. They have been copied from the originals, and require no commentary.

Copy of a letter from the Commission of Government to Marshal Prince d'Eckmuhl, Minister at War.

Paris, June 27th, 1815.

Sir,—Such is the state of affairs, that it is indespensable for Napoleon to decide on departing and proceeding to the Isle of Aix. If he does not determine to do, so on your notifying to him the annexed resolutions, you are to cause him to be watched at Malmaison to prevent his escape. For this purpose, you will place a requisite portion of gendarmerie and troops of the line, at the disposal of General Becker, so as to guard all the avenues leading to Malmaison in every direction. You will give orders to the chief inspector of gendarmerie to this effect. These measures must be kept as secret as possible.

This letter is intended for yourself; but General Becker, who will be charged with delivering the resolutions to Napoleon, will receive particular instructions from your excellency, and inform Napoleon that they have been drawn up with a view to the interest of the state, and for the safety of his person; that their prompt execution is indispensable; and finally, that his future interests make them absolutely necessary

(Signed) THE DUKE OF OTRANTO.

Copy of the resolutions entered into by the Commission of Government, extracted from the Minutes of the Secretary of State's department.

Paris, June 26th, 1815.

The Commission of Government resolves as follows:

Art. I. The Minister of Marine shall give orders for two frigates to be prepared at Rochfort, to convey Napoleon Bonaparte to the United States.

Art. II. Should he require it, a sufficient escort shall attend him to the place of embarkation under the orders of Lieutenant-General Becker, who will be instructed to provide for his safety.

Art. III. The Director-general of Posts will, on his part, give the necessary orders relative to the relays.

A sentiment the most base had dictated this choice; Fouché knew that General Becker had a private pique against the Emperor, and therefore did not doubt of finding in the former, one disposed to vengeance; it would be impossible for any man more groossly to deceive himself, as this officer constantly showed a degree of respect and attachment highly honourable to his own character.

Meanwhile time passed. When on the point of setting out, the Emperor sent a message to the Provisional Govern-

Art. IV. The Minister of Marine will issue the requisite orders for insuring the immediate return of the frigates, after the disembarkation.

Art. V. The frigates are not to quit Rochfort before the arrival of the safe-conducts.

Art. VI. The Ministers of Marine, War, and Finances, are each charged with the execution of that part of the present resolutions which concerns them respectively.

Signed, THE DUKE OF OTRANTO.

By order of the Commission of Government, the Assistant Secretary of State.

Signed, COUNT BERLIER.

Copy of the Duke of Otranto's letter to the Minister at War.

Paris, June 27th, 1815, at noon.

Sir—I transmit to you a copy of the letter I have just written to the Minister of Marine, relative to Napoleon. A perusal of it will convince you of the necessity of giving orders to general Becker not to separate himself from the person of Napoleon, whilst the latter remains in the roads of Aix.

Signed, THE DUKE OF OTRANTO.

Copy of the letter to the Minister of Marine alluded to in the foregoing.

Paris, June 27th, 1815, noon.

Sir,—The Commission reminds you of the instructions it transmitted to you an hour ago. The resolutions must be executed as prescribed by the Commission yesterday; and according to which, Napoleon Bonaparte will remain in the roads of Aix until the arrival of his passports.

The welfare of the State, which cannot be indifferent to him, requires that he should remain there until his fate and that of his family has been definitively regulated. Every means will be employed to render the result of the negotiation satisfactory to him. The honour of France is interested in it; but, in the meantime, all possible precautions must be taken for the personal security of Napoleon, and that he does not quit the place which is temporarily assigned him.

The President of the Commission of Government.

Signed, THE DUKE OF OTRANTO.

Letter from the Minister at War, to General Becker.

Paris, June 27th, 1815.

Sir,—I have the honour of transmitting to you the annexed resolutions which the Commission of Government charges you to notify to the Emperor Napoleon; observing to his Majesty that circumstances are so imperious as to make it indispensable he should decide on setting out for the Isle of Aix. These resolutions, observes the Commission, have been made as much for the safety of his person, as for the interest of the State, which must ever be dear to him.

If his Majesty does not make up his mind, on these resolutions being notified to him, it is the intention of the Commission of Government, that the necessary steps shall be taken to prevent the escape of his Majesty, and every attempt against his person

I have to repeat, General, that these resolutions have been adopted for the interest of the state, and for the personal safety of the Emperor; also, that the Commission of Government considers their prompt execution as indispensable for the future welfare of his Majesty and his family.

I have the honour to be, &c.

N. B. The above letter remained without any signature; at the moment of sending it off, the Prince of Eckmuhl observed to his secretary, "I will never sign this letter—sign it yourself, that will be sufficient." The secretary expressed himself equally incapable of putting his name to such a communication. Was it sent or not?—this is a point which I cannot decide.

ment, by General Becker, offering to place himself at the head of the army, merely in the rank of a citizen, adding, that after having repulsed Blucher, he would continue his route. On the refusal of this offer, we left Malmaison; the Emperor and a part of his suite taking the road to Rochfort by Tours; I and my son, with Messieurs Montholon, Planat, and Résigny, proceeded towards Orleans, as also two or three other carriages. We reached this place early on the 30th, and got to Chatellerault at midnight.

July 1st and 2d.—We passed through Limoges on the 1st, at four in the afternoon; dined at Rochefaucault on the 2d, and reached Jarnac about seven. We slept here, owing to the obstinacy of the post-master, which forced us to remain till next day.

3d.—We could not set out before five o'clock. On account of the misconduct of the post-master, who not content with detaining us all night had recourse to secret means for keeping us still longer; we were obliged to proceed almost at full speed to Cognac, where the post-master and inhabitants received us very differently. It was easy to perceive that our journey occasioned a great deal of agitation amongst all parties. On reaching Saintes, towards eleven o'clock, we nearly fell victims to the fury of some miscreants, collected by an officer of the royal guard, a native of that place, whom Napoleon's return had displaced. This person had prepared an ambuscade for us, and had even laid a plan for our assassination. We were arrested by them, but a part of the national guard interfered, and conducted us as prisoners to an adjoining inn. It was said that we were carrying off the treasures of the State, and therefore merited death. Some of them, who pretended to be the most distinguished inhabitants, and above all, the women, were the most outrageous, and called for our immediate execution.

We saw these females defile in succession before some windows that were open near our temporary prison, in order that their insults should not be lost on us. It will scarcely be credited that they went so far as to grind their teeth in sign of hatred, and from vexation at seeing the indifference we displayed; yet they formed the fashionable circle of Saintes! Could Real be in the right, when he told the Emperor, during the hundred days, that as for jacobins, he had a right to know something of them; protesting that the only difference between the blacks and whites was, that the former wore wooden shoes and the latter silk stockings.

Prince Joseph, who was passing through Saintes unknown to us, came to increase the interest of our adventure. He was also arrested, and conducted to the Prefecture; but highly respected

The windows of the inn faced a large square, which continued to be filled with an agitated and hostile rabble, who were extremely violent and abusive. I found an old acquaintance in the underprefect, who was thus enabled to state who we were. The carriage in which we travelled was next examined; while we were ourselves retained in a species of solitary confinement. I obtained leave, however, to visit the Prince about four o'clock.

While on my way to the prefecture, and though guarded by a non-commissioned officer, several individuals addressed me: some put notes secretly into my hands; others whispered something friendly; while all united in assuring me we might feel perfectly tranquil, for the patriots and well-intentioned inhabitants would protect us.

Towards the evening we were allowed to depart; and by this time things had so totally changed, that we left the inn amidst the most lively acclamations; females of the lower classes, in tears, kissed our hands; many persons offered to accompany us, that we might avoid the enemies of the Emperor, who, they said, lay in wait to murder us, at a short distance from the town. This singular transition was in some degree due to the arrival of numbers of country people and federates, who gave an immediate turn to public opinion.

4th.—On approaching Rochefort we met a party of gendarmerie, who, on the report of our reception at Saintes, had been despatched to meet us. We arrived at this place about two o'clock in the morning: the Emperor had reached it on the preceding evening.* Prince Joseph arrived in the afternoon; when I conducted him to the Emperor.

I profited by the first moment of leisure to inform the President of the Council of State why I absented myself. "Rapid and important events," said I, "obliged me to quit Paris without the necessary leave of absence. The peculiarity and importance of the case led to this irregularity: being in attendance on the Emperor at the moment of his departure, it was impossible to see the great man, who had governed us with so much splendour, and who banished himself to facilitate the tranquillity of France, of whose power nothing now remains but its glory and name;—I repeat, that I could not allow him to depart without yielding to the desire of following his steps. During the days of his prosperity he condescended to bestow some favours on me; I now owe him all that I can offer, whether of sentiment or of action."

* The following is the Emperor's Itinerary during the journey:—Left Paris on the 29th June, and slept at Rambouillet; at Tours on the 30th; and at Niort on the 1st July. Left Niort on the 2d, and reached Rochefort on the 3d; remained there till the 8th; embarked on board the Bellerophon on the 15th.

5th—7th.—At Rochefort the Emperor no longer wore a military dress. He lived at the prefecture: numbers were constantly grouped round the house: and acclamations continued to be frequently repeated. The Emperor appeared two or three times at the balcony. Numerous proposals were made to him, both by generals who came in person, and others who sent emissaries.

During our stay here, the Emperor has led the same sort of life as if at the Thuilleries: we do not approach his person more frequently: he scarcely receives any persons but Bertrand and Savary; so that we are reduced to reports and conjectures as to all that concerns him. It is however, evident, that, in the midst of this state of agitation, he continues calm and resolute, even to indifference, without manifesting the least anxiety.

A lieutenant of our navy, who commands a Danish merchant-ship, has generously offered to save the Emperor. He proposes to take him on board alone: engages to conceal his person in such a way that it will escape the severest scrutiny; and moreover, will immediately set sail for the United States. He demands but a small sum by way of indemnifying his owners for any loss they may sustain through his enterprise. Bertrand agrees under certain conditions which he has drawn out in my name. I have signed this fictitious bargain in presence, and under the eyes, of the maritime prefect.

Embarkation of the Emperor.

8th—The Emperor proceeded to Fouras in the evening, followed by the acclamations of the people wherever he passed. He slept on board the Saal,* which he reached about eight o'clock. I did not arrive till a much later hour, having had to accompany Madame Bertrand in another boat, and from a different point.

9th.—I attended the Emperor, who disembarked at an early hour in the Isle of Aix: he visited all the fortifications, and returned on board to breakfast.

10th.—I was despatched towards the British cruisers, with the duke de Rovigo, early in the morning, to know whether they had received the passes, which had been promised to us by the Provisional Government, to proceed to the United States. The answer was, that they had not; but that the matter should be instantly referred to the commander-in-chief. Having stated the supposition of the emperor's setting sail with the frigates under flags of truce, it was replied, that they would be attacked. We then spoke

* The name of one of the frigates destined to receive Napoleon on board.—Ed.

of his passage in a neutral bottom; and were told in reply, that all neutrals would be strictly examined, and, perhaps, even conducted to an English port; but we were recommended to proceed to England; and it was asserted that in that country we should have no ill usage to fear. We returned at two in the afternoon.

The Bellerophon, having followed, soon after anchored in Basque Roads, in order to be nearer us; so that the ships of both nations were now in view of and very near each other.

On reaching the Bellerophon, the captain had addressed us in French: I was not eager to inform him that I knew something of his own language. Some expressions which passed between him and his officers might have injured the negotiation, had I seemed to understand them. When, a short time after, it was asked, whether we understood English, I allowed the Duke of Rovigo to reply in the negative. Our situation was quite sufficient to remove any scruples I might have otherwise entertained, rendering this little deception very pardonable. I only mention this circumstance, because, as I remained a fortnight amongst these people, I was compelled to impose a tiresome restraint upon myself, to avoid disclosing what I had concealed in the first instance. In fact, though I could read the language with facility, yet, owing to an absence of thirteen years, and consequent want of practice, it was with considerable difficulty I understood English when spoken.

11th.—All the outlets being blockaded by English ships of war, the Emperor seemed extremely uncertain as to which plan he would pursue. Neutral vessels, and *chasse-marées*,* manned by young naval officers, were suggested for his conveyance; propositions also continued to be made from the interior.

12th.—The Emperor disembarked at the Island of Aix, amidst cries of exultation on every side. He quitted the frigates in consequence of the commandant's having refused to sail; whether from weakness of character, or owing to his having received fresh orders from the Provisional Government, is not known. Many were of opinion that the attempt might be made with some probability of success; but it must be allowed that the winds still continued unfavorable.

13th.—Prince Joseph visited his brother in the course of the day. Towards eleven at night the Emperor was on the point of embarking in one of the chasse-marées: two having been prepared, and some property and attendants already on board. M. de Planat was in one of them.

* Small vessels not unlike luggers, and usually employed as coasting vessels in France.—Ed.

14th.—I returned to the Bellerophon at four in the morning, accompanied by General Lallemand, to ascertain whether any answer had been received. The Captain told us he expected it every moment; adding, that if the Emperor would embark immediately for England, he had instructions to convey him thither. He still farther declared it as his private opinion, and several captains who were present expressed themselves to the same effect, that there was not the least doubt of Napoleon's meeting with all possible respect and good treatment; that there, neither the king nor his ministers exercised the same arbitrary authority as those of the Continent; that the English people possessed a generosity of sentiment and liberality of opinion, far above sovereignty itself. I replied, that I would return and communicate the Captain's offer to the Emperor, as well as the whole of his conversation. I added, that I thought I had a sufficient knowledge of the Emperor Napoleon's character to induce a belief, that he would not feel much hesitation in proceeding to England thus confidentially, so as to be able to continue his voyage to the United States. I described all France, south of the Loire, as being in a blaze; stated the propositions hourly made to him from various directions; his determination not to become either the cause or pretext of a civil war; the generosity shewn by him in abdicating, merely to render the conclusion of a peace more easy; and the firm resolution he had taken, to banish himself in order to make it more prompt and complete.

General Lallemand, who, from having been condemned to death, was interested on his own account in the determination that might be made, asked Captain Maitland, whom he formerly knew in Egypt, and whose prisoner, I think, he had been, if persons implicated in the civil dissensions of his country, like himself, and going thus voluntarily to England, had any reason to fear being ever delivered up to France. The Captain replied, that they had not: repelling the doubt as an insult. Previous to our separating, the conference was summed up, by my repeating, that it was possible, from the state of affairs and his own intentions, the Emperor would avail himself of Captain Maitland's offer, so as to get safe conducts for America. The latter begged it to be understood, that he would not guarantee the permission we demanded, being granted; upon which we departed. To say the truth, I did not myself think it would be given; but the Emperor, wishing to lead a life of tranquillity in future, had resolved to be a stranger to political concerns; we therefore conceived the probability of not being allowed to leave England without much uneasiness; but our fears and conjectures went no farther. It is very likely that Captain Maitland was of the same opinion: at all events, I will do him, as well as the other officers, the justice to believe, they were honest and sincere in the description they gave us of the sentiments of the people of England.

We reached the island at eleven o'clock; meanwhile the storm approached, and time became precious: it was necessary to decide one way or another. The Emperor having assembled us in a sort of council, all the chances of escape were discussed: that of the Danish vessel seemed impracticable, and the chasse-marées were no longer thought of; the English cruisers were not to be forced; so that there seemed only two alternatives—either to renew the war, or to accept the offers of Captain Maitland; the latter was chosen. On reaching the Bellerophon, we said, we shall be at once on British ground; the English will then find themselves bound by the ties of hospitality, which are held sacred amongst the most barbarous nations; we shall also be under the civil rights and privileges of the country. The people of England will not be so insensible to their glory as not to seize so fortunate a circumstance with avidity; upon this, Napoleon wrote the following letter to the Prince Regent:

"ROYAL HIGHNESS.—Exposed to the factions which divide my country, and to the hostility of the greatest powers of Europe, I have closed my political career. I come, like Themistocles, to seek the hospitality of the British nation. I place myself under the protection of their laws, which I claim from your Royal Highness, as the most powerful, the most constant, and the most generous of my enemies.

(Signed) "NAPOLEON."

I set out about four o'clock, with my son and General Gourgaud, to go on board the Bellerophon, whence I was not again to return. My mission was to announce the coming of his Majesty on the following morning; and moreover, to deliver the letter above quoted to Captain Maitland.—General Gourgaud was commissioned to carry the Emperor's letter to the Prince Regent immediately, and to present it in person. Captain Maitland read Napoleon's letter, which he greatly admired. Two other captains were permitted to take copies of it, to be kept secret till it became public; after which no time was lost in preparing to despatch Gourgaud in the Slaney, a sloop of war, forming part of the squadron.

Soon after the Slaney had parted company with the Bellerophon, and while I was seated in the captain's cabin of the latter with my son, Captain Maitland, who had gone to issue some orders, suddenly entered, and with a countenance expressive of deep concern, exclaimed, "Count Las Cases, I am deceived when I treat with you. The consequence of detaching one of my ships is, as I have just heard, that Napoleon has escaped. Should this be the case, it will place me in a dreadful situation with my Government."—These words startled me: I would have given the world had they been true. The Emperor had made no engagement; I was perfectly sincere; and would, therefore, have most willingly become the victim of an event of which I was quite innocent. I asked Captain Maitland, with the utmost coolness, at what hour the Emperor was said to have set out. He had been so astonished, that he had not given himself time to inquire; but went out again to ascertain this point, and, on returning, said, "at 12 o'clock." If that be the case, I replied, the Slaney's departure can do no harm, as you have only just sent her away; but do not be uneasy, for I left the Emperor in the island of Aix at four o'clock. "Are you sure of that?" said he. On my repeating the fact, he turned to some officers who were with him, and observed, in English, that the intelligence must be false, as I was too calm, and seemed to be sincere; and that I had, besides, pledged my word on the subject.

The English cruisers had numerous sources of information on our coast; I was subsequently enabled to ascertain that they were minutely informed of all our proceedings.*

Nothing was now thought of but preparing for the next day. Captain Maitland having asked whether I wished his boats to be sent for the Emperor, I replied, that the separation was too painful for the French seamen, not to let them have the satisfaction of attending him to the last moment.

Embarkation of Napoleon on board the Bellerophon.

15th.—At day-light, one of our brigs, the Epervier, was seen under weigh, and coming towards the Bellerophon, having a flag of truce flying. Both wind and tide being contrary, Captain Maitland sent his barge to meet her.—Seeing the boat return, the Captain was extremely anxious to discover, with his spy-glass, whether the Emperor was on

* While on our passage to St. Helena, Admiral Cockburn placed his library at our disposal. One of our party in turning over the leaves of a volume of the *Encyclopedia Britannica*, found a letter from La Rochelle, addressed to the commanding officer of the English squadron: it contained, word for word, the whole of our affair relative to the Danish ship, the moment of her projected departure, future intentions, &c. We passed this letter from hand to hand, taking care that it should be replaced where first discovered. It gave us very little information; we were aware of the understanding which existed both in and out of France, but were desirous of seeing a proof of it so much to the point. How did this letter happen to get on board the Northumberland? Captain Maitland had doubtless, when transferring us to that ship, also delivered up the documents concerning our capture. This was the letter which occasioned so much alarm on the part of the Captain, relative to the supposed escape of the Emperor, soon after my embarkation.

board; he frequently begged I would look myself, but I could not as yet reply with certainty: at length the matter was placed beyond farther doubt, as the Emperor came alongside, surrounded by all his attendants. I stood at the gangway to present Captain Maitland, to whom he said, "I come on board your ship, to place myself under the protection of the laws of England." The captain then led him into his cabin, of which the Emperor was immediately put in possession. All the officers of the Bellerophon were presented to him soon after: this ceremony over, he came out of the cabin, and visited every part of the ship during the morning. I related the alarm felt by Captain Maitland the preceding evening, relative to his escape; the Emperor did not see the matter in the light in which it had appeared to me—"What had he to fear?" he asked in an emphatic and dignified manner—"were not you in his power?"

Towards four o'clock, the Superb, a seventy-four gun ship, bearing the flag of Rear-admiral Hotham, the commander on the station, anchored close to the Bellerophon. The admiral came to visit the Emperor, and remained to dinner. From the questions asked by Napoleon relative to his ship, he expressed a wish to know whether his Majesty would condescend to go on board the following day; upon which the Emperor said he had no objection, and would therefore breakfast with the Admiral accompanied by all his attendants.

16th.—Accompanied the Emperor on board the Superb: all the honours, except those of firing cannon, were liberally done; we went round the ship, and examined the most trifling objects; every thing seemed to be in admirable order. Admiral Hotham evinced, throughout, all the refinement and grace of a man of rank and education. On our return to the Bellerophon she got under weigh, and made sail for England: this event took place twelve days after our departure from Paris.

On our leaving the Bellerophon in the morning to visit the Superb, the Emperor stopped short in front of the guard drawn up on the quarter-deck to salute him. He made them perform several movements, giving the word of command himself: having desired them to charge bayonets, and perceiving this motion was not performed altogether in the French manner, he advanced into the midst of the soldiers, put the weapons aside with his hands, and seized a musquet from one of the rear rank, with which he went through the exercise himself according to our method. A sudden movement and change of countenance amongst the officers and others who were present, sufficiently expressed their astonishment at seeing the Emperor thus carelessly place himself amidst English bayonets, some of which came in contact with his person. This circumstance produced a most striking effect. On returning from the Superb, we were indirectly questioned on the subject, and asked whether the Emperor had ever acted in the same way with his own soldiers; while the greatest surprise was expressed at his confidence. Not one amongst the officers had formed any idea of sovereigns who could thus explain and execute their own commands; it was therefore easy to perceive they had no just conception of the personage now before them, notwithstanding his having been so marked an object of attention and curiosity for above twenty years.

17th—18th.—Though nearly a calm, we lost sight of land.

19th.—The wind being very strong, though not favourable, we proceeded at the rate of nine miles an hour.

20th—22.—We continued our course, with winds that were by no means favourable.

The Emperor was not long amongst his most inveterate enemies, those who had been continually fed with rumours no less absurd than irritating, without exercising all the influence of glory over them. The captain, officers, and crew soon adopted the etiquette of his suite, shewing him exactly the same attention and respect: the Captain addressed him either as *Sire* or *your Majesty*; when he appeared on deck, every one took off his hat, and remained uncovered while he was present—this was not the case at first. There was no entering his cabin, except by passing the attendants: no persons but those who were invited appeared at his table. Napoleon was, in fact, an emperor, on board the Bellerophon. He often appeared on deck, conversing either with some of his suite or the officers of the ship.

Of all those who had followed the Emperor, I was perhaps the person of whom he knew the least: it has already been seen that, notwithstanding my employments near his person, I had enjoyed but little immediate intercourse with Napoleon; since our leaving Paris he had scarcely spoken to me, but I was now addressed very frequently.

The occasion and circumstances were highly favourable to me; I was sufficiently acquainted with the English language to be able to give various explanations as to what was passing around us. I had been in the navy, and could afford the Emperor any information he required relative to the manœuvres of the ship, and state of the weather. I had been ten years in England, and had formed definite notions of the laws, manners, and customs of the people, which enabled me to reply to the Emperor's questions with facility.

My Historical Atlas, too, had stored my mind with a number of facts, dates, and coincidences, upon which he always found me prepared to answer.

A part of my time was occupied in drawing up the following summary of our situation at Rochefort, and the notions which had dictated the determination of the Emperor.

Summary dictated by Napoleon himself.

The English squadron was not strong; there were two sloops of war off Bordeaux; they blockaded a French corvette, and gave chase to American vessels, which sailed daily in great numbers. At the Isle of Aix we had two frigates well armed; the Vulcan corvette, one of the largest vessels of its class, and a large brig, lay in the roads; the whole of this force was blockaded by an English seventy-four of the smallest class, and an indifferent sloop or two. There is not the least doubt that by risking the sacrifice of one or two of our ships, we should have passed, but the senior captain was deficient in resolution, and refused to sail; the second in command was quite determined, and would have made the attempt; the former had probably received secret instructions from Fouché, who already openly betrayed the Emperor, and wanted to give him up. However that may be, there was nothing to be done by sea. The Emperor then landed at the Isle of Aix.

"Had the mission been confided to Admiral Werhuel," said Napoleon, "as was promised on our departure from Paris, it is probable he would have sailed." The officers and crews of both frigates were full of attachment and enthusiasm. The garrison of Aix was composed of fifteen hundred seamen, forming a very fine regiment; the officers were so indignant at the frigate not sailing, that they proposed to fit out two chasse-marées of fifteen tons each: the midshipmen wished to navigate them; but when on the point of putting this plan into execution, it was said there would be great difficulty in gaining the American coast without touching on some point of Spain or Portugal.

Under these circumstances the Emperor composed a species of council, from amongst the individuals of his suite: here it was represented that we could no longer calculate on the frigates or other armed vessels; that the chasse-marées held out no probable chance of success, and could only lead to capture by the English cruisers in the open sea, or to falling into the hands of the allies: only two alternatives remained; that of marching towards the interior, once more to try the fate of arms; or that of seeking an asylum in England. To follow up the first there were fifteen hundred seamen, full of zeal and willing to act: the commandant of the Island was an old officer of the army of Egypt, entirely devoted to Napoleon: the Emperor would have proceeded at the head of these to Rochefort, where the corps would have been increased by the garrison, which was also extremely well disposed: the garrison of La Rochelle, composed of four battalions of federated troops, had offered their services: with these we might then have joined General Clausel, so firmly fixed at the head of the army at Bordeaux, or General Lamarque, who had performed prodigies, with that of La Vendée; both these officers expected and wished to see Napoleon: it would have been exceedingly easy to maintain a civil war in the interior. But Paris was taken, and the Chambers had been dissolved; there were, besides, from five to six hundred thousand of the enemy's troops in France; a civil war could therefore have no other result than leading to the destruction of all these generous men who were attached to Napoleon. This loss would have been severe and irreparable: it would have destroyed the future resources of the nation, without producing any other advantage than placing the Emperor in a position to treat and obtain stipulations favourable to his interests. But Napoleon had renounced sovereignty; he only wanted a tranquil asylum; he abhorred the thought of seeing all his friends perish to attain so trifling a result; he was equally averse to become the pretext for the provinces being ravaged; and above all, he did not wish to deprive the national party of its truest supports, which would sooner or later re-establish the honour and independence of France. Napoleon's only wish was to live as a private individual in future: America was the most proper place, and that of his choice. But even England, with its positive laws, might also answer; and it appeared, from the nature of my first interview with Captain Maitland, that the latter was empowered to convey the Emperor and suite to England to be equitably treated. From this moment we were under the protection of British laws: and the people of England were too fond of glory to lose an opportunity which thus presented itself, and that ought to have formed the proudest page of their history. It was therefore resolved to surrender to the English cruisers, as soon as Captain Maitland should positively declare his orders to receive us. On renewing the negotiation, he clearly stated that he had the authority of his Government to receive the Emperor, if he would come on board the Bellerophon, and to convey him as well as his suite to England. Napoleon went on board, not that he was constrained to it by events, since he could have remained in France; but because he wished to live as a private individual, would no longer meddle with public affairs, and had determined not to embroil those of France. He would, most assuredly, not have adopted this plan had he suspected the unworthy treatment which was preparing for him, as every body will readily feel convinced. His letter to the Prince Regent fully explains his confidence and persuasion on the subject. Captain Maitland, to whom it was officially communicated before the Emperor embarked on board his ship, having made no remarks on the above document, had, by this circumstance alone, recognized and sanctioned the sentiments it contained.

23d.—Saw Ushant at four in the morning, having passed it in the night. From the moment of approaching the Channel, ships of the line and frigates were seen sailing in various directions. The coast of England was discovered towards evening.

24th.—We anchored at Torbay about eight in the morning; the Emperor had risen at six, and went on the poop, whence he surveyed the coast and anchorage. I remained by his side to give the explanations he required.

Captain Maitland immediately dispatched a messenger to Lord Keith, the commander-in-chief at Plymouth. General Gourgaud rejoined us: he had been obliged to give up the letter for the Prince Regent; he had not only been refused permission to land, but prohibited from all communication. This was a bad omen, and the first indication of those numberless tribulations which followed.

No sooner had it transpired that the Emperor was on board the Bellerophon, than the bay was covered with vessels and boats full of people. The owner of a beautiful country-seat in sight of the ship sent his Majesty a present of various fruits.

25th.—The concourse of boats and crowds of spectators continued without intermission. The Emperor saw them from the cabin windows, and occasionally shewed himself on deck. On returning from the shore, Captain Maitland handed me a letter from Lady C, enclosing another from my wife. My surprise was extreme, and not less than my satisfaction; but the former ceased when I reflected that the length of the passage had given the French papers time to transmit an account of what had occurred to a considerable distance, so that whatever related to the Emperor and his suite was already known in England, where we had even been expected for five or six days before. My wife hastened to address Lady C on the subject, and the latter wrote to Captain Maitland, to whom she enclosed my letters, without knowing him.

My wife's letter bespoke feelings of tender affliction; but that of Lady C, who, from being in London, had heard our future destiny, was full of reproaches—"I was not my own master, thus to dispose of myself; it was a crime to abandon my wife and children," &c. Melancholy result of our modern systems of education, which tend so little to elevate our minds that we cannot conceive either the merit or charm of heroic resolutions! We think all has been said, and every plea justified, when the danger of private interests and domestic enjoyments is put forward,—little imagining that the first duty towards a wife is to place her in a situation of honour, and that the richest inheritance we can leave our children, is the example of some virtues, and a name to which a little true glory is attached.

26th—Orders had arrived in the night for the ship immediately to repair to Plymouth: having sailed at an early hour, we reached our new destination at four o'clock in the afternoon, ten days after our departure from Rochefort, twenty-seven after quitting Paris, and thirty-five from the Emperor's abdication. Our horrizon became greatly overcast from this day. Armed boats were placed round the ship; those whom curiosity had attracted were driven away, even by firing musquetry at them. Lord Keith, who was in the bay, did not come on board. Two frigates made the signal for sailing immediately; we were told that a courier extraordinary had brought dispatches for a distant quarter. In the morning, some of our party were distributed amongst other vessels. Every visage seemed now to look at us with a sullen interest; the most sinister reports had reached the ship; several destinations were mentioned, each more frightful than the other.

Imprisonment in the Tower of London was the least terrific, some spoke of St. Helena. Meanwhile the two frigates, which had greatly excited my attention, got under weigh, though the wind was contrary for leaving the roadstead, stood towards us, and anchored on each side, nearly touching the Bellerophon. Upon this, some person whispered to me that these ships were to receive us in the course of the night, and to sail for St. Helena.

Never can I pourtray the effect of these terrible words! A cold sweat overspread my whole frame: it was an unexpected sentence of death! Unpitying executioners had seized me: I was torn from all that attached me to life. I extended my arms sorrowfully towards those who were dear to me, but in vain; my fate was inevitable! This thought, together with a crowd of others which arose in equal disorder, excited a real tempest of the mind. It was like the struggle of a soul that sought to disengage itself from its earthly habitation! It turned my hair gray!—Fortunately the crisis was short, and, as it happened, the mind came forth triumphant; so much so, indeed, that from this moment I seemed above the world. I felt that I could thenceforth defy injustice, ill treatment, and sufferings. Above all, I vowed that neither complaints nor solicitation should escape me. But let not those of my companions to whom I appeared tranquil in those fatal circumstances, accuse me of being deficient in feeling! Their agony was prolonged in detail—mine operated all at once.

One of those coincidences, which is not the least extraordinary of my life, recurred to my thoughts soon after. Twenty years before, and during my emigration to England, without possessing any worldly goods, I had refused to seek a certain fortune in India, because it was too remote, and I thought myself too old. Now, at twenty years older, I was about to quit my family, friends, fortune, and enjoyments, to become a voluntary exile, two thousand miles off, in the midst of the ocean, *for nothing*. But no, I am mistaken! the sentiment that now impelled me was infinitely superior to the riches I then disdained; I followed him who had governed the world and will occupy the attention of posterity.

The Emperor continued to appear on deck as usual. I sometimes saw him in his cabin, but without communicating what I had heard: I wished to console him, and not to be his tormentor. The reports had, however, reached him; but he had come so freely and confidently on board the Bellerophon; he had been so strongly invited by the English themselves; he so completely regarded his letter to the Prince Regent, transmitted beforehand to Captain Maitland, as so many tacit conditions; he had, in fact, acted with so much magnanimity throughout the proceeding, that he repelled with indignation all the fears which were attempted to be excited in him, not even permitting those around him to entertain doubts.

27th—28th.—It would be difficult to describe our torments and anxiety at this moment; most of us were dumb and inanimate. The least circumstance which transpired from the shore—an opinion, however unimportant, expressed on board—an unmeaning paragraph in a daily paper, became the subjects of our most serious arguments, and the cause of perpetual oscillations between our hopes and fears. The most trifling reports were sought with avidity; whoever appeared was urged to give a favourable version of deceitful anticipations; so little do the ardour and activity of our national character contribute to endow us with that stoical resignation, that imperturbable composure which can only be acquired from settled principles and positive doctrines imbibed from early infancy.

The public papers, particularly those of the ministerial side, were let loose against us; it was the outcry of Ministers preparing the blow they were about to strike. It would not be easy to form an idea of the horrors, falsehoods, and imprecations accumulated on our heads; and there is always a portion communicated to the multitude, however well disposed it may be, so that the demeanour of those around us become less easy, while their politeness became embarrassed and their countenances more misgiving.

Lord Keith, after announcing himself for sometime before, had only just made his appearance. It was evident that our company was shunned; our conversation avoided. The papers contained an account of the measures which were about to be taken; but, as nothing official appeared, and there was some contradiction in the details, we were induced to flatter ourselves as to the final result; thus remaining in that state of suspense and uncertainty which is worse than a knowledge of the most painful truths. Nevertheless, our arrival in England had produced a singular sensation; the presence of the Emperor excited a curiosity bordering on delirium. It was the papers themselves that informed us of the circumstance, while they condemned it. All England seemed to hurry towards Plymouth. A person who had left London, on hearing of my arrival, was obliged to stop on the road for want of post-horses and accommodation. The Sound was covered with an immense number of boats; for some of which, we heard, above fifty pounds had been paid.

The Emperor, to whom I read all the newspapers, did not betray any decrease of composure, either by his conversation or general habits. It was known that he always appeared on deck towards five o'clock. A short time before this hour, all the boats collected along-side of each other; there were thousands, and so closely connected, that the water could no longer be seen between them; they looked more like a multitude assembled in a public square than any thing else. When the Emperor came out, the noise and gestures of so many people presented a most striking spectacle: it was, at the same time, very easy to perceive that nothing hostile was meant, and that if curiosity had brought them, they felt interested on going away; we could even see that the latter sentiment continued to increase;—at first, people merely looked towards the ship, they ended by saluting; some remained uncovered, and occasionally went so far as to cheer. Even our symbols began to appear amongst them. Several individuals of both sexes came decorated with red carnations, but this was only turned to our detriment in the eyes of the Ministry and its partisans, so that it rendered our agony more poignant.

It was under these circumstances that the Emperor, who, notwithstanding his calm demeanor, could not help being struck by what he heard, dictated a paper to me, worthy of serving as a model to jurists, discussing and defending his real political situation; we found means of conveying it on shore, but I have kept no copy.

Ministerial Decision.

29th—30th.—A report had circulated during the two previous days, that an under-secretary of state was coming from London officially to notify the resolutions of the Ministers with respect to the Emperor. Accordingly he appeared; it was Sir Charles Bunbury; he came on board, accompanied by Lord Keith, and delivered a dispatch ordering the removal of the Emperor to St. Helena, and limiting the number of persons who were to accompany Napoleon to three, excluding, however, the Duke de Rovigo and General Lallemand, comprised in the list of proscribed.

I was not called before the Emperor. The bearers of his sentence spoke and understood French; they were admitted alone. I have since heard, that he objected and protested, with no less energy than logic, against the violence exercised on his person. "He was the guest of England," said Napoleon, "and not its prisoner, he came of his own accord to place himself under the protection of its laws; the most sacred rights of hospitality were violated in his person; he would never submit voluntarily to the outrage they were preparing for him: violence alone should oblige him to do so, &c."

The Emperor gave me the ministerial document to translate for him, of which the following is a copy:

Communication made by Lord Keith, in the name of the English Ministers.

"As it may, perhaps, be convenient for General Buonaparte to learn, without farther delay, the intentions of the British Government with regard to him, your Lordship will communicate the following information.

"It would be inconsistent with our duty towards our country and the allies of his Majesty, if General Buonaparte possessed the means of again disturbing the repose of Europe. It is on this account, that it becomes absolutely necessary he should be restrained in his personal liberty, so far as this is required by the foregoing important object.

"The island of St. Helena has been chosen as his future residence; its climate is healthy, and its local position will allow of his being treated with more indulgence than could be admitted in any other spot, owing to the indispensable precautions which it would be necessary to employ for the security of his person.

"General Buonaparte is allowed to select amongst those persons who accompanied him to England, (with the exceptions of generals Savary and Lallemand) three officers, who, together with his surgeon, will have permission to accompany him to St. Helena; these individuals will not be allowed to quit the island without the sanction of the British Government.

"Rear-Admiral Sir George Cockburn, who is named Commander-in-chief at the Cape of Good Hope and seas adjacent, will convey General Buonaparte and his suite to St. Helena; and he will receive detailed instructions relative to the execution of this service.

"Sir G. Cockburn will, most probably, be ready to sail in a few days; for which reason it is desirable that General Buonaparte should make choice of the persons who are to accompany him without delay."

Although we expected our transportation to St. Helena, we were deeply affected by its announcement: it threw us all into a state of consternation. The Emperor did not however, fail to appear on deck as usual, with the same countenance; and, as before, tranquilly surveyed the crowds which seemed so eager to see him.

31st.—Our situation had now become truly frightful; our sufferings beyond every power of description; our existence was about to cease with regard to Europe, our country, families, and friends, as well as our enjoyments and habits. It is true, we were not forced to follow the Emperor; but our choice was that of martyrs; the question was a renunciation of faith, or death. Another circumstance was added, which greatly increased our torment: this was the exclusion of Generals Savary and Lallemand, whom it struck with the utmost terror: they saw nothing but a scaffold before them, and felt persuaded that the Ministers of England, making no distinction between the political acts of a revolution, and crimes committed in a moment of tranquillity, would give them up to their enemies to be sacrificed. This would have been such an outrage on all law, such an opprobrium for England herself, that her enemies would be almost tempted to invoke it; but it was only for those who were included in the same proscription to talk thus. At all events, we did not hesitate to desire that each of us might be amongst those whom the Emperor would choose; entertaining but one fear, that of finding ourselves excluded.

August 1st.—We still continued in the same state. I received a letter from London, in which it was strongly urged that I should be extremely wrong, nay that it would even be a crime, to expatriate myself. The person who thus wrote, also addressed Captain Maitland, begging he would assist by his efforts and counsel to dissuade me from such a resolution. But I stopped him short, by observing that, at my age, people generally acted on reflection.

I read the papers every day to the Emperor. Whether influenced by generosity, or that opinions began to be divided, there were two amongst the number that pleaded our cause with great warmth, compensating in some measure for the gross falsehoods and scurrilous abuse with which the others were filled. We gave ourselves up to the hope, that the hatred inspired by an enemy, would be succeeded by the interest which splendid actions ought naturally to excite; that England abounded in noble hearts and elevated minds, which would indubitably become our ardent advocates.

The number of boats increased daily. Napoleon continued to appear at his usual hour, and the reception became more and more flattering.

Numbers of every rank and condition had followed the Emperor; he was still with regard to most of us, as if at the Thuilleries; the Grand Marshal and Duke de Rovigo alone saw him habitually. Some had not approached or spoken to him more frequently than if we had been at Paris. I was called during the day, whenever there were any papers or letters to translate, until the Emperor insensibly contracted the habit of sending for me every evening towards eight o'clock, to converse with him a short time.

In the conversation of this evening, and after touching on various subjects, he asked me whether I would accompany him to St. Helena. I replied with great frankness, rendered more easy by my real sentiments, observing to his Majesty, that in quitting Paris I had disregarded every chance; and that therefore, that of St. Helena had nothing which could make it an exception. There were, however, a great many of us round his person, while only three were permitted to go out. As some people considered it a crime in me to leave my family, it was necessary with regard to the latter, and my own conscience, to know that I could be useful and agreeable to him—that, in fact, I required to be chosen; but that this last observation did not spring from any concealed motive, for my life was henceforth at his disposal without any restriction.

While thus engaged, Madame Bertrand, without having been called, and even without announcing her name, rushed into the cabin, and in a frantic manner, entreated the Emperor not to go to St. Helena, nor take her husband with him. But observing the astonishment, coolness, and calm answer of Napoleon, she ran out as precipitately as she had entered. The Emperor, still surprised, turned to me and said, "Can you comprehend all this? Is she not mad?" In a moment after, loud shrieks were heard, and every body seemed to be running towards the stern of the ship. Being desired to ring the bell, and to inquire the cause, I found it was Madame Bertrand, who, on leaving the cabin, had at-attempted to throw herself into the sea, and was prevented with the greatest difficulty. From this scene it is easy to judge of our general feelings!

Remarkable Words of the Emperor.

2d,—3d.—In the morning the Duke de Rovigo told me I was certainly to depart for St. Helena; while in conversation with the Emperor a short time before, his Majesty had said to him, that if there were only two to accompany him I should be one of the number, as he thought I could afford him some consolation. I am indebted to the candour and kindness of the Duke, for the satisfaction of being made acquainted with this flattering assurance, and am truly grateful, as, but for him, it would never have been known to me. The Emperor had not said a word in reply to my answer: this was his custom, as I shall have other opportunities of showing.

I had no particular acquaintance with any of those who had followed the Emperor, except General and Madame Bertrand, who had shown me great attention during my mission to Illyria, where he was Governor-General. I had until then never spoken to the Duke de Rovigo, certain prepossessions having induced me to keep at a distance; we had, however, scarcely exchanged a few words, when my scruples were completely removed. Savary was sincerely attached to the Emperor; I knew he possessed warmth of heart, sincerity, and uprightness of character, qualities which rendered him susceptible of real friendship: we should, therefore, I dare say have become very intimate.

I was again sent for by the Emperor; who, after alluding to different subjects, began to speak of St. Helena, asking me what sort of a place it could be? whether it was possible to exist there? and similar questions. "But," said he, "after all, am I quite sure of going there? Is a man dependent on others, when he wishes that his dependence should cease?"—We continued to walk to and fro in the cabin; he seemed calm, though affected, and somewhat absent.

"My friend," continued the Emperor, "I have sometimes an idea of quitting you, and this would not be very difficult; it is only necessary to create a little mental excitement, and I shall soon have escaped.—All will be over, and you can then tranquilly rejoin your families. This is the more easy, since my internal principles do not oppose any bar to it;—I am one of those who conceive that the pains of the other world were only imagined as a counterpoise to those inadequate allurements which are offered to us there. God can never have willed such a contradiction to his infinite goodness, especially for an act of this kind; and what is it after all, but wishing to return to him a little sooner?

I remonstrated warmly against such notions. Poets and philosophers had said that it was a spectacle worthy of the Divinity, to see men struggling with fortune: reverses and constancy had their glory. Such a great and noble character as his could not descend to the level of vulgar minds; he who had governed us with so much glory, who had excited the admiration, and influenced the destinies of the world, could not end like a desperate gamester or disappointed lover. What would then become of all those who looked up to and placed their hopes in him? Would he thus abandon the field to his enemies? The anxiety shown by the latter to drive him to it was surely sufficient to make him resist: who, besides, could tell the secrets of time, or dare assert what the future would produce. What might not the mere change of a ministry, death of a Prince, that of a confidant, the slightest burst of passion, or the most trifling dispute, bring about?

"Some of these suggestions have their weight," said the Emperor, "but what can we do in that desolate place?"—"Sire," I replied, "we will live on the past: there is enough of it to satisfy us. Do we not enjoy the life of Cæsar and that of Alexander? We shall possess still more, you will re-peruse yourself, Sire!" "Be it so!" rejoined Napoleon; "we will write our memoirs. Yes, we must be employed; for occupation is the scythe of time. After all, a man ought to fulfil his destinies; this is my grand doctrine:* let mine also be accomplished." Re-assuming from this instant an air of ease and even gaiety, he passed on to subjects totally unconnected with our situation.

* The following is a document, which the above circumstance contributes to render still more precious: it is an order of the day, issued by the Frst Consul to his guard, against suicide.

Order of the 22 Floreal, Year X.

"The grenadier Gobain has committed suicide from love: he was in other respects an excellent soldier. This is the second incident of the same nature that has occurred within a month.

"The first Consul directs it to be inserted in the order book of the Guard:—

"That a soldier ought to know how to vanquish the pangs and melancholy of the passions; that there is as much true courage in bearing up against mental sufferings with constancy, as in remaining firm on the wall of a battery.

"To give ourselves up to grief without resistance, or to kill ourselves to escape affliction, is to abandon the field of battle before the victory is gained."

Departure from Plymouth.—Continuance in the Channel.—Protest.

4th.—Orders had arrived during the night for us to sail at an early hour; when under weigh, our curiosity was greatly excited. The newspapers, official communications, and private conversations, told us we were to be conveyed to St. Helena by the Northumberland: we knew that this ship was still fitting out at Portsmouth or Chatham, so that we might still calculate on eight or ten day's delay. The Bellerophon was too old for the voyage, she had not provisions enough; moreover the wind was contrary; when therefore we saw the ship returning up Channel, our uncertainty and conjectures were renewed, but whatever these might be, every thing was welcome when compared to the idea of transportation to St. Helena.

Nevertheless, it occurred to us, that in such a decisive moment, the Emperor was bound to shew an official opposition to this violence; as to Napoleon himself, he attached but little importance to it, nor would he trouble himself about the matter. However, said we, it will be a weapon in the hands of our friends, and leave causes of remembrance as well as grounds of defence with the public. I ventured, therefore, to read a paper I had prepared to his Majesty, with the general sense of which he seemed pleased; after suppressing a few phrases, and correcting others, it was signed and sent to Lord Keith. The following is a literal copy of this document.

Protest.

"I hereby solemnly protest in the face of heaven and mankind, against the violence that is done me; and the violation of my most sacred rights, in forcibly disposing of my person and liberty. I voluntarily came on board the Bellerophon—I am not the prisoner, I am the guest of England. I came at the instigation of the Captain himself, who said he had orders from the Government to receive and convey me to England, together with my suite, if agreeable to me. I came forward with confidence to place myself under the protection of the laws of England. When once on board the Bellerophon, I was entitled to the hospitality of the British people. If the Government, in giving the Captain of the Bellerophon orders to receive me and my followers, only wished to lay a snare, it has forfeited its honour and disgraced its flag.

"If this act be consummated it will be in vain for the English henceforth to talk of their sincerity, their laws, and liberties. British faith will have been lost in the hospitality of the Bellerophon.

"I appeal to history: it will say, that an enemy who made war for twenty years against the English people came spontaneously, in the hour of misfortune to seek an asylum under their laws. What more striking proof could he give of his esteem and confidence? But how did England reply to such an act of magnanimity? It pretended to hold out a hospitable hand to this enemy; and on giving himself up with confidence, he was immolated!

"NAPOLEON."

Bellerophon, at Sea,
Friday, Aug. 4th, 1815

The Duke de Rovigo told me that the Emperor demanded permission to send me to the Prince Regent at London, but that it was obstinately refused.

The sea was rough, and the wind blew with violence. Most of us were affected with sea sickness. But what cannot the pre-occupation of the mind effect over physical infirmities? this was, perhaps, the only time in my life that I was not incommoded by such weather. On leaving Plymouth Sound, we stood to the eastward before the wind, but were soon after close-hauled, tacking backwards and forwards, without being able to comprehend the cause of this new source of torment.

5th.—The whole of this day was passed in the same manner. While conversing with the Emperor in the evening he gave me two proofs of confidence, but I cannot now confide them to paper.*

* There is, however, one of those proofs which I am now at liberty to disclose. While walking in the stern-gallery with the Emperor, at the usual hour, he drew from under his waistcoat, still conversing on a totally different subject, a species of girdle, which he handed to me, saying, "Take care of that for me;" without interrupting him, I placed it under my own waistcoat. The Emperor told me soon after, that it contained a diamond necklace, worth two hundred thousand francs, which Queen Hortensia forced him to accept on his leaving Malmaison. After our arrival at St. Helena I frequently spoke of returning the necklace, but never received any reply. Having ventured to mention the subject again when we were at Longwood, Napoleon drily asked, "Does it annoy you?"—"No Sire," was my answer;—"Keep it then," said he. From wearing the girdle so long, the necklace became as it were identified with my person; and I thought so little about it, that it was not till some days after my being torn from Longwood, and by the merest accident, it recurred to my memory; when I shuddered at the idea of depriving the Emperor of such a resource. For, how would it be possible now to make restitution? I was in the most rigorous confinement, surrounded by gaolers and sentinels, so that all communication was impracticable. I vainly endeavoured to contrive a plan; time pressed; only a few days were left, and nothing could be more distressing than thus to quit the island. In this predicament, I resolved to run all risks. An Englishman, to whom I had often spoken, came to the prison on a particular errand—and it was under the eyes of the governor himself or one of his most confidential agents whom he brought, that I ventured to communicate my wishes.

"I think you are a man of principle," said I, "and I am going to put it to the test;—though with nothing injurious or contrary to your honour—merely a rich deposit to be restored to Napoleon. If you accept the charge, my son will put it into your pocket."

He answered only by slackening his pace; my son, whom I had prepared for the scene, followed us, and the necklace was transferred into this man's possession, almost in sight of the military attendants. Before quitting the island, I had the inexpressible satisfaction of knowing that the necklace had reached the hands of the Emperor. How gratifying to the heart are the recollection and recital of such a trait on the part of an enemy, and under such circumstances!

Anchored off Start Point.—Persons allowed to accompany the Emperor.

6th.—We anchored about noon off Start Point, where there was no shelter whatever, though we had but a very short distance to go in order to anchor in Torbay: this circumstance excited great astonishment on our part. We had, however, heard that orders were given to meet the Northumberland, the departure of which vessel from Portsmouth was urged with all possible haste. Accordingly that ship soon appeared with two frigates full of troops, which were to compose the garrison of St. Helena. These three ships came to an anchor close to us; after which the communications amongst the whole squadron became very active. The precautions lest any boats should approach were still continued. Meanwhile the mystery of our precipitate sailing from Plymouth, and all the manœuvring that followed, was discovered. Lord Keith had, we were told, received notice by telegraph, that a public officer had just left London with a writ of *habeas corpus*, to claim the person of the Emperor in the name of the laws or of some competent tribunal. We could neither verify the motives nor details of this circumstance: the Admiral, it was added, had scarcely time enough to escape this difficulty; we heard that he was suddenly obliged to go on board a brig, and quit Plymouth Sound. This was the motive which kept us out of Torbay.

Admirals Keith and Cockburn came on board the Bellerophon; the flag of the latter was flying on board the Northumberland: they had a conference with the Emperor, to whom they delivered an extract from the instructions relative to our transportation to and stay at St. Helena. These stated, that all our effects were to be examined, for the purpose of taking away the money, bills, and diamonds, belonging to the Emperor, as well as ourselves, to be kept for us! we also heard that our arms would be taken from us at the same time, and that we were then to be transferred to the Northumberland. The documents were as follows:

Order from Lord Keith to Captain Maitland of the Bellerophon.

"All arms of every description are to be taken from the French, of whatever rank, who are on board his Majesty's ship under your command. These arms will be carefully packed, and are to remain in your charge so long as the persons to whom they belong continue on board the Bellerophon. They will then be under the charge of the captain of the ship to which the said individuals may be transferred."

Start Bay, August 6th, 1815.

Instructions of Ministers to Admiral Cockburn.

"When General Bonaparte leaves the Bellerophon to go on board the Northumberland, it will be the properest moment for Admiral Cockburn to have the effects examined which General Bonaparte may have brought with him. The Admiral will allow the baggage, wines, (*the wines!* an observation truly worthy of the English ministers,) and provisions which the General may have brought with him, to be taken on board the Northumberland. Among the baggage his table service shall be understood as included, unless it be so considerable as to seem rather an article to be converted into ready-money than for real use. His money, his diamonds, and his saleable effects (consequently bills of exchange also) of whatever kind they may be, must be delivered up. The Admiral will declare it to the General that the British government by no means intends to confiscate his property, but merely to take upon itself the administration of his effects, to hinder him from using them as a means to promote his escape.

"The examination shall be made in the presence of a person named by General Bonaparte, the inventory of the effects to be retained shall be signed by this person as well as by the Rear-admiral, or by the person whom he shall appoint to draw up the inventory. The interest or the principal (according as his property is more or less considerable) shall be applied to his support, and in this respect the principal arrangement is to be left to him. For this purpose he can from time to time signify his wishes to the admiral, till the arrival of the new governor of St. Helena, and afterwards to the latter: and if no objection is made to his proposal, the Admiral or the Governor can give the necessary orders: and the disbursement will be paid by bills on his Majesty's Treasury. In case of death, (*what foresight!*) he can dispose of his property by a last Will, and may be assured that the contents of his testament shall be faithfully executed. As an attempt might be made to make a part of his property pass for the property of the persons of his suite, it must be signified that the property of his attendants is subject to the same regulations.

"The Admiral is not to take any person on board for St. Helena, without the consent of such person, to whom he is previously to explain the necessity of being subjected to all the regulations which it may be thought proper to establish for securing the person of the General. It must be made known to the General, that if he make any attempt to escape, he will expose himself to close imprisonment; and that any of his suite who may be discovered in endeavouring to facilitate his escape, will incur the same punishment.

(Afterwards the Act of Parliament made the latter offence death.)

"All letters which shall be addressed to him, or to any of his suite, are to be delivered in the first place to the Admiral or the Governor, who is to read them previously to transmitting them: the same regulation is to be observed with respect to letters written by the General, or those of his suite.

"The General is to be informed, that the Governor and the Admiral have received positive orders to forward to his Majesty's Government any request or representation he may think proper to make: nothing is left to their discretion on this point; but the paper on which such representations shall be written is to remain open, in order that they may subjoin such observations as they may think expedient."

It would not be easy to conceive the intensity and nature of our feelings at this decisive moment, in which outrage, violence, and injustice were accumulated on our heads.

Constrained to reduce his suite to three persons, the Emperor selected the Grand Marshal, M. de Montholon, and myself. Gourgaud, in despair at the idea of being left behind, entered into a negotiation on the subject, and succeeded. As the instructions only allowed Napoleon to take three officers, it was agreed that I should be considered purely in a civil capacity, and to admit a fourth by the aid of this interpretation.

Conversation with Lord Keith.—Examination of the Emperor's effects.—He quits the Bellerophon.—Separation.—We sail for St. Helena.

7th.—The Emperor addressed to Lord Keith a species of new protest, against the violence done to his person in forcibly removing him from the Bellerophon. I took it on board the Tonnant. Admiral Keith, a fine looking old man, of highly polished manners, received me with great politeness; but he carefully avoided touching on the subject of the protest, observing that he would give an answer in writing.

This did not stop me. I stated the situation of Napoleon, who was very unwell, having his legs considerably swelled; and pointed out to his Lordship how desirable it was for the Emperor not to be sent off so suddenly. He replied, that I had been a sailor, and must therefore see the anchorage was unsafe, which was certainly true.

I explained the Emperor's repugnance to have his effects searched and tossed about as proposed; assuring him that

Napoleon would infinitely prefer seeing them thrown into the sea. The Admiral answered, that as this was a positive order, he could not infringe on it. Finally, I demanded whether it was probable those appointed to search would go so far as to deprive the Emperor of his sword. He said, that it would be respected, but that Napoleon was the only person exempted, as all his followers would be disarmed. I showed him that I was already so; my sword having been taken from me before I left the Bellerophon. A secretary who was writing near us, observed to Lord Keith, in English, that the order stated that Napoleon himself was to be disarmed; upon which the Admiral drily replied, also in English, as well as I could comprehend, "mind your own business, Sir, and leave us to ourselves."

Still continuing the conversation, I went over all that had occurred from the commencement. I had been the negociator, I said, and ought therefore to feel most acutely; and had the greater right to be heard. Lord Keith listened to me with marked impatience; we were standing, and his frequent bows were evidently to make me retire. When I told him that Captain Maitland said he had been authorised to bring us to England, without exciting a suspicion in our minds that we were to be prisoners of war; that the Captain could not deny we came on board voluntarily and in confidence; that the letter of the Emperor to the Prince of Wales, which I had previously communicated to Captain Maitland, must necessarily have created tacit conditions, since he made no remarks on it; at length the Admiral's ill humour and even anger broke forth, and he replied sharply, that if such were the case, Captain Maitland must have been a fool, for his instructions contained nothing of the kind; and he was quite sure of this, for it was from himself they had emanated. "But, my Lord," said I, "permit me to observe, in defence of Captain Maitland, that your Lordship speaks with a degree of severity for which you may become responsible; for not only Captain Maitland, but Admiral Hotham, and all the other officers whom we saw at the time, conducted and expressed themselves in the same way towards us; would it have been thus, if their instructions had been so clear and positive?" Saying this, I relieved the Admiral of my presence; he made no attempt to prolong a subject which, perhaps, his Lordship's conscience rendered somewhat painful to him.

Admiral Cockburn, aided by an officer of the customs, examined the effects of the Emperor; they seized four thousand Napoleons, and left fifteen hundred to meet present exigencies; this was all the Emperor's treasure. They were assisted, or rather impeded, in the operation by Marchand, the valet-de-chambre of his Majesty. This appeared to mortify the Admiral excessively; though requested to attend, not one amongst us would lend his presence to, or witness an act which we regarded as being at once mean and outrageous.

Meanwhile, the moment of quitting the Bellerophon arrived. The Grand Marshal had been sometime closeted with the Emperor, during which we remained in the outer cabin; on the door being opened, the Duke de Rovigo, bursting into tears, threw himself at the feet of Napoleon, who, still calm and collected, embraced the Duke, and continued his way towards the accommodation-ladder, graciously saluting all those who happened to be on the quarter-deck. The whole of our party whom we left behind, were in a state of the deepest anguish; nor could I help observing to Lord Keith, who stood near me at the time, "You see, my Lord, that the only persons who shed tears are those who remain."

We reached the Northumberland between one and two o'clock. The Emperor remained on deck conversing familiarly and cheerfully with those of the English who approached him. Lord Lowther and a Mr. Littleton had a long conversation with him on politics and government. I heard nothing of what passed: the Emperor seemed desirous that we should leave him to himself. I employed this moment of leisure in writing a last adieu to my wife and friends; indeed, I felt very unwell and much fatigued.

At the moment of getting under weigh, a cutter that was plying round the ship to keep off the people, ran down a boat full of spectators close to us. Fatality seems to have brought them from a great distance to become the victims of this accident; I understood that there were two women amongst those who perished. Thus were we at length under sail for St. Helena, thirteen days after our arrival at Plymouth, and forty from our quitting Paris.

Those of the attendants whom Napoleon was not allowed to take with him, were the last to quit the ship, bearing with them mingled proofs of satisfaction and regret. Their departure gave rise to a second scene, not less affecting than the first. The Emperor retired to the cabin allotted to him about seven o'clock.

The English Ministry warmly censured the respect which had been shewn to the Emperor on board the Bellerophon, and issued fresh orders in consequence; so that a totally different style of manner and expression was affected in the Northumberland. The crew seemed to betray a ridiculous anxiety to be covered before the Emperor; it had been strictly enjoined to give him no other title than that of *Gen-*

eral, and only to treat him as such. This was the ingenious contrivance, the happy conception engendered by the diplomacy of the English Ministers; and the title they thought proper to confer on him whom they had recognised as First Consul, whom they had so often styled head of the French Government, with whom they treated as Emperor at Paris, when Lord Lauderdale was employed to negotiate, and, perhaps, even signed articles at Chatillon. Hence, in a moment of warmth, the Emperor, in allusion to this regulation, observed: "They may call me whatever they choose, but they cannot prevent me from being *myself*." It was in fact no less whimsical than ridiculous to see the Ministers of England attach such importance to giving only the title of General to one who had governed so large a portion of Europe, and made seven or eight kings, of whom several still retained this title of his creation; who had been ten years Emperor of the French, and been annointed as well as consecrated in that quality by the head of the church; one who could boast two or three elections of the French people to the sovereignty; who had been acknewledged as Emperor by the whole of continental Europe; had treated as such with all the sovereigns; concluding every species of alliance both of blood and interest with them; so that he united in his person every title, civil, political, and religious, existing amongst men; and which, by a singular, though real, coincidence, not one of the reigning Princes of Europe could have shewn accumulated in an equal degree. Napoleon was not only the chief, but founder of his own dynasty. Nevertheless, his Majesty, who intended had he landed in England, to have assumed the name and title of Colonel Duroc or Muiron, no longer thought of it now that his legitimate titles were disputed.

Description of the Emperor's cabin on board the Northumberland.

8th.—9th.—The ship was in the greatest confusion, and seemed to be quite encumbered with men as well as stores and luggage; we sailed in so great a hurry, that there was scarcely any thing on board in its place, so that the whole crew were now occupied in restoring order, and preparing for the voyage.

The following particulars will afford some idea of the ship occupied by the Emperor and his suite. The space abaft the mizen-mast contained two public and two private cabins; the first was a dining-room, about ten feet broad, and extending the whole width of the ship, lighted by a porthole at each end, and a sky-light above. The drawing-room was composed of all the remaining space, diminished by two symmetrical cabins on the right and left, each having an entry from the dining or mess-room, and another from the drawing-room. The Emperor occupied that on the left, in which his camp-bedstead had been put up; that on the right was appropriated to the Admiral. It was, above all, promptly enjoined, that the drawing-room should be in common, and not given up to the Emperor; to such a ridiculous extent had the fears and solicitude of the Ministry been carried?

The form of the dining-table resembled that of the mess-room. The Emperor sat with his back to the drawing-room or after-cabin, and looking towards the head of the ship; on his left sat Madame Bertrand, and on his right, the Admiral. On the right of the Admiral sat Madame de Montholon; these filled one side of the table. At the end next that lady was Captain Ross, who commanded the ship; opposite whom, at the corresponding end, sat M. de Montholon, by Madame Bertrand; next him, the Admiral's secretary. The remaining space was the side of the table opposite the Emperor, which beginning from Captain Ross, was occupied by the Grand Marshal, the General commanding the 53d regiment, myself, and Baron Gourgaud.

The Admiral invited one or two of the officers every day, who were intermixed amongst us at table. I generally sat almost opposite the Emperor. The band of the 53d, which had been recently formed, exercised during dinner at the expense of our ears. We had two courses, but there was a want of provision; our tastes were, besides, very different from those of our hosts. It is true, they did their utmost; but, after all, it would not do to be difficult. I was lodged with my son on the starboard side, even with the main-mast, in a small cabin enclosed with canvas, and having a gun in it. We made as much sail as the wind would permit to get out of the Channel, and stood along the coast of England, communicating with all the ports in order to procure additional supplies of sea-stock, and complete the stores of the ship. A large quantity of articles was brought to us from Plymouth, off which port we were joined by several other vessels, as well as from Falmouth.

We lose sight of Land.—Reflections.—Argument against the English Ministers.

10th.—This day we cleared the Channel, and lost sight of land. We had now entered upon the dreary unknown course to which fate had doomed us. Again my agonies were renewed; again the dear connections I had abandoned resumed their influence over my heart. I indulged in the luxuriance of grief, and found a miserable satisfaction in its excess. "Objects of all my affections," I exclaimed, "friends of my heart, for whom alone I live, reflect that I am proving myself worthy of you. Let that thought support you also; and, oh! forget me not."

Meanwhile we advanced in our course, and were soon to be out of Europe. Thus, in less than six weeks, had the Emperor abdicated his throne, and placed himself in the hands of the English, who were now hurrying him to a barren rock in the midst of a vast ocean! This is certainly no ordinary instance of the chances of fortune, and no common trial of the firmness of the mind. Yet will posterity be better able to judge of these three leading circumstances, than we of the present day. They will have to pronounce on a clear horizon; whereas we are enveloped in clouds.

Scarcely had Napoleon descended from his throne, when those, who witnessed the misfortunes of the nation which followed, regarded his sacrifice as a capital error. When they heard of his being a prisoner at Plymouth, they censured his magnanimity: there was not a single incident, even to his suffering himself to be sent to St. Helena, which they did not make a subject of reproach. But such is the tendency of vulgar minds; never judging except on what they see at the moment! It is, however, impossible to judge of one resolution without considering, not only the evils which unavoidably attend it, but those which a contrary determination might have produced.

By abdicating, Napoleon rallied all the friends of their country round one point—that of its safety! He left France demanding, before all nations, nothing but the sacred rights of national independence; he took from the Allies every pretext to ravage and dismember our territory; he destroyed all idea of his personal ambition; terminating his career as the martyr of a cause of which he had been the hero. If all the advantages which might have been derived from his genius and talents as a citizen were not obtained, it is to be imputed to the weakness and treachery of the transitory government by which he was succeeded. When he arrived at Rochefort, and the commander of the frigates refused to sail, ought he to have abandoned the fruits of his abdication? Should he have returned to the interior, and placed himself at the head of mere bands, when he had renounced armies? or, ought he to have desperately encouraged a civil war which would lead to no beneficial result, but only serve to ruin the remaining pillars, the future hopes of the country? In this state of affairs, he formed a most magnanimous resolution, worthy of his life, and a complete refutation of the calumnies that for twenty years had been so ridiculously accumulated on his head. But what will history say of those ministers of a liberal nation, the guardians and depositories of popular rights—ever ardent in encouraging a Coriolanus, having only chains for a Camillus?

As to the reproach of suffering himself to be transported to St. Helena, it would be a disgrace to answer such a charge. To contend with an adversary in the cabin of a ship—kill some one with his own hand—or attempt to set fire to the powder-magazine, would have been, at best, the act of a buccaneer. Dignity in misfortune, submission to necessity, have also their glory: it is that which becomes great men overwhelmed by adversity.

When the English ministers found themselves in possession of Napoleon's person, passion had much more influence over them than justice or policy. They neglected the triumph of their laws, denied the rights of hospitality, disregarded their own honour, and compromised that of their country. They determined to exile their guest in the midst of the ocean, two thousand leagues from Europe, and far from all communion with mankind. It seemed that they wished to trust to the anguish of exile, the fatigues of a long voyage, privations of every kind, and the corroding influence of a burning climate, for effecting that which they feared to perform themselves. In order, however, to gain over the public voice, to make it appear that their conduct was indispensably necessary, the newspapers were instigated to irritate the passions of the multitude, by reviving former calumnies and falsehoods: while the ministers, on their side, represented their own determination as an engagement entered into with their allies. We presented ourselves at the moment of popular effervescence, just as every thing which could render us odious had been brought forward. The public journals were full of the most virulent declamations; maliciously raking up every act and expression of the previous struggle of twenty years, that could wound the national pride or re-kindle its hatred. Yet, when all England hurried to the south to see us, during our stay at Plymouth, the conduct and sentiments of the multitudes who came was enough to convince us that this factitious irritation would disappear of itself. Hence we were led to hope, on our departure, that the British people would daily grow more impartial in a cause to which they were no longer parties; that the current of public opinion would eventually turn against ministers; and that we had thus prepared formidable attacks and a terrible responsibility for them at a future day. Under these circumstances, what could these ministers have replied had any member of Parliament risen, and made use of the following argument:

"We have just been favoured by an unexampled instance of success! Fortune has caused our most constant and implacable enemy to surrender at discretion: we have suddenly found ourselves masters of the fate of the French sovereign and people: it was in our power to dispose of the future, or at least to enchain its unfavourable chances for a long period. Have our ministers profited by so many advantages? Have they ensured our interests, happiness, and glory? Have they guaranteed a durable peace—the first of our wishes, the most pressing of our wants? Have they extinguished that turbulent agitation, that warlike disposition throughout Europe, which keeps every nation in arms? Have they secured that happy political equilibrium, which prevents revolutions, and reduces war to a mere trifle? Have they strengthened and propagated our national principles? Have they secured for us the respect and affection of the European family, as the price of our efforts in its favour? Have they proved the excellence and superiority of our institutions and laws? Alas! I hear only negatives to all these questions. Europe was never more inflamed; its situation is at best only an armed truce; each power increases the number of its soldiers; the political balance is totally destroyed and broken. In a neighbouring state we have annihilated the very principles which form the sacred basis of our own political theory: universal jealousy animates the whole continent against us; and our civil laws have sustained an outrage calculated to leave an indelible stain on the nation."

"Do our Ministers flatter themselves that the destruction of our rival is a sufficient answer to every charge? But how are we so deeply interested in her destruction? In sound policy, is not her existence necessary to our glory and stability? For I am one of those who fear our own excesses, should we remain uncontrolled in the midst of prosperity. But what do I say? This very rival may be essentially necessary to us, either as an ally or counterpoise. It would be the height of folly to imagine, that the great struggle being over, the Continental States will not again give way to their natural jealousy of our maritime power, so prejudicial to their interests. In sincerely uniting themselves to us, they merely warded off the most pressing danger. New disputes and difficulties must infallibly arise; and if that system of universal monarchy, which has so often endangered us, and which we overturned when it extended from the south towards the north, should menace us again, by coming from the north towards the south, where would be our resource? How blind, then, is our policy, to annihilate France by imposing on her a government that our armies are obliged to defend and preserve! Above all, why have we drawn the personal animosity of its immense population on ourselves! If the weakening, or even destruction of France, was our real interest, it ought to have been effected; though justice might have censured the step, policy would have excused it; but it should have been frankly avowed: nations as well as individuals know how to submit to necessity. When the vanquished are plainly told that the rights of victory are exercised over them, their pride is soothed by reflecting on the vicissitudes of fortune; but their hearts are filled with bitterness and rage if they are plundered under the mask of hypocrisy and bad faith: this is to add outrage to violence. Why, therefore, say that you only seek the happiness of France, while you load her with contributions? Why pretend to have no other object in view but her deliverance from tyranny, and yet inflict intolerable sufferings on her? Why profess to have only made war against a single man, and yet trample on a whole nation? Why seize her fortresses, and strip her of the trophies of her victories? not because she had been vanquished in her turn, which would have been natural and just; but under the pretence that these possessions were only the result of robbery and plunder? Why so much contradiction between words and actions? Because the real object of these proceedings is one which those who aim at it dare not avow—because the doctrine which guides them is too unpopular to be acknowledged—because they endeavour to serve a party in Europe rather than eternal principles. Far be it from me to make any personal application: I wish to avoid passion and prejudice: I consider no other interest at this moment but that of my country. May our Ministers entertain the same sentiments! But how came they to place England amongst, or at the head of Powers who have shamelessly, and in the face of Europe, violated the sacred rights of national independence? How could they dare to sanction such doctrines? In their stay at the Congress of Vienna, did they intoxicate themselves over the cup of the old Continental doctrines? or did the arrival of the sovereigns in this country innoculate them with sentiments of absolute power; destroying the national maxim of the people's rights? What can have led them to overturn the solemn choice of a nation?

"Napoleon on his return had consecrated the very same public institutions and fundamental laws which we ourselves boast; all his strength and popularity arose from these acts; had he afterwards infringed on them, both would have been lost: he was too wise and too strong to be suspected of such a design. The institution of both nations would, therefore, have corresponded with each other, in spite of all obstacles. Perhaps this might have been the prelude to a knew and unknown system; when the people of two countries, which had, till now, only felt repugnance and hatred against each other, might have thenceforth formed a natural union, with common and inseparable interests. Instead of this, narrow and unjust views have thrown us into a position altogether forced and unnatural; Great Britain appears to stand in direct opposition to its manners, religion, constitution, and laws. We, a free people, impose chains on our neighbours! We, a sovereign people, must destroy the sovereignty of the people next us! We, the guardians of liberal ideas, employ our armies to extinguish those very ideas! We, the protectors and head of the protestant faith, permit the massacre of our brethren in France, and in sight of our national banners! Let not Ministers take credit to themselves for maintaining by this system a large army on the Continent, which will cost us nothing. I dread such an advantage much more than some reverses. In a foreign land, our soldiers will become foreigners; they will at last have no other country than the field of battle; the manners and maxims of our youth will become corrupted amidst the maxims and manners of other nations. If Ministers, the guardians of our constitution, had inherited the spirit of our forefathers, instead of thinking it important to preserve a large army, they would rather have been eager to reduce it. Will Ministers justify themselves on the plea that the Allies wished, once for all, utterly to destroy the revolutionary principle? But the Revolution had ended, and has been recommenced by the Allies themselves.

"The sovereigns, by insisting on prerogatives, and favouring the aristocratical faction to excess, have again awakened the jealousy and roused the passions of the people. Europe will soon be divided throughout, into the two extreme parties of Marius and Sylla. The cause of kings and their courts had been gained; they have hazarded it once more. Whither may not this lead us! There is no nation in Europe that suffers so much from the French Revolution, as France; will that unhappy country be destined to become a spectacle of the contrary excesses? I must notice a vulgar error propagated by our late measures: the very man who is now charged with all the crimes of the Revolution, is he who miraculously stopped it in its course, with the energy and force of an athletic champion stopping a chariot in the midst of its rapid career. It was he who replaced France in the European community; who re-established the manners, principles, and language of modern civilization; it was he who removed the stains of that very Revolution, by actions the most brilliant and glorious. On entering France, the Allies could not help doing homage to his monuments, institutions, and administration—an administration the most vigorous and enlightened hitherto known. What would have become of the sovereigns of Vienna and Berlin, if, on entering their capitals, he had revolutionized their subjects. It is well known that he rather kept down the germs of commotion found in these States; so much so indeed, that the revolutionists of the day considered him as an apostate from the Revolution. How does it happen, that circumstances and our injudicious conduct, now point him out as its martyr and Messiah to these very people? It was proper to make war against him while he was formidable to us; but we should have coalesced with his genius the moment our first object was attained. Let Ministers, therefore, no longer attempt to justify their conduct and measures, by telling us they were implicitly prescribed by the grand principle of legitimacy: what can they possibly mean by that?

"Is it the absolute prohibition of every new dynasty whatever? Can there be men ignorant of the fact, that this principle, however true in theory, is only decided by facts in the political world? Do they not know that crowns are in the hands of God, and in the winning of battles? If that of Waterloo had taken a different turn, what would have become of this famous principle? Would they have refused to treat *sine qua non*; and do they really and sincerely expect to make us believe that Europe could no longer exist, were a new dynasty to appear? Dare they maintain that the welfare of nations depends upon a religious belief, that the favour of Heaven has been entirely exhausted on the reigning families of the present day? But how long has this been the creed of our Ministers? How is it that they have become so difficult and scrupulous on this principle? Have their various communications and secret understandings with Vienna, not only established a coalition of Kings, but also a coalition of doctrines and Ministers; a conspiracy against fortune, and the irresistible force of events? We must then have been much less scrupulous when we acknowledged the First Consul, and received his Ambassadors; or when, at a later period, and while at war with him, we recognized him as head of the French Government; when we sent Lord Lauderdale to Paris for the purpose of treating with the Emperor of the French; when these very Ministers treated on the same footing at Chatillon, and, perhaps, even signed articles. If these had been ratified, what would then have become of the sanctity of the new principle? Why are they at this moment so indifferent to the events of Spain, where a son has dethroned his father? How do they happen to be the allies of Sweden, whence the legitimate Sovereign has been exiled, to call in a foreigner? But, what is still more extraordinary, how durst they adopt this new doctrine, without thinking of the family which governs us, of the glorious revolution which placed it upon the throne, of the excellent laws by which its sway has been distinguished, and which has ruled us with so much glory to the present time!

"But enough has been said of the errors of our Ministers abroad. I turn to an act of their domestic policy, which outrages our laws, and wounds our honour: I allude to the transportation of Napoleon. This noble adversary, by an act of magnanimity worthy of his life, disdaining to address himself to the Emperor of Russia, who had called himself his friend; disdaining to apply to the Emperor of Austria, whose son-in-law he was—selected an asylum in our island, in the bosom of a nation against which he had fought for twenty years: because, persecuted by all the sovereigns of Europe, he still wished, in all his misfortunes, to preserve his independence, and thought to find it in the stability and empire of our laws. What nobler triumph could England have—what greater homage could be paid to our institutions? Our Ministers laid a snare for him; they encouraged his sentiments; and when he placed himself in their power, they loaded him with chains: for it is a fact which no person can deny, that Napoleon came on board the Bellerophon freely and of his own accord. He was told that orders had been given to the Captain to receive and conduct him to England; these assurances were taken by him as an engagement of hospitality: his letter to the Prince Regent is a proof of this, and that engagement ought to have been valid for him, when the letter, which was communicated before he himself appeared, passed without any observation being made on it. It is in vain for Ministers to answer that they were forced to deliver him up to the ostracism of Kings; and that they had engaged to do so. Their answer leaves them in the following shameful dilemma:—either they made that engagement before his arrival, and by enticing him forfeited their honour; or, it was made after his coming, and therefore they betrayed their duty, in subjecting our laws and our dignity to foreign councils. I demand, therefore, that Napoleon be brought back, and that he be landed in this country, which he had chosen as an asylum. I demand this as a solemn reparation for the outrage offered to our laws, which, by this triumph, will become more renowned from their momentary violation."

The Emperor's mode of living on board the Northumberland.

11th—14.—Our course was shaped to cross the Bay of Biscay, and double Cape Finisterre. The wind was fair, though light, and the heat excessive; nothing could be more monotonous than the time we now passed. The Emperor breakfasted in his own cabin at irregular hours: we took our breakfast at ten o'clock, in the French style, while the English continued to breakfast in their own way at eight.

The Emperor sent for one of us every morning to know what was going on, the distance run, the state of the wind, and other particulars connected with our progress. He read a great deal, dressed towards four o'clock, and then came into the general cabin; here he played at chess with one of the party; at five o'clock, the Admiral having come out of his cabin a few minutes before, announced that dinner was on the table.

It is well known that Napoleon was scarcely ever more than fifteen minutes at his dinner; here the two courses alone occupied from an hour to an hour and a half; this was to him, a most serious annoyance, though he never mentioned it; his features, gestures, and manner, always evinced perfect indifference. Neither the new system of cookery, the difference or quality of the dishes, ever met with censure or approbation; he never expressed any wish or objection on the subject. He was attended by his two valets, who stood behind his chair. At first the Admiral was in the habit of offering to help the Emperor; but the acknowledgment of Napoleon was expressed so coldly, that this practice was discontinued. The Admiral continued very attentive, but thenceforth only pointed out to the servants what was preferable; they alone attended to these matters, to which the Emperor seemed totally indifferent, neither seeing, noticing, or seeking any thing. He was generally silent, remaining in the midst of conversation as if totally unacquainted with the language, though it was French. If he spoke, it was to ask some technical or scientific question, and to address a few words to those whom the Admiral occasionally asked to dinner. I was the person to whom the Emperor generally addressed his questions, in order to translate them.

I need scarcely observe, that the English are accustomed to remain a long time at table after the desert, drinking and conversing; the Emperor, already tired by the tedious dinner, could never have endured this custom, and he rose, therefore, from the first day immediately after coffee had been handed round, and went out on deck, followed by the

Grand Marshal and myself. This disconcerted the Admiral, who took occasion to express his surprise to his officers; but Madame Bertrand, whose maternal language is English, warmly replied—"Do not forget, Admiral, that your guest is a man who has governed a large portion of the world, and that kings once contended for the honour of being admitted to his table." "Very true," rejoined the Admiral; and this officer, who possesses good sense, a becoming pliability of manners, and sometimes much elegance, did his utmost from that moment to accommodate the Emperor in his habits. He shortened the time of sitting at table, ordering coffee for Napoleon and those who accompanied him, even before the rest of the company had finished their dinner. The moment Napoleon had taken his coffee, he left the cabin; upon which every body rose till he had quitted the room, and then continued to take their wine for another hour.

The Emperor remained walking on deck, till dark attended by the Grand Marshal and myself. This became a regular practice, and was seldom omitted. On returning to the after-cabin, he sat down to play *vingt-et-un* with us, and generally retired in about half an hour.

Singular good fortune of the Emperor.

15th.—We asked permission to be admitted into the Emperor's presence this morning, and all entered his cabin at the same time. He was not aware of the cause of this visit:—it was his birth-day, which seemed to have altogether escaped his recollection. We had been in the habit of seeing him on that anniversary, on a much larger stage, and in the midst of his power, but never were our vows more sincere, or our hearts more full of attachment than on the present occasion.

The days now exactly resembled each other: at night we constantly played at *vingt-et-un*; the Admiral and some of his officers being occasionally of the party. The Emperor used to retire after losing, according to custom, his ten or twelve Napoleons; this happened to him daily, because he would persist in leaving his stake on the table, until it had produced a considerable number. To-day he had gained from eighty to a hundred. The Admiral dealt the cards; the Emperor still wished to leave his winnings, in order to see how far he could reach; but thought he could perceive it would be quite as agreeable to the Admiral if he stopped where he was. The Emperor had won sixteen times, and might have won more than sixty thousand Napoleons. While all present were expatiating on his being thus singularly favoured by fortune, an English officer observed that it was the anniversary of his birth day.

Continuation of the voyage—Occupations—The Emperor's origin and family—Anecdotes.

16th—21st.—We doubled Cape Finisterre on the 16th, passed Cape St. Vincent on the 18th, and were opposite the Straits of Gibraltar next day. Continuing our course along the coast of Africa towards Madeira, nothing worthy of remark occurred, there being perfect uniformity in our habits and mode of passing the time; if there was any difference, it could only arise from the subject of our conversation.

The Emperor usually remained in his cabin during the whole morning: so excessive was the heat, that he only wore a very slight dress. He could not sleep, and frequently rose in the night. Reading was his chief occupation. I was sent for almost every morning, and translated from the "Encyclopædia Britannic," and such other books as were on board, whatever they contained relative to St. Helena, or the countries near which we were sailing. This led to my Historical Atlas being brought under review. Napoleon had merely glanced at it on board the Bellerophon, and before that time he had but a very indistinct notion of the work. I now had the satisfaction of seeing it in the Emperor's hands for several days, and of hearing him express the warmest approbation of my labours. The quantity and arrangement of the matter seemed more particularly to please him: he had, in fact, hitherto been but little acquainted with the book. Passing over all the others, his chief attention was attracted by the geographical charts; more especially the map of the world, which seemed principally to excite his notice and applause. I did not attempt to convince him that the geography was the weakest part of the work, displaying far less labour and research than other parts: the general tables could not easily be surpassed, either as to their method, symmetry, or facility for use; while each of the genealogical tables presented a miniature history of the country they concerned, and of which they were, in all respects, both a complete analysis, and a collection of elementary materials.

The Emperor asked me whether the work had been used in all our systems of education; adding, that had it been better known to him, all the schools and lyceums should have been furnished with it. I was also asked, why I had published it under the borrowed name of Le Sage. I replied, that a very imperfect sketch had been published in England, just after my emigration, at a time when we could not acknowledge our names without danger to our relations; "and, perhaps," said I laughing, "I was not then cured of the prejudices of my youth: like the nobles of

Bretagne, who deposited their swords with the registrar of the Civil Court, while engaged in trade, that they might not derogate from their family dignity."

As already observed, the Emperor always rose from table long before the rest of the company: the Grand Marshal and I always followed him to the quarter-deck, where I was frequently left alone with him; as General Bertrand had often to attend his wife, who suffered excessively from sea-sickness.

After the preliminary remarks on the weather, the ship's progress, and the winds, Napoleon used to start a subject of conversation, or revive that of the preceding or some other former day; and when he had taken eight or nine turns the whole length of the deck, he would seat himself on the second gun from the gangway on the larboard side. The midshipmen soon observed this habitual predilection, so that the cannon was thenceforth called the *Emperor's gun*.

It was there that Napoleon often conversed for hours together, and that I learned for the first time a part of what I am about to relate: in doing which, I wish to observe that I shall at the same time add whatever I collected in a variety of subsequent conversations; thus, presenting at one view, all that I have heard worth noting on the subject. This is, perhaps, the proper place to repeat, once for all, that if little order or method be found in my journal, it arises from the manner in which I am pressed for time: my contemporaries expect the work, and the state of my health precludes all application; thus situated, I am fearful of not having time to finish it. Such are my excuses, unfortunately too valid:—such are my claims to indulgence, as to the style and arrangement of my facts. What was set down at the moment, is here hastily re-produced, nearly in the same state as when first committed to paper.

The name of Bonaparte may be spelt either *Bonaparte* or *Buonaparte;* as all Italians know. Napoleon's father always introduced the *u;* and his uncle, the Archdeacon Lucien, (who survived Napoleon's father, and was a parent to Napoleon and his brothers) at the same time, and under the same roof, wrote it *Bonaparte.* During his youth, Napoleon followed the example of his father. On attaining the command of the army of Italy, he took good care not to alter the orthography, which agreed with the spirit of the language; but at a later period, and when amongst the French, he wished to adopt their orthography, and thenceforth wrote his name Bonaparte.

This family for many years made a distinguished figure in the Bolognese territory: it was very powerful at Trevisa; and is to be found inscribed on the golden book of Bologna, as also amongst the patricians of Florence.

When Napoleon, as General-in-chief of the army of Italy, entered Trevisa, at the head of his victorious army, the principal inhabitants came to meet him, bringing title-deeds and records, which proved that his family had once been one of the most eminent in their city.

At the interview of Dresden, before the Russian campaign, the Emperor Francis one day told Napoleon, then his son-in-law, that his family had governed as sovereigns at Trevisa: a fact of which there could be no doubt, as Francis had caused all the documents proving it to be drawn up and presented to him. Napoleon replied with a smile, that he did not wish to know any thing about it, and that he would greatly prefer being the Rodolph of Hapsburg, of the Austrian family. Francis attached much more importance to the matter: he said, that it was of very little consequence to have fallen from wealth to poverty; but that it was above all price to have been a sovereign, and that the fact must be communicated to Maria Louisa, to whom it would afford infinite pleasure.

When during the campaign of Italy, Napoleon entered Bologna, Marescalchi, Caprara, and Aldini, since so well known in France, and at that time deputies in the senate of their native city, came of their own accord to present the golden book, in which the name and arms of his ancestors were inscribed.

There are several houses at Florence which attest the former existence of the Bonaparte family there; many houses are even still bearing the escutcheons of the family.

Cesari, a Corsican or Bolognese, residing in London, who was shocked at the manner in which the British government had received Napoleon's pacific letter on assuming the Consulate, published a genealogical notice, wherein he established the Emperor's alliance with the ancient house of *Este*, *Welf*, or *Guelf*, supposed to be the parent stem of the present royal family of England.*

The Duke de Feltre, French ambassador in Tuscany, brought the portrait of a Bonaparte who had married a princess of the Grand Duke's family. The mother of Pope Nicholas V. or Paul V. of Sarzana, was also a Bonaparte.

* This paragraph was in such a state in the manuscript, as to excite doubts; and I was on the point of suppressing it: I must, therefore, state my reasons for its insertion. What is my object? chiefly to leave materials behind me. When I indicate how these were collected, and say that I obtained them from a mere conversation—that I may have disfigured them in thus suddenly seizing their sense—when I admit their probable inaccuracy, and place the reader in the way of rectifying my errors—have I not sufficiently fulfilled my object and duty? Besides, I am at this moment endeavouring to verify many of these points, and if the results reach me in time, they will be found at the end of the work, under the head of errata, or in the form of an Appendix.

It was a Bonaparte who negotiated the treaty by which Leghorn was exchanged for Sarzana. It is to a Bonaparte that we are indebted for one of the oldest comedies written at the period of the revival of letters, entitled *The Widow*. It may still be seen in the Royal Library at Paris.*

When Napoleon marched against Rome at the head of the French army, and received the propositions of the pope at Tolentino, one of the negotiators of the enemy observed, that he was the only Frenchman who had marched against Rome since the Constable de Bourbon; but what rendered this circumstance still more singular was, that the history of the first expedition was written by an ancestor of him who executed the second, that is to say, Monsignor Nicolas Bonaparte, who has in reality left us a work, called *The Sacking of Rome by the Constable de Bourbon*.†

Hence, perhaps, or from the pope mentioned above, the name of Nicolas, which the writer of certain pamphlets pretended to be that of the Emperor, instead of Napoleon. This work is to be found in most libraries; it is preceded by a history of the house of Bonaparte, printed about forty or fifty years ago, edited by Dr. Vaccha, a professor of Pisa.

M. de Cetto, ambassador of Bavaria, has often told me that the archives of Munich contained a great number of documents, in Italian, which proved the antiquity and importance of the Bonaparte family.

During the continuance of his power, Napoleon always refused to take any pains, or even enter into conversation on the subject. The first attempt to excite his attention to this matter occurred in the time of his Consulate, and was so much discouraged, that no one ever attempted to renew the discussion. Some one published a genealogy, in which it was contrived to connect the family of Napoleon with certain northern kings. Napoleon caused this specimen of flattery to be ridiculed in the public papers, in which the writers concluded by observing, that the nobility of the First Consul only dated from *Montenotte*, or from the 18th of Brumaire.

* Verified at the Royal Library: the manuscript being really there, and the play itself printed.

† Also verified at the Royal Library where the account of the sacking of Rome is deposited, but by *James Buonaparte*, and not *Nicholas*. James was a contemporary and an occular witness of the event: his manuscript was printed for the first time at Cologne, in 1756; and the volume actually contains a genealogy of the Bonapartes, which is carried back to a very remote period, and describes them as one of the most illustrious houses of Tuscany

The above genealogy presents a fact which is certainly of a very singular nature: it is that of the first Bonaparte having been exiled from his country as a *Ghibeline*. Was it, then, the destiny of this family, in all times, and at every epoch, that it must yield to the malignant influence of the *Guelfs!*

The Cologne editor sometimes writes *Buonaparte*, and at others *Bonaparte*.

This Monsignor Nicolas Bonaparte, named in the text as the historian, is only the uncle; he is, however, mentioned in the genealogy as a very distinguished man of learning, and as having founded the class of jurisprudence in the University of Pisa.

This family suffered, like many others, from the numerous revolutions which desolated the cities of Italy. The troubles of Florence placed the Buonapartes amongst the *fuorusciti*, or emigrants. One of the family retired to Sarzana in the first instance, and thence went to Corsica, from which island his descendants always continued to send their children to Tuscany, where they were educated under the care of the branch that remained at San Miniato. The second sons of this branch had borne the name of Napoleon for several generations, which was derived from an ancestor thus named, celebrated in the annals of Italy.

When on his way to Florence, after the expedition to Leghorn, Napoleon slept at the house of an old Abbé Buonaparte, at San Miniato, who treated the whole of his staff with great magnificence. Having exhausted all the family reminiscences, the Abbè told the young General that he was going to bring forth the most precious document of all. Napoleon thought he was about to show him a fine genealogical tree, well calculated to gratify his vanity, (said he, laughing); but it was a memorial regularly drawn up in favour of father Buonaventura Buonaparte, a Capuchin friar of Bologna, long since beatified, but who had not yet been canonized, owing to the enormous expense it required. "The Pope will not refuse you," said the good Abbé, "if you ask him; and should it be necessary to pay the sum now, it will be a mere trifle for you." Napoleon laughed heartily at this simplicity, so little in harmony with the manners of the day: the old man never dreamt that the saints were no longer in fashion.

On reaching Florence, Napoleon conceived it would be very satisfactory to his namesake to send him the ribbon of the order of St. Stephen, of which he was merely a knight; but the pious Abbé was much less anxious about the favours of this world, than the religious justice which he so pertinaciously claimed; and, as it afterwards appeared, not without reason. The Pope, when he came to Paris to crown the Emperor, also recurred to the claims of Father Buonaventura. "It was doubtless he," said the Pope, "who, from his seat amongst the blessed, had led his relative, as it were by the hand, through the glorious earthly career he had traversed; and who had preserved Napoleon in the midst of so many dangers and battles. The Emperor, however, always turned a deaf ear to these remarks: leaving it to the holy father's own discretion to provide for the glory of Buonaventura. As to the old Abbè of San Miniato, he left his fortune to Napoleon, who presented it to one of the public establishments in Tuscany.

It would, however, be very difficult to connect any genealogical data in this place, from the conversations of the Emperor; who used often to say, he had never looked at one of his parchments: these having always remained in the hands of his brother Joseph, whom he styled the "genealogist of the family." And, lest I may forget it, I will here mention the fact of Napoleon's having, when on the point of embarking, delivered a packet to his brother, containing all the original letters addressed to him by the sovereigns of Europe in their own hand writing. I frequently expressed my regret to the Emperor at his parting with such a precious historical manuscript.*

Charles Buonaparte, the father of Napoleon, was extremely tall, handsome, and well made; his education had been well conducted at Rome and Pisa, where he studied the law: he is said to have possessed great spirit and energy. It was he who, on its being proposed to submit to France, in the public assembly of Corsica, delivered a speech which electrified the whole country: he was not more than twenty years of age at this period. "If it only depended on the will to become free," said he, "all nations would be so; yet history teaches us, that very few have attained the blessings of liberty, because few have had energy, courage and virtue enough to deserve them."

When the island was conquered, he wished to accompany Paoli in his emigration; but an old uncle, the Archdeacon Lucien, who exercised the authority of a parent over him, prevented his departure.

In 1779, Charles Buonaparte was elected deputy to represent the nobles of Corsica at Paris, where he brought young Napoleon with him, then only ten years old. He passed through Florence on his way, and obtained a letter of introduction from the Grand Duke Leopold, to his sister the Queen of France. It was to his known rank and the respectability of his name and family in Tuscany, that he was indebted for this mark of attention.

There were two French generals in Corsica, at the above period, so inimical to each other that their quarrels formed two parties; one was M. de Marbeuf, a mild and popular character, and the other, M. de Narbonne Pellet, distinguished for haughtiness and violence. The latter, from his birth and superior interest, must have been a dangerous man for his rival: fortunately for M. de Marbeuf, he

*On my return to Europe, I did not fail to inquire for the invaluable deposit, and hastened to suggest the importance of making another copy to Prince Joseph, in order to become still more sure of its existence. What was my grief to hear, that this historical monument had been mislaid, and that no person knew what had become of it! Into whose hands can it have fallen? May they know how to appreciate such a collection, and preserve it for history?

was much more beloved in the island. When the deputation headed by Charles Bonaparte arrived at Versailles, he was consulted on the dispute, and the warmth of his testimony obtained a triumph for Marbeuf. The Archbishop of Lyons, nephew to Marbeuf, thought it his duty to wait on the deputy, and thank him for the service he had rendered. On young Napoleon's being placed in the military school of Brienne, the Archbishop gave him a special recommendation to the family of Brienne, which lived there during the greater part of the year; hence the friendly demeanor of the Marbeufs and Briennes towards the children of the Bonaparte family. Calumny has assigned another cause, but the simple examination of dates is fully sufficient to prove its absurdity.

Old M de Marbeuf, who commanded in Corsica, lived at Ajaccio, where the family of Charles Bonaparte was one of the principal. Madame Bonaparte being the most fascinating and beautiful woman in the town, it was very natural for the General to frequent her house in preference to many other places of resort.

Charles Bonaparte died at the age of thirty-eight, of an induration in the glands of the stomach. He had experienced a temporary cure during one of his visits to Paris; but became the victim of a second attack at Montpelier, where he was interred in one of the convents of the city.

During the Consulate the notables of Montpelier, through the medium of their compatriot Chaptal, minister of the interior, solicited the permission of the Frst Consul to erect a monument to the memory of his father. Napoleon thanked them for their good intentions, but declined acceding to their solicitation. "Let us not disturb the repose of the dead," said he; "let their ashes remain in peace. I have also lost my grandfather and great-grandfather; why not erect monuments to them? It is going too far back. Had my father died yesterday, it would be proper and natural that my grief should be accompanied by some signal mark of respect. But his death took place twenty years ago: it is an event of no public interest, and it is useless to revive the recollection of it." At a subsequent period Louis Bonaparte, without the knowledge of Napoleon, had his father's remains disinterred, and removed to Saint Leu, where he erected a monument to his memory.

Charles Bonaparte had been the very reverse of devout; he had even written some anti-religious poems; and yet at the period of his death, said the Emperor, there were not priests enough for him in Montpelier. In this respect he was very different from his brother Archdeacon Lucien, a very pious and orthodox ecclesiastic, who died long after him, at a very advanced age. On his death-bed, he took great umbrage at Fesch, who, being by this time a priest, ran to him in his stole and surplice to assist him in his last moments. Lucien begged that he would suffer him to die in peace, and he breathed his last surrounded by the members of his family, giving them philosophic counsel and patriarchal benedictions.

The Emperor frequently spoke of his old uncle, who had been a second father to him, and who was, for a length of time, the head of the family. He was Archdeacon of Ajaccio, one of the pricipal dignities of the island. His prudence and economy re-established the affairs of the family, which had been much deranged by the extravagance of Charles. The old uncle was much revered, and enjoyed considerable authority in the district; the peasantry voluntarily submitted their disputes to his decision, and he freely gave them his advice and his blessing.

Charles Bonaparte married Mademoiselle Letitia Ramolini, whose mother, after the death of her first husband, married Captain Fesch, an officer in one of the Swiss regiments which the Genoese usually maintained in the island. Cardinal Fesch was the issue of this second marriage, and was consequently step-brother to Madame and uncle to the Emperor.

Madame was one of the most beautiful women of her day, and she was celebrated throughout Corsica. Paoli, in the time of his power, having received an embassy from Algiers or Tunis, wished to give the savage envoys some notion of the attractions of the island, and for this purpose he assembled together all the most beautiful women in Corsica, among them Madame took the lead. Subsequently, when she travelled to Brienne to see her son, her personal charms were remarked even in Paris.

During the war for Corsican liberty, Madame Bonaparte shared the dangers of her husband, who was an enthusiast in the cause. In his different expeditions she frequently followed him on horseback, while she was pregnant with Napoleon. She was a woman of extraordinary vigour of mind, joined to considerable pride and loftiness of spirit. She was the mother of thirteen children, and she might have had many more, for she was a widow at thirty. Of these thirteen, only five boys and three girls lived, all of whom played distinguished parts in the reign of Napoleon.

Joseph, the eldest of the family, was originally intended for the church, on account of the influence possessed by Marbeauf, archbishop of Lyons, who had the patronage of numerous livings. He went through the regular course of study; but when the moment arrived for taking orders, he refused to enter the ecclesiastical profession. He was successively King of Naples and Spain.

Louis was King of Holland, and Jerome King of Westphalia. Eliza was grand duchess of Tuscany; Caroline, queen of Naples; and Pauline, Princess Borghese. Lucien, who through his marriage, and a mistaken direction of character, doubtless forfeited a crown, atoned for all his past errors, by throwing himself into the arms of the Emperor on his return from Elba, at a moment when Napoleon was far from relying on the certainty of his prospects. Lucien, the Emperor used to say, passed a turbulent career in his youth; at the age of fifteen he was taken to France by M. Semonville, who soon made him a zealous revolutionist, and an ardent clubist. On this subject, the Emperor said, that in the numerous libels published against him were some addresses or letters bearing, among other signatures, that of Brutus Bonaparte, which were attributed to him, Napoleon; he would not affirm, he added, that these addresses were not written by some individual of the family, but he could declare that they were not his production.

I had the opportunity of rendering myself acquainted with the sentiments of Prince Lucien, on the Emperor's return from Elba, and am enabled to say, that it would have been difficult for any man to have been more upright and steady in his political views, or to have evinced greater devotedness and good will towards his brother.

Madeira, &c.—Violent Gale.—Chess.

22d—26th.—On the 22d we came within sight of Madeira, and at night arrived off the port. Only two of the vessels cast anchor, to take on board supplies for the squadron. The wind blew very hard, and the sea was exceedingly rough. The Emperor found himself indisposed, and I was also ill. A sudden gale arose; the air was excessively hot, and seemed to be impregnated with small particles of sand; we were now assailed by the emanations of the terrible winds from the deserts of Africa. This weather lasted throughout the whole of the following day. Our communication with the shore became extremely difficult. The English Consul came on board, and informed us that for many years there had not been such a hurricane at Madeira; the vintage was entirely destroyed, all the windows in the town were broken, and it had been found scarcely possible to breathe in the streets. All this time we continued tacking about before the town; which we continued to do throughout the whole of the following night, and the 24th, when we took on board several oxen, and stores of other provisions, such as unripe oranges, bad peaches, and tasteless pears; the figs and grapes were however excellent. In the evening we made way with great rapidity; the wind still blowing hard. On the 25th and 26th we lay-to during a portion of each day, to distribute provisions among the vessels composing the squadron; during the rest of the time, we sailed on smoothly and rapidly.

Meanwhile nothing occurred to interrupt the uniformity of the scene. Each day crept slowly on, and added to the past interval, which, as a whole, seemed brief because it was void of interest, and not characterized by any remarkable incident.

The Emperor had added to the number of his amusements by a game at piquet, which he regularly played about three o'clock. This was succeeded by a few games at chess with the Grand Marshal, M. de Montholon, or some other individual, until dinner-time. There was no very good chess-player on board the vessel. The Emperor was but an indifferent player; he gained with some and lost with others, a circumstance which one evening led him to say, "How happens it that I frequently lose with those who are never able to beat him whom I almost always beat? Does not this seem contradictory? How is this problem to be solved?" said he, winking his eye, to shew that he was not the dupe of the constant politeness of him who was really the best player.

We no longer played at *Vingt-et-un* in the evening: we gave up this game on account of our having played too high, at which the Emperor appeared displeased, for he was a great enemy to gaming. On returning from his afternoon walk on deck, Napoleon played two or three games at chess, and retired to rest early.

The Canaries.—Passing the Tropic.—Details of the Emperor's childhood.—Napoleon at Brienne.—Pichegru.—Napoleon at the Military School in Paris.—In the Artillery.—His companions.—Napoleon at the commencement of the Revolution.

27th—31st.—At daybreak on Sunday, 27th, we found ourselves among the Canaries, which we passed in the course of the day, sailing at the rate of ten or twelve knots an hour, without having perceived the famous Peak of Teneriffe—a circumstance the more extraordinary, since in clear weather it is visible at the distance of sixty leagues.

On the 29th we crossed the tropic, and observed many flying fish round the ship. On the 31st, at eleven at night, one of the sailors threw himself overboard: he was a negro, who had got drunk, and was fearful of the flogging that awaited him. He had several times, in the course of the evening, attempted to jump overboard, and at last succeeded. He, however, soon repented, and uttered loud cries. He swam very well; but though a boat was immediately sent off, and every endeavour used to rescue him, he was lost.

The cries of this man in the sea excited a powerful sensation on board the vessel. In a moment the crew were hurrying about in every direction; the noise was very great, and the agitation universal.

As I was descending from deck to the cabin, a midshipman, an interesting youth between ten and twelve years of age, thinking I was going to inform the Emperor of what had occurred, seized hold of my coat, and in a tone expressive of the tenderest interest, exclaimed, "Ah, Sir, do not alarm the Emperor! Tell him the noise is nothing at all; that it is only a man fallen overboard." Amiable and innocent youth! he expressed his sentiments rather than his thoughts!

In general the midshipmen, of whom there were several on board the ship, behaved with marked respect and attention to the Emperor. They every evening repeated a scene that made a deep impression on our feelings. Early in the morning the sailors carried up their hammocks, and put them in the large nettings at the sides of the ship; and about six in the evening they carried them away at the signal of a whistle. Those who were tardy in the performance of this duty, received a certain punishment. On the signal being given a great bustle ensued: and it was gratifying to see the midshipmen at this moment form a circle round the Emperor, whether he might be standing in the middle of the deck or resting on his favourite gun. They watched his motions with an anxious eye, and either by signs or words directed the sailors to avoid incommoding him. The Emperor frequently observed this conduct, and remarked that youthful hearts were always inclined to enthusiasm.

I will now proceed with the details, which I collected at various times, respecting the early years of the Emperor's life.

Napoleon was born about noon on the 15th of August, (the Assumption Day,) in the year 1769. His mother, who was possessed of great bodily as well as mental vigour, and who had braved the dangers of war during her pregnancy, wished to attend mass on account of the solemnity of the day; she was however, taken ill at church, and on her return home was delivered before she could be conveyed to her chamber. The child as soon as it was born was laid on the carpet, which was an old-fashioned one, representing at full length the heroes of fable, or, perhaps, of the Iliad:—this child was Napoleon.

In his boyhood Napoleon was turbulent, adroit, lively and agile in the extreme. He had gained, he used to say, the most complete ascendency over his elder brother Joseph. The latter was beaten and ill-treated; complaints were carried to the mother, and she would begin to scold before poor Joseph had even time to open his mouth.

At the age of ten, Napoleon was sent to the military school at Brienne. His name, which in his Corsican accent he pronounced as if written Napoilloné, from the similiarty of the sound procured for him, among his youthful companions, the nick-name of *la paille au nez* (straw in his nose.) At this period a great change took place in Napoleon's character. In contradiction to all the apochryphal histories, which contain anecdotes of his life, he was when at Brienne, mild, quiet, and susceptible. One day the quarter-master, who was a man of harsh disposition, and who never took the trouble of considering the physical and moral shades of character in each individual scholar, condemned Napoleon, by way of punishment, to wear the serge coat, and to take his dinner on his knees at the door of the refectory. Napoleon, who had a vast share of pride and self-conceit, was so mortified by this disgrace, that he was seized with a violent retching, and suffered a severe nervous attack. The head master of the school happening accidentally to pass by, relieved him from the punishment, reproving the quarter-master for his want of discernment; and Father Patrault, the professor of mathematics, was very indignant on finding that his first mathematician had been treated with so little respect.

*"On attaining the age of puberty, Napoleon's temper became morose and reserved; his passion for reading was carried to excess; and he eagerly devoured the contents of every book that fell in his way. Pichegru was at this time his quarter-master and his tutor in the four rules of arithmetic.

"Pichegru was a native of the Franche-Compté, where his family were farmers. The Minime monks of Champagne were appointed to superintend the military school of Brienne. Owing to their poverty, however, so few individuals were induced to enter their order, that they found themselves inadequate to the task imposed on them; and they solicited the assistance of the Minime monks of the Franche-Comtè, of whom Father Patrault was one. An aunt of Pichegru, a nun of La Charitè, followed Patreult, for the purpose of superintending the infirmary, and she was accompanied by her nephew, a youth who was admitted to

* These lines were dictated by the emperor himself:—how and when will be hereafter explained.

the school to receive his education gratuitously. Pichegru, who was extremely clever, was, on his attaining a suitable age, made quarter-master and tutor under Father Patrault, who had taught him mathematics. He intended to become a monk, which was the sole object of his ambition and of his aunt's wishes. But Father Patrault dissuaded him from this idea, assuring him that the profession was not suited to the age; and that he should look forward to something better: he prevailed on him to enlist in the artillery, where the revolution found him a sub-officer. His military career is known:—he was the conqueror of Holland. Thus Father Patrault had the honour of counting among his pupils the two greatest generals of modern France.

Father Patrault was subsequently secularized by M. de Brienne, archbishop of Sens, and cardinal de Lomenie, who made him one of his grand vicars, and intrusted him with the management of his numerous benefices.

"At the time of the Revolution, Father Patrault, though his opinions were widely opposite to those of his patron, nevertheless exerted every endeavour to save him, and with this view applied to Danton, who was a native of the same part of France to which the Cardinal and himself belonged. But all was unavailing; and it is supposed that Patrault, after the manner of the ancients, rendered to the Cardinal the service of procuring for him a poisoned draught to save him from the scaffold.

Madame de Lomenie, the cardinal's niece, before her life was sacrificed by the revolutionary tribunal, intrusted Father Patrault with the care of her two daughters, who were yet in their childhood. The moment of terror having passed away, their aunt, Madame de Brienne, who had escaped the storm and preserved a considerable portion of her fortune, applied to Father Patrault for the children; but he refused to give them up, on the ground that their mother had directed him to withdraw them from the world, and devote them to the occupation of peasants. He had conceived the design of literally executing these figurative commands, and was on the point of uniting them to two of his own nephews. "I was then," said Napoleon, "general of the army of the interior, and I became the mediator for the restoration of the two children, an object which was accomplished not without difficulty. Patrault employed every possible means of resistance. These daughters of Madame de Lomenie were the two ladies whom you have since known by the names of Madame de Marnesia, and the beautiful Madame de Canisy, Duchess de Vicenza."

"Father Patrault having renewed his acquaintance with his old pupil, followed him and joined the army of Italy;

where he proved himself better able to calculate projectiles, than to meet their effects. At Montenotte, Millesimo, and Dego, he evinced the most puerile cowardice. He did not like Moses fall to praying when he ought to have been fighting; but he passed his time in weeping. The general-in-chief appointed him administrator of domains at Milan, from which he derived considerable profits.—On Napoleon's return from Egypt he presented himself to him: he was no longer the little Minime Monk of Champagne, but a corpulent financier, possessed of upwards of a million. Two years afterwards he again sought an interview with the First Consul at Malmaison: he now looked mean, dejected, and shabbily dressed. 'How is this?' inquired the consul. 'You see before you a ruined man,' replied Patrault: 'one who is reduced to beggary: the victim of severe misfortune.' The First Consul determined to investigate the truth of this statement: he discovered that Father Patrault had commenced the trade of an usurer. The great calculator had lost his fortune through bankruptcies, in lending at great risk for a high interest. 'I have already paid my debt,' said the First Consul, at his next interview with him; 'I can do no more for you: I cannot make a man's fortune twice.' He contented himself with granting Patrault a pension sufficient for his subsistence.

"Napoleon retained but a faint idea of Pichegru; he remembered that he was a tall man, rather red in the face. Pichegru, on the contrary, seems to have preserved a striking recollection of young Napoleon. When Pichegru joined the royalist party, he was asked whether it would not be possible to gain over the General-in-chief of the army of Italy. 'To attempt that would only be wasting time,' he said: 'from my knowledge of him when a boy I am sure he must be a most inflexible character: he has taken his resolutions, and he will not change them."

The Emperor has often been much amused at the tales and anecdotes that are related of his boyhood, in the numerous little publications which he had happened to peruse: he acknowledged scarcely any of them. There is one, relative to his confirmation at the military school of Paris, which, however, he admitted to be true. It is as follows:—the archbishop who confirmed him, manifesting his astonishment at the name of Napoleon, said he did not know of any such saint, and that there was no such name in the calendar; the boy quickly replied, that that could be no rule, since there were an immense number of saints and only 365 days.

Napoleon never observed his festival-day until after the Concordat; his patron saint was a stranger to the French calendar, and even where his name is recorded, the date of his festival is a matter of uncertainty. The Pope, however, fixed it for the 15th of August, which was at once the Emperor's birth-day, and the day of the signing of the Concordat.

*"In 1783, Napoleon was one of the scholars who, at the usual competition at Brienne, were fixed upon to be sent to the military school at Paris, to finish their education. The choice was made annually by an inspector, who visited the twelve military schools. This office was filled by the Chevalier de Keralio, a general officer, and the author of a work on military tactics. He was also the tutor of the present king of Bavaria, who in his youth bore the title of Duke de Duex-Ponts. Keralio was an amiable old man, and well adapted to discharge the duty of Inspector of the military schools. He was fond of the boys, played with them when they had finished their examinations, and permitted those who had acquitted themselves most to his satisfaction to dine with him at the table of the monks. He was particularly attached to young Napoleon, and took a pleasure in stimulating him to exertion. He singled him out to be sent to Paris, though it would appear he had not at that time attained the requisite age. The lad was not very far advanced in any branch of education except mathematics, and the monks suggested that it would be better to wait till the following year, to afford time for further improvement. But this the Chevalier de Keralio would by no means agree to: 'I know what I am about,' said he, 'and if I am transgressing the rules, it is not on account of family influence: I know nothing of the friends of this youth. I am actuated only by my own opinion of his merit. I perceive in him a spark of genius which cannot be too early fostered.' The worthy chevalier died suddenly, before he had time to carry his determination into effect; but his successor, M. de Regnaud, who would not perhaps have evinced half his penetration, nevertheless fulfilled his decision, and young Napoleon was sent to Paris."

At this period he began to develope qualities of a superior order: decision of character, profound reflection, and vigorous conceptions. It would appear, that from his earliest childhood his parents rested all their hopes on him. His father, when on his death-bed at Montpelier, though Joseph was beside him, spoke only of Napoleon, who was then at the military school. In the delirium with which he was seized in his last moments, he incessantly called Napoleon to come to his aid with his *great sword*. The grand uncle, Lucien, who on his death-bed was surrounded by all his

* Dictated by the Emperor.

relatives, said, addressing himself to Joseph, "You are the eldest of the family; but there is the head of it, (pointing to Napoleon). Never lose sight of him." The Emperor used to laugh and say, "This was a true disinheritance: it was the scene of Jacob and Esau."

Having myself been educated at the military school of Paris, though at an earlier period than that at which Napoleon attended it, I was enabled on returning from my emigration, to converse about the Emperor with the masters who had been common to us both.

M. de l'Eguille, our teacher of history, used to boast that the records of the military school contained proofs of his having foretold the great career which his pupil was destined to fill; and that he had frequently, in his notes, eulogized the depth of his reflection, and the shrewdness of his judgment. He informed me that the First Consul used often to invite him to breakfast at Malmaison, and that he always took pleasure in conversing about his old lessons:—"That which made the deepest impression on me," said he, one day to M. de l'Eguille, "was the revolt of the Constable de Bourbon, though you did not present it to us precisely in its proper light. You made it appear that his great crime was his having fought against his king; which certainly was but a trifling fault, in those days of divided nobility and sovereignty; particularly considering the scandalous injustice of which he was the victim. His great, his real, his only crime, and that on which you did not sufficiently dwell, was his having come with foreigners to attack his native soil."

M. Domairon, our professor of belles-lettres, informed me that he had always been struck with the singularity of Napoleon's amplifications, which he said were like flaming granites poured from a volcano.

Only one individual formed a mistaken idea of him; that was M. Bauer, the dull heavy German master. Young Napoleon never made much advancement in the German language, which offended M. Bauer, and he in consequence formed a most contemptible opinion of his pupil's abilities. One day Napoleon not being in his place, M. Bauer inquired where he was, and was told that he was attending his examination in the class of artillery. "Oh! so he does learn something?" said M. Bauer ironically. "Why, Sir, he is the best mathematician in the school," was the reply. "Ah! I have always heard it remarked, and I have always believed, that none but a fool could learn mathematics." "It would be curious," said the emperor, "to know whether M. Bauer, lived long enough to ascertain my real character, and to enjoy the confirmation of his own judgment."

Napoleon was scarcely eighteen years of age when the Abbé Raynal, struck with the extent of his acquirements, appreciated his merit so highly as to make him one of the ornaments of his scientific *déjeuners*. Finally, the celebrated Paoli, who had long inspired Napoleon with a sort of veneration, and who found that the latter had headed a party against him, whenever he showed himself favourable to the English, was accustomed to say—"This young man is formed on the ancient model. He is one of Plutarch's men."

In 1785, Napoleon, who was created at once a cadet and an officer of artillery, quitted the military school to enter the regiment of La Fère, in the rank of second-lieutenant; whence he was promoted to the rank of first-lieutenant in the regiment of Grenoble.

Napoleon on quitting the military school went to join his regiment at Valence. The first winter he spent there his comrades at the mess-table were Lariboissiére, who, during the empire, was appointed inspector-general of the artillery; Sorbier, who succeeded Lariboissiére in that post; d'Hedouville, junior, afterwards minister plenipotentiary at Frankfort; Mallet, the brother of him who headed the tumult in Paris in 1813; an officer named Mabille, whom, on his return from emigration, the Emperor appointed postmaster-general; Rolland de Villarceaux, afterwards prefect of Nismes; Desmazzis, senior, his companion at the military school and the friend of his early years, who, after Napoleon ascended the throne, became keeper of the Imperial wardrobe.

There were in the corps, officers more or less easy in their circumstances; Napoleon ranked among the former. He received from his family 1200 francs a-year, which was then an officer's full pay. There were two individuals in the regiment who could afford to keep cabriolets, or carriages of some kind, and they were looked upon as very great men. Sorbier was one of these two; his companions got him to drive them about, and they repaid the obligation by jokes and puns. Sorbier was the son of a physician at Moulins.

At Valence, Napoleon got an early introduction to Madame du Colombier, a lady about fifty years of age, who was endowed with many rare and inestimable qualities, and who was the most distinguished person in the town. She entertained a great regard for the young artillery-officer, and through her connexion he mingled in all the best company in Valence and its neighbourhood. She introduced him to the Abbé de Saint-Rufe, a man of considerable property, who was frequently visited by the most distinguished persons in the country. Napoleon was indebted for the favour he enjoyed to his extensive information, joined to the facility and force with which he turned it to account. Madame du Colombier often foretold that he would be a distinguished man. The death of this lady happened about the time of the breaking out of the Revolution: it was an event in which she took great interest, and in her last moments was heard to say, that if no misfortune befel young Napoleon, he would infallibly play a distinguished part in the events of the time. The Emperor never spoke of Madame du Colombier but with expressions of the tenderest gratitude; and he did not hesitate to acknowlege, that the valuable introductions and superior rank in society which she procured for him had great influence over his destiny.

The gaiety which Napoleon enjoyed at this period of his life, excited great jealousy on the part of his fellow-officers. They were displeased at seeing him absent himself so frequently from among them, though his doing so could be no reasonable ground of offence to them. Fortunately the commandant, M. d'Urtubie, had formed a just estimate of his character; he shewed him great kindness, and afforded him the means of fulfilling his military duties, and at the same time of mingling in the pleasures of society.

Napoleon conceived an attachment for Mademoiselle du Colombier, who, on her part, was not insensible to his merits. It was the first love of both; and it was that kind of love which might be expected to arise at their age and with their education. "We were the most innocent creatures imaginable," the Emperor used to say; "we contrived little meetings together; I well remember one which took place on a midsummer morning, just as daylight began to dawn. It will scarcely be believed that all our happiness consisted in eating cherries together."

It has been said that the mother wished to bring about this marriage, and that the father opposed it on the ground that they would ruin each other by their union; while each was destined separately to a fortunate career. But this story is untrue, as is likewise another anecdote relative to a marriage with Mademoiselle Clary, afterwards Madame Bernadotte, now Queen of Sweden.

In 1805, the Emperor when about to be crowned King of Italy, on passing through Lyons, again saw Mademoiselle du Columbier, who had now changed her name to Madame de Bressieux. She gained access to him with some difficulty, surrounded as he was by the etiquette of royalty. Napoleon was happy to see her again; but he found her much altered for the worse. He did for her husband what she solicited, and placed her in the situation of lady of honour to one of his sisters.

Mademoiselles de Laurencin and St. Germain were at that time the reigning toasts in Valence, where they divided the general admiration. The latter married Monsieur de Montalivet, who was also known to the Emperor at that time, and who was afterwards made Minister of the Interior. "He was an honest fellow," said Napoleon, "and one who, I believe, remained firmly attached to me."

When about eighteen or twenty years of age, the Emperor was distinguished as a young man of extensive information, possessing a reflective turn of mind and strong reasoning powers. He had read an immense deal, and had profoundly meditated on the fund of knowledge thus acquired, much of which, he used to say, he had probably since lost. His sparkling and ready wit, and energetic language, distinguished him wherever he went: he was a favourite with every one, particularly with the fair sex, to whom he recommended himself by the elegance and novelty of his ideas, and the boldness of his arguments. As for the men, they were often afraid to engage with him in those discussions into which he was led by a natural confidence in his own powers.

Many individuals, who knew him at an early period of life, foresaw his extraordinary career; and they viewed the events of his life without astonishment. At an early age he gained anonymously a prize at the Academy of Lyons, on the following question, proposed by Raynal:—"*What are the principles and institutions calculated to advance mankind to the highest possible degree of happiness?*" The anonymous memorial excited great attention: it was perfectly in unison with the ideas of the age. It began by inquiring in what happiness consisted; and the answer was, in the perfect enjoyment of life in the manner most conformable with our moral and physical organization. After he became Emperor, Napoleon was one day conversing on this subject with M. de Talleyrand: the latter, like a skillful courtier, shortly after presented to him the famous memorial, which he had procured from the archives of the Academy at Lyons. The Emperor took it, and after reading a few pages, threw into the fire this first production of his youth, saying, "One can never observe every thing." M. de Talleyrand had not had an opportunity of transcribing it.

The Prince de Condé one day communicated his intention of visiting the Artillery School at Auxonne; and the cadets considered it a high honour to be examined by that military Prince. The commandant, in spite of the hierarchy, placed young Napoleon at the head of the polygon, in preference to others of superior rank. It happened, that on the day preceding the examination, all the cannons of the polygon were spiked: but Napoleon was too much on the alert to be caught by this trick of his comrades, or it may, perhaps, be said, he was too keen to suffer himself to be entrapped in the snare of the illustrious traveller.

It is generally believed that Napoleon, in his boyhood, was taciturn, sullen, and morose; on the contrary, he was of a very lively turn. He never appeared more delighted than when relating to us the various tricks he was accustomed to play when at the School of Artillery. In describing the joyous moments of his early youth, he seems to forget the misfortunes which hold him in captivity.

There was an old commandant, upwards of eighty years of age, for whom the cadets entertained a very high respect, notwithstanding the many jokes they played upon him. One day, while he was examining them in their cannon exercise, and watching every discharge with his eye-glass, he asserted they were far from hitting the mark, and asked those near him if they had seen the ball strike. Nobody had observed the youths slipping aside the ball every time they loaded. The old general was rather sharp; after five or six discharges, he took it into his head to count the balls. The trick was discovered. The general thought it a very good one; but nevertheless ordered all who had participated in it to be put under arrest.

The cadets would occasionally take a pique at some of their captains, or determine to revenge themselves on others to whom they owed a grudge. They then resolved to banish them from society, and to reduce them to the necessity of putting themselves under a sort of arrest. Four or five of the cadets undertook to execute the design. They fastened on their victim; pursued him into every company, and he was not suffered to open his mouth without being methodically and logically contradicted, though always with a strict regard to politeness: at length the poor fellow found that retirement was his only alternative.

"On another occasion," Napoleon used to relate, "one of my comrades who lodged above me unluckily took a fancy to learn to play the horn, and made such a hideous noise as completely disturbed the studies of those who were within hearing. We met each other one day on the stairs; 'Are you not tired of practising the horn?' said I. 'Not at all,' he replied. 'At any rate, you tire other people.' 'I am sorry for it.' 'It would be better if you went to practise elsewhere.' 'I am master of my own apartment.' 'Perhaps you may be taught to entertain a doubt on that point.' 'I scarce think any one will be bold enough to attempt to teach me that.' A challenge ensued; but before the antagonists met, the affair was submitted to the consideration of a council of the cadets, and it was determined that the one should practise the horn at a greater distance, and that the other should be more accommodating.

In the campaign of 1814, the Emperor again met his horn-player in the neighbourhood of Soissons or Laon: he was residing on his estate, and gave some important information respecting the enemy's position. The Emperor made him one of his aides-de-camp; this officer was Colonel Bussy.

When attached to his artillery-regiment, Napoleon seized every opportunity of mingling in company, where he invariably made an agreeable impression. Women at that time, attached a high value to talent in the other sex; it was a quality which never failed to win their good graces. Napoleon, at this period, performed what he termed his Sentimental Journey from Valence to Mont Cenis in Burgundy, and he intended to write an account of it after the manner of Sterne. The faithful Desmazzis was of the party; he was constantly with him, and his narrative of Napoleon's private life, if combined with the details of his public career, would form a perfect history of the Emperor. It would then be seen that, however extraordinary his life might be with respect to its incidents, yet nothing could be more simple or natural than its course.

Circumstances and reflection have considerably modified his character. Even his style of expression, now so concise and laconic, was in his youth diffuse and emphatic. At the time of the Legislative Assembly, Napoleon assumed a serious and severe demeanour, and became less communicative than before. The army of Italy also marked another epoch in his character. His extreme youth, when he went to take the command of the army, rendered it necessary that he should evince great reserve, and the utmost strictness of morals. "This was indispensably necessary," said he, "to enable me to command men so much above me in point of age. I pursued a line of conduct truly irreproachable and exemplary. I proved myself a sort of Cato. I must have appeared such in the eyes of all. I was a philosopher and a sage." In this character he appeared on the theatre of the world.

Napoleon was in garrison at Valence when the Revolution broke out. At that time it was a point of particular importance to cause the artillery officers to emigrate; and the officers, on their part, were very much divided in opinion. Napoleon, who was imbued with the notions of the age, possessing a natural instinct for great actions and a passion for national glory, espoused the cause of the Revolution; and his example influenced the majority of the regiment. He was an ardent patriot under the Constituent Assembly; but the Legislative Assembly marked a new period in his ideas and opinions.

He was at Paris on the 21st of June, 1792, and witnessed the insurrection of the people of the Faubourgs, who traversed the garden of the Thuilleries, and forced the palace. There were but 6000 men; a mere disorderly mob, whose language and dress proved them to belong to the very lowest class of society.

Napoleon was also a witness of the events of the 10th of August, in which the assailants were neither higher in rank nor more formidable in number.

In 1793, Napoleon was in Corsica, where he had a command in the National Guards. He opposed Paoli as soon as he was led to suspect that the veteran, to whom he had hitherto been so much attached, entertained the design of betraying the island to the English. Therefore it is not true, as has been generally reported, that Napoleon, or some of his family, were at one time in England, proposing to raise a Corsican regiment for the English service.

The English and Paoli subdued the Corsican patriots, and burnt Ajaccio. The house of the Bonapartes was destroyed in the general conflagration, and the family were obliged to fly to the Continent. They fixed their abode at Marseilles, whence Napoleon proceeded to Paris. He arrived just at the moment when the federalists of Marseilles had surrendered Toulon to the English.

Cape Verd Islands.—Napoleon at the siege of Toulon.—Rise of Duroc and Junot.—Napoleon quarrels with the Representatives of the People.—Quarrels with Aubry.—Anecdotes relative to Vendemiaire.—Napoleon General of the Army of Italy.—Integrity of his military administration.—His disinterestedness.—Nicknamed Petit-Corporal.—Difference between the system of the Directory and that of the General of the Army of Italy.

September 1st—6th. On the 1st of September we found from our latitude that we should see the Cape Verd Islands in the course of the day. The sky was, however, overcast, and at night we could see nothing. The Admiral, convinced that there was a mistake in the reckoning of our longitude, was preparing to bear westward to the right, in order to fall in with the islands, when a brig, which was a-head of us, intimated by a signal that she had discovered them on the left. During the night the wind blew violently from the south-east, and if our mistake had been the reverse of what it was, and the Admiral had really borne to the right, it is not improbable that we should have been thrown out of our course; a proof that, notwithstanding the improvements in science, mistakes are very apt to take place, and that the chances of navigation are very great. As the wind continued to blow strong, and the sea was boisterous, the Admiral preferred continuing his course, rather than waiting to take in water, of which he believed he had already a sufficient store. Every thing now promised a prosperous passage; we were already very far advanced on our course. Every circumstance continued favorable; the weather was mild, and we might even have thought our voyage agreeable, had it been undertaken in the pursuit of our own plans and in conformity with our own inclinations; but how could we forget our past misfortunes, or close our eyes on the future?

Occupation alone could enable us to support the languor and tedium of our days. I had undertaken to teach my son English: and the Emperor to whom I mentioned the progress he was making, expressed a wish to learn also. I endeavoured to form a very simple plan for his instruction, in order to save him trouble. This did very well for two or three days; but the *ennui* occasioned by the study was at least equal to that which it was intended to counteract, and the English was laid aside. The Emperor occasionally reproached me with having discontinued my lessons; I replied that I had the medicine ready, if he had the courage to take it. In other respects, particularly before the English, his manners and habits were always the same: never did a murmur or a wish escape his lips; he invariably appeared contented, patient and good-humoured.

The Admiral, who, I suppose, thought it necessary, on the strength of our reputation, to fortify himself well on our departure from England, gradually laid aside his reserve and every day took greater interest in his captive. He represented the danger incurred by coming on deck after dinner, owing to the damp of the evening; the Emperor would then sometimes take his arm and prolong the conversation, which never failed to gratify him exceedingly. I have been assured that the Admiral carefully noted down every particular that he could collect. If this be true, the remarks which the Emperor one day made, during dinner on naval affairs—on the French resources in the south; those which he had already created, and those which he contemplated; and on the ports and harbours of the Mediterranean; to all of which the Admiral listened with deep attention, and as if fearful of interruption—will compose a chapter truly valuable to a seaman.

I will now return to the details collected during our ordinary conversation. The following relate to the siege of Toulon.

In September 1793, Napoleon Bonaparte, then in his twenty-fourth year, was yet unknown to the world which was destined to resound with his name. He was a lieutenant-colonel of artillery, and had been only a few weeks in Paris; having left Corsica, where political events had forced him to yield to the faction of Paoli. The English had taken possession of Toulon; an experienced artillery-officer was wanting to direct the operations of the siege, and Napoleon was fixed on. There will history take him up, never more to leave him;—there commences his immortality.

I refer to the Memoirs of the Campaign of Italy, for the plan of attack which he adopted, and the manner in which that plan was carried into effect. It will there be seen that it was he, and he alone, who took the fortress. This was a great triumph, no doubt; but to appreciate it justly, it would be necessary to compare the plan of the attack with the account of the evacuation; the one is the literal prediction, and the other is the fulfilment word for word. From this moment the young commander of artillery enjoyed the highest reputation. The Emperor never looks back to this period without pleasure, and always mentions it as the happiest portion of his life. The taking of Toulon was his first successful achievement, and it naturally excites the fondest recollections. The history of the campaign of Italy will present a faithful picture of the three generals-in-chief who succeeded each other during the siege: the inconceivable ignorance of Cartaux, the gloomy brutality of Doppet, and the honest courage of Dugommier. Of them I shall here say nothing.

At the first breaking out of the revolution, there was nothing but disorder in the *materiel* and ignorance in the *personnel* of the French army, which was owing both to the confusion of the times, and the rapidity and irregularity with which the promotions had been made. The following story will afford an idea of the state of affairs and of the manners of the time:—

On his arrival at head-quarters, Napoleon waited on General Cartaux, a haughty man, covered with gold lace from head to foot, who asked him what duty he had been sent upon. The young officer modestly presented the letter which directed him to superintend, under the general's command, the operations of the artillery. "This was quite unnecessary," said the general, twirling his whiskers; "we want no assistance to retake Toulon: but, however, you are welcome, and you may share the glory of burning the town to-morrow, without having experienced any of the fatigue." And he made him stay to sup with him.

A party of thirty sat down to table; the general alone was served like a prince, while every one else was dying of hunger; a circumstance which, in those days of equality, strangely shocked the new guest. The next morning, at break of day, the general took him out in his cabriolet, to admire, as he said, the preparations for attack. As soon as he had crossed the height, and came within sight of the road and harbour, they got out of the carriage, and threw themselves down among some vines. The commandant of artillery then perceived some pieces of ordnance, and some digging, for which it was literally impossible for him in the slightest degree to account. "Dupas," said the general haughtily, turning to his aid-de-camp, his confidential man, "are those our batteries?"—"Yes, General."—"And our park?"—"There, close at hand."—"And our red-hot balls?"—"In yonder houses, where two companies have been employed all the morning in heating them."—"But how shall we be able to carry these red-hot balls?" This consideration seemed to puzzle them both completely, and they turned to the officer of artillery, and begged to know whether, through his scientific knowledge, he could not explain how the thing was to be managed. Napoleon, who would have been very much tempted to take the whole for a hoax, had his interrogators evinced less simplicity, for they were more than a league and a half from the object of attack, summoned to his aid all the gravity he was master of, and endeavoured to persuade them, before they troubled themselves about red-hot balls, to try the range of the shot with cold ones. After a great deal of trouble, he at length prevailed on them to follow his advice, but not till he had very luckily made use of the technical term *coup d'épreuve* which took their fancy, and brought them over to his opinion. They then made the experiment, but the shot did not reach to a third of the distance required; and the general and Dupas began to abuse the Marseillais and the Aristocrats, who had, they said, maliciously spoiled the powder. In the mean time the representative of the people came upon horseback; this was Gasparin: an intelligent man, who had served in the army. Napoleon, perceiving how things were going on, and, boldly deciding on the course he should pursue, immediately assumed great confidence of manner, and urged the representative to intrust him with the whole direction of the affair. He exposed, without hesitation, the unparalleled ignorance of all who were about him, and from that moment took upon himself the entire direction of the siege.

Cartaux was a man of such limited intellect, that it was impossible to make him understand, that to facilitate the taking of Toulon, it would be necessary to make tho attack at the outlet of the road. When the commandant of artillery sometimes pointed to this outlet on the map, and told him there was Toulon, Cartaux suspected he knew very little of geography: and when, in spite of his opposition the authority of the representative decided on the adoption of this distant point of attack, the general was haunted by the idea of treasonable designs, and he would often remark, with great uneasiness, that Toulon did not lie in that direction.

Cartaux wanted one day to oblige the commandant to erect a battery, with the rear of the guns so close against the front of a house as to leave no room for the recoil. On another occasion, on his return from the morning parade, he sent for the commandant to tell him that he had just discovered a position, from whence a battery of from six to twelve pieces would infallibly carry Toulon in a few days: it was a little hillock which would command three or four forts, and several points of the town. He was enraged at the refusal of the commandant of artillery, who observed to him, that if a battery could command every point, it followed that every point would be able to bear upon it; that the twelve guns would have one hundred and fifty to oppose them: and that simple subtraction would suffice to show him his disadvantage. The commandant of the engineer department was called on for his opinion, and as he concurred without hesitation, in that of the commandant of artillery, Cartaux said that it was impossible to do any thing with those learned corps, as they all went hand-in-hand. At length, to put a stop to difficulties which were continually recurring, the representative decided that Cartaux should communicate to the commandant of artillery his general plan of attack, and that the latter should execute the details, according to the rules of his department. The following was Cartaux's memorable plan :—

"The general of artillery shall batter Toulon during three days, at the expiration of which time I will attack it with three columns, and carry it."

At Paris, however, the engineer committee found this hasty measure much more humorous than wise, and it was one of the causes which led to Cartaux's recall. There was indeed no want of plans; for the retaking of Toulon having been proposed as a subject for competition in the popular societies, plans poured in from all quarters. Napoleon says he must have received at least six hundred during the siege. It was to the representative Gasparin, that Napoleon was indebted for the triumph of his plan, (that which gained Toulon,) over the objections of the Committee of the Convention. He preserved a grateful recollection of this circumstance: it was Gasparin, he used to say, who had first opened his career.*

In all the disputes between Cartaux and the commandant of artillery, which usually took place in the presence of the general's wife, the latter uniformly took the part of the officer of artillery, saying with great *naiveté* to her husband, "Let the young man alone, he knows more about it than you do, for he never asks your advice; besides, are not you the responsible person: the glory will be yours."

This woman was not without some share of good sense. On her return to Paris, after the recall of her husband, the jacobins of Marseilles gave a splendid fête in honour of the disgraced family. In the course of the evening the conversation happened to fall on the commandant of artillery, who was enthusiastically praised. "Do not reckon on him," said she; "that young man has too much understanding to remain long a *sansculotte*." On which the general exclaimed, with the voice of a Stentor, "Femme Cartaux, would you make us all out fools then?" "No, I do not say that, my dear; but . . . I must tell you, he is not one of your sort."

One day, at head quarters, a superb carriage arrived from the Paris road; it was followed by a second and a third; at length no less than fifteen appeared. It may be imagined how great was the astonishment and curiosity occasioned by such a circumstance in those times of republican simplicity. The *grand monarque* himself could not have travelled with greater pomp. The whole cavalcade had been procured by a requisition in the capital: several of the carriages had belonged to the Court. About sixty soldiers, in fine condition, alighted from them, and inquired for the general-in-chief, they marched up to him with the important air of ambassadors:—"Citizen General," said the orator of the party, "we come from Paris; the patriots are indignant at your inactivity and delay. The soil of the Republic has long since been violated; she trembles to think that the insult still remains unavenged: she asks, why is Toulon not yet retaken? Why is the English fleet not yet destroyed? In her indignation, she has appealed to her brave sons; we have obeyed her summons, and burn with impatience to fulfil her expectation. We are volunteer gunners from Paris: furnish us with arms, tomorrow we will march upon the enemy." The general, disconcerted at this address, turned to the commandant of

* The Emperor has, in his will, paid a tribute of gratitude to the representative Gasparin, for the special protection he received from him.

He has honoured with a similar tribute General Duteil, the head of his School of Artillery, and General Dugommier, for the attention and kindness he had experienced from them.

artillery, who promised, in a whisper, to rid him of the heroes next morning. They were well received, and at daybreak the commandant of artillery led them to the sea-shore, and put some guns at their disposal. Astonished to find themselves exposed from head to foot, they asked whether there was no shelter, or epaulement. They were told that those things were out of fashion: that patriotism had abolished them. Meanwhile an English frigate fired a broadside, and put all the braggadocios to flight. There was nothing but tumult in the camp: some openly fled, and the rest quietly slipped after them.

Disorder and anarchy now prevailed. Dupas, the factotum of the general-in-chief, a man of no ability, made himself busy, and was continually meddling with the artillerymen in the arrangement of their field-train and batteries. A plan was formed to get rid of him. They turned him into ridicule, and urged each other on till they became very vehement in their jokes. On a sudden Dupas appeared among them with all his usual confidence, giving orders and making inquiries about every thing he saw. He got uncivil answers, and high words arose. The tumult spread on every side; cries of *l'aristocrate* and *la lanterne* were echoed from every mouth; and Dupas clapped both spurs to his horse, and never returned to annoy them.

The commandant of artillery was to be seen every where. His activity and knowledge gave him a decided influence over the rest of the army. Whenever the enemy attempted to make a sortie, or compelled the besiegers to have recourse to rapid and unexpected movements, the heads of the columns and detachments were always sure to exclaim, "Run to the commandant of artillery, and ask him what we are to do; he understands the localities better than any one." This advice was uniformly adopted without a murmur. He adopted no precautions for ensuring his own safety; he had several horses killed under him, and received from an Englishman a bayonet-wound in his left thigh, which for a short time threatened him with the necessity of amputation.

Being one day in a battery where one of the gunners was killed, he seized the rammer, and with his own hands loaded ten or twelve times. A few days after he was attacked with a violent cutaneous disease. No one could conceive where he had caught it, until Mairon, his adjutant, discovered that the dead gunner had been infected with it. In the ardour of youth, and the activity of service, the commandant of artillery was satisfied with slight remedies, and the disorder disappeared: but the poison had only entered the deeper into his system, it long affected his health and well nigh cost him his life. From this disorder proceeded the thinness, the feebleness of body, and sickly complexion which characterized the general-in-chief of the army of Italy, and of the army of Egypt.

It was not till a much later period that Corvisart succeeded, by the application of numerous blisters on his chest, in restoring him to perfect health; and it was then that he acquired the corpulency for which he has since been remarked.

From being the commandant of artillery in the army of Toulon, Napoleon might have become general-in chief before the close of the siege.—The very day of the attack on *le Petit Gibraltar*, General Dugommier, who had delayed it for some days, wished to delay it still longer; about three or four o'clock in the afternoon the representatives sent for Napoleon: they were dissatisfied with Dugommier, particularly on account of his delay; they wished to deprive him of the command, and to transfer it to the chief of the artillery, who declined accepting it. Napoleon went to the general, whom he esteemed and loved, informed him of what had occurred, and persuaded him to decide on the attack. About eight or nine in the evening, when all the preparations were completed, and just as the attack was about to commence, a change took place in the state of affairs, and the representatives countermanded the attack. Dugommier, however, still influenced by the commandant of artillery, persisted: had he failed, he must have forfeited his head.—Such was the train of affairs and the justice of the times.

The notes which the Committees of Paris found in the office of the artillery department respecting Napoleon, first called their attention to his conduct at the siege of Toulon. They saw that in spite of his youth and the inferiority of his rank, as soon as he appeared there he was master.—This was the natural effect of the ascendancy of knowledge, activity, and energy, over the ignorance and confusion of the moment. He was, in fact, the conqueror of Toulon, and yet he is scarcely named in the official despatches. He was in possession of the town before the army had scarcely dreamt of it. After taking *le Petit Gibraltar*, which he always looked upon as the key of the whole enterprise, he said to old Dugommier, who was worn out with fatigue,—"Go and rest yourself—we have taken Toulon—you may sleep there the day after to-morrow." When Dugommier found the thing actually accomplished—when he reflected that the young commandant of artillery had always foretold exactly what would happen, he became all enthusiasm and admiration; he was never tired of praising him. It is perfectly true, as some of the publications of the period relate, that Dugommier informed the Committees of Paris that he had with him a young man who merited particular notice; for that whichever side he might adopt, he was certainly destined to throw great weight into the balance. When Dugommier joined the army of the Eastern Pyrenees, he wished to take with him the young commandant of artillery; but this he was unable to do. He however spoke of him incessantly; and at a subsequent period, when this army was, on the conclusion of peace with Spain, sent to reinforce the Army of Italy, of which Napoleon soon after became general-in-chief, he found on his arrival, that in consequence of all Dugommier had said of him, the officers had, to use his own expression, scarcely eyes enough to look at him.

With regard to Napoleon, his success at Toulon did not much astonish him; he enjoyed it, he says, with a lively satisfaction, unmingled with surprise. He was equally happy the following year at Saorgio, where his operations were admirable: he accomplished in a few days what had been attempted in vain for two years. "Vendemiaire and even Montenotte," said the Emperor, "never induced me to look upon myself as a man of a superior class; it was not till after Lodi that I was struck with the possibility of my becoming a decided actor on the scene of political events.—It was then that the first spark of my ambition was kindled." He however mentioned that subsequently to Vendemiaire, during his command of the army of the interior, he drew up the plan of a campaign, which was to terminate by a treaty of peace on the summit of the Simmering, which plan he shortly afterwards carried into execution at Leoben. It is perhaps still to be found in the official archives. The well known fury of the times was still farther increased under the walls of Toulon, by the assembling of two hundred deputies from the neighbouring popular associations, who had proceeded thither for the purpose of instigating the most atrocious measures. To them must be attributed the excesses which were then committed, and of which the whole army complained. When Napoleon afterwards rose to distinction, attempts were made to throw the odium of these atrocities on him. It would be a degradation to seek to reply to such calumnies.

As soon as Napoleon took the command of the artillery at Toulon, he availed himself of the necessity of circumstances to procure the reinstatement of many of his old companions, who had been removed from the service on account of their birth or political principles. He obtained the appointment of Colonel Gassendi to the post of keeper of the arsenal of Marseilles. The obstinacy and severity of this ma-are well known; they frequently placed him in danger: it more than once required all Napoleon's vigilance and care, to save him from the effects of the irritation which his conduct excited.

The ascendancy which Napoleon had acquired, through his services, in the port and arsenal of Toulon, afforded him the means of saving several unfortunate members of the emigrant family Chabriant, or Chabrillan, who had been overtaken by storms at sea, and driven on the French shore.—They were about to be put to death, for the law was decisive against the emigrants who might return to France.—They urged in their defence, that their return had been purely the effect of accident, and was contrary to their own wishes; the only favour they solicited was to be permitted to depart; but all was vain: they would have perished had not the commandant of the artillery hazarded his own safety and procured for them a covered boat, which he sent off from the French coast under the pretence of business relative to his department. During the reign of Napoleon, these individuals took an opportunity of expressing their gratitude to him, and informing him that they had carefully preserved the order which saved their lives.

Napoleon was himself, at various times, exposed to the fury of revolutionary assassins.—Whenever he established a new battery, the numerous patriotic deputations, who were at the camp, solicited the honour of having it named after them. Napoleon named one the battery of the *Patriots of the South*: this was a sufficient ground for his being denounced and accused of federalism; and had he been a less useful person, he would have been put under arrest, or, in other words, he would have been sacrificed. In short, language is inadequate to describe the phrenzy and horror of the times. The Emperor, for example, has told us, that while engaged in fortifying the coasts at Marseilles, he was a witness to the horrible condemnation of the merchant Hugues, a man of eighty-four years of age, deaf and nearly blind. In spite of his age and infirmities, his atrocious executioners pronounced him guilty of conspiracy: his real crime was his being worth eighteen millions. This he was himself aware of, and he offered to surrender his wealth to the tribunal, provided he might be allowed to retain five hundred thousand francs, which, he said, he could not live long to enjoy. But this proposition was rejected, and he was led to the scaffold. "At this sight," said Napoleon, "I thought the world was at an end!"—an expression which he was accustomed to employ on any extraordinary occasion. Barras and Fréron were the authors of these atrocities.—The Emperor did Robespierre the justice to say, that he had seen long letters written by him to his brother, Robespierre the younger, who was then the Representative to the Army of the South, in which he warmly opposed and disavowed these excesses, declaring that they would disgrace and ruin the Revolution.

Napoleon, when at Toulon, formed a friendship with many individuals who subsequently became very noted. He distinguished in the train a young officer, whose talent he had at first much difficulty in forming, but from whom he afterwards derived the greatest services: this was Duroc, who, with a very unprepossessing person, was endowed with talent of the most solid and useful kind; he loved the Emperor for himself, was devoted to his interests, and at the same time knew how to tell him the truth at proper seasons. He was afterwards created Duke de Frioul and Grand Marshal of the Palace. He placed the Imperial household on an excellent footing, and preserved the most perfect order. At his death, the Emperor thought he had sustained an irreparable loss, and many other persons were of the same opinion. The Emperor told me that Duroc was the only man who shared his intimacy and possessed his entire confidence.

During the erection of one of the first batteries which Napoleon on his arrival at Toulon, directed against the English, he asked whether there was a sergeant or corporal present who could write. A man advanced from the ranks, and wrote to his dictation on the epaulment. The note was scarcely ended, when a cannon ball, which had been fired in the direction of the battery, fell near the spot, and the paper was immediately covered by the loose earth thrown up by the ball. "Well," said the writer, "I shall have no need of sand." This remark, together with the coolness with which it was made, fixed the attention of Napoleon, and made the fortune of the sergeant. This man was Junot, afterwards Duke of Abrantes, colonel-general of the Hussars, commandant in Portugal, and governor-general in Illyria, where he evinced signs of mental alienation, which increased on his return to France, where he wounded himself in a horrible way.—He died the victim of the intemperance which destroyed both his health and his reason.

Napoleon, on being created General of the Artillery, and Commandant of that department in the Army of Italy, carried thither all the superiority and influence which he had acquired before Toulon; still, however, he experienced reverses and even dangers. He was put under arrest for a short time at Nice, by the representative Laporte, because he refused to crouch to his authority. Another representative pronounced sentence of outlawry upon him, because he would not suffer him to employ his artillery-horses for the service of the post. Finally, a decree, which was never executed, summoned him to the bar of the Convention, for having proposed certain military measures relative to the fortifications at Marseilles.

When attached to the Army of Nice or of Italy, he became a great favourite with the representative Robespierre the younger, whom he described as possessing qualities very different from his brother: the latter Napoleon never saw. Robespierre the younger, on being recalled to Paris by his brother, sometime before the 9th of Thermidor, exerted every endeavour to prevail on Napoleon to accompany him. "If I had not firmly resisted," observed the Emperor, "who knows whither this first step might have led me, and for what a different destiny I might have been reserved?"

At the Army of Nice there was another Representative, an insignificant man. His wife, who was an extremely pretty and fascinating woman, shared and even usurped his authority; she was a native of Versailles. Both husband and wife paid great attention to the General of artillery; they became extremely fond of him, and treated him in the handsomest manner. This was a great advantage to the young general, for, at that time, during the absence or inefficiency of the laws, a representative of the people was a man of immense power.

The individual here alluded to, was one of those who in the Convention, most contributed to bring Napoleon into notice, at the crisis of Vendemiaire: this was the natural consequence of the deep impressions produced by the character and capacity of the young general.

The Emperor relates that after he had ascended the throne, he again saw his old acquaintance the fair representative of Nice. She was so much altered as to be scarcely recognisable; her husband was dead, and she was reduced to extreme indigence. The Emperor readily granted every thing she solicited: "He realized," he said, "all her dreams, and even went beyond them." Although she lived at Versailles, many years had elapsed before she had succeeded in gaining access to him. Letters, petitions, solicitations of every description had proved unavailing: "So difficult it is," said the Emperor, "to reach the sovereign, even when he does not wish to deny himself." At length, one day when he was on a hunting excursion at Versailles, Napoleon happened to mention this lady to Berthier, who was also a native of that place, and had known her in her youth; and he who had never yet deigned to mention her, and still less to regard her petitions, on the following day presented her to the sovereign. "But why did you not get introduced to me through our mutual acquaintances in the Army of Nice?" inquired the Emperor: "many of them are now great men, and are on a constant footing of intimacy with me." "Alas! sire," replied she, "our acquaintance ceased when their fortune was advanced, and I was overtaken by misfortune."

The Emperor one day communicated to me some details respecting this old friendship:—"I was," said he, "very young when I first knew this lady; I was proud of the favourable impression I had made on her, and seized every opportunity of shewing her all the attention in my power. I will mention one circumstance, to shew for what trivial causes men sometimes abuse the authority on which the fate of their fellow-creatures depends, for I am no worse than the rest. I was walking about one day with the Representative's wife, inspecting our positions in the neighbourhood of the Col de Tende, when I suddenly took it into my head to give her an idea of an engagement, and for this purpose ordered the attack of an advanced post. We were the conquerors, it is true; but the affair could be attended by no advantage. The attack was a mere whim, and yet it cost the lives of several men. I have never failed to reproach myself whenever I look back on this affair."

The events of Thermidor having produced a change in the Committees of the Convention, Aubry, formerly a captain of artillery, was appointed to direct the Committee of War, and he remodelled the army. He did not forget himself; he obtained the rank of general of artillery, and he favoured several of his old comrades to the injury of the inferior officers, whom he disbanded. Napoleon, who was at this time scarcely twenty-five years of age, became a general of infantry, and he was chosen for the service of La Vendée. This circumstance induced him to quit the Army of Italy, in order to protest against the change, which, on every account, was dissatisfactory to him. Finding Aubry inflexible, and even offended at his just representations, he gave in his resignation. The narrative of the Campaigns of Italy shew that only a short time elapsed before he was again employed in the topographic committee, by which the movements of the army and the plans of the campaigns were arranged: here he was on the 13th of Vendemiaire.

Napoleon's expostulations with Aubry on the subject of his new appointment formed a perfect scene: he vehemently insisted, because he had facts to bear him through; Aubry was obstinate and bitter, because he had power in his hands. He told Napoleon that he was too young, and that he must let older men go before him; Napoleon replied, that a soldier soon grew old on the field of battle, and that he should speedily attain the suitable age. They came to very high words.

I informed the Emperor that, on returning from my emigration, I occupied for a considerable time, in the Rue St. Florentin, the identical apartment in which this scene took place. I had frequently heard it spoken of; and though it was described by unfriendly tongues, each, nevertheless, took great interest in relating the details, and in trying to guess the part of the room in which any particular gesture was made or any remarkable word spoken.

The history of the famous day of Vendemiaire, which had so important an influence on the fate of the Revolution and of Napoleon, will shew that he hesitated for some time before he undertook the defence of the Convention.

On the night succeeding that day, Napoleon presented himself to the Committee of Forty, which was established at the Thuilleries. He wanted to procure mortars and ammunition from Meudon; but such was the circumspection of the President (Chambaceres) that in spite of the dangers which had marked the day, he refused to sign the order; and merely, by way of accommodating the matter, requested that the guns and ammunition might be placed at the disposal of the general.

During his command of Paris, subsequently to the 13th of Vendemiaire, Napoleon had to encounter a great scarcity, which occasioned several popular commotions. One day when the usual distribution had not taken place, crowds of people collected round the bakers' shops. Napoleon was parading about the city with a party of his staff to preserve public tranquillity. A crowd of persons, chiefly women, assembled round him, loudly calling for bread. The crowd augmented, the outcries increased, and the situation of Napoleon and officers became critical. A woman, of monstrous robust appearance, was particularly conspicuous by her gestures and exclamations. "Those fine epauletted fellows," said she, pointing to the officers, "laugh at our distress: so long as they can eat and grow fat, they care not if the poor people die of hunger." Napoleon turned to her, and said, "Good woman, look at me; which is fattest, you or I?" Napoleon was at that time extremely thin: "I was a mere slip of parchment," said he. A general burst of laughter disarmed the fury of the populace, and the staff-officers continued their round.

The Memoirs of the Campaign of Italy shew how Napoleon became acquainted with Madame de Beauharnais, and how he contracted the marriage which had been so greatly misrepresented in the accounts of the time. As soon as he got introduced to Madame de Beauharnais, he spent almost every evening at her house, which was frequented by the most agreeable company in Paris. When the majority of the party retired, there usually remained M. de Montesquiou, the father of the Grand Chamberlain; the Duke de Nivernais, so celebrated for the graces of his wit; and a few others. They used to look round to see that the doors were all shut, and they would then say, "Let us sit down and chat about the old court; let us make a tour to Versailles."

The poverty of the treasury and the scarcity of specie were so great during the Republic, that on the departure of General Bonaparte for the army of Italy, all his efforts, joined to those of the Directory, could only succeed in raising 2000 louis, which he carried with him in his carriage.—With this sum he set out to conquer Italy, and to march upon the empire of the world. The following is a curious fact: An order of the day was published, signed Berthier, directing the general-in-chief, on his arrival at the head-quarters at Nice, to distribute to the different generals, to enable them to enter on the campaign, the sum of four louis in specie. For a considerable time no such thing as specie had been seen. This order of the day displays the circumstances of the times more truly and faithfully than whole volumes written on the subject.

As soon as Napoleon joined the army, he proved himself to be a man born for command. From that moment he filled the theatre of the world*; he occupied all Europe; he was a meteor blazing in the firmament; he concentrated all eyes, rivetted all thoughts, and formed the subject of all conversations. From that time every Gazette, every publication, every monument, became the record of his deeds. His name was inscribed in every page and in every line, and echoed from every mouth.

His appearance in the command produced a revolution in his manners, conduct, and language. Decres has often told me, that he was at Toulon when he first heard of Napoleon's appointment to the command of the army of Italy. He had known him well in Paris, and thought himself on

* CHRONOLOGICAL RECAPITULATION.

The Emperor was born	Aug. 15, 1769
Entered the military school of Brienne	1779
Transferred to the school of Paris	1783
Lieutenant in the 1st Artillery regiment of la Fere	Sep. 1, 1785
Captain	Feb. 6, 1792
Chief of Battalion	Oct. 19, 1793
General of Brigade	Feb. 6, 1794
General of Division	Oct 16, 1795
General-in-Chief of the army of the Interior	Oct. 26, 1795
General-in-Chief of the army of Italy	Feb. 23, 1796
First Consul	Dec. 13, 1799
Consul for life	Aug. 2, 1802
Crowned Emperor	May 18, 1804
First abdication at Fontainebleau	April 11, 1814
Resumed the reins of government	Mar. 20, 1815
Second abdication at l'Elysee	June 21, 1815

terms of perfect intimacy with him. "Thus," said he, "when we learned that the new General was about to pass through the city, I immediately proposed to introduce my comrades to him, and to turn my connexion to the best account. I hastened to him full of eagerness and joy; the door of the apartment was thrown open, and I was on the point of rushing towards him with my wonted familiarity, but his attitude, his look, the tone of his voice, suddenly deterred me. There was nothing offensive either in his appearance or manner; but the impression he produced was sufficient to prevent me from ever again attempting to encroach upon the distance that separated us."

Napoleon's generalship was, moreover, characterized by the skill, energy, and purity of his military administration; his constant dislike of peculation of any kind, and his total disregard of his own private interest. "I returned from the campaign of Italy," said he, "with but 300,000 francs in my possession. I might have easily carried off 10 or 12 millions; that sum might have been mine. I never made out any accounts, nor was I ever asked for any. I expected on my return to receive some great national reward. It was publicly reported that Chambord was to be given to me, and I should have been very glad to have had it; but the idea was set aside by the Directory. I had, however, transmitted to France at least 50,000,000 for the service of the State. This, I imagine, was the first instance in modern history of an army contributing to maintain the country to which it belonged, instead of being a burthen on it."

When Napoleon was in treaty with the Duke de Modena, Salicetti, the Government commissary with the army, who had hitherto been on indifferent terms with him, entered his cabinet.—"The Commander d'Este," said he, "the Duke's brother, is here with four millions in gold, contained in four chests. He comes in the name of his brother to beg you to accept them, and I advise you to do so. I am a countryman of yours, and I know your family affairs. The Directory and the Legislative body will never acknowledge your services. This money belongs to you; take it without scruple and without publicity. A proportionate diminution will be made in the Duke's contribution, and he will be very glad to have gained a protector."—"I thank you," coolly answered Napoleon, "I shall not for that sum place myself in the power of the Duke de Modena:—I wish to continue free."

A Commissary-in-chief of the same army used often to relate that he had witnessed an offer of seven millions in gold made in like manner to Napoleon by the Government of Venice, to save it from destruction, which offer was refused.—The emperor smiled at the transports of admiration evinced by this financier, to whom the refusal of his General appeared superhuman—an action much more difficult and noble than the gaining of victories. The Emperor dwelt with a considerable degree of complacency on these anecdotes of his disinterestedness. He however observed, that he had been in the wrong, and that such a course of conduct was the most improvident he could have pursued, whether his intention had been to make himself the head of a party, and to acquire influence, or to remain in the station of a private individual; for, on his return, he found himself almost destitute; and he might have continued in a career of absolute poverty, whilst his inferior generals and commissaries were amassing large fortunes. "But," added he, "if my commissary had seen me accept the bribe, who can tell to what lengths he might have gone? My refusal was at least a check upon him."

"When I was placed at the head of affairs, as Consul, it was only by setting an example of disinterestedness, and employing the utmost vigilance, that I could succeed in changing the conduct of the Administration, and putting a stop to the dreadful spectacle of Directorial peculations. It cost me an immense deal of trouble to overcome the inclinations of the first persons in the State, whose conduct at length became strict and irreproachable. I was obliged to keep them constantly in fear. How often did I not repeat in my councils, that if my own brother were found to be in fault, I should not hesitate to dismiss him."

No man in the world ever had more wealth at his disposal, and appropriated less to himself.—Napoleon, according to his own account, possessed as much as four hundred millions of specie in the cellars of the Thuilleries. His extraordinary domain amounted to more than seven hundred millions. He has said that he distributed upwards of five hundred millions on endowments to the army. And, what is very extraordinary, he who circulated such heaps of wealth, never possessed any private property of his own! He had collected in the Museum, treasures which it was impossible to estimate, and yet he never had a picture or a curiosity of his own.

On his return from Italy, and on the eve of his departure for Egypt, he became possessed of Malmaison, and there he deposited nearly all his property. He purchased it in the name of his wife, who was older than himself, and consequently, in case of his surviving her, he must have forfeited all claim to it. The fact is, as he himself has said, that he never had a taste nor desire for riches.

"If I now possess any thing,"* continued he, "it is owing to measures which have been adopted since my departure; but even in that case it must depend on a hair's-breadth chance whether there be any thing in the world I can call my own or not. But every one has his relative ideas. I have a taste for founding, and not for possessing. My riches consisted in glory and celebrity: the Simplon and the Louvre were, in the eyes of the people and of foreigners, more my property than private domains could have been. I purchased diamonds for the crown, I repaired and adorned the Imperial palaces; and I was often surprised to find that the expenses lavished by Josephine on her green-houses and her gallery, were a real injury to my *Jardin des Plantes* and my *Musee de Paris*."

On taking the command of the army of Italy, Napoleon, notwithstanding his extreme youth, immediately impressed the troops with a spirit of subordination, confidence, and the most absolute devotedness. The army was subdued by his genius, rather than seduced by his popularity; he was, in general, very severe and reserved. During the whole course of his life he has uniformly disdained to court the favour of the multitude by unworthy means; perhaps he has even carried these feelings to an extent which may have been injurious to him. A singular custom was established in the army of Italy, in consequence of the youth of the commander, or from some other cause. After each battle, the oldest soldiers used to hold a council, and confer a new rank on their young General, who, when he made his appearance in the camp, was received by the veterans, and

* The deposit at the house of Lafitte.

On the Emperor's second abdication, somebody who loved him for his own sake, and who knew his improvident disposition, eagerly enquired whether any measures had been taken for his future support. Finding that no provision had been made, and that Napoleon remained absolutely destitute, a contribution was made, and four or five millions were raised for him, of which M. Lafitte became the depository.

At the moment of his departure from Malmaison, the solicitude of Napoleon's real friends was no less serviceable to him.—An individual, aware of the disorder and confusion of our situation, wished to ascertain whether the little treasure had been forwarded to its destination. What was his astonishment on learning that the carriage in which it had been placed, was left in a coach-house at Malmaison. A new difficulty arose: the key of the coach-house was not to be found; and the embarrassment occasioned by this unexpected circumstance delayed our departure for some moments. M. Lafitte wished immediately to give the Emperor a receipt for the sum; but Napoleon would not accept it—saying, "I know you, M. Lafitte—I know you did not approve of my government; but I consider you as an honest man."

M. Lafitte seems to have been doomed to be the depository of the funds of unfortunate Monarchs. Louis XVIII., on his departure for Ghent, also placed a considerable sum of money in his hands. On Napoleon's arrival, on 20th March, M. Lafitte was sent for by the Emperor, and questioned respecting the deposit, which he did not deny. On his expressing his apprehension lest a reproach should be intended to be conveyed in the questions which had been put to him—"None" said the Emperor: "that money belonged personally to the King, and private affairs are totally distinct from political matters."

saluted with his new title. They made him a Corporal at Lodi, and a Sergeant at Castiglione; and hence the surname of "*Petit Caporal*," which was for a long time applied to Napoleon by the soldiers. How subtle is the chain which unites the most trivial circumstances to the moss important events!—Perhaps this very nickname contributed to his miraculous success on his return in 1815.—While he was haranguing the first battalion which he found it necessary to address, a voice from the ranks exclaimed—"*Vive notre petit Caporal!*—we will never fight against him!"

The administration of the Directory, and that of the general-in-chief of the army of Italy, seemed two distinct Governments. The Directory put the emigrants to death: the army of Italy never inflicted capital punishment on any one of them. The Directory, on learning that Wurmser was besieged in Mantua, wrote to Napoleon, to remind him that he was an emigrant; but Napoleon, on making him prisoner, eagerly sought to render an affecting homage of respect to his old age. The Directory adopted the most insulting forms in communicating with the Pope: the General of the army of Italy addressed him by the words "Most Holy Father," and wrote to him with respect. The Directory endeavoured to overthrow the authority of the Pope: Napoleon preserved it. The Directory banished and proscribed Priests: Napoleon commanded his soldiers, wherever they might fall in with them, to remember that they were Frenchmen and their brothers. The Directory would have exterminated every vestige of aristocracy: Napoleon wrote to the democracy of Genoa, blaming their violence; and did not hesitate to declare that if the Genoese attached any value to the preservation of his esteem, they must learn to respect the Statue of Doria, and the institutions to which they were indebted for their glory.

The Emperor determines to write his Memoirs.

7th—9th.—We continued our course, and nothing occurred to interrupt the uniformity which surrounded us. Our days were all alike; the correctness of my journal alone informed me of the day of the week or of the month. Fortunately my time was employed, and therefore the day usually slipped on with a certain degree of facility. The materials which I collected in the afternoon conversation afforded me no idle time till next day.

Meanwhile the Emperor osberved that I was very much occupied, and he even suspected the subject on which I was engaged. He determined to ascertain the fact, and obtained sight of a few pages of my journal: he was not displeased with it. Having alluded several times to the subject, he observed that such a work would be interesting rather than useful. The military events, for example, thus detailed, in the ordinary course of conversation, would be meagre, incomplete, and devoid of end or object: they would be mere anecdotes, frequently of the most puerile kind, instead of grand operations and results. I early seized the favourable opportunity: I entirely concurred in his opinion, and ventured to suggest the idea of his dictating to me the campaigns of Italy. "It would," I observed, "be a benefit to the country—a true moment of national glory. Our time is unemployed, our hours are tedious; occupation will help to divert us, and some moments may not be devoid of pleasure." This idea became the subject of various conversations.

At length the Emperor came to a determination, and on Saturday the 9th of September he called me into his cabin, and dictated to me, for the first time, some details respecting the siege of Toulon; they will be found in the campaigns of Italy, which will form a separate work, without at all interfering with the anecdotes which I shall continue to note down here whenever an opportunity occurs.

Trade Wind.—The Line.

10th—13th.—On approaching the line, we fell in with what are called the trade-winds, that is to say, winds blowing constantly from the east. Science explains this phenomenon in a way sufficiently satisfactory. When a vessel sailing from Europe first encounters these winds, they blow from the north-east; in proportion as the ship approaches the line, the winds become more easterly. Calms are generally to be expected under the line. When the line is crossed, the winds gradually change to the south, until they blow in the direction of the south-east. At length, after passing the tropics, the trade-winds are lost, and variable winds are met with, as in our European regions. A ship sailing from Europe to St. Helena, is always driven a westerly direction by these constant easterly winds. It would be very difficult to gain that island by a direct course; and, indeed, this is never attempted. The ship stands away to the variable winds in the southern latitude, and then shapes her course towards the Cape of Good Hope, so as to fall in with the trade winds from the south-east, which bring her, with the wind astern, to St. Helena.

Two different courses are taken to gain the variable winds of the southern latitudes; the one is to cross the line about the 20th or 24th degree of longitude, reckoning from the meridian of London: those who prefer this course, affirm that it is less exposed to the equatorial calms, and that though it frequently has the disadvantage of carrying the vessel within sight of Brazil, yet it enables her to make that part of her voyage in a short time. Admiral Cockburn, who was inclined to regard this course as a prejudice and a routine, determined in favour of the second method, which consisted in steering more to the east, and followed particular examples with which he was acquainted, he endeavoured to cross the line about the 2d or 3d degrees of longitude. He doubted not that standing towards the variable winds, he should pass sufficiently near St. Helena, to shorten his passage considerably, if even he did not succeed in reaching the island by tacking without leaving the trade-winds.

The winds, to our great astonishment, veered to the west, (a circumstance which the Admiral informed us was more common than we supposed,) and this tended to favour his opinion. He abandoned the bad sailers of his squadron, in proportion as they lagged behind; and he determined on gaining the place of his destination with all possible speed.

A Storm.—Examination of certain Libel supon the Emperor. General reflections.

14th—18th.—After a few slight gales and several calms, we had on the 16th a considerable fall of rain, to the great joy of the crew. The heat was very moderate; it may, indeed, be said, that with the exception of the storm at Madeira, we had uniformly enjoyed mild weather. But water was very scarce on board the ship; and, for the sake of economy, the crew took advantage of the opportunity of collecting the rain-water, of which each sailor laid by a little store for his own use. The rain fell heavily just as the Emperor had got upon deck to take his afternoon walk. But this did not disappoint him of his usual exercise: he merely called for his famous grey great coat, which the English regarded with deep interest. The grand Marshal and I attended the Emperor in his walk. The rain descended heavily for upwards of an hour; when the Emperor left the deck, I had great difficulty in stripping off my wet clothes; almost every thing I wore was soaked through.

For several succeeding days the weather continued very rainy; this somewhat impeded my labours, for the damp penetrated into our wretched little cabin; and on the other hand, it was not very agreeable to walk on deck. This was the first time during our passage that we had had any thing like a continuance of wet weather; and it quite disconcerted us. I filled up the intervals between my hours of occupation, in conversing with the officers of the ship. I was not on intimate terms with any of them; but I was in the habit of observing civility and politeness to them all. They loved to talk with us on French affairs, and their ignorance of all that concerned France and the French people was almost incredible. We excited mutual astonishment in each other; they surprised us by their degenerate political principles, and we astonished them by the novelty of our ideas and manners, of which they had previously formed no conception. They certainly knew infinitely less of France than of China.

One of the principal officers of the ship, in a familiar conversation, happened to say—"I suppose you would be very much alarmed if we were to land you on the coast of France."—"Why so?" I enquired.—"Because," replied he, "the King would perhaps make you pay dearly for having left your country to follow another Sovereign; and also because you wear a cockade which he has prohibited."—"And is this language becoming an Englishman!" observed I. "You must be degenerated indeed! You are, it is true, far removed from the period of your revolution, to which you so justly apply the epithet *glorious*. But we, who are nearer to ours, by which we have gained so much, may tell you that every word you say is heresy. In the first place, our punishment depends not on the King's pleasure; we are subject only to the law. Now, there exists no law against us; and if any law were to be violated for the purpose of applying to our case, it would be your duty to protect us. Your general has pledged himself to do so by the capitulation of Paris, and it would be an eternal disgrace to the English Ministry, were they to permit the sacrifice of lives which their public faith had solemnly guaranteed."

"In the next place, we are not following another sovereign. That the Emperor Napoleon was our sovereign is an undeniable fact; but he has abdicated, and his reign is at an end. You are confounding private actions with party measures; love and devotedness, with political opinions. Finally, with regard to our colours, which seem to have dazzled you much, they are but a remnant of our old costume. We wear them to-day, only because we wore them yesterday. One cannot with indifference lay aside things to which one is attached; that can only be done from constraint or necessity. Why did you not deprive us of our colours when you deprived us of our arms?—the one act would have been as reasonable as the other. We are here only as private men: we do not preach sedition. We cannot deny that these colours are dear to us: we are attached to them because they have seen us victorious over all our enemies; because we have paraded them in triumph through every capital in Europe; and because we wore them while we were the first nation in the world."

On another occasion, one of the officers, after glancing at the extraordinary vicissitude of recent events, said—"Who knows whether we may not yet be destined to repair the misfortunes which we have occasioned to you? What would be your astonishment if Wellington should one day conduct Napoleon back to Paris?" "I should be astonished indeed," I replied; "but I should certainly decline the honour of being one of the party: at such a price, I would not hesitate to abandon Napoleon himself! But I may rest easy on that score; for I can swear Napoleon will never put me to such a trial. It is from him I imbibe these sentiments: it was he who cured me of the contrary doctrine, which I call the error of my youth."

The English were also very fond of asking us questions concerning the Emperor, whose character and disposition, as they afterwards avowed, had been described to them in the falsest colours. It was not their fault, they observed, if they formed an erroneous estimate of his character: they knew him only through the works published in England, which were all greatly exaggerated, and much to his prejudice: they had several of these publications on board the ship.—One day I happened to cast my eyes on one of a most malignant character: on another occasion, when I was about to look on a book which one of the officers was reading, he suddenly closed it, observing it was so violent against the Emperor, that he could not prevail on himself to let me see it. Another time, the Admiral questioned me respecting certain imputations contained in different works in his library, some of which he said enjoyed a degree of credit, while all had produced a great sensation in England. This circumstance suggested to me the idea of successively examining all the works of this kind that were on board the ship, in order to note down my opinion of them in my journal—conceiving that so favourable an opportunity might never again occur of obtaining, if I chose, information on these points, which it might be worth while to enquire into.

Before I commence my review of these works, I must beg to offer a few general remarks: they will suffice to answer in anticipation many of the numberless accusations that will fall in my way. Calumny and falsehood are the arms of the civil or political, the foreign or domestic enemy. They are the resource of the vanquished and the feeble, of those who are governed by hatred or fear.—They are the food of the drawing-room, and the garbage of the public place: they rage with the greater fury in proportion as their object is exalted: there is nothing which they will not venture to propagate. The more absurd, ridiculous, and incredible calumnies and falsehoods may be, the more eagerly are they received and repeated from mouth to mouth. Triumph and success are but fresh causes of irritation: a moral storm will invariably gather; and bursting in the moment of adversity, it will precipitate and complete the fall, and will become the immense lever of public opinion.

No man was ever so much assailed and abused as Napoleon. No individual was ever the subject of so many pamphlets, libels, atrocious and absurd stories and false assertions. This may be because he rose from the common rank of life to supreme distinction, and advanced at the head of a revolution which he himself had civilized. These two circumstances plunged him into a deadly contest with the rest of Europe—a contest in which he was subdued only because he wished to terminate it too speedily. Napoleon the conqueror of his neighbours, and in some measure a universal Monarch—hated by the aristocrats of Europe as a Marius, by the demagogues as a Sylla, and by the republicans as a Cæsar;—raised against himself a burricane of passions both at home and abroad; while he had on his side only the genius, the force, and the destiny of his own power.

Despair, policy, and fury, in every country, painted him as an object of detestation and alarm. Thus, all that has been said against him can excite no astonishment: it is only surprising that more calumny has not been uttered, and that it has not produced a much greater effect. When in the enjoyment of his power, he never would permit any one to reply to the attacks that were made upon him. "Whatever pains might have been bestowed on such answers," said he, "they would only have given additional weight to the accusations they were intended to refute. It would have been said that all that was written in my defence was ordered and paid for. The ill-managed praise of those by whom I was surrounded, had already in some instances been more prejudicial to me than all the abuse of which I was the object. Facts were the most convincing answers. A fine monument, another good law, or a new triumph, were sufficient to defeat thousands of such falsehoods. Declamation passes away, but deeds remain!"

This is unquestionably true with regard to posterity. The great men of former times are handed down to us free from the ephemeral accusations of their contemporaries. But it is not thus during the lifetime of the individual; and in 1814, Napoleon was convinced by cruel experience, that even deeds may vanish before the fury of declamation. At the moment of his fall, he was absolutely overwhelmed by a torrent of abuse. But it was reserved for him whose life had been so fertile in prodigies to surmount this adverse stroke of fate, and almost immediately to arise resplendent from amidst his own ruins. His miraculous return is certainly unparalleled, both in its execution or its results. The transports which it called forth, penetrated into neighbouring countries, where prayers for his success were offered up, either publicly or in secret; and he who, in 1814, was defeated and pursued as the scourge of human nature, suddenly re-appeared in 1815, as the hope of his fellow-creatures.

Calumny and falsehood, in this instance, lost their prey by having overshot their mark. The good sense of mankind in a great measure rendered justice to Napoleon, and the abuse that had been heaped upon him was thenceforth discredited. "Poison lost its effect on Mithridates," said the Emperor, as he was the other day glancing over some new libels upon himself, "and since 1814, calumny cannot injure me."

In the universal clamour which was directed against him when in the enjoyment of his power, England bore the most conspicuous part.

In England, two great machines were mentioned in full activity; the one conducted by the emigrants, for whom nothing was too bad; and the other under the control of the English ministers, who had established a system of defamation, and who had regularly organized its action and effects. They maintained in their pay pamphleteers and libelists in every corner of Europe; their tasks were marked out to them; and their plans of attack were regularly laid and combined.

The English ministry multiplied the employment of these potent engines in England more than elsewhere. The English, who were more free and enlightened than other nations, stood the more in need of excitement. From this system the English ministers derived the two-fold advantage of rousing public opinion against the common enemy, and withdrawing attention from their own conduct, by directing popular clamour and indignation to the character and conduct of others; by this means their own character and conduct were screened from that investigation and recrimination which they might not have found very agreeable.

Thus the assassination of Paul at St. Petersburgh, and of our envoys in Persia; the seizure of Naper-Tandy in the free city of Hamburgh; the capture, in time of peace, of two rich Spanish frigates; the acquisition of the whole of India; the retaining of Malta and the Cape of Good Hope, against the faith of treaties; the machiavelian rupture of the treaty of Amiens; the unjust seizure of our ships previously to a new declaration of war; the Danish fleet seized with such cold and ironical perfidy, &c. &c.; all these aggressions were overlooked in the general agitation which had been artfully stirred up against a foreign power.

In order to take a just view of the accusations which have been heaped upon Napoleon, by the numerous publications written against him, it is necessary to make allowance for passions and circumstances; to reject with contempt all that is apocryphal, anonymous, and purely declamatory; and to adhere solely to the facts and proofs which would doubtless have been produced by those, who, after the overthrow of their enemy, became possessed of the authentic documents, the archives of the public departments and courts of law; in short, of all the sources of truth which are usually to be found in society. But nothing has been published; nothing has been brought forward; and, therefore, how much of this monstrous scaffolding falls to the ground. And to be still more rigidly equitable, if we wish to judge Napoleon by the example of his peers, or great men in analogous circumstances; that is to say, by comparing him with the founders of dynasties; or those who have ascended thrones by dint of popular commotions, it may then confidently be said that he is unequalled, and that he shines purely from amidst all that is opposed to him. It would be a loss of time to cite the numberless examples furnished by ancient and modern history: they are accessible to every one. It is only necessary to refer to the two countries which are here under consideration.

Did Napoleon, like Hugues-Capet, raise his arm against his sovereign? Did he cause him to perish in captivity?

Has Napoleon acted like the princes of the present house of Brunswick, who in 1715 and 1745 loaded the scaffold with victims—victims to whom the present English ministers, through their inconsequential policy and the principles they now profess, leave no other qualification than that of faithful subjects dying for their lawful sovereign!

The course by which Napoleon advanced to supreme power, is perfectly simple and natural; it is single in history; the very circumstances of his elevation render it unparalleled. "I have not usurped the crown," said he one day to the Council of State, "I have raised it out of the mire: the people placed it on my head: let their acts be respected!"

By thus raising up the crown, Napoleon restored France to her rank in European society, terminated her horrors, and revived her character. He freed us of all the evils of our fatal crisis, and reserved to us all the advantages arising out of it. "I ascended the throne unsullied by any of the crimes of my situation," said he, on one occasion. "How few founders of dynasties can say as much!"

Never during any period of our history were favours distributed with so much impartiality; merit so indiscriminately sought out and rewarded; public money so usefully employed; the arts and sciences better encouraged, or the glory and lustre of the country raised to so high a pitch. "It is my wish," said he one day to the Council of State, "that the title of Frenchman should be the best and most desirable on earth; that a Frenchman travelling through any part of Europe may think and find himself at home."

If liberty seemed occasionally to suffer encroachments, if authority seemed sometimes to overstep its limits, circumstances rendered those measures necessary and inevitable. Our present misfortunes have, though too late, made us sensible of this truth; we now render justice, though also too late, to the courage, judgment, and foresight which then dictated those steps. It is certain that in this respect, the political fall of Napoleon has considerably increased his influence. Who can now doubt that his glory and the lustre of his character have been infinitely augmented by his misfortunes?

If the works which have fallen in my way should present any circumstances connected with these general considerations, they will be the object of my particular attention. I do not intend to enter upon a political controversy; I shall not address myself to party men, whose opinions are founded on their interests and passions; I speak only to the cool friend of truth, or to the unprejudiced writer, who in future times may impartially seek for materials: to them alone I address myself; in their eyes my testimony will be superior to anonymous evidence, and will rank on an equality with that which bears a creditable character.

The first work that I looked into was the *Anti-Gallican*, of which I shall speak hereafter.

Employment of our time.

19th—22d.—We continued our course with the same wind, the same sky, and the same temperature. Our voyage was monotonous, but pleasant: our days were long, but employment helped them to glide away. The Emperor now began regularly to dictate to me his Campaigns in Italy. I had already written several chapters. For the first few days, the Emperor viewed this occupation with indifference; but the regularity and promptitude with which

I presented to him my daily task, together with the progress we made, soon excited his interest, and at length the pleasure he derived from this dictation, rendered it absolutely necessary to him. He was sure to send for me about eleven o'clock every morning, and he seemed himself to await the hour with impatience. I always read to him what he had dictated on the preceding day, and he then made corrections and dictated farther. In this way the time passed rapidly till four o'clock arrived, when he summoned his valet-de-chambre. He then proceeded to the state-cabin, and passed the time until dinner in playing at piquet or chess.

The Emperor dictates very rapidly, almost as fast as he speaks in ordinary conversation. I was, therefore, obliged to invent a kind of hieroglyphic writing; and I, in my turn, dictated to my son. I was happy enough to be able to collect almost literally every sentence that fell from him. I had now not a moment to spare: at dinner-time somebody was sure to come and tell me that all the company were seated at table. Fortunately my seat was near the door, which always stood open. I had some time since changed my place at the request of captain Ross, the commander of the vessel, who, as he did not speak French, took the opportunity of occasionally asking me the meaning of words: I therefore took my seat between him and the Grand Marshal. Captain Ross was a man of agreeable manners, and was exceedingly kind and attentive to us. I had learnt, according to the English custom, to invite him to take a glass of wine, drinking mine to the health of his wife, and he would then drink to the health of mine. This was our daily practice.

After dinner, the Emperor never failed to allude to his morning dictation, as if pleased with the occupation and amusement it had afforded him. On these occasions, as well as whenever I happened to meet him in the course of the day, he would address me in a jocular tone with—"Ah! sage Las Cases!—Illustrious memorialist!—the Sully of St. Helena;" and other similar expressions. Then he would frequently add: "My dear Las Cases, these memoirs will be as celebrated as any that have preceded them. You will survive as long as any previous memoir-writer. It will be impossible to dwell upon the great events of our time, or to write about me without referring to you." Then resuming his pleasantry, he would add:—"After all, it will be said, he must have known Napoleon well; he was his Councillor of State, his Chamberlain, his faithful companion. We cannot help believing him, for he was an honest man and incapable of misrepresentation."

Accidental Phenomenon.—Passage of the Line.—Christening.

23d—25th.—The west wind still continued, to our great astonishment; it was a sort of phenomenon in these regions, and had hitherto been very much in our favour. But with regard to phenomena, chance produced one of a much more extraordinary kind on the 23d, when we crossed the Line in O_0 latitude, O° longitude, and O_0 declination. This is a circumstance which chance alone may perhaps renew only once in a century, since it is necessary to arrive precisely at the first meridian about noon, in order to pass the line at that same hour, or to arrive there at the same time with the sun.

This was a day of great merriment and disorder among the crew: it was the ceremony which the English sailors call *the Christening*. The sailors dress themselves up in the most grotesque way; one is disguised as Neptune, and all persons on board the ship who have not previously crossed the Line, are formally presented to him; an immense razor is passed over their chins, with a lather made of pitch; buckets of water are thrown over them, and the loud bursts of laughter which accompany their retreat, complete their initiation into the grand mystery. No one is spared; and the officers are generally more roughly used than the lowest of the sailors. The Admiral, who had previously amused himself by endeavouring to alarm us with the anticipation of this awful ceremony, now very courteously exempted us from the inconvenience and ridicule attending it. We were with every mark of attention and respect presented to the rude god, who paid to each of us a compliment after his own fashion; and thus our trial ended.

The Emperor was scrupulously respected during the whole of this saturnalian festivity, when respect is usually shewn to no one. On being informed of the decorum which had been observed with respect to him, he ordered a hundred Napoleons to be distributed to the grotesque Neptune and his crew, which the Admiral opposed, perhaps from motives of prudence as well as politeness.

Examination of the Antigallican.—Sir Robert Wilson's writings.—Plague at Jaffa.—Anecdotes of the French army in Egypt.—Feelings of the army in the Egyptian Campaign. Berthier.—Jests of the soldiery.—Dromedaries.—Death of Kleber.—The young Arab.—Singular coincidences respecting Philipeaux and Napoleon.—Circumstances on which Fate depends.—Caffarelli's attachment to Napoleon.—Reputation of the French army in the East.—Napoleon quitting Egypt to assume the government of France.—The English expedition. Kleber and Desaix.

26th—30th. The weather still continued favourable.—Having passsed the Line, we momentarily expected to fall in with an east or south-east wind. The continuance of the west wind was extraordinary, and it was impossible it could last much longer. The resolution which the Admiral had adopted of bearing considerably to the East, rendered our situation very favourable, and we had every reason to hope for a short passage.

One afternoon, the sailors caught an enormous shark.—The Emperor enquired the cause of the great noise and confusion which he suddenly heard overhead; being informed of what had occurred, he expressed a wish to have a sight of the sea-monster. He accordingly went up to the poop, and incautiously approached too near the animal, which by a sudden movement knocked down four or five of the sailors, and had well nigh broke the Emperor's legs.—He descended the larboard gangway, covered with blood; we thought he was severely hurt, but it proved to be only the blood of the shark.

My labours advanced with the greatest regularity. The Antigallican, which was the first work I undertook to read, was a volume of five hundred pages, comprising all that had been written in England at the time when that country was menaced with the French invasion. It was the object of the English government to nationalize opposition to that event, and to rouse the whole nation against her dangerous enemy. The book contained a collection of public speeches, exhortations, patriotic appeals of zealous citizens, satirical songs, sarcastic productions, and highly-coloured newspaper articles, all pouring a torrent of odium and ridicule upon the French and their First Consul, whose courage, genius, and power excited the greatest alarm. This was all perfectly natural and allowable. Productions of this sort are like a shower of arrows thrown by combatants before they come to a close action: some hit, and some are carried away by the wind. Such writings will never afford satisfactory evidence to a man of judgment, and they scarcely merit contradiction.

Pamphleteers are little regarded, because their character is the antidote of their poison: it is not so with the historian. The latter, however, degrades himself to a level with the pamphlet-writer when he departs from the calm dignity and impartiality required for his office, to indulge in declamation, and to steep his pen in gall.

With these feelings I arose from the perusal of the different productions of Sir Robert Wilson, which I read after the Antigallican. This writer did us the greater injury, because his talents, his courage, and his numerous and brilliant services gave him importance in the eyes of his countrymen. A circumstance which I am about to state caused the writings of Sir R. Wilson to be particularly known and spoken of on board the ship.

Sir Robert had a son among the young midshipmen on board the Northumberland, and my son, whose similarity of age occasioned him to be much in the society of these youths, could easily observe the change which took place in their opinions with respect to us. They were at first very much prejudiced against us. When the Emperor came on board, they regarded him as an ogre ready to devour them. But on a better acquaintance with us, truth soon exercised over them the same influence which it produced on the rest of the crew. This was, however, at the expense of young Wilson, who was scouted by his companions, by way of expiation for the stories which his father had circulated.

. . . .

At this part of the manuscript a great number of leaves are struck out; the reason was explained on the margin as follows:

"I had collected numerous offensive statements from the writings of Sir Robert Wilson, to which I had perhaps replied with too much bitterness; a recent circumstance has induced me to suppress this portion of my Journal.

"Sir Robert Wilson has lately acted a conspicuous part in a cause which does honour to the hearts of all who were concerned in it: I allude to the saving of Lavalette. Being asked before a French tribunal, whether he had not formerly published works respecting our affairs? he replied in the affirmative, and added, that he had stated in them what he *then* believed to be true. These words are more to the purpose than any thing I could say; and I therefore hasten to cancel what I have already written; happy in thus having an opportunity to render justice to Sir Robert Wilson, on whose sincerity and good intentions I had, in my indignation, cast reflections."*

* After my removal from Longwood, Sir Hudson Lowe, who had seized my papers, looked over this Journal, with my permission. He, of course, met with parts which were very displeasing to him; and he said to me: "What a pretty legacy you are preparing for my children, Count!"—"That is not my fault," replied I;

I therefore set aside the works of Sir Robert Wilson, and the various accusations contained in them; I also suppress the numerous refutations I had collected. I shall merely stop to consider one circumstance which has been repeated in a hundred different works; the report of which has been circulated through Europe, and has obtained credit even in France. I allude to the poisoning of the men infected with the plague at Jaffa.

Certainly nothing can better prove how easily calumny may effect its object. If the voice of slander be bold and powerful, and can command numerous echoes, no matter how far probability, reason, common sense, and truth be violated—the wished-for end is sure to be attained.

A general, a hero, a great man, hitherto respected by fortune, as well as by mankind, at that moment rivetting the attention of three quarters of the globe, commanding admiration even from his enemies, was suddenly accused of a crime declared to be unheard of and unparalleled; of an act pronounced to be inhuman, atrocious, and cruel; and what is above all extraordinary, he could have no possible object in committing that crime.

The most absurd details, the most improbable circumstances, the most ridiculous episodes were invented, to give a colouring to this first falsehood. The story was circulated through Europe; malevolence seized it, and exaggerated its enormity; it was published in every newspaper; recorded in every book; and thenceforward was looked upon as an established fact:—indignation was at its height, and clamour universal. It would have been vain to reason, or attempt to stem the torrent, or to show that no proofs of the fact had been adduced, and that the story contradicted itself. It would have been vain to bring forward opposite

"it depends only on yourself to render it otherwise; I shall be happy to have reason to strike out any thing respecting you, as I did the other day with regard to Sir Robert Wilson." Upon which he asked me what I had written about Sir Robert, and I pointed out the place. After reading all that had been written, and my reasons for cancelling it, he said, with a thoughtful and mortified air: "Yes, I see; but I can't tell what to make of it; for I know Wilson well, and he has proved himself a warm friend of the Bourbons."

We leaped for joy when we heard of the deliverance of Lavalette. Some one observed, that his deliverer, Wilson, could not be the same individual who had written so many offensive things concerning the Emperor. "And why not?" said Napoleon. "You know but little of men, and the passions that actuate them.—What leads you to suppose that Sir Robert Wilson is not a man of enthusiasm and violent passions, who wrote what he then believed true? And while we were enemies we contended with each other; but in our present adversity he knows better: he may have been abused and deceived, and may be sorry for it; and he is perhaps now as sincere in wishing us well as he formerly was in seeking to injure us."

Either sagacity or chance so happily led the Emperor to his conclusion, that it may be said he was enabled to read character at a distance. Sir R Wilson was indeed the man who wrote against Napoleon. Vexed to see a great people deprived of their natural rights, he reproached the allies as bitterly as though they had imposed chains on himself and no one has manifested stronger indignation at the treatment of Napoleon, or testified a more ardent wish to see it end.

and incontrovertible evidence—the evidence of those very medical men who were said to have administered, or to have refused to administer, the poison. It would have been vain to expose the unreasonableness of accusing of inhumanity the man who, but a short time before, had immortalized the hospitals of Jaffa by an act of the sublimest heroism; risking his own safety by solemnly touching the troops infected with the plague, to deceive and soothe the imaginations of the sick men. In vain might it have been urged that the idea of such a crime could not be affixed on him, who, when consulted by the medical officers as to the expediency of burning or merely washing the clothes worn by the invalids, and being reminded of the enormous loss attendant on the former measure, replied:—"Gentlemen, I came here to fix the attention and to recall the interests of Europe to the centre of the ancient world, and not with the view of amassing wealth." In vain would it have been shown that there could be no object, no motive whatever for this supposed crime. Had the French General any reason to suspect a design for corrupting his invalids and converting them into reinforcements against himself? Did he hope that this barbarous act would completely rid him of the infection? He might have effected that object equally well by leaving his invalids to be overtaken by the enemy's troops, which would moreover have been the means of spreading the contagion among the latter. It would have been vain to show that an unfeeling and selfish chief might have freed himself from all embarrassment by merely leaving the unfortunate men behind him: they would have been massacred, it is true; but no one would ever have thought of addressing a reproach to him.

These and every other argument would have been vain and useless, so powerful and infallible are the effects of falsehood and declamation when the passions of mankind are interested in their propagation. The imaginary crime was repeated by every mouth, was engraven on every heart, and to the common mass of mankind it will perhaps for ever continue a positive and incontrovertible fact.

A circumstance, which will not a little surprise those who have yet to learn how little credit is due to public report, and which will also serve to show the errors that may creep into history, is, that Marshal Bertrand, who was himself with the army in Egypt, (though certainly in a rank which did not enable him to come into immediate contact with the General-in-chief) firmly believed, up to the period of his residence at Saint Helena, the story of poison having been administered to sixty invalids. The report was circulated and believed even in our army; therefore, what answer could be given to those who triumphantly asserted "it is a fact, I assure you, I have it from officers who served in the French army at the time!" Nevertheless, the whole story is false. I have collected the following facts from the highest source, from the mouth of Napoleon himself.

1st. That the invalids in question who were infected with the plague, amounted, according to the report made to the General-in-chief, only to *seven* in number.

2d. That it was not the General-in-chief, but a professional man, who at the moment of the crisis, proposed the administering of opium.

3d. That the opium was not administered to a single individual.

4th. That the retreat having been effected slowly, a rear-guard was left behind in Jaffa for three days.

5th. That on the departure of the rear-guard, the invalids were all dead, except one or two, who must have fallen into the hands of the English.

N. B. Since my return to Paris, having had opportunities of conversing with those whose situation and profession naturally rendered them the first actors in the scene—those whose testimony must be considered as official and authentic, I have had the curiosity to enquire into the most minute details, and the following is the result of my enquiries.

"The invalids under the care of the Surgeon-in-chief, that is to say, the wounded, were all, without exception, removed, with the help of the horses belonging to the staff, not excepting even those of the General-in-chief, who proceeded for a considerable distance on foot, like the rest of the army. These, therefore, are quite out of the question.

"With regard to the rest of the invalids, about twenty in number, who were under the care of the Physician-in-chief, and who were in an absolutely desperate condition, totally unfit to be removed, while the enemy was advancing, it is very true that Napoleon asked the Physician-in-chief whether it would not be an act of humanity to administer opium to them. It is also true, that the physician replied, his business was to cure and not to kill; an answer which, as it seems to have reference to an order rather than to a subject of discussion, has, perhaps, furnished a basis on which slander and falsehood might invent and propagate the fabrication which has since been circulated on this subject.

"Finally, the details which I have been able to collect, afford me the following incontestible results:—

"1st. That no order was given for the administration of opium to the sick.

Refuted poison in Egypt

"2d. That there was not at the period in question, in the medicine-chest of the army, a single grain of opium for the use of the sick.

"3d. That even had the order been given, and had there been a supply of opium, temporary and local circumstances, which it would be tedious to enumerate here, would have rendered its execution impossible.

"The following circumstances have probably helped to occasion, and may, perhaps, in some degree excuse, the mistake of those who have obstinately maintained the truth of the contrary facts. Some of our wounded men, who had been put on board ship, fell into the hands of the English. We had been short of medicines of all kinds in the camp, and we had supplied the deficiency by compositions formed from indigenous trees and plants. The ptisans and other medicines had a horrible taste and appearance. The prisoners, either for the purpose of exciting pity, or from having heard of the opium story, which the nature of the medicines might incline them to believe, told the English that they had miraculously escaped death, having had poison administered to them by their medical officers." So much for the invalids under the care of the Surgeon-in-chief.

Now for the others.—"The army unfortunately had, as Apothecary-in-chief, a wretch who had been allowed the use of five camels to convey from Cairo the quantity of medicines necessary for the expedition. This man was base enough to supply himself on his own account, instead of medicines, with sugar, coffee, wine, and other provisions, which he afterwards sold at an enormous profit. On the discovery of the fraud, the indignation of the General-in-chief was without bounds, and the offender was condemned to be shot; but all the medical officers, who were so distinguished for their courage, and whose attentive care had rendered them so dear to the army, implored his pardon, alleging that the honour of the whole body would be compromised by his punishment; and thus the culprit escaped. Some time after, when the English took possession of Cairo, this man joined them, and made common cause with them; but, having attempted to renew some of his old offences, he was condemed to be hanged, and again escaped by slandering the General-in-chief, Bonaparte, of whom he invented a multitude of horrible stories, and by representing himself as the identical person who had, by the General's orders, administered opium to the soldiers infected with the plague. His pardon was the condition and the reward of his calumnies. This was doubtless the first source whence the story was derived, by those who were not induced to propagate it from malevolent motives.

"Time has, however, fully exposed this absurd calumny, as well as many others which have been applied in the same direction, and that with so great a rapidity, that on revising my manuscript, I have been surprised at the importance I have attached to the refutation of a charge which no one would now dare to maintain. Still, I thought it best to preserve what I had written, as a testimony of the impression of the moment; and if I have now added some farther details, it is because they happened to lie within my reach, and I thought it important to record them as historical facts."

Sir Robert Wilson has, in his work, boasted with seeming complacency of having been the first to make known and to propagate these odious charges in Europe. His countryman, Sir Sydney Smith, may perhaps dispute this honour with him, particularly as he may, in a great measure at least, justly lay claim to the merit of their invention. To him, and to the system of corruption he encouraged, Europe is indebted for all the false reports with which she has been inundated, to the great detriment of our brave army of Egypt.

It is well known that Sir Sydney Smith did every thing in his power to corrupt our army. The false intelligence from Europe—the slander of the General-in-chief—the powerful bribes held out to the officers and soldiers,—were all approved by him: the documents are published, his proclamations are known. At one time they created sufficient alarm in the French General, to induce him to seek to put a stop to them; which he did by forbidding all communication with the English, and stating in the order of the day, that their Commodore had gone mad. This assertion was believed in the French army; and it so much enraged Sir Sydney Smith, that he sent Napoleon a challenge. The General replied, that he had business of too great importance on his hands to think of troubling himself about such a trifle: had he received a challenge from the great Marlborough, then indeed he might have thought it worth while to consider of it: but if the English seaman really felt inclined to amuse himself at a tilting-match, he would send him a tall, bullying grenadier, and neutralize a few yards of the sea coast, where the mad Commodore might come ashore, and enjoy his heart's content of it.

As I am on the subject of Egypt, I will here note down all the information I collected in my detached conversations, and which may possibly not be found in the campaign of Egypt, dictated by Napoleon to the Grand Marshal.

The campaign of Italy exhibits all the most brilliant and decisive results to which military genius and conception ever gave birth. Diplomatic views, administrative talents, legislative measures, are there uniformly blended in harmony with the prodigies of war. But the most striking, and the finishing touch in the picture, is the sudden and irresistible ascendancy which the young General acquired: the anarchy of equality—the jealousy of republican principles—every thing vanished before him: there was not a power, even to the ridiculous sovereignty of the Directory, which was not immediately suspended. The Directory required no accounts from the General-in-chief of the army of Italy; it was left to himself to send them: no plan, no system, was prescribed to him; but accounts of victories, and conclusions of armistices, of the destruction of old states, and the creation of new ones, were constantly received from him.

In the expedition of Egypt may be retraced all that is admired in the campaign of Italy. The reflecting observer will even perceive, that in the Egyptian expedition, the points of resemblance are of a more important nature, from the difficulties of every kind which gave character to the campaign, and required greater genius and resources on the part of its conductor. In Egypt, a new order of things appeared: climate, country, inhabitants, religion, manners, and mode of fighting, all were different.

The Memoirs of the Campaign of Egypt, will determine points which at the time formed only the subjects of conjecture and discussion to a large portion of society.

1st. The expedition of Egypt was undertaken at the earnest and mutual desire of the Directory and the General-in-chief.

2d. The taking of Malta was not the consequence of a private understanding, but of the wisdom of the General-in-chief. "It was in Mantua that I took Malta," said the Emperor one day; "it was the generous treatment observed towards Wurmser, that secured to me the submission of the Grand Master and his Knights."

3d. The conquest of Egypt was calculated with as much judgment as it was executed with skill. If Saint Jean d'Acre had surrendered to the French army, a great revolution would have taken place in the east; the General-in-chief would have established an empire there, and the destinies of France would have taken a different turn.

4th. On its return from the campaign of Syria, the French army had scarcely sustained any loss: it remained in the most formidable and prosperous condition.

5th. The departure of the General-in-chief for France was the result of a grand and magnanimous plan. How ridiculous is the imbecility of those who consider that departure as an evasion or a desertion.

6th. Kleber fell a victim to Musulmanic fanaticism.—There is not the slightest foundation for the absurd calumny which would have attributed this catastrophe to the policy of his predecessor, or to the intrigues of his successor.

7th, and lastly. It is pretty well proved that Egypt would have remained for ever a French province, if any other but Menou had been appointed for her defence; nothing but the gross errors of that general could have lost us the possession of Egypt.

The emperor said, that no army in the world was less fit for the Egyptian expedition than that which he led there—the army of Italy. It would be difficult to describe the disgust, the discontent, the melancholy, the despair of that army, on its first arrival in Egypt. The Emperor himself saw two dragoons run out of the ranks and throw themselves into the Nile. Bertrand had seen the most distinguished generals, such as Lannes, and Murat, in momentary fits of rage, throw their laced hats on the sand, and trample on them in the presence of the soldiers. The Emperor explained these feelings surprisingly well. "This army," said he, "had fulfilled its career. All the individuals belonging to it were satiated with wealth, rank, pleasure, and consideration; they were not fit for the Deserts and the fatigues of Egypt; and," continued he, "had that army been placed in other hands than mine, it is difficult to say what excesses might not have been committed."

More than one conspiracy was formed to carry away the flags to Alexandria, and other things of the same sort. The influence, the character, and the glory of the General, could alone restrain the troops. One day Napoleon, losing his temper in his turn, rushed among a group of discontented generals, and addressing himself to the tallest, "You have held mutinous language," said he with vehemence, "take care that I do not fulfil my duty; your five foot ten* should not save you from being shot in a couple of hours."

With regard, however, to their conduct before the enemy, the Emperor said that this army never ceased to be the army of Italy; that it still preserved the same admirable character. The most difficult party to manage was that which the Emperor used to call "the faction of the *sentimentalists*," whom it was impossible to keep under any restraint; their minds were diseased; they spent the night in gazing on the moon for the reflected image of the idols they had left in Europe. At the head of this party was Berthier, the weak and spiritless Berthier, who, when the General-in-chief was preparing to sail from Toulon, posted night and

* French feet are of course here alluded to.

day from Paris to tell him that he was unwell, and could not follow him, though he was the head of the staff. The General-in-chief took not the smallest notice of what he said; and Berthier, finding himself no longer at the feet of the fair one who had despatched him with the excuse, set sail along with him! On his arrival in Egypt, he became a prey to *ennui*, and was unable to subdue his tender recollections; he solicited and obtained permission to return to France. He took leave of Napoleon, and bade him a formal adieu; but shortly returned again with his eyes full of tears, saying, that he would not after all dishonour himself, and that he could not separate his destiny from that of his General.

Berthier's love was mingled with a kind of worship.—Adjoining the tent destined for his own use, he always had another prepared, and furnished with the magnificence of the most elegant boudoir; this was consecrated to the portrait of his mistress, before which he would sometimes even go so far as to burn incense. This tent was pitched even in the deserts of Syria. Napoleon said with a smile, that his temple had oftener than once been profaned by a worship less pure, through the clandestine introduction of foreign divinities.

Berthier never relinquished his passion, which sometimes carried him to the very verge of idiocy. In his first account of the battle of Marengo, young Visconti, whose highest rank was that of a captain, was mentioned five or six times in remembrance of his mother. "One would have thought," said Napoleon, "that the youth had gained the battle."—Surely the General-in-chief must have been ready to throw the paper in the writer's face.

The Emperor calculated that he had given Berthier forty millions during his life; but he supposed that from this weakness of his mind, his want of regularity, and his ridiculous passion, he had squandered away a great part of it.

The discontent of the troops in Egypt happily vented itself in sarcastic jokes: this is the humour which always bears a Frenchman through difficulties. They had a great spite at General Caffarelli, whom they believed to have been one of the promoters of the expedition. Caffarelli had a wooden leg, having lost one of his limbs on the banks of the Rhine; and whenever the soldiers saw him bobbling past, they would say, loud enough for him to hear—"That fellow does not care what happens; he is certain, at all events, to have one leg in France."

The men of science, who accompanied the expedition, also came in for their share of the jests. Asses were very numerous in Egypt; almost all the soldiers possessed one or two, and they used always to call them their *demi-savans*.

The General-in-chief, on his departure from France, had issued a proclamation, in which he informed the troops that he was about to take them to a country where he would make them all rich; where they should each have seven acres of land at their disposal. The soldiers, when they found themselves in the midst of the Desert, surrounded by the boundless ocean of sand, began to question the generosity of their general: they thought he had observed singular moderation in having promised only seven acres. "The rogue," said they, "might with safety make us a more unlimited offer; we should not abuse his good nature."

While the army was passing through Syria, there was not a soldier but was heard to repeat these lines from Zaire:—

Les Francais sont lasses de chercher desormais
Des climats que pour eux le destin n'a point faits,
Ils n'abandonnent point leur fertile patrie,
Pour languir aux deserts de l'aride Arabie.

On one occasion, the general-in-chief, having a few moments of leisure to look about the country, took advantage of the ebb-tide, and crossed on foot to the opposite coast of the Red Sea. Night surprised him on his return, and he lost his way in the midst of the rising tide. He was in the greatest danger, and very narrowly escaped perishing precisely in the same manner as Pharaoh. "This," said Napoleon, "would have furnished all the preachers of Christianity with a splendid text against me." On reaching the Arabian coast of the Red Sea, he received a deputation of the Cenobites of Mount Sinai, who came to implore his protection, and to request him to inscribe his name on the ancient register of their charters. Napoleon inscribed his name on the same list with those of Ali, Saladin, Abraham, and others! In allusion to this circumstance, or something of a similar kind, the emperor observed, that he had in the course of one year received letters from Rome and Mecca; the Pope addressing him as his dearest son, and the Sherif styling him the protector of the holy Kaaba.

This singular coincidence, however, is scarcely surprising, with reference to him who has led armies both through the burning sands of the Tropic, and over the frozen *Steppes* of the North; who, while he narrowly escaped being swallowed up in the waves of the Red Sea, and might have perished in the flames of Moscow, threatened the Indies from those two extreme points.

The general-in-chief shared the fatigues of the soldiers. The privations endured by every individual in the army were sometimes so great, that they were compelled to dispute with each other for the smallest enjoyments, without the least distinction of rank. To such extremities were they reduced, that in the Desert, the soldiers would hardly relinquish their places to allow the General to dip his hands in the muddy stream. On one occasion, as they were passing by the ruins of Pelusium, and were almost suffocated with the heat, some one resigned to him the fragment of an ancient door, beneath which he contrived to shade his head for a few minutes; "and this," said Napoleon, "was no trifling concession." It was on this very spot, while removing some stones at his feet, that chance rendered him the possessor of a superb antique, well known in the learned world.*

In proceeding to Asia, the French army had to cross the Desert which separates that continent from Africa. Kleber, who commanded the advance-guard, mistook his road, and lost his way in the Desert. Napoleon, who was following at the distance of half a day's march, attended by a slender escort, found himself at night-fall in the midst of the Turkish camp: he was closely pursued, and escaped only because, it being night, the Turks suspected an ambush was intended. The next source of uneasiness was the doubtful fate of Kleber and his detachment, and the greater part of the night was passed in the most cruel anxiety. At length they got information respecting them from some Arabs of the deserts, and the General-in-chief hastened, on his dromedary, in quest of his troops. He found them overwhelmed with despair, and ready to perish from thirst and fatigue; some of the young soldiers had, in a moment of frenzy, even broken their musquets. The sight of their general seemed to give them new life, by reviving their hopes. Napoleon informed them that a supply of provisions and water was coming up behind him; "but," said he to the troops, "if relief had been longer delayed, would that have excused your murmuring and loss of courage? No, soldiers, learn to die with honour."

Napoleon travelled the greater part of the way through the Desert, on a dromedary. The physical hardihood of this animal renders it unnecessary to pay the least attention to his sustenance; he scarcely eats or drinks;—but his moral sensibility is extreme, harsh treatment provokes his resentment, and renders him furious. The Emperor observed that the roughness of his trot created nausea, like the motion of a ship. The animal will travel twenty leagues

* A cameo of Augustus, a mere sketch, but admirably designed. Napoleon gave it to General Andreossi, who was a great collector of antiquities; but M. Denon, who was at that time absent, having afterwards seen this cameo, was struck with its resemblance to Napoleon, who then had the stone returned to him and kept it. It afterwards fell into the possession of Josephine, and M. Denon does not know what has since become of it. *(This information was furnished to me by M. Denon since my return to France.)*

a-day. The Emperor formed some dromedary regiments, and the use he made of them in the army soon proved the destruction of the Arabs. The rider squats himself on the back of the animal, through whose nostrils a ring is passed, which serves to guide him: he is very obedient, and on a certain signal made by the voice of the rider, the animal kneels down to allow him to alight. The dromedary will carry very heavy burdens, and he is never unloaded during the whole of the journey. On his arrival at evening stations, his load is propped up, and the animal lies down and goes to sleep: at day-break he rises—his burden is on his back, and he is ready to continue his journey. The dromedary is only a beast of burden, and not at all fit for draught. In Syria, however, they succeeded in yoking them to field-pieces, and thus rendering them essentially serviceable.

Napoleon became very popular among the Egyptains, who gave him the name of Sultan Kebir (father of the Fire.) He inspired particular respect; wherever he appeared, the people rose in his presence; and this deference was paid to him alone. The uniform consideration with which he treated the Sheiks, and the adroitness by which he gained their confidence, rendered him truly the sovereign of Egypt, and more than once saved his life. But for the connexion he maintained with the Egyptians, he would have fallen a victim to fanaticism, like Kleber, who, on the contrary, rendered himself odious to the Sheiks, and perished, in consequence of subjecting one of them to the punishment of the bastinado. Bertrand was one of the judges who condemned the assassin, and on his telling us this fact one day at dinner, the Emperor observed :—"If slanderers, who accuse me of having caused the death of Kleber, were acquainted with the fact you have mentioned, they would not hesitate to call you the assassin or the accomplice, and would take it for granted that your title of Grand Marshal, and your residence at Saint Helena, are the reward and the punishment of the crime."

Napoleon willingly conversed with the people of the country, and always revealed sentiments of justice which struck them with wonder. On his way back to Syria, an Arab tribe came to meet him, for the double purpose of showing him respect and of selling their services as guides. "The chief of the tribe was unwell, and his place was filled by his son, a youth of the age and make of 'your boy here,'" said the Emperor to me; "he was mounted on his dromedary, riding close beside me, and chatting to me with great familiarity.—'Sultan Kebir,' said he, I could give you good advice, now that you are returning to Cairo.'—'Well! speak, my friend, and if your advice is good, I will follow it.'—'I'll tell you what I would do, if I were in your place. As soon as I got to Cairo, I would order the richest slave-merchant into the market, and I would choose twenty of the prettiest women for myself; I would next send for the richest jewellers, and would make them give up a good share of their stock; I would then do the same with all the other merchants; for what is the use of reigning or being powerful, if not to acquire riches!'—'But, my friend, suppose it were more noble to preserve them for others!'—This sentiment seemed to make him reflect a little, without convincing him. The young man was evidently very promising, for an Arab: he was lively and courageous, and led his troop with dignity and order. He is perhaps destined one day or other to carry his advice into execution in the market-place of Cairo."

On another occasion, some Arabs who were on friendly terms with the army, penetrated into a village on the frontier, and an unfortunate Fellah (peasant) was killed. The Sultan Kebir flew into a great passion; and vowing that he would have vengeance, gave orders that the tribe should be pursued into the Desert to extinction. This order was given in the presence of the Grand Sheiks, one of whom could not refrain from laughing at his anger and his determination.—"Sultan Kebir," said he, "you are playing a bad game just now; do not quarrel with these people; they can do you ten times more harm than you can do them. And besides, what is it all about? Because they have killed a miserable peasant? Was he your cousin (a proverbial expression among them)?"—"He was more than my cousin," replied Napoleon; "all those whom I govern are my children: power is given to me only that I may ensure their safety." On hearing these words, all the Sheiks bowed their heads, and said, "Oh! that is very fine!—you have spoken like the prophet."

The decision of the Grand Mosque of Cairo in favour of the French army, was a masterpiece of skill on the part of the General-in-chief, who induced the synod of the Grand Sheiks to declare, by a public act, that the Musulmans should obey and pay tribute to the French general. It is the first and only example of the sort since the establishment of the Koran, which forbids submission to infidels. The details of this transaction are invaluable: they will be found in the Campaigns of Egypt.

Saint Jean d'Acre doubtless presented a singular spectacle, when two European armies met with hostile intentions in a little town of Asia, with the mutual purpose of securing the possession of a portion of Africa; but it is still more extraordinary, that the persons who directed the efforts of each party were both of the same nation, of the same age, of the same rank, of the same corps, and of the same school.

Phelippeaux, to whose talents the English and the Turks owed the preservation of Saint Jean d'Acre, had been the companion of Napoleon at the Military School of Paris: they had been there examined together, previous to their being sent to their respective corps. "His figure resembled yours," said the Emperor to me, after having dictated his eulogium in the Memoirs, and mentioned all the ill he had done him. "Sire," I answered, "there were many other points of affinity between us: we had been intimate and inseparable companions at the Military School. When he passed through London with Sir Sydney Smith, who by his assistance had been enabled to escape from the Temple, he sought for me in every direction. I called at his lodgings only half an hour after he had gone: had it not been for this accident, I should probably have accompanied him. I was at that time without occupation: the prospect of adventure might have tempted me; and how strangely might the course of my destinies have been turned into a new direction!"

"I am well aware," said Napoleon, "of the influence which chance usurps over our political determinations; and it is the knowledge of that circumstance which has always kept me free from prejudice, and rendered me very indulgent with regard to the party adopted by individuals in our political convulsions. To be a good Frenchman, or to wish to become so, was all that I look for in any one."—The Emperor then went on to compare the confusion of our troubles to battles in the night-time, where each man attacks his neighbour, and friends are often confounded with foes; but when day-light returns, and order is restored, every one forgives the injury which he has sustained through mistake. "Even for myself," said he, "how could I undertake to say that there might not have existed circumstances sufficiently powerful, notwithstanding my natural sentiments, to induce me to emigrate? The vicinity of the frontier, for instance, a friendly attachment, or the influence of a chief. In revolutions, we can only speak with certainty to what we have done: it is silly to affirm that we could not have acted otherwise." The Emperor then related a singular example of the influence of chance over the destinies of men. Serrurier and the younger Hedouville, while travelling together on foot to emigrate to Spain, were met by a military patrol Hedouville, being the younger and more active of the two, cleared the frontier, thought himself very lucky, and went to spend a life of mere vegetation in Spain. Serrurier, on the contrary, being obliged to return into the interior, bewailed his unhappy fate, and became a marshal: —such is the uncertainty of human foresight and calculations!

At Saint Jean d'Acre, the General-in-chief lost Caffarelli, of whom he was extremely fond. Caffarelli entertained a sort of reverential respect for the General-in-chief. The influence of this sentiment was so great, that though he was delirious for several days previous to his death, when Napoleon went to see him, the announcement of his name seemed to recall him to life: he became more collected, his spirits revived, and he conversed coherently; but he relapsed into his former state immediately after Napoleon's departure. This singular phenomenon was renewed every time the General-in-chief paid him a visit.

Napoleon received, during the siege of Saint Jean d'Acre, an affecting proof of heroic devotedness. While he was in the trenches, a shell fell at his feet; two grenadiers who observed it, immediately rushed towards him, placed him between them, and raising their arms above his head, completely covered every part of his body. Happily the shell respected the whole group; nobody was injured.

One of these brave grenadiers afterwards became General Dumesnil, who lost a leg in the campaign of Moscow, and commanded the fortress of Vincennes at the time of the invasion in 1815. The capital had been for some weeks occupied by the Allies, and Dumesnil still held out. Nothing was then talked of in Paris but his obstinate defence, and his humorous reply when summoned by the Russians to surrender:—"Give me back my leg, and I will give up my fortress."

The French soldiers acquired extraordinary reputation in Egypt, and not without cause; they had dispersed and dismayed the celebrated Mamelucks, the most formidable militia of the East. After the retreat from Syria, a Turkish army landed at Abukir: Murat-Bey, the most powerful and brave of the Mamelucks, left Upper Egypt, whither he had fled for safety, and reached the Turkish camp by a circuitous route. On the landing of the Turks, the French detachments had fallen back in order to concentrate their forces. The Pacha who commanded the Turks was delighted at this movement, which he mistook for the effect of fear; and on perceiving Murat-Bey, he exultingly exclaimed:—"So! these are the terrible French whom you dare not face; see, the moment I make my appearance, how they fly before me!" The indignant Murat-Bey furiously replied;—"Pacha, render thanks to the Prophet that it has pleased these Frenchmen to retire; if they should return, you will disappear before them like dust before the wind."

This prophecy was fulfilled:—some days after, the French poured down upon the Turkish army and put it to flight.—Murat-Bey, who had interviews with several of our generals, could not recover from his surprise at their diminutive stature and pitiful condition. The Oriental nations attach high importance to the formation of the body, and they were unable to conceive how so much genius could exist within such small dimensions. The appearance of Kleber alone came up to their ideas; he was an uncommonly fine-looking man, but his manners were extremely offensive. The discrimination of the Egyptians induced them to think that he was not a Frenchman; in fact, though a native of Alsace, Kleber had spent the early part of his life in the Prussian army, and might very well have passed for a German. Some one here observed that he had been a Janissary in his youth; on which the Emperor burst into a fit of laughter, and said somebody had been hoaxing him.

The Grand-Marshal told the Emperor that at the battle of Abukir he was for the first time placed in his army, and near his person. He was then so little accustomed to the boldness of his manœuvres, that he scarcely understood any of the orders he heard him give. "Particularly, Sire," added he, "when I heard you call out to an officer of the Guards, 'Hercule, take twenty-five men and charge that rabble;' I really thought I had lost my senses; your Majesty pointed at the time to a detachment of perhaps a thousand Turkish horse."

After all, the losses sustained by the army in Egypt were far from being so considerable as might have been expected in a country to which the troops were unaccustomed; particularly when the insalubrity of the climate, the remoteness of the resources of the country, the ravages of the plague, and the numerous actions which have immortalized that army, are taken into account. The French force, at its landing in Egypt, amounted to 30,000 men; it was augmented by the wrecks of the battle of Abukir, and probably also by some partial arrivals from France; and yet the total loss sustained by the army, from the commencement of the campaign to two months after the departure of the General-in-chief for Europe, that is to say, during the space of seven or eight and twenty months, amounted only to 8915, as is proved by the official report of the Muster-master-general of the army.*

* Killed in battle	3614
Died of their wounds	854
Died through various accidents	290
Died from common disorders	2468
Died from the pestilential fever	1689
Total	8915

Signed,
Sartelon, Muster-master-general,

Cairo, 10 Frimaire, year IX.

The life of a man must indeed be replete with prodigies, when one of his acts, which is without parallel in history, scarcely arrests our attention. When Cæsar passed the Rubicon, he possessed an army, and was advancing towards his defending forces. When Alexander, urged by the ardour of youth and the fire of genius, landed in Asia, to make war on the great King, he, Alexander, was the son of a king, a king himself, and courted the chances of ambition and glory at the head of the forces of his kingdom. But that a private individual, whose name three years before was unknown to the world, who at that moment had nothing to aid him but the reputation of a few victories, his name, and the consciousness of his genius, should have dared to conceive the project of taking into his own hands the destinies of thirty millions of men, of protecting them from external defeats and internal dissensions;—that, roused by the recital of the troubles which were described to him, and by the idea of the disasters which he foresaw, he should have exclaimed, "France will be lost through these fine talkers, these babblers; now is the time to save her!"—that he should have abandoned his army, and crossed the seas, at the risk of his liberty and reputation, have reached the French soil and flown to the capital;—that he should there have seized the helm, and stopped short a nation intoxicated with every excess;—that he should have suddenly brought her back to the true course of reason and justice; that he should from that moment have prepared for himself a mould of power and glory till then unknown;—and that all this should have been accomplished without the shedding of a single tear or a drop of blood;—such an undertaking may be regarded as one of the most gigantic and sublime that ever was heard of; it will fill calm and dispassionate posterity with astonishment and admiration; though at the present day it may be qualified with the title of a desperate flight, and an infamous desertion. The army, however, which Napoleon left behind him, continued to occupy Egypt for the space of two years longer. It was the opinion of the Emperor, that it ought never to have been forced unwillingly to remain there; and the Grand Marshal, who accompanied the army to the last moment, concurred in that opinion.

After the departure of the General-in-chief, Kleber, who succeeded him, deceived and misled by intrigues, treated for the evacuation of Egypt; but when the enemy's refusal compelled him to seek for new glory, and to form a more just estimate of his own force, he totally altered his opinions, and declared himself favourable to the occupation of Egypt; and this had even become the general sentiment of the army. He now thought only of maintaining himself in the country; he dismissed those who had influenced him in forming his first design, and collected around him only those who favoured the contrary measure. Had he lived, Egypt would have been secure; to his death her loss must be attributed. The command of the army was afterwards divided between Menou and Regnier. It then became a mere field of intrigue: the energy and courage of the French troops continued unabated; but they were no longer employed and directed as they had been by Kleber.

Menou was totally inefficient; the English advanced to attack him with twenty thousand men; his force was much more considerable, and the general spirit of the two armies was not to be compared. By an inconceivable infatuation, Menou hastily dispersed his troops, as soon as he learned that the English were about to appear; the latter advanced in a mass, and were attacked only in detail. "How blind is fortune!" said the Emperor; "by the adoption of contrary measures, the English would infallibly have been destroyed; and how many new chances might not that event have brought about!"

Their landing was admirable, said the Grand Marshal; in less than five or six minutes five thousand five hundred men appeared in the order of battle: it was a truly theatrical movement; and it was thrice repeated. Their landing was opposed by only twelve hundred men, who did them considerable damage. Shortly after, this mass, amounting to between thirteen and fourteen thousand, was intrepidly attacked by General Lanusse. The General had only three thousand troops; but fired with ambition, and not doubting that his force was adequate to fulfil the object he had in view, he would not wait for reinforcements; at first he overthrew every thing in his way, and after causing immense slaughter to the enemy, he was at length defeated. Had his force been two or three thousand stronger, he would have attained his object.

The English were greatly astonished when they had an opportunity of judging for themselves of our real situation in Egypt; and they considered themselves extremely fortunate in the turn which affairs had taken.

General Hutchinson, who reaped the glory of the conquest, said, on his return to Europe, that had the English known the real state of things, they would certainly never have attempted to land; but in England it was believed that there were not six thousand French troops in Egypt. This mistake arose out of the intercepted letters, as well as the intelligence that was collected in Egypt. "So natural is it to Frenchmen," said Napoleon, "to exaggerate, murmur, and misrepresent, when they are dissatisfied. These reports, however, were created merely by ill-humour or diseased imaginations: it was said that there was a famine in Egypt; that the French had all been destroyed, at every new battle; that the plague had swept away the whole army; that there was not a man left," &c.

Through the repetition of these reports, Pitt was at length persuaded of their reality; and how could it be otherwise? The First Consul saw the despatches from his successor addressed to the Directory; and also letters from various persons in the French army. Who can explain the contradictions they contained? Who will henceforth trust to individual authority for the support of his opinion? Kleber, the General-in-chief, informed the Directory, that he had only six thousand men; while in the same packet the accounts of the inspector at reviews exhibited upwards of twenty thousand. Kleber declared that he was without money, and the treasury accounts display vast sums. The General-in-chief alleged that the artillery was merely an intrenched park, destitute of ammunition; while the estimates of that department made mention of provisions for several campaigns. "Thus, if Kleber, by virtue of the treaty he commenced, had evacuated Egypt," said the Emperor, "I should undoubtedly have brought him to trial on his return to France. All these contradictory documents had been submitted to the examination and opinion of the Council of State."

From the letters of Kleber, the General-in-chief, an idea may be formed of the tone of those written by persons of inferior rank, and by the common soldiers. Such, however, were the communications daily intercepted by the English; which they printed and which guided them in their operations—a circumstance that must frequently have led them into grievous errors. The Emperor observed, that in all his campaigns he had seen the same effect produced by intercepted letters, which sometimes had proved of great advantage to him.

Among the letters which at this period fell into his hands, he found odious attacks upon himself, which he felt the more sensibly, because several of them were written by persons whom he had loaded with benefits, in whom he had reposed full confidence, and whom he believed to be strongly attached to him. One of these individuals, whose fortune he had made, and in whom he trusted with the utmost sincerity, alleged that the General-in-chief had decamped, after robbing the treasury of two millions. Fortunately, in these same despatches the accounts of the Paymaster proved that the General had not even received the whole amount of the pay due to him. "On reading this statement," said the Emperor, "I felt really disgusted at mankind. This was the first moral revulsion I had ever experienced; and if it has not been the only one, it has, perhaps, been at least the most severe. Many individuals in the army thought me ruined, and they were already eagerly seeking to pay their court in the proper quarter at my expense." The author of the assertion above alluded to, subsequently endeavoured to restore himself to favour. The Emperor signified that he should have no objection to his being employed in a subordinate situation; but that he would never see him again. To every application he constantly replied, that he did not know him: this was the only vengeance he took.

The Emperor never ceased to repeat that Egypt ought to have remained in the possession of the French, which would infallibly have been the case had the country been defended by Kleber or Desaix. "These were my two most distinguished lieutenants," said he; "both possessed great and rare merits, though their characters and dispositions were very different." Their portraits will be found in the Memoirs of the Campaign of Italy.

Kleber's was the talent of nature; Desaix's was entirely the result of education and assiduity. The genius of Kleber was only called forth at particular moments, when roused by the importance of the occasion; and then it immediately slumbered in the bosom of indolence and pleasure. The talent of Desaix was always in full activity; he lived only for noble ambition and true glory: his character was formed on the true ancient model. The Emperor said, that his death was the greatest loss he could possibly have sustained. Their conformity of education and principles would always have preserved a good understanding between them. Desaix would have been satisfied with secondary rank, and would have remained ever devoted and faithful. Had he not been killed at the battle of Marengo, the First Consul would have given him the command of the army of Germany, instead of continuing it to Moreau. A very extraordinary circumstance in the destiny of these two lieutenants of Napoleon was, that on the very day and at the very hour when Kleber was assassinated at Cairo, Desaix was killed by a cannon-ball at Marengo.

The Emperor's method of dictating.

October 1st—3d. The wind, the sea, and the temperature still continued without variation. The westerly wind, which had at first been so much in our favour, now began to be adverse. We had taken an easterly direction, in the hope of falling in with the trade-winds; but we now found ourselves to the leeward of the place of our destination, through the continuance of the westerly winds, a circumstance which surprised every body, and excited dissatisfaction among the crew.

The Emperor every morning regularly continued his dictation, in which he daily took a deeper interest: consequently his hours henceforth seemed less tedious.

The vessel had been sent so hurriedly out of port, that many repairs remained to be completed after we had put to sea, and the painting of the ship had only recently been finished. The Emperor's sense of smelling is extremely delicate; and he found the paint so extremely offensive, that he was forced to confine himself to his cabin for two days.

Every evening, when taking his walk on deck, he loved to revert to the occupation of the morning. At first he was assisted by no other document than a wretched work entitled *Guerres des Francais en Italie*, written without end or object, and devoid of any connected chronological plan.—The Emperor glanced through it, and his memory supplied all deficiencies: this faculty indeed appeared to me the more extraordinary, since it always seemed to be in readiness when needed, and as if at command.

When the Emperor commenced his daily dictations, he always complained that the circumstances to which he wished to recur were no longer familiar to him. After considering for a few moments he would rise and walk about, and then begin to dictate. From that moment he was quite another man: every thing flowed smoothly; he spoke as if by inspiration; places, dates, phrases, he stopped at nothing.

On the following day I read to him what he had dictated. After making the first correction he continued to go on with the same subject, as though he had said nothing about it the day before.—The difference between the first and the second version was very great: the latter was more positive and diffuse, and better arranged; indeed it sometimes materially differed from the first.

On the day succeeding the first correction, the same operation was repeated, and the Emperor commenced his third dictation for the purpose of setting the two former ones right. But after that, had he dictated a fourth, a seventh, or a tenth time, as he in some instances did, it would have been a repetition of precisely the same ideas, the same construction of phrases, and almost the same words. It was needless to take the trouble to write, though before his eyes: he paid no attention to what was doing, and continued to the end of his subject. It would have been vain to ask him to repeat any thing that might not have been distinctly heard; and as he dictated with great rapidity, I never ventured to interrupt him, lest I should lose still more, and render him unable to recover the thread of the subject.

A singular Accident.

4th—7th. The continuance of the south-west wind was truly unfortunate. We were now going back instead of forward, and we had completely entered the Gulf of Guinea. There we perceived a ship, with which we spoke. She proved to be a French ship, driven out of her course like ourselves. She had sailed from a port in Brittany, and was bound for the Isle of Bourbon. The Emperor had been much distressed for want of books; and I jokingly said that perhaps I might have a box-full on board that ship, as I had despatched one to the Isle of Bourbon about two months previously. I spoke truly. Such is the caprice of chance! Had I been in quest of this ship, I might have traversed the ocean in vain. This was the identical vessel: I learned her name next day from the officer who had visited her. This officer strangely surprised the French captain, by telling him that the Emperor Napoleon was on board the ship which he then saw making way to St. Helena. The poor fellow shook his head sorrowfully and said, "You have robbed us of our treasure: you have taken away him who knew how to govern us according to our tastes and manners."

Complaints of the Crew against the Admiral.—Examination of another work.—Refutations.—Reflections.

8th—11th.—The weather continued obstinately settled. We every evening consoled ourselves for the unfavourable state of the day, with the hope of a change during the night; but we arose in the morning with the same disappointment. We had been almost within sight of the Congo, and we stood off. Every one manifested discontent and *ennui*. The crew complained of the Admiral: had he taken the usual course, said they, we should have reached our destination long before; his caprice, they observed, had led him, in spite of reason, to try an experiment, of which they knew not what might be the consequence. Their murmurs were not, however, so vehement as those raised against Christopher Columbus; we should not have been ill pleased had he been reduced to the necessity of finding another Saint-Salvador, in order to evade the crisis. Being for my own part fully occupied, this circumstance engrossed but little of my attention; and after all, one prison was as good as another. As to the Emperor, he was still more unconcerned by this delay; he merely looked upon it as so many days spent.

Les Mémoires de Napoleon Bonaparte, par quelqu'un qui ne l'a jamais quitté pendant 15 *ans*, (*The Memoirs of Napoleon Bonaparte, by one who was constantly near him, during fifteen years*,) was the title of a work which I began to examine after the writings of Sir Robert Wilson. It is a volume of three hundred pages, by an anonymous author, a circumstance in itself sufficient to inspire distrust at the first outset. But the composition and style of the work soon create more positive doubts in the mind of the reflecting reader, who is accustomed to judge of books. Finally, he who has seen and known but little of the Emperor, will not hesitate to affirm, that this work is a mere romance written at pleasure; that the author has never approached the Emperor; and that he is a hundred leagues distant from his language, habits, and every thing concerning him. The Emperor never said to a minister: "Count, do this,"—"Count, execute that." Ambassadors never attended his levee. Napoleon could not, at fourteen years of age, have made to a lady in company, the reply attributed to him, relative to the Vicomte de Turenne; because from the age of ten to eighteen he was attending the Military school, where he could not possibly have been introduced to the company of ladies. It was not Perignon, who did not know him, but Dugommier, who had been his general, who recommended him in so marked a way to the Directory. It was a letter for restoring the Democracy, and not the Bourbons, which an officer addressed to the First Consul, &c.

The Emperor, who in Europe was universally acknowledged to have preserved the most impenetrable secresy with regard to his plans and views, never indulged in gestures, and still less in monologues, which would have been likely to betray him:—nor did his anger ever throw him into fits of insanity or epilepsy, an absurd fabrication which was long circulated in the saloons of Paris, but which was relinquished when it was found that those accidents never occurred on important occasions. These memoirs have unquestionably been an ordered work, the speculation of some bookseller, who has furnished the title. Be this as it may, it might have been supposed, that in adverting to a career so public as that of the Emperor and those who surrounded him, the author might have evinced more accuracy and knowledge of his subject. He is aware of his insufficiency on this head, and seeks to defend himself by saying that he was under the necessity of altering names, and that he did not wish to render certain portraits too striking; but he also observes this circumspection with regard to facts, so that they are not recognisable. They are for the most part entirely the creations of his own fancy. Thus, the paper whose loss cost the general-in-chief so much anxiety in Egypt; the recommendation of the young Englishman, who transported Bonaparte with joy by opening to him so brilliant a perspective of fortune at Constantinople; the melodrama of Malmaison, where the heroism of Madame Bonaparte (who is described as an absolute amazon) so promptly secures the safety of her husband, may perhaps excite the interest of the reader; but they are only so many fables; and the story of Malmaison shows, that the author knew no more of the character and disposition of the Empress Josephine than of those of the Emperor. The writer, however, by extolling certain traits, praising certain actions, and refuting certain falsehoods, assumes an air of impartiality, which, joined to his pretended situation, near the Emperor, during fifteen years, produces a wonderful effect in the eyes of common readers. Most of the Englishmen on board the vessel looked upon this work as a kind of oracle. Their opinion was not changed on finding the Emperor's character so different from that attributed to him in this romance. They were inclined to believe that adversity and constraint had wrought an alteration in the Emperor, rather than to suppose that these printed statements were false. To my observations they constantly replied:—"But the author was an impartial man, and one who was about the Emperor for fifteen years?"—"But," said I, "what is this man's name? If he had personally injured you in his book, how could you bring him to justice? Any body here might have written it!" These arguments were of course unanswerable; but the English found great difficulty in overcoming their first impressions: such are the common mass of readers, and such is the effect inevitably produced by printed falsehoods!

But I shall no longer continue my examination of a work which is not deserving of farther notice; I therefore dispense with the remainder. On revising my manuscript in Europe, I found that public opinion had made such progress, that I should be ashamed to waste time in refuting allegations and facts, which judgment and common sense have long since rejected, and which are now repeated only by fools.

In endeavouring to subvert the erroneous notions which this author thought proper to create respecting the character of Napoleon, it will perhaps be thought that I should substitute my own opinions in their stead; but this I shall carefully avoid. I shall content myself with noting down all that I saw and heard: I will report his conversations, and nothing more must be expected.

12th—13th.—By dint of patience, and with the help of a few trifling variations, we gradually approached the termination of our voyage; and though deprived of the natural monsoon, we had now advanced within a short distance of our place of destination. As we continued our course, the weather gradually improved, and at length the wind became perfectly favourable; but this change did not take place until twenty-four hours before our arrival.

14th.—The Admiral had previously informed us that he expected to come within sight of Saint-Helena this day. We had scarcely risen from table when our ears were saluted with the cry of *Land!* This was just within a quarter of an hour of the moment that had been fixed on. Nothing can better prove the advancement of navigation, than this sort of miracle, by which seamen are enabled to foretell the hour at which they shall arrive at a particular point in the vast expanse. The Emperor went on the forecastle to see the island; he thought he perceived it, but I could see nothing. We lay-to all night.

Arrival at Saint-Helena.

15th.—At day-light I had a tolerably near view of the island. At first I thought it rather extensive; but it seemed to diminish considerably as we approached. At length, about seventy days after our departure from England, and a hundred and ten after our departure from Paris, we cast anchor about noon. This was the first link of the chain that was to bind the modern Prometheus to his rock.

We found at anchor several of the vessels of our squadron, which had separated from us, or which we had left behind. They had, however, arrived several days before us: another proof of the extreme uncertainty attending nautical calculations.

The Emperor, contrary to custom, dressed early and went upon deck; he went forward on the gangway to view the island. We beheld a kind of village surrounded by numerous barren and naked hills towering to the clouds. Every platform, every aperture, the brow of every hill, was planted with cannon. The Emperor viewed the prospect through his glass. I stood behind him. My eyes were constantly fixed on his countenance, in which I could perceive no change; and yet he saw before him, perhaps his perpetual prison!—perhaps his grave! . . . . How much, then, remained for me to feel and to witness!

The Emperor soon left the deck. He desired me to come to him, and we proceeded to our usual occupation.

The Admiral, who had gone ashore very early, returned about six o'clock, much fatigued. He had been walking about various parts of the island, and at length thought he had found a habitation that would suit us. The place, however, stood in need of repairs, which might occupy two months. We had now been confined to our wooden dungeon for nearly three months; and the precise instructions of the ministers were, that we should be detained there until our prison on shore was ready for our reception. The Admiral, to do him justice, was incapable of such barbarity; he informed us, at the same time betraying a sort of inward satisfaction, that he would take upon himself the responsibility of putting us ashore next day.

RESIDENCE AT BRIARS,

FROM THE 16TH OF OCTOBER, 1815, THE DAY OF OUR LANDING AT SAINT-HELENA, TO THE 9TH OF DECEMBER, THE DAY PRECEDING THAT OF OUR REMOVAL TO LONGWOOD.

An interval of a Month and Twenty-four days.

Landing of the Emperor at Saint-Helena.

October 16th.—After dinner, the Emperor, accompanied by the Grand Marshal, got into a boat to go ashore. By a remarkable and irresistible impulse, the officers all assembled on the quarter deck, and the greater part of the crew on the gangways. This was not the effect of curiosity which an acquaintance of three months duration could not fail to have removed, and which was now succeded by the liveliest interest. The Emperor, before he stepped into the boat, sent for the Captain of the vessel, and took leave of him, desiring him at the same time to convey his thanks to the officers and crew. These words appeared to produce a great sensation on all by whom they were understood, or to whom they were interpreted. The remainder of the Emperor's suite landed about eight o'clock. We were accompanied by several of the officers, and every one on board seemed to be sincerely affected at our departure.

We found the Emperor in the apartment which had been assigned to him; a few minutes after our arrival he went up-stairs to his chamber, where we were called to attend him. His situation here was no better than it had been on board the vessel; we found ourselves lodged in a sort of inn or hotel.

The town of Saint-Helena consists only of one very short street, or row of houses, built along a very narrow valley, formed between two hills, on the summit of a barren rock.

The Emperor fixes his abode at Briars.—Description of the place.—Miserable situation.

17th.—At six o'clock in the morning the Emperor, the Grand Marshal, and the Admiral, rode out on horseback to visit Longwood, a house which had been chosen for the Emperor's residence, and was more than two leagues from the town. On their return they saw a small villa situated in the valley about two miles from the town. The Emperor was extremely reluctant to return to the place where he had passed the preceding night, and where he felt himself more completely secluded from the world than he had been when on board the vessel. What with the sentinels who guarded his doors, and the crowds of persons whom curiosity had attracted beneath his windows, he had been obliged to confine himself to his chamber. A small pavilion, attached to the villa above mentioned, pleased him, and the Admiral was of opinion that he would be more agreeably situated there than in the town. In this place, therefore, the Emperor fixed his residence, and immediately sent for me. He had become so much interested in his work on the campaigns of Italy, that he could not suspend it:—I immediately proceeded to join him.

The little valley, in which the village of Saint-Helena is situated, extends to a considerable distance up the island, winding along between two chains of barren hills which enclose it on either side. A good carriage-road runs through this valley to the distance of about two miles; after which it is traced along the brow of the hill which rises on the left, while nothing but precipices and gulfs are discoverable on the right. The rugged aspect of the country here gradually diminishes, and the road opens on a small level height, on which are several houses interspersed with trees and different kinds of vegetation; this is a little oasis amidst the rocky desert. Here is situated the modest residence of Mr. Balcombe, a merchant of the island. At the distance of thirty or forty paces from the dwelling-house, on a pointed eminence, stood a little summer-house, or pavilion, to which, in fine weather, the family were accustomed to retire to take tea and amuse themselves: this was the obscure retreat hired by the Admiral, as the temporary residence of the Emperor; and he took possession of it in the morning. As I was ascending the winding path leading to the pavilion, I thought I perceived the Emperor, and stopped to look at him. It was Napoleon himself: his body was slightly bent, and his hands behind his back; he wore his usual neat and simple uniform, and his celebrated little hat. He was standing at the threshold of the door when I advanced to salute him. "Ah!" said he, "here you are! why have you not brought your son?"—"Sire," I replied, "the respect, the consideration I owe you, prevented me." "Oh, you must learn to dispense with that," continued he; "bring your son to me."

In none of his campaigns, perhaps in no situation of his past life, had the Emperor been so wretchedly lodged, or subject to so many privations. The summer-house contained one room nearly square on the ground-floor, having two doors facing each other on two of its sides, and two windows on each of the other sides. These windows had neither curtains nor shutters, and there was scarcely a seat in the room. The Emperor was at this moment alone; his two valets-de-chambre were bustling about to prepare his bed. He took a fancy to walk a little; but there was no level ground on any side of the pavilion, which was surrounded by huge pieces of stone and rock. He took my arm, and began to converse in a cheerful strain. Night was advancing; profound silence, undisturbed solitude, prevailed on every side;—what a crowd of sensations and sentiments overwhelmed me at this moment!—I was in this desert, *tête-à-tête*, and enjoying familiar conversation with the man who had ruled the world!—with Napoleon! What were my feelings!—But to understand them it would be necessary to revert to the days of his past glory; to the time when one of his decrees sufficed to subvert thrones and create kings! It would be necessary to reflect on what he was to all who surrounded him at the Thuilleries: the timid embarrassment, the profound respect, with which he was approached by his ministers and officers; the anxiety, the dread of ambassadors, princes, and even kings! With me all these sentiments remained in full force.

When the Emperor was about to retire to rest, we found that one of the windows (which, as I have already observed, had neither shutters nor curtains) was close upon his bed, nearly on a level with his face. We barricadoed it as well as we could, so as to exclude the air, of the effects of which the Emperor is very susceptible, the least draught being sufficient to give him cold or the tooth-ache. For my part I ascended to the upper story, immediately above the Emperor's room. In this place, the dimensions of which were about seven square feet, there was only a bed, and not a single chair: this served as a lodging for me and my son, for whom a mattress was spread out upon the floor. But how could we complain, being so near the Emperor! we could hear the sound of his voice and distinguish his words! The valets-de-chambre slept on the ground, across by the door, wrapped up in their cloaks. Such is the faithful description of the first night which Napoleon passed at Briars.

Description of Briars.—The Garden.—The Emperor meets the young ladies of the house.

18th.—I breakfasted with the Emperor: he had neither table-cloth nor plates; and the remains of the preceding day's dinner were brought to him for breakfast.

The English officer was lodged in the neighbouring house, as our guard, and two inferior officers marched up and down with an air of military parade before our eyes, for the purpose of watching our motions. Breakfast being over, the Emperor proceeded to his dictation, which occupied him some hours. He afterwards took a fancy to explore our new domain, and to take a view of the surrounding grounds.

Descending our hillock on the side facing the principal house, we found a path bordered by a hedge, and running at the foot of precipices. After walking along the path to the distance of two hundred paces, we arrived at a little garden, the door of which was open. This garden is long and narrow, and formed on very uneven ground; but a tolerably level walk extends the whole length of it. At the entrance there is a sort of arbour at one extremity; and at the other, are two huts for the negroes whose business it is to look after the garden. It contains some fruit-trees and a few flowers. We had no sooner entered the garden, than we were met by the daughters of the master of the house, girls about fourteen or fifteen years of age: the one sprightly, giddy, and caring for nothing; the other more sedate, but, at the same time, possessing great *naïvetè* of manner; both speak a little French. They had walked through the garden, and put all the flowers under contribution, to present them to the Emperor, whom they overwhelmed with the most whimsical and ridiculous questions. The Emperor was much amused by this familiarity, to which he was so little accustomed. "We have been to a masked ball," said he, when the young ladies had taken their leave.

The youth of France.—The Emperor visits Mr. Balcombe's house.

19th—20th. The Emperor invited my son to breakfast: it may be easily imagined that he was greatly overjoyed at this honour! It was, perhaps, the first time he had ever been so near the Emperor, or had spoken to him; and he was not a little flurried on the occasion.

The table still remained without a cloth; the breakfast continued to be brought from the town, and consisted of only two or three wretched dishes. To-day a chicken was brought: the Emperor wished to carve it himself, and to help us. He was astonished at finding that he succeeded so well; it was long, he said, since he had done so much; for all his politeness, he added, had been lost in the business and cares of his Generalship of Italy.

Coffee is almost a necessary of life to the Emperor; but here it proved so bad, that on tasting it he thought himself poisoned. He sent it away, and made me send away mine also.

The Emperor was at this moment using a snuff-box set with several ancient medals, which were surrounded by Greek inscriptions. The Emperor, not being certain of the name of one of the heads, asked me to translate the inscription; and on my replying that it was beyond my powers, he laughed and said, "I see you are no better scholar than myself." My son then tremblingly undertook the task, and read Mithridates, Demetrius-Poliorcetes, and some other names. The extreme youth of my son, and this circumstance, attracted the Emperor's attention. "Is your son so far advanced?" said he; and he began to question him at great length respecting his Lyceum, his masters, his lessons, &c. Then turning to me, "What a rising generation I leave behind me!" said he. "This is all my work! The merits of the French youth will be a sufficient revenge to me. On beholding the work, all must render justice to the workman! and the perverted judgment or bad faith of declaimers must fall before my deeds. If I had thought only of myself, and securing my own power, as has been continually asserted, I should have endeavoured to hide learning *under a bushel;* instead of which I devoted myself to the propagation of knowledge. And yet the youth of France have not enjoyed all the benefits which I intended they should. My University, according to the plan I had conceived, was a master-piece in its combinations, and would have been such in its national results. But an evil-disposed person spoiled all; and in so doing he was actuated by the worst of feelings, and doubtless, by a calculation of consequences."

In the evening the Emperor went to visit our neighbours. Mr. Balcombe, who was suffering under a fit of the gout, lay stretched on a sofa; his wife and the two young ladies, whom we had met in the morning, were beside him. The *masked ball* was resumed again with great spirit. Our guests liberally dealt out all their store of knowledge. The conversation turned on novels. One of the young ladies had read Madame Cottin's *Mathilde*, and was delighted to find that the Emperor was acquainted with the work. An Englishman, with a great round face, to all appearance a true *vacuum plenum*, who had been listening earnestly, in order to turn his little knowledge of French to the best account, modestly ventured to ask the Emperor whether the Princess, the friend of Matilda, whose character he particularly admired, was still living? The Emperor with a very solemn air replied, "No, sir; she is dead and buried:" and he was almost tempted to believe he was himself hoaxed, when he found that the melancholy tidings drew tears from the great staring eyes of the Englishman.

The young ladies evinced no less simplicity, though in them it was more pardonable; however, I was led to conclude that they had not studied chronology very deeply.— One of them turning over Florian's *Estelle*, to show us that she could read French, happened to light on the name of Gaston de Foix, and finding him distinguished by the title of General, she asked the Emperor whether he had been satisfied with his conduct in the army, whether he had escaped the dangers of war, and whether he was still living.

21st.—In the morning the Admiral came to visit the Emperor. He knocked at the door; and had I not been present, the Emperor must have been reduced to the alternative of opening it himself, or suffering the Admiral to wait on the outside.

All the scattered members of our little colony, likewise, came from the town, and we were for a short time collected together. Each described the wretchedness of his situation, and received the sympathy of the Emperor.

Horror and misery of our situation.—The Emperor's indignation.—Note to the English Government.

23d—24th. The English ministers, in violating the rights of hospitality, to which we had trusted with such implicit confidence, seem to have omitted nothing to make us feel this violation the more bitterly. By banishing us to the farther extremity of the world, and reducing us to every kind of privation and ill-treatment, they wish to make us drain the cup of misery to the very dregs. Saint-Helena is a true Siberia: the only difference is its limited extent, and the climate being warm instead of cold.

The Emperor Napoleon, who but lately possessed such boundless power, and disposed of so many crowns, now occupies a wretched hovel, a few feet square, perched upon a rock, unprovided with furniture, and without either shutters or curtains to the windows. This place must serve him for bed-chamber, dressing-room, dining-room, study, and sitting-room; and he is obliged to go out when it is necessary to have this one apartment cleaned. His meals, consisting of a few wretched dishes, are brought to him from a distance, as though he were a criminal in a dungeon. He is absolutely in want of the necessaries of life: the bread and wine are not such as we have been accustomed to, and are so bad that we loathe to touch them: water, coffee, butter, oil, and other articles, are either not to be procured, or are scarcely fit for use: a bath, which is so necessary to the

Emperor's health, is not to be had; and he is deprived of the exercise of riding on horseback.

His friends and servants are two miles distant from him, and are not suffered to approach his person without being accompanied by a soldier. They are deprived of their arms, and are compelled to pass the night at the guard-house, if they return beyond a certain hour, or if any mistake occur in the pass-word, which happens almost daily. Thus, on the summit of this frightful rock, we are equally exposed to the severity of man and the rigour of nature! And how easy would it have been to procure us a more suitable retreat and more courteous usage.

Assuredly, if the Sovereigns of Europe decreed this exile, private enmity has directed its execution. If policy alone dictated this measure as indispensable, would it not have been essential, in order to render the fact evident to the world, to have surrounded with every kind of respect and consideration the illustrious victim, with regard to whom it had been found necessary to violate law and principle?

We were all assembled round the Emperor; and he was recapitulating these facts with warmth: "For what infamous treatment are we reserved!" he exclaimeed. "This is the anguish of death! To injustice and violence, they now add insult and protracted torment. If I were so hateful to them, why did they not get rid of me? A few musquet balls in my heart or my head would have done the business; and there would at least have been some energy in the crime! Were it not for you, and, above all, for your wives, I would receive from them nothing but the pay of a private soldier. How can the monarchs of Europe permit the sacred character of sovereignty to be violated in my person? Do they not see that they are, with their own hands, working their own destruction at Saint-Helena? I entered their capitals victorious, and had I cherished such sentiments, what would have become of them? They styled me their brother; and I had become so by the choice of the people, the sanction of victory, the character of religion, and the alliances of their policy and their blood. Do they imagine that the good sense of nations is blind to their conduct? and what do they expect from it? At all events, make your complaints, gentlemen, let indignant Europe hear them! Complaints from me would be beneath my dignity and character; I must command, or be silent."

Next morning an officer, gently opening the door, introduced himself, without farther ceremony, into the Emperor's room; where I was engaged with him. He had come, however, with good intentions. He was the captain of one of the small vessels which had formed our squadron. He was now about to return to Europe, and came to enquire whether the Emperor had any commands. Napoleon immediately recurred to the subject of our conversation on the preceding evening, and, becoming animated by degrees, gave utterance to sentiments of the loftiest and most energetic character, which he charged him to communicate to the British government. I interpreted what he said in the same spirit and with great rapidity. The officer seemed astonished at what he heard, and left us with a promise punctually to fulfil his commission. But he could not have described the expression, and particularly the tone, of which I was a witness.—The Emperor, however, directed me to make a memorandum of what he had said, which the officer must have found very feebly expressed compared with what he had just heard. The note was as follows:—

Memorandum.—"The Emperor desires, by the return of the next vessel, to receive some account of his wife and son, and to be informed whether the latter is still living. He takes this opportunity of repeating and conveying to the British government the protestations which he has already made against the extraordinary measures adopted towards him.

"1st. That Government has declared him a prisoner of war. The Emperor is not a prisoner of war. His letter to the Prince Regent, which he wrote and communicated to Captain Maitland, before he went on board the Bellerophon, sufficiently proves, to the whole world, the resolutions and the sentiments of confidence which induced him freely to place himself under the English flag.

"The Emperor might, had he pleased, have agreed to quit France only on stipulated conditions with regard to himself; but he disdained to mingle personal considerations with the great interests with which his mind was constantly occupied. He might have placed himself at the disposal of the Emperor Alexander, who had been his friend, or of the Emperor Francis, who was his father-in-law. But, confiding in the justice of the English nation, he desired no other protection than its laws afforded; and, renouncing public affairs, he sought no other country than that which was governed by fixed laws, independent of private will.

"2d. Had the Emperor really been a prisoner of war, the rights which civilized governments possess over such a prisoner, are limited by the law of nations, and terminate with the war itself.

"3d. If the English government considered the Emperor, though arbitrarily, as a prisoner of war, the right of that government was then limited by public law, or else, as there existed no cartel between the two nations during the war, it might have adopted towards him the principles of savages, who put their prisoners to death. This proceeding would have been more humane, and more conformable to justice, than that of sending him to this horrible rock; death inflicted on board the Bellerophon, in the Plymouth roads, would have been a blessing compared with the treatment to which he is now subjected.

"We have travelled over the most desolate countries of Europe, but none is to be compared with this barren rock. deprived of every thing that can render life supportable, it is calculated only to renew perpetually the anguish of death. The first principles of Christian morality, and that great duty imposed on man to pursue his fate, whatever it may be, may withhold him from terminating with his own hand a wretched existence: the Emperor glories in being superior to such a feeling. But if the British ministers should persist in their course of injustice and violence towards him, he would consider it a happiness if they would put him to death."

The vessel which sailed for Europe, with this document, was the Redpole, Captain Desmond.

The reader must pardon the insipid monotony of our complaints: they will be found to be always the same, no doubt; but let it be remembered how much more pain must have been felt in repeating them, than can possibly be experienced in their perusal.

Mode of living at Briars.—Cabinet which the Emperor had with him at Austerlitz.—The Emperor's large Cabinet.—Its Contents.—Articles of Vertu, Libels against Napoleon, &c. infamous conduct of persons at the Thuilleries.

25th—27th.—The Emperor dressed very early; he took a short walk out of doors; we breakfasted about ten o'clock; he walked again, and then we proceeded to business. I read to him what he had dictated on the preceding evening, and which my son had copied in the morning; he corrected it, and then continued his dictation. We went out again about five o'clock, and returned at six, the hour appointed for dinner, that is to say, if the dinner should be brought from the town by that time. The days were very long, and the evening still longer. Unfortunately I did not understand chess; at one time I had an idea of studying it by night, but where could I find a teacher? I pretended to a little knowledge of piquet; but the Emperor soon discovered my ignorance; he gave me credit for my good intentions, yet he gave up playing. Want of occupation would sometimes lead him to the neighbouring house, where the young ladies made him play at whist. But his more usual practice was to remain at table after dinner, and to converse sitting in his chair; for the room was too small to admit of his walking about.

One evening he ordered a little travelling cabinet to be brought to him, and after minutely examining every part of it, he presented it to me, saying, "I have had it in my possession a long time, I made use of it on the morning of the battle of Austerlitz. It must go to young Emanuel," said he, turning to my son: "when he is thirty or forty years old, we shall be no more. This will but enhance the value of the gift; he will say when he shows it, the Emperor Napoleon gave this to my father at St. Helena." I received the precious gift with a kind of reverential feeling, and I preserve it as a valuable relic.

Passing from that to the examination of a large cabinet, he looked over some portraits of his own family, and some presents which he had personally received. These consisted of the portraits of Madame, of the Queen of Naples, of the daughters of Joseph, of his brothers, of the King of Rome &c. An Augustus and a Livia, both exceedingly rare; a Continence of Scipio and another antique of immense value given to him by the pope; a Peter the Great on a box; another box with a Charles V; another with a Turenne; and some, which were in daily use, covered with a collection of medallions of Cæsar, Alexander, Sylla, Mithridates, &c. Next came some snuff-boxes, ornamented with his own portrait set in diamonds. He then looked for one without diamonds, and not finding it, he called his valet-de-chambre, to enquire about it: unfortunately this portrait still remained in the town along with the greater part of his effects; I felt mortified at receiving this intelligence, I could not help thinking that I had been a loser by this mischance.

The Emperor then examined several snuff-boxes which Louis XVIII had left on his table at the Thuilleries at the time of his precipitate departure. On one of these were represented on a black ground, the portraits of Louis XVI, of the Queen, and of Madame Elizabeth, executed in paste in imitation of ivory, and fantastically arranged. They formed three crescents placed back to back in the shape of an equilateral triangle, and groups of cherubs closely interwoven composed the external border. Another box presented a water-colour sketch of a hunt, which had no other claim to merit than the circumstance of its being attributed to the pencil of the Duchess of Angoulême. A third was surmounted with a portrait, which appeared to be that of the Countess de Provence. These three boxes were of simple and even ordniary execution; and could possess no other value than that which their history attaches to them."

On the Emperor's arrival in Paris on the evening of the 20th of March, he found the King's study precisely in the state in which it had been used; all his papers still remained on the tables. By the Emperor's desire, these tables were pushed into the corners of the apartment, and others brought. He gave orders that nothing should be touched, intending to examine the papers at his leisure; and as the Emperor himself quitted France without returning to the Thuilleries, the King must have found his study and his papers nearly as he had left them.

The Emperor took a hasty glance at some of the papers. He found among them several letters from the king to M. d'Avarai at Madeira, where the latter died; they were written in the King's own hand, and had doubtless been sent back to him. He found also some confidential letters of the King, likewise in his own hand. But how came they there? How had they been returned to him? That would be difficult to explain? They consisted of five or six pages, written in very elegant language, and displaying some sense; but very abstract and metaphysical. In one of them the Prince said to the lady whom he addressed:—"*Judge, Madame, how much I love you; I have left off mourning for your sake.*" "And here," said the Emperor, "the idea of mourning was followed up by a succession of long paragraphs, quite in an academic style." The Emperor could not imagine to whom it had been written, or what the *mourning* alluded to; I could not assist his conjectures on either of these points.

Two or three days after the Emperor had replaced a certain individual at the head of a celebrated institution, he found on one of the tables a memoir from that very person, which, from the terms in which it was couched with reference to himself and the whole of his family, would certainly have prevented him from signing the reappointment.

There were also many other documents of the same nature; but the most complete records of baseness, deceit, and villany, were found in the apartments of M. Blacas, grand-master of the wardrobe, and minister of the household: these were filled with plans, reports, and petitions of every kind. There were few of these papers in which the writers did not put themselves forward at the expense of Napoleon, whom they were far from expecting to return. They formed altogether such a mass, that the Emperor was obliged to appoint a committee of four persons to examine them; he now thinks he was to blame in not having confided that office to a single individual, and with such injunctions that he might have felt confident nothing was suffered to escape. He has since had reason to believe that these papers might have afforded some salutary hints respecting the treachery which surrounded him on his return from Waterloo.

Among the rest there was a long letter from one of the female attendants of the Princess Pauline. This voluminous letter was expressed in very coarse language with regard to the princess and her letters; and described the Emperor, to whom the writer always alluded under the title of *that man*, in the worst possible colours. This had not been thought sufficient; part of it had been erased and interlined by another hand, in order to bring forward Napoleon in the most scandalous manner; and on the margin, in the hand of the interlineator, [illegible]e written the words, *fit to be printed*. A few days aft[illegible]ards, probably, this libel was published.

An upstart woman [illegible]eld a distinguished rank in the state, and who had [illegible]verwhelmed with acts of kindness from the Emperor, wrote in a great hurry to her friend to acquaint her with the famous decision of the Senate respecting the forfeiture and proscription of Napoleon. The letter contained the following: "My dear friend, my husband has just returned: he is tired to death; but his efforts have carried it; we are delivered from *that man*, and we shall have the Bourbons. Thank God, we shall now be real Countesses!" &c.

Among these papers, Napoleon experienced the mortification to meet with some containing very improper remarks respecting himself personally; and those too in the very hand-writing of individuals who only the day before had assembled round him, and were already in the enjoyment of his favours.

The first impulse of his indignation was to determine that they should be printed, and to withdraw his protection: a second thought restrained him. "We are so volatile, so inconstant, so easily led away," said he, "that after all, I could not be certain that those very people had not really and spontaneously come back to my service: in that case, I should have been punishing them at the very time when they were returning to their duty. I thought it better to seem to know nothing of the matter, and I ordered all their letters to be burnt."

The Emperor commences the Campaign of Egypt with the Grand Marshal.—Anecdotes of Brumaire, &c.—Letter of the Count de Lille.—The beautiful Duchess de Guiche.

28th—31st. My son and I prosecuted our labours without intermission. His health, however, began to be affected: he felt a pain in his chest. My eyes also grew weak: these were really the effects of our excessive occupation. Indeed, we had gone through an amazing quantity of work: we had already nearly arrived at the end of the Campaign of Italy. The Emperor, however, did not yet find that he had sufficient occupation. Employment was his only resource, and the interest which his first dictations had assumed furnished an additional motive for proceeding with them. The Campaign of Egypt was now about to be commenced. The Emperor had frequently talked of employing the Grand Marshal on this subject.

Those of our party who were lodged in the town were badly accommodated, and were dissatisfied at being separated from the Emperor. They were harassed by the constraint and mortifications to which they were subjected. I suggested to the Emperor that he should set us to work altogether, and proceed at once with the Campaigns of Italy and Egypt, the history of the Consulate, the return from the Island of Elba, &c. The time, I observed, would then pass more quickly; the great work, the glory of France, would advance more rapidly, and the gentlemen who resided in the town would be less unhappy. The idea pleased the Emperor, and from that moment one or two of his suite came regularly every day to write to his dictations, the transcript of which they brought to him next morning.—They then stayed to dinner, and thus afforded the Emperor a little more amusement than usual.

We made such arrangements that the Emperor insensibly found himself more comfortably situated in many respects. A tent, which had been given to me by the Colonel of the 53d regiment, was spread out so as to form a prolongation of the room occupied by the Emperor. Our cook took up his abode at Briars. The table-linen was taken from the trunks, the plate was set forth, and our first dinner after these preparations was a sort of *fete*. The evenings however always hung heavily on our hands. The Emperor would sometimes visit the adjoining house; at other times he would endeavour to leave his chamber to walk; but more frequently he remained within-doors, and tried to pass the time in conversation until ten or twelve o'clock. He avoided retiring to bed too early; for when he did so, he awoke in the night; and in order to divert his mind from sorrowful reflections, he was obliged to rise and read.

One day at dinner, the Emperor cast his eyes on one of the dishes of his own campaign-service, on which the Imperial arms were engraved. "How they have spoiled this!" he exclaimed emphatically; and he could not refrain from observing that the King had been in a great hurry to take possession of the Imperial plate, which he certainly could not claim as his property, since it unquestionably belonged to him; for, he added, that when he ascended the throne he found not a vestige of royal property. At his abdication, he left to the crown five millions in plate, and between forty and fifty millions in furniture, which was all his own property, purchased out of his civil list.

In a conversation one evening, the Emperor related the circumstances attending the event of Brumaire. I suppress the particulars, because they were afterwards dictated to General Gourgaud; and a detailed account of this remarkable affair will be found in the Memoirs.

Sieyes, who was one of the Provisional Consuls along with Napoleon, astonished to hear his colleague, on the very first conference, discussing questions relative to finance, administration, the army, law, and politics, left him quite disconcerted, and ran to his friends, saying, "Gentlemen, you have got a master! This man knows every thing, wants every thing, and can do every thing."

I was in London at that time, and I told the Emperor that the emigrants there had formed great hopes and placed much confidence on the events of the 18th of Brumaire and on his Consulate. Several of us, who had formerly been acquainted with Madame de Beauharnais, immediately set out for Paris, hoping, through her means, to exercise some influence, or give some direction to affairs, which then appeared under a new aspect.

Our general opinion at the time was, that the First Consul had waited for propositions from the French Princes. We rested our hopes on the circumstance of his having been so long without coming to a decision respecting them; which, however, he did some time afterwards in a way the most overwhelming, by means of a proclamation. We attributed this result to the stupid conduct of the Bishop of Arras, the counsellor and director of our affairs: who, according to his own confession, went to work with his eyes shut, and boasted of not having read a single newspaper for a series of years, ever since they had been filled, as he said, with the successful enterprises and the falsehoods of that wretched party. On the first establishment of the Consulate, some one having attempted to persuade the Bishop to enter into negotiations with the Consul, through the mediation of Madame Bonaparte, he rejected the proposition with indignation, and in language of so coarse and disgusting a nature, as induced the person to tell him that his expressions were far from being episcopal, and that he certainly had never learned them from his breviary.

About the same period he made use of some gross invectives against the Duc de Choiseuil,—that too at the table of the Prince, where he was smartly reprimanded for them; and all this was only because the Duke, on being released from imprisonment at Calais, and escaping death through the protection of the Consul, concluded his reply to the enquiries made by the Prince relative to Bonaparte, by protesting that, for his part, he should never cease to acknowledge his personal gratitude towards him.

To all this the Emperor replied, that he had never bestowed a thought on the Princes; that the observations to which I had alluded, proceeded from one of the other Consuls, and were made without any particular motive; that we, who were abroad, seemed to have no idea of the opinions of those at home; and that even if he had been favourably disposed towards the Princes, it would not have been in his power to carry his intentions into execution. He had, however, received overtures, about that period, both from Mittare and London.

The King, he said, wrote him a letter, which was conveyed to him by Lebrun, who had it from the Abbè de Montesquiou, the secret agent of the Prince at Paris. This letter, which was written in a very laboured style, contained the following paragraph; "You delay long to restore me my throne. It is to be feared that you may allow favourable moments to escape. You cannot complete the happiness of France without me, nor can I serve France without you. Hasten, then, and specify yourself the places which you would wish your friends to possess."

To this letter the First Consul replied:—"I have received your Royal Highness's letter; I have always felt deep interest in your misfortunes and those of your family. You must not think of appearing in France; you could not do so without passing over a hundred thousand dead bodies. I shall, however, be always eager to do every thing that may tend to alleviate your fate, or enable you to forget your misfortunes."

The overtures made by the Count d'Artois possessed still more elegance and address. He commissioned as the bearer of them the Dutchess de Guiche, a lady whose fascinating manners and personal graces were calculated to assist her in the important negotiation. She easily got access to Madame Bonaparte, with whom all the individuals of the old Court came easily in contact. She breakfasted with her at Malmaison; and the conversation turning on London, the emigrants, and the French princes, Madame de Guiche mentioned that as she happened a few days before to be at the house of the Count d'Artois, she had heard some person ask the Prince what he intended to do for the First Consul, in the event of his restoring the Bourbons; and that the Prince had replied:—"I would immediately make him Constable of the kingdom, and every thing else he might choose. But even that would not be enough; we would raise on the Carrousel a lofty and magnificent column, surmounted with a statue of Bonaparte crowning the Bourbons."

As soon as the First Consul entered, which he did very shortly after breakfast, Josephine eagerly repeated to him the circumstance which the Duchess had related. "And did you not reply," said her husband, "that the corpse of the First Consul would have been made the pedestal of the column!"—The charming Duchess was still present; the beauties of her countenance, her eyes, and her words, were directed to the success of her commission. She said she was so delighted, she did not know how she should ever be able sufficiently to acknowledge the favour which Madame Bonaparte had procured her, of seeing and hearing so distinguished a man—so great a hero. It was all in vain: the Duchess de Guiche received orders that very night to quit Paris. The charms of the emissary were too well calculated to alarm Josephine, to induce her to say any thing very urgent in her favour, and next day the Duchess was on her way to the frontier.

It is, however, absolutely false that Napoleon, on his part, at a subsequent period, made overtures or propositions to the Princes touching the cession of their rights, or their renunciation of the crown; though such statements have been made in some pompous declarations, profusely circulated through Europe.—"How was such a thing possible?" said the Emperor;—"I, who could only reign by the very principle which excluded them—that of the sovereignty of the people—how could I have sought to possess through them, rights which were proscribed in their persons? That would have been to proscribe myself. The absurdity would have been too palpable, too ridiculous; it would have ruined me for ever in public opinion. The fact is, that neither directly nor indirectly, at home or abroad, did I ever do any thing of the kind; and this will, no doubt, in the course of time, be the opinion of all persons of judgment, who allow me to have been neither a fool nor a madman.

"The prevalence of this report, however, induced me to seek to discover what could have given rise to it, and these are the facts which I collected:—At the period of the good understanding between France and Prussia, and while that state was endeavouring to ingratiate herself in our favour, she caused enquiry to be made, whether France would take umbrage at her allowing the French Princes to remain in the Prussian territories, to which the French government answered in the negative. Emboldened by this reply, Prussia next enquired whether we should feel any great repugnance to furnishing them, through her medium, with an annual allowance. To this our Government also replied in the negative, provided that Prussia would be responsible for their remaining quiet, and abstaining from all intrigue. The negotiation of this affair being once set on foot between the two countries, Heaven knows what the zeal of some agent, or even the doctrines of the Court of Berlin, which did not accord with ours, may have proposed.—This furnished, no doubt, the motive and pretext, if, indeed, any really existed, for the fine letter of Louis XVIII, to which all the members of his family so ostentatiously adhered. The French Princes eagerly seized that opportunity of reviving the interest and attention of Europe, which had been by this time totally withdrawn from them."

Occupations of the day.—Council of State.—Disgrace of Portalis.—Dissolution of the Legislative Body in 1813.—The Senate.

November 1—4. Our days now passed away in the same uniformity as those which we spent on board the vessel. The Emperor summoned me to breakfast with him about ten or eleven o'clock. That meal being concluded, after half an hour's conversation, I read to him what he had dictated the evening before, and he renewed his dictations. The Emperor discontinued his practice of dressing as soon as he rose, and walking before breakfast, which had broken up his day too much, and rendered it too long. He never dressed now till about four o'clock. He then walked out, to give the servants an opportunity of making his bed, and cleaning his room. We walked in the garden, which he particularly liked, on account of its solitude. I had the little arbour covered with a canvass, and ordered a table and chairs to be placed in it; and the Emperor henceforward chose this spot for dictating to any of the gentlemen who might come from the town for that purpose.

In front of Mr. Balcombe's house there was a walk bordered by some trees. It was here that the two English soldiers had posted themselves for the purpose of watching us. They were, however, at length removed, at the desire of Mr Balcombe, who felt offended at the circumstance on his own account. Nevertheless, they still continued for some time to move about, so as to get a sight of the Emperor; either attracted by curiosity, or acting in obedience to their orders. At length they entirely disappeared, and the Emperor gradually took possession of this lower walk. This was quite an acquisition to his domain; and he walked here every day before dinner. The two young ladies, with their mother, joined him in this walk, and told him the news. He sometimes returned to the garden after dinner, when the weather permitted; he was then enabled to spend the evening without paying a visit to his neighbours, which he never did when he could avoid it, nor ever till he was satisfied no stranger was there, which I always ascertained previously, by peeping through the window.

In one of his walks, the Emperor conversed a great deal on the subject of the Senate, the Legislative Body, and particularly the Council of State. I will here note down some remarks relative to the Council of State, the more readily, as it was very little understood at the time in the drawing-rooms of Paris; and as it does not now exist on the same footing as formerly, I shall insert, as I proceed, a few lines on its mechanism and prerogatives.

"The Council of State," said the Emperor, "was generally composed of well-informed, skilful, and honest men. Fermont and Boulay, for example, were certainly of this class. Notwithstanding the immense law-suits which they conducted, and the vast emoluments they enjoyed, I should not be surprised to learn that they are not now in very flourishing circumstances." The Emperor employed the counsellors of state individually in every case, and with advantage. As a whole, they were his real council—his mind in deliberation, as the ministers were his mind in execution. At the Council of State were prepared the laws which the Emperor presented to the Legislative Body, a circumstance which rendered it altogether one of the elements of the legislative power. In the Council, the Emperor's decrees and his rules of public administration were drawn up; and there the plans of his ministers were examined, discussed, and corrected.

The Council of State received appeals and pronounced finally on all administrative judgments; and incidentally on those of all other tribunals, even those of the Court of Cassation. There were examined, complaints against the ministers, and appeals from the Emperor to the Emperor better informed. Thus the Council of State, at which the Emperor uniformly presided, being frequently in direct opposition to the ministers, or occupied in reforming their acts and errors, naturally became the point of refuge for persons or interests aggrieved by any authority whatever. All who were ever present at the meetings of the council, must know with what zeal the cause of the citizens was there defended. A committee of the Council of State received all the petitions of the empire, and laid before the sovereign those which deserved his attention.

With the exception of lawyers and persons employed in the administration, it is surprising how far the rest of society were ignorant of our political legislation. No one had a correct idea of the Council of State, of the Legislative Body, or of the Senate. It was received, for example, as an established fact, that the Legislative Body, like an assembly of mutes, passively adopted, without the least opposition, all the laws which were presented to it; that which belonged to the nature and excellence of the institution, was attributed to its complaisance and servility.

The laws which were prepared in the Council of State, were presented by commissaries chosen from that council to a committee of the Legislative Body appointed to receive them; they were there amicably discussed, and were often quietly refered back to the Council of State to receive some modifications. When the two deputations could not come to an understanding, they proceeded to hold regular conferences, under the presidency of the arch-chancellor or the arch-treasurer; so that before these laws reached the Legislative Body, they had already received the assent of the two opposite parties. If any difference existed, it was discussed by the two committees, in the presence of the whole of the Legislative Body, performing the functions of a jury; which, as soon as its members had become sufficiently acquainted with the facts, pronounced its decision by a secret scrutiny. Thus every individual had an opportunity of freely giving his opinion, as it was impossible to know whether he had put in a red or a white ball. No plan," said the Emperor, "could have been better calculated to correct our national effervescence and our inexperience in matters of political liberty."

The Emperor asked me whether I thought the discussion perfectly free in the Council of State, or whether his presence did not impose a restraint on the deliberations? I reminded him of a very long debate, during which he had remained throughout singular in his opinion, and had at last been obliged to yield. He immediately recollected the circumstance. "Oh, yes," said he, "that must have been in the case of a woman of Amsterdam, [illegible] had been tried for her life and acquitted three several times by the Imperial Courts, but against whom a fresh trial was demanded in the Court of Cassation." The Emperor hoped that this happy concurrence of the law might have exhausted its severity in favour of the prisoner; that this lucky fatality of circumstances might have turned to her advantage. It was urged in reply, that he possessed the beneficient power of bestowing pardon; but that the law was inflexible, and must take its course. The debate was a very long one. M. Muraire spoke a great deal, and very much to the point; he persuaded every one except the Emperor, who still remained singular in his opinion, and at length yielded, with these remarkable words:—"Gentlemen, the decision goes by the majority here, I remain single, and must yield; but I declare, in my conscience, that I yield only to forms. You have reduced me to silence, but by no means convinced me."

So little was the nature of the Council of State understood by people in general, that it was believed no one dared utter a word in that assembly in opposition to the Emperor's opinion. Thus I very much surprised many persons, when I related the fact, that one day, during a very animated debate, the Emperor, having been interrupted three times in giving his opinion, turned towards the individual who had rather rudely cut him short, and said in a sharp tone: "I have not yet done; I beg you will allow me to continue. I believe every one here has a right to deliver his opinion." The smartness of this reply, notwithstanding the solemnity of the occasion, excited a general laugh, in which the Emperor himself joined.

"Yet," said I to him, "the speakers evidently sought to discover what might be your Majesty's opinion: they seemed to congratulate themselves when their views coincided with yours, and to be embarrassed on finding themselves maintaining opposite sentiments. You were accused, too, of laying snares for us, in order to discover our real opinion." However, when the question was once started, self-love and the warmth of argument contributed, along with the freedom of discussion which the Emperor encouraged, to induce every one to maintain his own opinion. "I do not mind being contradicted," said the Emperor; I seek to be informed. Speak boldly," he would repeat; whenever the speaker expressed himself equivocally, or the subject was a delicate one; "tell me all that you think; we are alone here; we are all *en famille*."

I have been informed, that under the Consulate, or at the commencement of the Empire, the Emperor opposed an opinion of one c[illegible] members, and through the warmth and obstinacy of the [illegible]ter, the affair at length amounted absolutely to a personal misunderstanding. Napoleon commanded his temper, and was silent; but a few days after, seeing his antagonist at one of the public audiences, he said to him in a half-earnest manner, "You are extremely obstinate; and what if I were equally so!——— At all events, you are in the wrong to put power to the trial! You should not be unmindful of human weakness!"

On another occasion, he said in private to one of the members who had likewise driven him to the utmost extreme, "You must take a little more care to manage my temper. You were lately very much out: you obliged me to have recourse to scratching my forehead. That is a very ominous sign with me: you had better not urge me so far for the future."

Nothing could equal the interest which the presence and the words of the Emperor excited in the Council of State. He presided there regularly twice a week when he was in town, and then none of us would have been absent for the whole world.

I told the Emperor that there were two sittings in particular which had made the deepest impression on me: one relating to internal regulation on the expulsion of a member, when the whole council was of one opinion; the other was on the occasion of the dissolution of the Legislative Body by a Constitutional decision.

A religious party was fomenting civil discord in the State, by secretly circulating bulls and letters from the Pope.— They were shown to a Counsellor of State, appointed to superintend religious worship; and who, if he did not himself circulate them, at least neither prevented nor denounced their circulation. This was discovered, and the Emperor suddenly challenged him with the fact in open Council.— "What could have been your motive, sir?" said he: "were you influenced by your religious principles? If so, why are you here? I use no control over the conscience of any man. Did I force you to become my Counsellor of State? On the contrary, you solicited the post as a high favour. You are the youngest member of the Council, and perhaps the only one who has not some personal claim to that honour; you had nothing to recommend you but the inheritance of your father's services. You took a personal oath to me; how could your religious feelings permit you openly to violate that oath, as you have just now done? Speak, however; you are here in confidence: your colleagues shall be your judges. Your crime is a great one, sir. A conspiracy for the commission of a violent act is stopped as soon as we seize the arm that holds the poinard. But a conspiracy to influence the public mind has no end: it is like a train of gunpowder. Perhaps, at this very moment, whole towns are thrown into commotion through your fault!" The Counsellor, quite confused, said nothing in reply: the first appeal was sufficient to establish the fact. The members of the council, to the majority of whom this event was quite unexpected, were struck with astonishment, and observed profound silence.—"Why," continued the Emperor, "did you not, according to the obligation imposed by your oath, discover to me the criminal and his plots? Am I not at all times accessible to every one of you?" "Sire," said the Counsellor, at length venturing to reply, "he was my cousin." "Your crime is then the greater, sir," replied the Emperor sharply: "your kinsman could only have been placed in office at your solicitation: from that moment all the responsibility devolved on you. When I look upon a man as entirely devoted to me, as your situation ought to render you, all who are connected with him, and all for whom he becomes responsible, from that time require no watching. These are my maxims." The accused member still remained silent, and the Emperor continued: "The duties which a Counsellor of State owes to me are immense. You, sir, have violated those duties, and you hold the office no longer. Begone: let me never see you here again!"—The disgraced Counsellor, as he was withdrawing, passed very near the Emperor: the latter looked at him and said, "I am sincerely grieved at this, sir, for the services of your father are still fresh in my memory." When he was gone, the Emperor added, "I hope such a scene as this may never be renewed; it has done me too much harm.—I am not distrustful, but may become so! I have allowed myself to be surrounded by every party; I have placed near my person even emigrants and soldiers of the army of Condé; and though it was wished to induce them to assassinate me; yet, to do them justice, they have continued faithful. Since I have held the reins of Government, this is the first individual employed about me, by whom I have been betrayed." And then turning towards M. Locré, who took notes of the debates of the Council of State, he said, "write down *betrayed*—do you hear?"

What an interesting collection were those reports of M. Locré! What has become of them? All that I have here related would be found in them word for word.

With respect to the dissolution of the Legislative Body, the Council of State was convoked either on the last day, or the last day but one, of December, 1813. We knew that the debate would be an important one, without, however, knowing its object: the crisis was of the most serious nature, the enemy was entering on the French territory.

"Gentlemen," said the Emperor, "you are aware of the situation of affairs, and the dangers to which the country is exposed. I thought it right, without being obliged to do so, to forward a private communication on the subject to the Deputies of the Legislative Body. I wished thus to have associated them with their dearest interests; but they have converted this act of my confidence into a weapon against me; that is to say, against the country. Instead of assisting me with all their efforts, they seek to obstruct mine. Our attitude alone would be sufficient to check the advance of the enemy, while their conduct invites him; instead of showing him a front of brass, they unveil to him our wounds. They stun me with their clamorous demands for peace, while the only means to obtain it was to recommend war; they complain of me, and speak of their grievances; but what time, what place do they select for so doing? These are subjects to be discussed in private, and not in the presence of the enemy. Was I inaccessible to them? Did I ever show myself incapable of arguing reasonably? It is time, however, to come to a resolution: the Legislative Body, instead of assisting me in saving France, wishes to accelerate her ruin. The Legislative Body has betrayed its duty—I fulfil mine—I dissolve it!"

He then ordered the reading of a decree, the purport of which was that two-fifths of the Legislative Body had already gone beyond their power; that on the 1st of January another fifth would be in the same situation, and that consequently the majority of the Legislative Body would then be composed of members who had no right to be in it; that, in consideration of these circumstances, it was, from that moment, prorogued and adjourned until fresh elections should be made.

After the reading of this document, the Emperor continued: "Such is the decree which I issue; and were I assured that it would bring the people of Paris in a crowd to the Thuilleries to murder me this very day, I would still issue it; for such is my duty. When the people of France placed their destinies in my hands, I took into consideration the laws by which I was to govern them: had I thought those laws insufficient, I should not have accepted them. I am not a Louis XVI. Daily vacillations must not be expected from me. Though I have become Emperor, I have not ceased to be a citizen. If anarchy were to resume her sway, I would abdicate and mingle with the crowd to enjoy my share of the sovereignty, rather than remain at the head of a system in which I should only compromise all, without being able to protect any one. Besides," concluded he, "my determination is conformable to the law; and if every one here will do his duty this day, I shall be invincible behind the shelter of the law as well as before the enemy."—But, alas! every one did not perform his duty!

Contrary to the received opinion, the Emperor was far from being of an arbitrary temper, and he was so willing to make concessions to his Council of State, that he has frequently been known to submit to discussion, or even to annul a decision that he had adopted, because one of the members might afterwards privately advance new arguments, or hint that the personal opinion of the Emperor had influenced the majority. Let the chiefs of the sections be referred to on this head.

The Emperor was accustomed to communicate to members of the Institute every scientific idea that occurred to him, and also to submit his political ideas to Counsellors of State: he often did this with private, and even secret views. It was a sure way, he said, to try a question; to ascertain the powers of a man and his political inclination; to take measure of his discretion, &c. I know that in the year XII he submitted to three Counsellors of State the consideration of a very extraordinary question: namely, the suppression of the Legislative Body. It was approved by the majority; but one opposed it strenuously; he spoke at great length, and much to the purpose. The Emperor, who had listened to the discussion with great attention and gravity, without uttering a single word, or suffering any indication of his opinion to escape him, closed the sitting by observing, "A question of so serious a nature deserves to be maturely considered; we will resume the subject." But it was never again brought forward.

It would have been well had he adopted the same precautions at the time of the suppression of the Tribunate; for that has always continued to be a great subject of declamation and reproach. As for the Emperor, he viewed it merely as the suppression of an expensive abuse, and an important economical measure.

"It is certain," said he, "that the Tribunate was absolutely useless, while it cost nearly half a million; I therefore suppressed it. I was well aware that an outcry would be raised against the violation of the law; but I was strong: I possessed the full confidence of the people, and I considered myself a reformer. This at least is certain, that I did all for the best. I should, on the contrary, have created the Tribunate, had I been hypocritical or evil disposed; for, who can doubt that it would have adopted and sanctioned, when necessary, my views and intentions? But that was what I never sought after in the whole course of my administration. I never purchased any vote or decision by promises, money, or places! and if I distributed favours to ministers, counsellors of state, and legislators, it was because there were things to give away, and it was natural and even just that they should be dealt out among those whose avocations brought them in contact with me.

"In my time, all constituted bodies were pure and irreproachable; and I can firmly declare that they acted from conviction. Malevolence and folly may have asserted the contrary; but without ground. If those bodies were condemned, it was by persons who knew them not, or wished not to know them; and the reproaches that were levelled at them, must be attributed to the discontent or opposition of the time; and above all, to that spirit of envy, detraction, and ridicule, which is so peculiarly natural to the French people.

"The Senate has been much abused; great outcry has been raised against its servility and baseness; but declamation is not proof. What was the Senate expected to do? To refuse conscripts? Was it wished that the Committees of personal liberty and the liberty of the press should have brought disgrace upon the Government? or that the Senate should have done what was done in 1813 by a committee of the Legislative Body? But where did that measure lead us! I doubt whether the French people are now very grateful for it. The truth is, that we were placed in forced and unnatural circumstances: men of understanding knew this, and accommodated themselves to the urgency of the moment. It is not known that in almost every important measure, the senators, before they gave their vote, came to communicate to me privately, and sometimes very decidedly, their objections, and even their refusal; and they went away convinced either by my arguments or by the necessity and urgency of affairs. If I never gave publicity to this fact, it was because I governed conscientiously, and because I despised quackery, and every thing like it.

"The votes of the Senate were always unanimous, because their conviction was universal. Endeavours were made at the time to cry up an insignificant minority, whom the hypocritical praises of malevolence, together with their own vanity, or some other perversity of character, excited to harmless opposition. But did the individuals composing that minority evince, in the last crisis, either sound heads or sincere hearts? I once more repeat, that the character of the Senate was irreproachable; the moment of its fall was alone disgraceful and culpable. Without right, without power, and in violation of every principle, the Senate surrendered France, and accomplished her ruin. That body was the sport of high intriguers, whose interest it was to discredit and degrade it, and to ruin one of the great bases of the modern system. It may be truly said they succeeded completely; for I know of no body that can be recorded in history with more ignominy than the French Senate. However, it is but just to observe, that the stain rests not on the majority, and that among the delinquents there was a multitude of foreigners, who will henceforth at least be indifferent to our honour and interests."

On the arrival of the Count d'Artois, the Council of State exerted every effort to attract his attention, and secure his favour. A deputation of the Council was twice presented to him, and permission was solicited to send one to meet the King at Compiègne. To this solicitation the Lieutenant-general of the kingdom replied, that the King would willingly receive the individual members of the Council; but that the sending a deputation was a thing not to be thought of. It is true that the *gros bonnets*, that is to say, the Chiefs of the Sections, were absent. All this agitation had no other object than to insure the payment of their salary, and, perhaps, the retainment of their places. Thus the Council of State immediately signed its adherence to the resolutions of the Senate, avoiding, it is true, every expression that might be offensive to Napoleon: "And you signed it?" said the Emperor. "No, Sire, I declined signing that adherence, on the ground that it was an egregious piece of folly to endeavour to remain successively the counsellor and the confidential servant of two antagonists; and that, besides, if the conqueror were wise, the best pledge that could be offered to his notice, would be fidelity and respect towards the conquered party."—"And you reasoned rightly," observed Napoleon.

5th.—Nearly all our party were assembled round the Emperor in the garden. Those who were lodged in the town complained much of the inconvenience and continual vexations to which they were exposed. The Emperor, for the last fortnight, had laid down the rule of making no communication on this head, except by writing, which he conceived to be the manner most suitable and best calculated to produce the wished-for result. He had drawn up a note on this subject, which should have been delivered some days ago, but which had been neglected. He alluded several times to this business, and in a tone of displeasure. All his indirect arguments and observations applied to the Grand Marshal. The latter at length took umbrage: for, who is not rendered irritable by misfortune? He expressed himself in rather pointed language. His wife, who was standing near the garden-gate, despairing of being able to appease the storm, withdrew. I had now an opportunity of observing how the impressions produced by this circumstance succeeded each other in the Emperor's mind. Reason, logic, and, it may be added, sentiment, always prevailed.—"If," said he, "you did not deliver the letter because you considered it to be couched in offensive terms, you performed a duty of friendship; but surely this did not require a delay of more than twenty-four hours. A fortnight has elapsed without your mentioning it to me. If the plan was faulty, if the letter was ill-expressed, why not have told me so? I should have assembled you all to discuss the matter with me."

We all stood near the arbour at the extremity of the path, while the Emperor walked back and forward before us. At a moment, when he had gone to a little distance from us, and was out of hearing, the Grand Marshal, addressing himself to me, said:—"I fear I have expressed myself improperly, and I am sorry for it."—"We will leave you alone with him," said I; "you will soon make him forget the offence." I accordingly beckoned the other individuals who were present to leave the garden.

In the evening, the Emperor, conversing with me about the events of the morning, said:—"It was after we had made it up with the Grand Marshal—It was before the misunderstanding with the Grand Marshal,"—and other things of the same sort, which proved that the affair had left no impression on his heart.

The General's of the Army of Italy.—Ancient Armies.—Gengiskan.—Modern Invasions.—Character of Conquerors.

6th.—The Emperor was somewhat unwell, and employed himself in writing in his chamber. He dictated to me the portraits of the Generals of the army of Italy—Massena, Augereau, Serrurier, &c. Massena was endowed with extraordinary courage and firmness, which seemed to increase in excess of danger. When conquered, he was always as ready to fight the battle again as though he had been the conqueror. Augereau was a cross-grained character: he seemed to be tired and disheartened by victory, of which he always had enough. His person, his manners, and his language, gave him the air of a braggadocio, which, however, he was far from being. He was satiated with honours and riches, which he had received at all hands, and in all ways. Serrurier, who retained the manners and severity of an old major of infantry, was an honest and trust-worthy man; but a bad general, &c.—Further details of these individuals will be found in the Campaigns of Italy.

Among the various subjects of the day's conversation, I note down what the Emperor said respecting the armies of the Ancients. He asked whether the accounts of the great armies mentioned in history were to be credited. He was of opinion that those statements were false and absurd. He placed no faith in the descriptions of the innumerable armies of the Carthaginians in Sicily." "Such a multitude of troops," he observed, "would have been useless in so inconsiderable an enterprise; and if Carthage could have assembled such a force, a still greater one would have been raised in Hannibal's expedition, which was of much greater importance, but in which not more than forty or fifty thousand men were employed." He did not believe the accounts of the millions of men composing the forces of Darius and Xerxes, which might have covered all Greece, and which would doubtless have been subdivided into a multitude of partial armies. He even doubted the whole of that brilliant period of Greek history: and he regarded the famous Persian war only as a series of undecided actions, in which each party laid claim to the victory. Xerxes returned triumphant, after taking, burning, and destroying Athens; and the Greeks exulted in their victory, because they had not surrendered at Salemis. "With regard to the pompous accounts of the conquests of the Greeks, and the defeat of their numberless enemies, it must be recollected," observed the Emperor, "that the Greeks, who wrote them, were a vain and hypocritical people; and that no Persian chronicle has ever been produced to set our judgment right by contrary statements."

But the Emperor attached credit to Roman history, if not in its details, at least in its results; because these were facts as clear as daylight. He also believed the descriptions of the armies of Gengiskan and Tamerlane, however numerous they are said to have been; because they were followed by gregarious nations, who, on their part, were joined by other wandering tribes as they advanced; "and it is not impossible," obsrved the Emperor, "that this may be the case in Europe. The revolution produced by the Hunts, the cause of which is unknown, because the tract is lost in the desert, may at a future period be renewed."

The situation of Russia is admirably calculated to assist her in bringing about such a catastrophe. She may collect at will numberless auxiliaries and scatter them over Europe. The wandering tribes of the north will be better disposed, and the more impatient to engage in such enterprises, in proportion as their imaginations have been fired, and their avarice excited by the successes of those of their countrymen who lately visited us.

The conversation next turned on conquests and conquerors; and the Emperor observed, that to be a successful conqueror, it was necessary to be ferocious, and that if he had been such, he might have conquered the world. I presumed to dissent from this opinion, which was doubtless expressed in a moment of vexation. I represented that he, Napoleon, was precisely a proof of the contrary; that he had not been ferocious, and yet had conquered the world; and that with the manners of modern times, ferocity would certainly never have raised him to so high a point. I added, that at the present day, terror could never subject us to the control of an individual man; and that dominion was to be secured only by good laws, joined to greatness of character, and that degree of energy which is proof against every trial, in him who is charged with the execution of the laws. These, I affirmed, were precisely the causes of Napoleon's success, and of the submission and obedience of the people over whom he ruled.

The Convention was ferocious, and inspired terror: it was submitted to, but could not be endured. Had the power been vested in an individual, his overthrow would soon have been accomplished. But the Convention was a hydra, yet how many attempts were hazarded for its destruction! how many dangers did it escape as if by miracle! It was reduced to the necessity of burying itself amidst its triumphs.

For a conqueror to be ferocious with success, he must of necessity command troops who are themselves ferocious, and he must wield dominion over unenlightened people. In this respect Russia possesses an immense superiority over the rest of Europe. She has the rare advantage of possessing a civilized government, and barbarous subjects. There, information directs and commands, while ignorance executes and destroys. A Turkish Sultan could not long govern any enlightened European nation; the empire of knowledge would be too strong for his power.

Speaking on another subject, the Emperor observed, that if the French people had less energy than the Romans, they at least evinced greater decorum. We should not have killed ourselves, as the Romans did under the first emperors; but at the same time we should have afforded no examples of the turpitude and servility that marked the later periods of the Roman empire. "Even in our most corrupt days," said he, "our baseness was not without certain restrictions: courtiers whom the sovereign could have prevailed on to do any thing in his own palace, have refused to bend the knee to him at his levee."

I have already mentioned, that we had with us scarcely any document relative to French affairs during the Emperor's time. The books that had been brought among his effects were merely a few classics which he carried about with him in all his campaigns. I received from Major Hudson, a resident of the island, a political compendium from 1793 to 1807, entitled "The Annual Register," which contains the succession of political events during each year, together with some of the most important official documents. In our destitute circumstances this was a valuable acquisition.

Ideas.—Plans.—Political Suggestions, &c.

7th.—The Emperor breakfasted alone, and was engaged during the day in dictating to the Grand Marshal and M. de Montholon.

In the evening, as the Emperor and I were walking together in the lower path, which had now become the favourite resort, I informed him that a person of consequence, whose ideas and statements might become the channel of mediation between ourselves and the ruling world, and influence our future destiny, had, with sufficiently significant forms and preambles, invited us to tell him conscientiously what we believed to be the Emperor's notions on certain political subjects:—whether he had granted his last constitution with the intention of maintaining it;—whether he would have consented to leave England in the enjoyment of her maritime supremacy, without envying her the tranquil possession of India;—whether he would have been willing to renounce the Colonies, and to purchase colonial goods from the English alone, at the regular market price;—whether he would not have formed an alliance with the Americans, in case of their rupture with England;—whether he would have consented to the existence of a great kingdom in Germany, for that branch of the English royal family, who must immediately forfeit the throne of Great Britain on the accession of the Princess Charlotte of Wales, or, in default of Germany, whether he would have consented to the establishment of that dominion in Portugal, in case England should conclude arrangements with the Court of Brazil.

These questions did not rest on vague ideas or idle opinions; the individual supported them on positive facts. "We want," said he, "a long and lasting peace on the Continent—we want the tranquil enjoyment of our present advantages, to help us out of the critical circumstances in which we are now involved, and to relieve us from the enormous debt with which we are burthened. The present state of France and of Europe," added he, "cannot bring about these results. The victory of Waterloo ruined you; but it was far from saving us: every sensible man in England, every one who escapes the momentary influence of passion, either does think, or will think, as I do."

The Emperor doubted a part of this statement, and treated the rest as a reverie; then changing his tone, he said to me, "Well, what is your opinion? Come, now, you are one of the Council of State."—"Sire," I replied, "people often indulge in reveries on the most serious subjects; and our being imprisoned at St. Helena does not hinder us from composing romances. Here then is one. Why not form a political marriage between the two nations, in which the one would bring the army as a dowry, and the other the navy? This will doubtless appear an absurd idea in the eyes of the vulgar, and will perhaps be thought too bold by well-informed people, because it is entirely novel and out of the usual routine. But it is one of those unforeseen, luminous, and useful creations of plans which characterize your Majesty. You alone are capable of attending to it, and perhaps of carrying it into effect."

Going even beyond the ideas of our English interlocutor, I said: "Would not your Majesty give to-morrow, if you could, the whole French navy to purchase Belgium and the bank of the Rhine? Would you not give one hundred and fifty millions to purchase tens of thousands of millions? Besides, such a bargain would procure to both nations at once the object for which they have been wrangling and fighting for so many years; it would reduce both countries to the necessity of mutually assisting each other, instead of maintaining perpetual enmity. Would it be nothing for France that her merchants in the English colonies should henceforward be on the footing of Englishmen: and thus secure, without striking a blow, the enjoyment of the trade of the whole world? Would it be nothing for England, on the other hand, for the sake of insuring to herself the sovereignty of the ocean, the universality of trade (for obtaining and preserving which she has incurred so many risks,) to attach France to a system by which the latter would become the regulator and arbiter of the Continent?

Henceforth secure from danger, and strengthened by all the power of her ally, England might disband her army, in return for the sacrifice which France would make of her navy. She might even reduce considerably the number of her ships. She would thus pay her debt, relieve her people, and prosper; and far from envying France, she would (the system being once fairly understood, and passion having given place to real interests) herself labour for the Continental aggrandizement of her neighbour; for France would then be merely the advance-guard, while England would be the resource and the reserve. Unity of legislation between the two nations, their common interests, results so visibly advantageous, would make amends for all the obstacles and difficulties which the passions of rulers might oppose to the fulfilment of this plan."

The Emperor heard me, but made no reply; it is seldom that one can ascertain his private opinions, and he rarely enters into political conversations. Lest I should not have expressed myself with sufficient clearness, I requested that he would permit me to unfold my ideas in writing. He consented, and said no more. It was now very late, and he retired to rest.

8th.—The Emperor dictated in the garden to MM. Montholon and Gourgaud, and then walked on his favourite path. He was fatigued and indisposed. He observed some females about to advance on the path, and to throw themselves awkwardly in his way, for the sake of being introduced to him; this annoyed him, and he turned away to avoid meeting them.

I suggested that riding on horseback might be beneficial to him; we had three horses at our disposal. The Emperor replied, that he never could reconcile himself to the idea of having an English officer constantly at his side; that he decidedly renounced riding on such conditions; adding that every thing in life must be reduced to calculation, and that if the vexation arising from the sight of his jailor were greater than the advantage he might derive from riding, it was of course advisable to renounce the recreation altogether.

The Emperor ate but little dinner. During the dessert he amused himself in examining the paintings on some plates of very beautiful Sevres porcelaine. They were *chefs-dœuvre* in their kind, and were worth thirty Napoleons each. The paintings represented views or objects of antiquity in Egypt.

The Emperor closed the day with a walk on his favourite path. He remarked that he had been very dull all day. After several broken conversations, he looked at his watch, and was very glad to find it was half-past ten.

The weather was delicious, and the Emperor insensibly recovered his usual spirits. He complained of his constitution, which, though vigorous, occasionally exposed him to fits of indisposition. He, however, consoled himself with the thought, that if in imitation of the ancients, he should ever feel inclined to escape from the disgusts and vexations of life, his moral opinions were not of a nature to prevent him. He said that sometimes he could not reflect without horror on the many years he might still have to live, and on the inutility of a protracted old age; and that if he were convinced France was happy and tranquil, and not needing his aid, he should have lived long enough.

14*

We ascended to the pavilion, it was past midnight, and we thought we had gained a signal victory over time.

9th.—I called on Mr. Balcombe very early, to deliver to him my letters for Europe, as a vessel was on the point of sailing. At Mr. Balcombe's house I met the officer who had been appointed as our guard. Struck with the dejection which I had observed in the Emperor the day before, and convinced of the necessity of his taking exercise, I told the officer that I suspected the reason which prevented the Emperor from riding on horseback; I added, that I would speak to him the more candidly and openly, since I had noticed the very delicate way in which he discharged his duty. I enquired what were his instructions, and whether it would be necessary to observe them literally in case the Emperor merely took a ride round the house; adverting to the repugnance which he must naturally feel for arrangements that were calculated every moment to revive the recollection of the situation in which he was placed. I assured the officer that I intended to cast no reflections on him personally, and that I was convinced, when the Emperor wished to take long rides, he would prefer that some one should accompany him. The officer replied, that his instructions were to follow the Emperor; but that as he made it a rule not to do any thing that might be offensive to him, he would take upon himself not to ride beside him.

At breakfast I communicated to the Emperor the conversation I had had with the Captain. He replied that it was all very well as far as regarded him; but that he should not avail himself of the indulgence, as it was not conformable with his sentiments to enjoy an advantage which might be the means of compromising an officer.

This determination was very fortunate. When I went to Mr. Balcombe's in the evening, the Captain took me aside to inform me, that he had been to the town, in the course of the day, to speak with the Admiral respecting our morning's conversation, and that he had been enjoined to conform with his instructions. I could not refrain from replying, somewhat sharply, that I was certain the Emperor would immediately send back the three horses that had been assigned for his use. The officer, to whom I had also communicated the reply which the Emperor had given me in the morning relative to him, observed, that it would be very right to send back the horses, and that he thought nothing better could be done. This remark appeared to me to be prompted by the mortification he himself experienced at the part that was imposed on him.

When we left Mr Balcombe's, the Emperor walked up and down the path in the garden. I mentioned to him what I had heard from the English officer. He seemed to expect it. I was not deceived in my conjecture; he ordered me to send away the horses. This vexed me exceedingly; and I said, perhaps rather sharply, that with his leave I would go and fulfil his orders immediately. On which he replied, with great gravity and a very peculiar tone of voice:—"No, Sir, you are now out of temper. It rarely happens that any thing is done well under such circumstances; it is always best to let the night pass over after the offence of the day."

We continued our walk till nearly midnight: the weather was delightful.

10th.—To-day, when our usual task was ended, the Emperor strolled out in a new direction. He proceeded towards the town, until he came within sight of the road and shipping. As he was returning, he met Mrs. Balcombe, and a Mrs. Stuart, a very pretty woman about twenty years of age, who was returning from Bombay to England. The Emperor conversed with her respecting the manners and customs of India, and the inconveniences of a sea-voyage, particularly for females. He also spoke of Scotland, which was Mrs. Stuart's native country; said a great deal about Ossian, and complimented the lady on the climate of India not having spoiled her clear Scottish complexion.

At this moment some slaves, carrying heavy boxes, passed us on the road; Mrs. Balcombe desired them, in rather an angry tone, to keep back; but the Emperor interfered, saying: "Respect the burden, Madame!" At these words, Mrs. Stuart, who had been attentively observing the Emperor's features, said in a low tone of voice to her friend: "Heavens! what a countenance, and what a character. How different from what I had been led to expect!"

Midnight conversations by moonlight.—The two Empresses.—Maria-Louisa's marriage.—Her house-hold.—The Duchess de Montebello.—Madame de Montesquiou.—The Institute of Meudon.—Sentiments of the House of Austria, with regard to Napoleon.—Anecdotes collected in Germany, since my return to Europe.

11th—13th. We led a most regular life at Briars. Every day, after dictating to me, the Emperor walked out between three and four o'clock. He descended to the garden, where he walked up and down, and dictated to one of the gentlemen who came from the town for that purpose, and who wrote in the little arbour. About half-past five o'clock, he passed Mr Balcombe's house, and went into the lower walk, to which he became every day more and more attached. At this time the family were at dinner, and he could enjoy his promenade without interruption. I joined the Emperor here, and he continued his walk until dinner was announced.

After dinner, the Emperor again returned to the garden, where he sometimes had his coffee brought to him. My son then visited Mr. Balcombe's family, and the Emperor and I walked up and down. We frequently remained in the garden until the night was far advanced and the moon rose to light us. In the mildness and serenity of the night we forgot the burning heat of the day. The Emperor never was more talkative, nor seemed more perfectly to forget his cares, than during these moonlight walks. In the familiarity of the conversations which I thus enjoyed with him, he took pleasure in relating anecdotes of his boyhood, in describing the sentiments and illusions which diffused a charm over the early years of his youth, and in detailing the circumstances of his private life, since he had played so distinguished a part on the great theatre of the world. I have elsewhere noted down what I conceived myself at liberty to repeat. Sometimes he seemed to think he had spoken too much at length, and had detailed things too minutely. He would then say to me: "Come, it is your turn now; let me have a little of your history; but you are not a tale-teller." Indeed, I took especial care to be silent; I was too much afraid of losing a syllable of what so deeply interested me.

In one of our nightly walks, the Emperor told me that he had in the course of his life been much attached to two women of very different characters. The one was the votary of art and the graces; the other was all innocence and simple nature: and each, he observed, had a very high degree of merit.

The first, in no moment of her life ever assumed a position or attitude that was not pleasing or captivating; it was impossible to take her by surprise, or to make her feel the least inconvenience. She employed every resource of art to heighten natural attractions; but with such ingenuity as to render every trace of allurement imperceptible. The other, on the contrary, never suspected that any thing was to be gained by innocent artifice. The one was always somewhat short of the truth of nature; the other was altogether frank and open, and was a stranger to subterfuge.—The first never asked her husband for any thing, but she was in debt to every one; the second freely asked whenever she wanted, which, however, very seldom happened; and she never thought of receiving any thing without immediately paying for it. Both were amiable and gentle in disposition, and strongly attached to their husbands. But it must already have been guessed who they are; all those who have ever seen them will not fail to recognise the two Empresses.

The Emperor declared that he had uniformly experienced from both the greatest equality of temper and most implicit obedience.

The marriage of Maria-Louisa was consummated at Fontainebleau, immediately after her arrival. The Emperor, setting aside all the etiquette that had previously been arranged, went to meet her, and in disguise got into her carriage. She was agreeably surprised when she discovered him. She had always been given to understand that Berthier, who had married her by proxy at Vienna, in person and age exactly resembled the Emperor: she, however, signified that she observed a very pleasing difference between them.

The Emperor wished to spare her all the details of domestic etiquette, customary on such occasions. She had received careful instructions at Vienna relative to the ceremonies to be observed at her marriage. The Emperor enquired what directions she had received from her illustrious relatives with regard to him personally. To be entirely devoted to him, and to obey him in all things, was the reply. This declaration, and not the decisions of certain cardinals and bishops, as was reported, proved the solution of all the Emperor's scruples of conscience. Besides, Henry IV acted in the same way on a similar occasion.

Maria-Louisa's marriage, said the Emperor, was proposed and concluded under the same forms and conditions, as that of Marie-Antoinette, whose contract was adopted as a model. After the repudiation of Josephine, negotiations were entered into with the Emperor of Russia, for the purpose of soliciting the hand of one of his sisters: the difficulties rested merely in the settling of certain points relative to religion. Prince Eugéne, conversing with M. de Schwartzenberg, learned that the Emperor of Austria would not object to a union between Napoleon and his daughter; and this information was communicated to the Emperor. A council was convoked to decide whether an alliance with Russia or Austria would be most advantageous. Eugéne and Talleyrand were for the Austrian alliance, and Cambacérès against it. The majority were in favour of an Archduchess. Eugène was appointed to make the official overture, and the Minister for Foreign Affairs was empowered to sign it that very day if an opportunity should present itself; which proved to be the case.

Russia took umbrage at this; she thought herself trifled with, though without just ground. Nothing of an obligatory nature had yet transpired; both parties remained perfectly free. Political interests predominated over every thing.

The Emperor appointed the Duchess de Montebello to be lady of honour to Maria-Louisa; the Count de Beauharnais to be her gentleman of honour, and the Prince Aldobrandini to be her equery. In the misfortunes of 1814, these individuals, said the Emperor, did not evince the devotedness which the Empress was entitled to expect from them. Her equery deserted her without taking his leave; her gentleman of honour refused to follow her; and her lady of honour, notwithstanding the attachment which the Empress entertained for her, thought she had completely fulfilled her duty in attending her mistress as far as Vienna.

The appointment of the Duchess de Montebello to the post of lady of honour, was one of those happy selections which, at the time it was made, excited universal approbation. The Duchess was a young and beautiful woman, of irreproachable character, and the widow of a marshal, called the *Orlando* of the army, who had recently fallen on the field of battle. This choice was very agreeable to the army, and encouraged the national party, who were alarmed at the marriage and the number and rank of the chamberlains who were appointed. This retinue was, by many, looked upon as a step towards the counter-revolution; and endeavours were made to represent it as such. As for the Emperor, he had acted in ignorance of the character of Maria-Louisa, and had been principally influenced by the fear that she would be filled with prejudices respecting birth, that might be offensive at the court. When he came to know her better, and found that she was wholly imbued with the prevailing notions of the day, he regretted not having made another choice. He conceived he would have done better to have selected the Countess de Beauvean, a woman of amiable, mild, and inoffensive manners, who would have been influenced only by the family considerations of her numerous relatives, and who might thus have introduced a kind of useful tradition, and have occasioned the appointment of well-recommended inferiors. She might also have rallied about the court many persons who were at a distance; and that, without any inconvenience, because these arrangements could only have been brought about by the sanction of the Emperor who was not the sort of man to allow himself to be abused.

The Empress conceived the tenderest affection for the Duchess de Montebello. This lady had at one time a chance of being Queen of Spain. Ferdinand VII, when at Valency, requested the Emperor's permission to marry Mademoiselle de Tascher, cousin-german of Josephine; he even proposed to marry the young lady, in her own name, after the example of the Prince of Baden, who married Mademoiselle de Beauharnais. The Emperor, who already contemplated a separation from Josephine, refused his consent to the match, not wishing by this connection to add to the difficulties that already stood in the way of his divorce. Ferdinand then solicited the hand of the Duchess de Montebello, or of any other French lady whom the Emperor might think proper to adopt. The Emperor subsequently gave Mademoiselle de Tascher in marriage to the Duke d'Aremberg, intending to create her husband Governor of the Netherlands; with the view of ultimately compensating Brussels for the loss of her old court. The Emperor moreover wished to appoint the Count de Narbonne, who had taken part in the Empress's marriage, Gentleman of honour, in room of the Count de Beauharnais; but the extreme aversion which Maria-Louisa evinced for this change, deterred the Emperor from carry it into effect. The Empress's dislike to the Count de Narbonne was, however, only occasioned by the intrigues of the individuals composing her household, who had nothing to fear from M. de Beauharnais, but who very much dreaded the influence and talent of M. de Narbonne.

The Emperor informed us, that when he had to make appointments to difficult posts, he usually asked the persons about him to furnish him with a list of candidates; and from these lists, and the information he obtained, he privately deliberated on his choice. He mentioned several individuals who were proposed as lady of honour to the Empress: they were the Princess de Vaudemont, Madame de Rochefoucault, afterwards Madame de Castellanes, and some others. He then asked us to tell him whom we should have proposed; which occasioned us to take a review of a good part of the court. One of us mentioned Madame de Montesquiou; upon which the Emperor replied, "She would have done well, but she had a post which suited her still better. She was a woman of singular merit; her piety was sincere, and her principles excellent; she had the highest claims on my esteem and regard. I wanted half a dozen like her; I would have given them all appointments equal to their deserts. She discharged her duties admirably when with my son at Vienna."

The following anecdote will afford a correct idea of the manner in which Madame de Montesquiou managed the King of Rome. The apartments of the young Prince were on the ground floor and looked out on the court of the Thuilleries. At almost every hour in the day, numbers of people were looking in at the window, in the hope of seeing him. One day when he was in a violent fit of passion, and rebelling furiously against the authority of Madame de Montesquiou, she immediately ordered all the shutters to be closed. The child, surprised at the sudden darkness, asked *Maman Quiou*, as he used to call her, what it all meant. "I love you too well," she replied, "not to hide your anger from the crowd in the court-yard. You, perhaps, will one day be called to govern all those people, and what would they say if they saw you in such a fit of rage? Do you think they would ever obey you, if they knew you to be so wicked!" Upon which, the child asked her pardon, and promised never again to give way to such fits of anger.

"This," observed the Emperor, "was language very different from that addressed by M. de Villeroi to Louis XV. '*Behold all those people, my Prince,*' said he, '*they belong to you; all the men you see yonder are yours.*'"

Madame de Montesquiou was adored by the young King of Rome. At the time of her removal from Vienna, it was found necessary to employ stratagems to deceive the child: it was even supposed that his health would suffer from the separation.

The Emperor had conceived many novel ideas relative to the education of the King of Rome. For this important object, he decided on the *Institute de Meudon*, of which he had already laid down the principle, with the view of farther developing it at his leisure. There he proposed to assemble the Princes of the Imperial house, particularly the sons of those branches of the family who had been raised to foreign thrones. In this institution he intended that the Princes should receive the attentions of private tuition, combined with the advantages of public education. "These children," said the Emperor, "who were destined to occupy different thrones, and to govern different nations, would thus have acquired conformity of principles, manners, and ideas. The better to facilitate the amalgamation and uniformity of the federative parts of the Empire, each Prince was to bring with him from his own country ten or twelve youths about his own age, the sons of the first families in the state. What an influence would they not have exercised on their return home! I doubted not," continued the Emperor, "but that Princes of other dynasties, unconnected with my family, would soon have solicited, as a great favour, permission to place their sons in the Institute of Meudon. What advantages would thence have arisen to the nations composing the European association! All these young Princes," said he, "would have been brought together early enough to be united in the tender and powerful bonds of youthful friendship; and they would, at the same time, have been separated early enough to obviate the fatal effects of rising passions—the ardour of partiality—the ambition of success—the jealousy of love.

The Emperor wished that the education of the Princes should be founded on general information, extended views, summaries, and results. He wished them to possess knowledge rather than learning; judgment rather than attainments; he preferred the application of details to the study of theories. Above all, he objected to the pursuing of any particular study too deeply, for he regarded perfection or too great success in certain things, whether in the arts or sciences, as a disadvantage to a prince. A nation, he said, will never gain much by being governed by a poet, a virtuoso, a naturalist, a turner, a locksmith, &c. &c.

Maria-Louisa confessed to the Emperor, that when her marriage with him was first proposed, she could not help feeling a kind of terror, owing to the accounts she had heard of Napoleon from the individuals of her family. When she mentioned these reports to her uncles, the Archdukes, who were very urgent for the marriage, they replied,—"that was all very true, while he was our enemy; but the case is altered now."

"To afford an idea of the sympathy and good will with which the different members of the Austrian family were taught to regard me," said the Emperor, "it is sufficient to mention that one of the young Archdukes frequently burned his dolls, which he called *roasting Napoleon*. He afterwards declared he would not roast me any more, for he loved me very much, because I had given his sister Louisa plenty of money to buy him playthings."

Since my return to Europe, I have had an opportunity of ascertaining the sentiments entertained by the House of Austria towards Napoleon. In Germany, a person of distinction informed me, that having had a private audience of the Emperor Francis, during his tour in Italy in 1816, the conversation turned on Napoleon. Francis spoke of him in the most respectful terms. One might almost have supposed, said my informant, that he still regarded him as the ruler of France, and that he was ignorant of his captivity at Saint-Helena. He never alluded to him by any other title than the Emperor Napoleon.

I learned from the same individual that the Archduke John, when in Italy, visited a rotunda, on the ceiling of which was painted a celebrated action of which Napoleon was the hero. As he raised his head to look at the painting, his hat fell off, and one of his attendants stooped to pick it up. "Let it be," said he: "it is thus that I should contemplate the man who is there portrayed."

Now that I am on this subject, I will note down a few particulars which I collected in Germany since my return to Europe; and to mark the degree of credit to which they are entitled, I may mention that I obtained them from individuals holding high diplomatic posts. Every one knows that these members of diplomatic corps form among themselves a sort of family, a kind of free-masonry, and that their sources of information are of the most authentic kind.

The Empress Maria-Louisa complained that when she quitted France, M. de Talleyrand reserved to himself the honour of demanding from her the restitution of the crown-jewels, and ascertaining whether they had been restored with the most scrupulous exactness.

In 1814, during the disasters of France, many tempting and brilliant proposals were made to Prince Eugène. An Austrian General offered him the crown of Italy, in the name of the allies, on condition of his joining them. This offer afterwards came from a still higher source, and was several times repeated. During the reign of the Emperor, there had been some idea of raising the Prince to a throne; and those of Portugal, Naples, and Poland, were thought of.

In 1815, men of high influence in European diplomacy, endeavoured to sound his opinions, with the view of ascertaining whether, in case Napoleon should again be constrained to abdicate, and the choice should fall on him, he would accept the crown. On this occasion, as on every other, the Prince steadily pursued a line of duty and honour which will immortalize him. *Honour and fidelity* was his constant reply; and posterity will make it his device.

On the distribution of States in 1814, the Emperor Alexander, who frequently visited the Empress Josephine at Malmaison, signified a wish to procure for her son the sovereignty of Genoa. Eugène, however, declined this proposition, at the instigation of the ruling diplomatists, who falsely flattered him with the hope of something better.

At the Congress of Vienna, the Emperor Alexander, who honoured Prince Eugène with particular marks of favour, insisted that he should be made the Sovereign of at least three hundred thousand subjects. He testified the sincerest friendship for him, and they were every day seen walking about together arm-in-arm. The landing at Cannes put a period, if not to the sentiment, at least to the manifestation of it; and changed the political interests of the Emperor of Russia. The Austrian government even entertained the idea of seizing the person of Prince Eugène, and sending him a prisoner to a fortress in Hungary; but the King of Bavaria, his father-in-law, indignantly represented to the Emperor of Austria, that Eugène had gone to Vienna under his protection and guarantee, and that they should not be violated. Thus Eugène remained free on his own private parole and that of the King his father-in-law.

So late as 1814, gold twenty and forty-franc pieces were struck at Milan with the head of Napoleon and the date of 1814. Either from motives of economy or some other cause, no new die had yet been engraved.

After the fall of Napoleon, Alexander on several occasions manifested a marked and decided dislike to him. In 1815 he was the promoter of the second crusade against Napoleon; he directed every hostile measure with the utmost degree of malice, and seemed to make it almost a personal affair; alleging, as the cause of his aversion, that he had been deceived and trifled with. If this tardy resentment was not a mere pretence, there is every reason to believe that it was stirred up by an old confidant of Napoleon, who, in private conversations, had artfully wounded the vanity of Alexander, by statements, true or false, of the private opinion of Napoleon with regard to his illustrious friend.

In 1814 there appeared reason to believe that Alexander would not be averse to see young Napoleon placed on the throne of France. After the Emperor's second abdication, he seemed far less favourably disposed to the continuance of Napoleon's dynasty.

In the second crusade, the Emperor Alexander marched at the head of innumerable forces. He was heard to declare at that period, that the war might last for three years; but that Napoleon would nevertheless be subdued in the end.

On the first intelligence of the battle of Fleurus, the chiefs of all the Russian columns received orders immediately to halt; while all the Austrian and Bavarian corps instantly turned off, with the view of detaching themselves and forming a separate force. Had the Congress of Vienna been broken up on the 20th of March, it is almost certain that the crusade would not have been renewed; and had Napoleon been victorious at Waterloo, it is also tolerably certain that the Congress would have been dissolved.

The news of Napoleon's landing at Cannes was a thunderbolt to the French Plenipotentiary at Vienna. He indeed drew up the famous declaration of the 13th of March; and however virulent it might be, the first draught was still more so: it was amended by other ministers. The countenance of this Plenipotentiary, as he gradually learned the advance of Napoleon, was a sort of thermometer, which excited the risibility of all the members of the Congress.

Austria soon knew what part to act: her couriers admirably well informed her of all that was passing. The members of the French Legation alone were involved in doubt: they, however, circulated a magnanimous letter from the King to the other Sovereigns, informing them that he was resolved to die at the Thuilleries, though it was known that Louis had already left the capital, and was on his way to the frontier.

A member of the Congress and Lord Wellington held a confidential conversation with the members of the French Legation; and with the map in their hands, assigned the 20th or 21st for Napoleon's entrance into Paris.

As the Emperor Francis received the official publications from Grenoble and Lyons, he regularly forwarded them to Schœnbrunn, to Maria-Louisa, to whom they afforded extreme joy. It is very true that at a somewhat later period an idea was entertained of seizing young Napoleon, in order to convey him to France.

The French Plenipotentiary at length quitted Vienna, and proceeded to Frankfort and Wisbad, whence he could more conveniently negotiate either with Ghent or Paris.—Never was a courtier thrown into greater embarrassment and anxiety by the turn of events. The ardour with which he had been inspired on receiving the intelligence of Napoleon's landing at Cannes, was very much abated when he heard of the Emperor's arrival at Paris; and he entered into an understanding with Fouché, that the latter should be his guarantee with Napoleon, pledging himself, on the other hand, to be Fouché's guarantee with the Bourbons. There is good ground for believing that the offers made by this Plenipotentiary to the new Sovereign, went very great lengths indeed; but Napoleon indignantly rejected them, lest, as he said, he should degrade his policy too far.

In 1814, before M. de Talleyrand declared himself for the Bourbons, he was for the Regency; in which, however, he himself wished to play the principal part. Events fatal to the Napoleon dynasty prevented this moment of uncertainty from being turned to good account. Every thing tends to prove, that the result which was at that period adopted, was far from being agreeable to the intentions of Austria; that power was duped, betrayed, or at least carried by assault.

The fatality attending the military movements was such, that the Allies entered Paris without the concurrence of the Austrian Cabinet. Alexander's famous declaration against Napoleon Bonaparte and his family was also made without the Austrian Power being consulted; and the Count d'Artois only entered France by contriving to slip in secretly in spite of the orders at the Austrian head-quarters, where he had been refused passports.

It appears that Austria, on the retreat from Moscow, exerted sincere efforts in London for negotiating a peace with Napoleon; but the influence of the Russian Cabinet was all-powerful in London, and no proposals for peace were listened to. The armistice of Dresden then arrived, and Austria declared herself favourable to war.

During this interval, the Austrian minister in London could never obtain a hearing. He however remained for a considerable time in the English capital, and left it only when the Allies had reached the heart of France, and when Lord Castlereagh felt a momentary foreboding that the heroic success of Napoleon might render negotiations indispensable.

If this minister had not previously been sent to London, he would have been destined for Paris; and there probably his influence might have brought about a turn of negotiations different from those which arose during his absence between the Thuilleries and Vienna.

In the height of the crisis he found himself detained in England as if by force. In his impatience to reach the grand centre of negotiations, he quitted his post, and proceeded to Holland, braving the fury of the tempest. No sooner had he arrived on the theatre of events, than he fell into the hands of Napoleon at Saint-Dizier; but the fate of France was then decided, though the fact was not yet known at the French head-quarters. Alexander was entering Paris.

The Austrian minister in London exerted every endeavour to procure a passport to enable him to join his Sovereign by passing through Calais and Paris; but in vain.—This circumstance, whether accidental, or premeditated, was another fatality. But for this disappointment the Austrian minister would have reached Paris before the Allies, would have joined Maria-Louisa, would have defeated the last projects of M. de Talleyrand, and would have altogether produced new combinations.

Opinion was divided in the Austrian Cabinet. One party was for the union with France; the other was for the alliance with Russia. Intrigue or chance decided in favour of Russia, and Austria was thus merely led on.

14th.—The coffee that was served at our breakfast this morning was better than usual; it might even have been called good. The Emperor expressed himself pleased with it. Some moments after he observed, placing his hand on his stomach, that he felt the benefit of it. It would be difficult to express what were my feelings on hearing this simple remark. The Emperor by thus, contrary to his custom, appreciating so trivial an enjoyment, unconsciously proved to me the effect of all the privations he had suffered, but of which he never complained.

When we returned from our evening walk, the Emperor read to me a chapter on the *Provisional Consuls,* which he had dictated to M. de Montholon. Having finished reading, the Emperor took a piece of ribbon, and began to tie together the loose sheets of paper. It was late; the silence of night prevailed around us. My reflections at this moment took a melancholy turn. I gazed on the Emperor. I looked on those hands which had wielded so many sceptres, and which were now tranquilly, and, perhaps, not without some degree of pleasure, occupied in the humble task of tying together a few sheets of paper. On these sheets, indeed, were traced events that will never be forgotten; portraits that will decide the judgment of posterity. It is the book of life or death to many whose names are recorded in it. These were the reflections that passed in my mind. "And the Emperor," thought I, "reads to me what he writes; he familiarly asks my opinion, and I freely give it! After all, am I not rather to be envied than pitied in my exile at Saint-Helena?"

15th. Immediately after dinner the Emperor walked in his favourite path. He had his coffee carried down to him in the garden, and he drank it as he walked about. The conversation turned on love. I must have made some very fine and sentimental remarks on this important subject; for the Emperor laughed at what he styled my prattle, and said that he understood none of my romantic verbiage. Then speaking with an air of levity, he wished to make me believe that he was better acquainted with sensations than sentiments. I made free to remark, that he was trying to be thought worse than he was described to be in the authentic but very secret accounts that were circulated about the palace. "And what was said of me?" resumed he, with an air of gaiety. "Sire," I replied, "it is understood, that when in the summit of your power, you suffered yourself to be enslaved by the chains of love; that you became a hero of romance.—In short, that you conceived an attachment for a lady in humble circumstances; that you wrote her above a dozen love-letters; and that her power over you prevailed so far as to compel you to disguise yourself, and to visit her secretly and alone, at her own residence in the heart of Paris."—"And how came this to be known?" said he, smiling; which of course amounted to an admission of the fact. "And it was doubtless added," continued he, "that that was the most imprudent act of my whole life; for had my mistress proved treacherous, what might not have been my fate—alone and disguised, in the circumstances in which I was placed, amidst the snares with which I was surrounded! But what more is said of me?"—"Sire, it is affirmed that your Majesty's posterity is not confined to the King of Rome. The secret chronicle states that he has two elder brothers: one, the offspring of a fair foreigner, whom you loved in a distant country; the other, the fruit of a connexion nearer at hand, in the bosom of your own capital. It was asserted, that both had been conveyed to Malmaison, before our departure; the one brought by his mother, and the other introduced by his tutor; and they were described to be the living portraits of their father."*

The Emperor laughed much at the extent of my information, as he termed it; and being now in a merry vein, he began to take a frank retrospect of his early years, relating many of the love-affairs and humorous adventures in which he had been engaged. He mentioned a supper that took place in the neighbourhood of the Saone at the commencement of the Revolution, and at which he had been present in company with Demazis. He described the whole with the utmost pleasantry. Demazis, he observed, was a good-natured fellow, or his patriotic eloquence might have proved fatal when opposed to the contrary doctrines of the other guests, and might even have brought him into some serious scrape. "You and I," he continued, "were at that time very far from each other."—"Not so very far, in point of distance, Sire," I replied, "though certainly very remote with respect to doctrines. At that time I was also in the neighbourhood of the Saone, on one of the quays of Lyons, where crowds of patriots were declaiming against the cannon which they had just discovered in some boats, and which they termed a counter-revolution. I very unopportunely proposed that they should make sure of the cannon, by administering to them the *civic oath*. However, I narrowly escaped being hanged for my folly. You see, Sire, that I might at that time have balanced your account, had any disaster befallen you among the aristocrats." This was not the only curious approximation that was mentioned in the course of the evening. The Emperor having related to me an interesting circumstance that took place in 1788, said, "Where were you at that time?"—"Sire," replied I, after a few moments recollection, "I was then at Martinique, supping every evening with the future Empress Josephine."

A shower of rain came on, and we were obliged to retire from our favourite path, which, the Emperor observed, we might probably at a future period look back to with pleasure. "Perhaps so," I replied; "but certainly that will

* It is said, that a codicil in the Emperor's will, which, however, must remain secret, completely confirms the above conjectures.

not be until we have forsaken it for ever. Meanwhile we must content ourselves with naming it the path of Philosophy, since it cannot be called the path of Lethe."

The Fauxbourg Saint-Germain, &c.—The Emperor's freedom from prejudice and ill-will.—The Characteristic language.

16th.—To-day the Emperor put some questions to me relative to the Fauxbourg Saint-Germain; the last bulwark of the old aristocracy, that refuge of old-fashioned prejudices; the *Germanic league*, as he called it. I told him, that before his last misfortune, his power had extended into every part of it: it had been invaded, and its name alone remained; it had been shaken and vanquished by glory; and that the victories of Austerlitz and Jena, and the triumph of Tilsit, had achieved its conquest. The younger portion of the inhabitants, and all who had generous hearts, could not be insensible to the glory of their country. The Emperor's marriage with Maria-Louisa gave the finishing stroke to this conversation. The few malcontents who remained, were either those whose ambition had not been gratified, and who are to be found in all classes, or some obstinate old men, and silly old women, bewailing their past influence. All reasonable and sensible persons had yielded to the superior talents of the Head of the State, and endeavoured to console themselves for their losses in the hope of a better prospect for their children. This was the point towards which all their ideas were directed. They gave the Emperor credit for his partiality to old family names; they agreed that any one else in his place would have annihilated them. They prized very highly the confidence with which the Emperor had collected individuals of ancient families about his person; and they valued him no less for the language he had made use of in making choice of their children to serve in the army:—"These names belong to France and to History; I am the guardian of their glory; I will not allow them to perish." These and other such expressions had gained him numbers of proselytes. The Emperor here expressed his apprehension that sufficient favour had not been shown to this party. "My system of amalgamation," said he, "required it: I wished and even directed favours to be conferred on them; but the ministers, who were the great mediators, never properly fulfilled my real intentions in that respect; either because they had not sufficient foresight, or because they feared that they might thus create rivals for favour, and diminish their own chances. M. Talleyrand, in particular, always showed great opposition to such a measure, and always resisted my favourable intentions towards the old nobility." I observed, however, that the greater part of those whom he had placed near him, had soon shown themselves attached to his person; that they had served him conscientiously, and had, generally speaking, remained faithful to him at the critical moment. The Emperor did not deny it, and even went so far as to say that the two-fold event of the King's return and his own abdication must naturally have had great influence on certain doctrines; and that, for his own part, he could see a great difference between the same conduct pursued in 1814 and in 1815.

And here I must observe, that since I have become acquainted with the Emperor's character, I have never known him to evince, for a single moment, the least feeling of anger or animosity against those individuals who had been most to blame in their conduct towards him. He gives no great credit to those who distinguished themselves by their good conduct: they had only done their duty. He is not very indignant against those who acted basely; he partly saw through their characters: they yielded to the impulse of their nature. He speaks of them coolly, and without animosity; attributing their conduct in some measure to existing circumstances, which he acknowledged were of a very perplexing nature, and threw the rest to the account of human weakness. Vanity was the ruin of Marmont: "Posterity will justly cast a shade upon his character," said he; "yet his heart will be more valued than the memory of his career. The conduct of Augereau was the result of his want of information, and the baseness of those who surrounded him; that of Berthier, of his want of spirit, and his absolute nullity of character."

I remarked, that the latter had let slip the best and easiest opportunity of rendering himself for ever illustrious, by frankly rendering his submission to the King, and entreating his Majesty's permission to withdraw from the world, and mourn in solitude the fate of him who had honoured him with the title of his companion in arms, and had called him his friend. "Yes," said the Emperor: "even this step, simple as it was, was beyond his power."—"His talents, his understanding," said I, "had always been a subject of doubt with us. Your Majesty's choice, your confidence, your great attachment, surprised us exceedingly."—"To say the truth," replied the Emperor, "Berthier was not without talent, and I am far from disavowing his merit, or my partiality for him; but his talent and merit were special and technical; beyond a limited point he had no mind whatever: and then he was so undecided."—I observed, that "he was, notwithstanding, full of pretensions and pride in his conduct towards us."—"Do you think, then, that the title of Favourite stands for nothing?" said the emperor. I added, that "he was very harsh and overbearing." "And what," said he, "my dear Las Cases, is more overbearing than weakness which feels itself protected by strength? Look at women, for example."

Berthier accompanied the Emperor in his carriage during his campaigns. As they drove along, the Emperor would examine the order-book and the report of the positions, whence he formed his resolutions, adopted his plans, and arranged the necessary movements. Berthier noted down his directions, and at the first station they came to, or during the first moments allotted to rest, whether by night or by day, he made out, in his turn, all the orders and individual details with admirable regularity, precision and despatch. This was a kind of duty at which he shewed himself always ready and indefatigable. "This was the special merit of Berthier," said the Emperor: "it was most valuable to me; no other talent could have made up for the want of it."

I now return to notice some characteristic traits of the Emperor. He invariably speaks with perfect coolness, without passion, without prejudice, and without resentment, of the events and the persons connected with his life. He seems as though he could be equally capable of becoming the ally of his most cruel enemy, and of living with the man who had done him the greatest wrong. He speaks of his past history as if it had occurred three centuries ago; in his recitals and observations he speaks the language of past ages; he is like a spirit discoursing in the Elysian fields; his conversations are true dialogues of the dead. He speaks of himself as of a third person; noticing the Emperor's actions, pointing out the faults with which history may reproach him, and analysing the reasons and the motives which might be alleged in his justification.

He never can excuse himself, he says, by throwing blame on others, since he never followed any but his own decision. He may complain, at the worst, of false informations, but never of bad counsel. He surrounded himself with the best possible advisers, but he always adhered to his own opinion, and he was far from repenting of so doing. "It is," said he, "the indecision and anarchy of agents which produce anarchy and feebleness in results. In order to form a just opinion respecting the faults produced by the sole personal decision of the Emperor, it will be necessary to throw into the scale the great actions of which he would have been deprived, and the other faults which he would have been induced to commit, by those very counsels which he is blamed for not having followed."

In viewing the complicated circumstances of his fall, he looks upon things so much in a mass, and from so high a point, that individuals escape his notice. He never evinces the least symptom of virulence towards those of whom it might be supposed he has the greatest reason to complain. His greatest mark of reprobation, and I have had frequent occasion to notice it, is to preserve silence with respect to them, whenever they are mentioned in his presence. But how often has he not been heard to restrain the violent and less reserved expressions of those about him? "You are not acquainted with men," he said to us; "they are difficult to comprehend, if one wishes to be strictly just. Can they understand or explain even their own characters? Almost all those who abandoned me, would, had I continued to be prosperous, never, perhaps, have dreamed of their own defection. There are vices and virtues which depend on circumstances. Our last trials were beyond all human strength! Besides, I was forsaken rather than betrayed; there was more of weakness than of perfidy around me. It was the *denial of St. Peter*: tears and repentance are probably at hand. And where will you find, in the page of history, any one possessing a greater number of friends and partizans? Who was ever more popular and more beloved? Who was ever more ardently and deeply regretted? Here from this very rock, on viewing the present disorders in France, who would not be tempted to say that I still reign there? The Kings and Princes, my allies, have remained faithful to me to the last, they were carried away by the people in a mass; and those who were around me, found themselves overwhelmed and stunned by an irresistible whirlwind .... No! human nature might have appeared in a more odious light, and I might have had greater cause of complaint!"

On the Officers of the Emperor's household, in 1814.—Plan of address to the King.

17th.—The Emperor asked me some questions to-day relative to the officers of his household. With the exception of two or three, at the most, who had drawn upon themselves the contempt of the very party to which they had gone over, nothing could be said against them; the majority had even evinced an ardent devotion to the Emperor's interests. The Emperor then made enquiries respecting some of these individuals in particular, calling them by their names; and I could not but express my approbation of them all. "What do you tell me?" said he, interrupting me hastily while I was speaking of one of them; "and yet I gave him so bad a reception at the Thuilleries on my return! Ah!

I fear I have committed some involuntary acts of injustice! This comes of being obliged to take for granted the first story that is told, and of not having a single moment to spare for verification! I fear too that I have left many debts of gratitude in arrear! How unfortunate it is to be incapable of doing every thing one's self!"

I replied—"Sire, it is true that if blame be attached to the officers of your household, it must be shared equally by all; a fact, however, which must humble us strangely in the eyes of foreign nations. As soon as the King appeared, they hastened to him, not as to the sovereign whom your abdication had left us, but as to one who had never ceased to be our sovereign. Not with the dignity of men proud of having always fulfilled their duties, but with the equivocal embarrassment of unskilful courtiers. Each individual sought only to justify himself: your majesty was from that instant disavowed and abjured; the title of Emperor was dropped. The Ministers, the Nobles, the intimate friends of your Majesty, styled you simply '*Bonaparte*,' and blushed not for themselves or their nation. They Excused themselves by saying that they were compelled to serve; that they could not do otherwise, through dread of the treatment they might have experienced." The Emperor here recognised a true picture of our national character. He said we were still the same people as our ancestors the Gauls; that we still retained the same levity, the same inconstancy, and, above all, the same vanity. "When shall we," said he, "exchange this vanity for a little pride!"

"The officers of your Majesty's household," said I, "neglected a noble opportunity of acquiring both honour and popularity. There were above one-hundred and fifty officers of the household; a great number of them belonged to the first families, and were men of independent fortune. It was for them to have set an example, which, being followed by others, might have given another impulse to the national attitude, and afforded us a claim on public esteem."—"Yes," said the Emperor, "if all the upper classes had acted in that way, affairs might have turned out very differently. The old editors of the public journals would not then have indulged in their chimeras of the good old times; we should not then have been annoyed with their dissertations on the straight line and the curve line; the King would have adhered honestly to his charter; I should never have dreamed of quitting the Island of Elba; the head of the nation would have been recorded in history with greater honour and dignity; and we should all have been gainers."

The Emperor's idea of reserving Corsica.—His opinion of Robespierre.—His idea respecting public opinion.—Expiatory intention of the Emperor with regard to the victims of the Revolution.

18th.—After the accustomed occupation of the day, I accompanied the Emperor to the garden about four o'clock. He had just completed his dictation on the subject of Corsica. Having concluded every thing he had to say relative to that island, and to Paoli, he adverted to the interest which he himself excited there, while yet so young at the time of his separation from Paoli. He added, that latterly he might to a certainty have united in his favour the wishes, the sentiments, and the efforts of the whole population of Corsica: and that, had he retired to that island on quitting Paris, he would have been beyond the reach of any foreign power whatever. He had an idea of doing so when he abdicated in favour of his son. He was on the point of reserving to himself the possession of Corsica during his life. No obstacle at sea would have obstructed his passage thither. But he abandoned that design for the sake of rendering his abdication the more sincere and the more advantageous to France. His residence in the centre of the Mediterranean, in the bosom of Europe, so near France and Italy, might have furnished a lasting pretext to the Allies. He even preferred America to England, from the same motive and the same idea. It is true that in the sincerity of his own measures, he neither did, nor could foresee, his unjust and violent banishment to Saint Helena.

The Emperor, next proceeded to take a review of different points of the Revolution, dwelt particularly on Robespierre, whom he did not know, but whom he believed to be destitute of talent, energy, or system. He considered him, notwithstanding, as the real scape-goat of the Revolution, sacrificed as soon as he attempted to arrest it in its course: the common fate, he observed, of all who, before himself, (Napoleon) had ventured to take that step. The Terrorists and their doctrine survived Robespierre; and if their excesses were not continued, it was because they were obliged to bow to public opinion. They threw all the blame on Robespierre; but the latter declared shortly before his death, that he was a stranger to the recent executions, and that he had not appeared in the Committees for six weeks previously. Napoleon confessed that while he was with the army of Nice, he had seen some long letters addressed by Robespierre to his brother, condemning the horrors of the Commissioners of the Convention, who, as he expressed it, were ruining the Revolution by their tyranny and atrocities. "Cambacérès, who," observed the Emperor, "must be a good authority on subjects relating to that period, answered an enquiry which I one day addressed to him respecting the condemnation of Robespierre, in these remarkable words: 'Sire, that was a sentence without a trial;' adding that Robespierre had more foresight and conception than was generally imagined. That after he should have succeeded in subduing the unbridled factions which he had to oppose, his intention was to restore a system of order and moderation. 'Some time previous to his fall,' added Cambacérès, 'he delivered a most admirable speech on this subject: it was not thought proper to insert it in the Moniteur, and all trace of it is now lost.'"

This is not the first instance I have heard of omissions and want of accuracy in the Moniteur. In the reports inserted in that journal relative to the proceedings of the Assembly, there must be a period remarkable for incorrectness; as the minutes of these proceedings were for a time arbitrarily drawn up by one of the Committees.

Those who are induced to believe that Robespierre was at once wearied, satiated, and alarmed by the Revolution, and had resolved on checking it, affirm that he would not take any decided step until after he had read his famous speech. He considered it so fine, that he had no doubt of its effect on the Assembly. If this be true, his mistake or his vanity cost him dear. Those who think differently, assert that Danton and Camille-des-Moulins had precisely the same views; and yet that Robespierre sacrificed them. To these it is replied, that Robespierre sacrificed them to preserve his popularity, because he judged that the decisive moment had not yet arrived; or because he did not wish to resign to them the glory of the enterprise.

Be this as it may, it is certain that the nearer we approach to the instruments and the agents in that catastrophe, the greater obscurity and mystery we find; and this uncertainty will but increase with time. Thus the page of history, will on this point as on many others, become the record, not so much of the events which really occurred, as of the statements which are given of them.

In the course of our conversation, relative to Robespierre, the Emperor said, that he had been very well acquainted with his brother, the younger Robespierre, the representative to the Army of Italy. He said nothing against this young man, whom he had inspired with great confidence and considerable enthusiasm for his person. Previously to the 9th of Thermidor, young Robespierre being recalled by his brother, who was then secretly laying his plans, insisted on Napoleon's accompanying him to Paris. The latter experienced the greatest difficulty in ridding himself of the importunity, and at length only escaped it by requesting the interference of the General-in-chief, Dumerbion, whose entire confidence he possessed, and who represented that it was absolutely necessary he should remain where he was." Had I followed young Robespierre," said the Emperor, "how different might have been my career! On what trivial circumstances does human fate depend!—Some office would doubtless have been assigned to me; and I might at that moment have been destined to attempt a sort of Vendemiaire. But I was then very young; my ideas were not yet fixed. It is probable, indeed, that I should not have undertaken any task that might have been allotted to me; but supposing the contrary case, and even admitting that I had been successful, what results could I have hoped for? In Vendemiaire the revolutionary fever was totally subdued; in Thermidor it was still raging in its utmost fury and at its greatest height."

"Public opinion," said the Emperor on another occasion, when conversing on another subject, "is an invisible and mysterious power which it is impossible to resist: nothing is more unsteady, more vague, or more powerful; and capricious as it may be, it is, nevertheless, just and reasonable more frequently than is supposed. On becoming Provisional Consul, the first act of my administration was the banishment of fifty anarchists. Public opinion, which had at first been furiously hostile to them, suddenly turned in their favour, and I was forced to retract. But some time afterwards, these same anarchists, having shown a disposition to engage in plots, were again assailed by that very public opinion, which had now returned to support me. Thus, through the errors that were committed at the time of the restoration, popularity was secured to the regicides, who but a moment before had been proscribed by the great mass of the nation.

"It belonged to me," continued the Emperor, "to shed a lustre over the memory of Louis XVI in France, and to purify the nation of the crimes with which she had been sullied by frantic acts and unfortunate fatalities. The Bourbons, being of the royal family, and coming from abroad, merely avenged their own private cause, and augmented the national opprobrium. I, on the contrary, being one of the people, should have raised the character of the nation, by banishing from society, in her name, those whose crimes had disgraced her. This was my intention, but I proceeded prudently in the fulfilment of it. The three expiatory altars at St. Denis were but a prelude to my design. The Temple of Glory, on the site of the *Magdelaine*, was to have been devoted to this object with still greater solemnity.

There, near the tomb and over the very bones of the political victims of our revolution, human monuments and religious ceremonies would have consecrated their memory in the name of the French people. This is a secret that was not known to above ten individuals: though it would have been necessary to communicate a hint of the design to those who might have been intrusted with the arrangement of the edifice. I should not have executed my scheme in less than ten years; but what precautions had I not adopted; how carefully had I smoothed every difficulty, and removed every obstruction! All would have applauded my design, and no one would have suffered from it. So much depends on circumstances and forms," added he, "that in my reign, Carnot would not have dared to write a memorial, boasting the death of the King, though he did so under the Bourbons. I should have leagued with public opinion in punishing him; while public opinion sided with him in rendering him unassailable."

Cascade at Briars.

19th.—My son and I rose very early. Our task had been finished on the preceding day; and as the Emperor could not want me for some time, we availed ourselves of the fineness of the morning to explore the neighbourhood of our abode.

Passing through the valley of James-Town, on the right of our little level height at Briars, was a deep ravine, the sides of which were intersected by numerous perpendicular clefts. We descended into the ravine, not without difficulty, and found ourselves at the edge of a little limpid streamlet, beside which grew abundance of cresses. We amused ourselves by gathering them as we passed along; and after a few windings we soon reached the extremity of the valley and the streamlet, which are closed transversely by a huge pointed mass of rock, from the summit of which issues a pretty cascade, produced from the waters of the surrounding heights. This waterfall descending into the valley forms the streamlet, along which we had just passed, and which sometimes rolls in a torrent to the sea. The water of the cascade was at this moment dispersed above our heads in small rain or light vapour; but in stormy weather it rushes forth in a torrent, and furiously dashes through the ravine till it reaches the sea. To us the scene presented a gloomy, solitary, and melancholy aspect; and it was altogether so interesting that we quitted it with regret.

To-day was Sunday, and we all dined with the Emperor: he good-humouredly observed that we formed a state party.

After dinner the circle of our amusements was not very extensive: he asked us whether we would have a comedy, an opera, or a tragedy. We decided in favour of a comedy, and he himself read a portion of Moliere's *Avare*, which was continued by other individuals of the party. The Emperor had a cold, and was slightly feverish. He withdrew early from his walk in the garden, and desired me to see him again that evening if he should not have gone to bed. My son and I accompanied the rest of the gentlemen to the town; and on our return the Emperor had retired to rest.

First and only excursion during our abode at Briars.—The Admiral's Ball.

20th.—The Emperor, after dictating as usual with one of the gentlemen, called me about five o'clock. He was alone; the rest of the gentlemen and my son having gone to the town, where the Admiral was that evening to give a ball. The Emperor and I walked along the road leading to the town, until we came within sight of the sea and shipping. On the left, in the depth of the valley, was a pretty little house. The Emperor stood for a considerable time with his glass at his eye, examining the garden, which appeared to be very well cultivated, and in which a group of beautiful children were at play, attended by their mother. We were informed that this house belonged to Major Hudson, a resident of the Island; the same gentleman who had lent me the *Annual Register*. The house was situated at the bottom of the ravine which commences in the vicinity of Briars, and near the curious cascade which I have already noticed. The Emperor took a fancy to go down to the house, though it was now nearly six o'clock. The road was extremely steep: we found it longer and more difficult of descent than we had expected; and we reached the bottom of the ravine quite out of breath. We took a survey of the little domain, which had evidently been laid out as the residence of a permanent occupant, and not as the mere temporary abode of a traveller passing to a foreign land; and after receiving the attentions of the master of the house, and paying a few compliments to the mistress, the Emperor took his leave.

But the evening was already far advanced, and we were very much fatigued; we therefore accepted the horses that were offered us, and speedily returned to our hut and our dinner. This little excursion, and the exercise of riding on horseback which had been so long relinquished, seemed to do the Emperor good.

He desired that I would go to the Admiral's ball, in spite of my reluctance to leave him. At half-past eight o'clock, he observed that the night was dark, the road bad, and that it was time I had set out. He insisted on my leaving him, and he entered his room, where I saw him undress and retire to bed. He again desired me to go; and I unwillingly obeyed. I left him alone; and thus, for the first time, violated a custom which had become most dear to me.

I proceeded on foot to the town. The Admiral had given great *eclat* to his ball. It had been talked of for a considerable time before. He wished it to be understood that the entertainment was given solely on our account, and we had been formally invited. Was it most advisable to accept or to decline the invitaton? Something might be said on both sides. Political misfortunes did not require that we should assume the appearance of domestic sorrow; it might be proper, and even useful, to mingle cheerfully in company with our jailors. We might, therefore, adopt either resolution indifferently. We determined to go. But what sort of conduct were we to observe? Should we assume pride, or employ address? The first might be attended with inconvenience; in our situation, every wounded pretension became an insult. In the second there could be no impropriety: to receive marks of politeness as though we were accustomed to them, and as though they were our due, and to overlook any little want of respect, was certainly the wisest course. I arrived at the ball very late, and left it very early. I was very much pleased with the entertainment in every respect.

My comduct while the Emperor was at Elba.

21st—22d.—The Emperor, who had often questioned me on the line of conduct pursued by many of his ministers, members of his council, and officers of his household, during his residence at the Island of Elba, at length called me to account in my turn, saying:—"But you yourself, Las Cases, what did you do after the arrival of the King? What happened to you all that time? Come, give me an account of your conduct: you know this is my way; and it is the only plan by which we can properly classify what we say, or what we wish to learn. Besides, it will furnish you with another article for your journal. And, don't you see?" added he, jokingly, "your biographers will only have the trouble of extracting; the thing will be all ready written to their hands."

"Sire," I replied, "you shall have a literal statement of every thing; though I have but little to say. I commanded, on the 31t of March, the 10th legion of the National Guard of Paris, that which was appointed as the guard of the Legislative Body. We lost, during the day, a considerable number of men. At night I heard of the capitulation; I wrote to the officer next in rank to myself, and transferred to him the command of my legion, informing him, that though in my quality of member of the Council of State, I had previously received orders to proceed elsewhere, yet I had not wished to abandon my legion at the moment of danger; but that the event which had just occurred having changed the aspect of affairs, I must now proceed forthwith to fulfil new duties.

"At day-break I set out on the road to Fontainebleau, and found myself in the midst of the wrecks of Marmont's and Mortier's detachments. I was on foot, but I doubted not I should be able to purchase a horse. I soon, however, discovered that soldiers in retreat are neither just nor civil. At that disastrous moment, my uniform of a National Guard was insulted, and I was myself ill-treated.

"After an hour's walk, overpowered by the fatigue of the journey, joined to the want of rest which I had experienced for two or three nights previously; seeing around me no face that I knew, and having no hope of procuring a horse, I determined, with a sorrowful heart, to return to the capital.

"The National Guard was ordered out to assist in the triumphant entry of the enemy: there was even a probability of its being selected as a guard of honour to the Sovereigns who had conquered us. I determined to be absent from my home. I had conveyed my wife and children safely out of Paris a week or two before, and for a few days had recourse to the hospitality of a friend. I never went out of doors but in a shabby great-coat, visiting the coffee-houses and public places, and joining the different groups which were formed in the streets. My object was to make observations on persons and things, and above all, to learn the real feelings of the people. How many extraordinary occurrences did I not witness in the course of my rambles!

"I saw, in front of the residence of the Emperor of Russia, men distinguised by their rank, and calling themselves Frenchmen, exerting their utmost endeavours to induce the rabble to call out '*Long live Alexander, our deliverer!*'

"I saw, Sire, your monument on the Place Vendôme resist the efforts of a few wretches, belonging to the lowest dregs of the people, who had been hired by persons of note.

"Finally, in one of the corners of the Place Vendôme, before the hotel of the Commandant of the place, I saw one of the officers of your household trying to prevail on young conscripts to enter another service than yours; but he received from them a lesson that might have made him blush for his own conduct.

"Doubtless, those to whom I here allude will exclaim that I mingled with the *rabble*; and yet it may be with justice affirmed that the acts of baseness which then disgraced France did not originate with the rabble. These acts were far from obtaining the countenance of the lower classes of the people; on the contrary, they were decidedly censured by the uprightness, generosity, and nobleness of sentiment manifested in the public streets. What reproaches might I not convey, were I to repeat all that I heard on this subject!

"Your Majesty abdicated. I had refused my signature to the act of adherence of the Council of State; but I thought I might make amends for this by an additional act of adherence. The Moniteur was every day filled with articles of this kind; yet mine was not deemed worthy the honour of insertion.

"At length the King arrived: he was henceforth our Sovereign. He appointed a day for the reception of those individuals who had been presented to Louis XVI. I proceeded to the Thuilleries to avail myself of this prerogative. What were my reflections on entering those apartments which had so lately been filled with your glory and power! And yet I presented myself to the King sincerely and in good faith; my foresight never led me even to think of your return.

"Deputations to the King were multiplied beyond number: a meeting of the officers of the naval establishment was proposed. To the person who communicated this fact to me, I replied, that nothing could be more gratifying to my heart than to join my old comrades, none of whom could entertain sentiments purer than I did; but that the offices I had filled placed me in a peculiar and delicate situation, and that motives of prudence must deter me from appearing where the zeal of a president might lead him to employ expressions which I neither could nor would sanction by my opinion or presence.

"Subsequently, however, in spite of my mortification and disgust, I determined, at the solicitation of some friends, to think of something for myself. The Council of State was recomposed; several members of the last Council assured me, in spite of my recent conjectures on that point, that nothing was easier than to retain my office; that they had succeeded merely by an application to the Chancellor of France. I had not courage to venture a moment's encroachment on his Lordship's time; and therefore contented myself with writing to acquaint him that I had been Master of requests to the last Council of State; and that if that circumstance were not sufficient to exclude me from becoming a member of the new assembly, I begged him to recommend me to the King as a Councillor of State. I observed that I would not advance as claims to favour, my eleven years' emigration, or the loss of my patrimony in the King's cause. In these respects I conceived I had only done my duty; which I had at all times, to the best of my knowledge, fulfilled faithfully and to the utmost. This language, as may well be supposed, deprived me even of the honour of a reply.

"Meanwhile the new situation of Paris, the sight of the foreign troops, the acclamations of every kind were more than I could endure; and I adopted the determination of going for a short time to London, where I should meet with old friends, who might afford me all the consolation of which I was susceptible. Then, again, I recollected that I might find in London the same tumult and the same exultation that had driven me from Paris: this proved to be the fact. London was the scene of festivity and rejoicing, to celebrate the triumphs of the English and our humiliation.

"During my stay in London, the marine establishment was re-modelled at Paris, and the Chevalier de Grimaldi, one of my old comrades, whom I had not seen or heard of for a length of time, was appointed a member of the Committee. He called on my wife, and expressed his surprise that I had not put in my claims; observing that I was entitled by law to return to the corps, or to retire on a certain pension. He advised my wife to bring me to a decision on the subject, and to rely on his friendship; adding, that there was no time to be lost. I attached higher value to this mark of attention, than to the favour which it was intended to procure me. However, I wrote to the Committee, requesting, that as I was desirous of wearing a uniform to which I had become attached, I might be allowed to enjoy the honorary title of *Capitane de Visseau*; while at the same time I renounced the pension, to which I did not conceive myself entitled.

"I returned to Paris. The diversity of opinion and the irritation of the public mind were extreme. I had for a long time lived in the greatest retirement. I now confined myself entirely to the domestic circle of my wife and children. Never at any former period of my life did I prove myself a better husband or a better father; and never, perhaps, was I more physically happy.

"As I was one day reading, in the *Journal des Debats*, an an account of a work of M. Beauchamp, I found mentioned the names of several gentlemen who were stated to have assembled on the Place Louis XV on the 31st March, to excite sentiments in favour of royalty; and my name was among the number. It was in good company, no doubt; but at the same time the statement was untrue; and I should have been considerably lowered in the estimation of many if it had been believed. I wrote to request a correction of the error, which was calculated to render me the subject of congratulations to which I was in no way entitled.

I observed, that it was out of my power to have acted in the way described, whatever might have been my inclination. As the commander of a legion of the National Guard, I had contracted obligations from which no consideration on earth could free me; and I sent my letter to the Deputy Chabaud-Latour, one of the proprietors of the *Journal des Debats*, a man for whom I entertained a great esteem. He declined publishing my letter, purely from good intentions towards me. I then addressed it to the editor; but he refused to insert it on account of difference of opinion.

Meanwhile, the state of the public mind indicated an inevitable and speedy catastrophe. Every thing foreboded that the Bourbons would share the fate of the Stuarts. My wife and I used every evening to amuse ourselves in reading Hume's History of England. We began at Charles I, and your Majesty arrived before we had got to James II." (Here the Emperor could not repress his laughter.)

"Your Majesty's advancement and arrival," continued I, "were to us a subject of the greatest astonishment and anxiety. I was far from foreseeing the honourable voluntary exile which it would gain for me in the end; for I was then unknown to your Majesty; and circumstances arising out of that event alone brought me to your presence. Had I filled the most trivial post under the King; had I even been a frequent attendant at the Thuilleries, which would have been very natural and consistent with propriety, I should not have appeared for a length of time in your Majesty's presence. Not, indeed, that I should have had any thing to reproach myself with, or that my attachment to you would have been the less sincere; but because I should not have wished to pass for a piece of court furniture, or to seem always ready to offer incense at the shrine of power. I should have awaited an oppointment, instead of pressing forward to solicit one. But as it was, I felt myself so much at liberty, every thing about me was in such perfect harmony, that I seemed to form a part of the great event. I, therefore, eagerly hastened to meet the first glance of your Majesty; I felt as though I had claims on your kindness and favour. On your return from Waterloo, the same sentiments brought me immediately and spontaneously near your person, which I have never since quitted. If I was then attracted by your public glory, I am now attached by your private virtues; and if it be true, that the gratification of my feelings then cost me some sacrifice, I now find myself repaid a hundred-fold, by the happiness I enjoy in being able to tell you so.

"It would, however, be difficult to describe the extreme disgust I felt at every thing during the ten months of your absence. I felt an utter contempt for mankind and worldly vanities. Every illusion was destroyed, all interest had vanished. Every thing appeared to be at an end, or to be undeserving of the smallest value. During my emigration, I had received the cross of St. Louis; an ordinance decreed that it was to be legitimatized by a new brevet. I had not spirit to put in my claim. Another ordinance directed that the titles bestowed by your Majesty should be sent in to be confirmed; but I felt indifferent with regard to compromising those which I had obtained during the Empire. In fine, I received a letter from the Marine department, informing me that my captain's commission had just been forwarded thither, and there it still remains.

"Your Majesty's absence was to me a widowhood, the affliction and grief of which I concealed from no one. But on your return I was repaid for all by the testimony borne by those who surrounded you, and to whom I had previously been scarcely known. At your Majesty's first levee, the individual who was *ad interim* at the head of the department of foreign affairs, coming from the presence, took me aside to a window, and told me to go home and prepare, as I should probably have to set out on a journey. He had just, he said, proposed me to your Majesty, adding that he had represented me as a madman, but mad for love of you. I wished to know whither I was to be sent; but that, he said, he neither would nor could tell me. I never heard any thing more of the matter.

"M. Regnault de Saint-Jean d'Angeli placed me on the list of the Imperial Commissioners whom your Majesty sent to the departments. I assured him that I was ready to do any thing; but I observed that I was *noble* and an *emigrant*, and that these two words pronounced by the first comer would be sufficient to annul me, in case of necessity, at any time or in any place. He acknowledged the justice of my observation, and relinquished his intention.

"A Senator next solicited that your Majesty would appoint me to the perfecture of Metz, his native town. He requested me to make this sacrifice for only three months, in order, as he said, to conciliate the popular mind, and set things to rights. At length Decrès and the Duke of Bassano proposed me as a Councillor of State; and, the third day after your arrival, your Majesty signed my appointment."

23d.—The Emperor was still indisposed: he confined himself to his room, and would see nobody. He sent for me at 9 o'clock in the evening. I found him very low-spirited and melancholy. He scarcely spoke to me, and I did not dare to say any thing to him. If I regarded his illness as merely physical, it grieved me sincerely:—if he laboured under mental affliction, how much more was I grieved that I could not employ all the resources of consolation with which the heart naturally overflows for those whom we truly love. The Emperor dismissed me in about half an hour.

24th.—The Emperor continued indisposed, and still declined seeing any body. He sent for me to dine with him at a late hour. Dinner was served on a littl table beside the sofa on which he was lying. He ate heartily. He said that he stood in need of some sudden revulsion of the constitution, which he should soon obtain; so well did he understand his own temperament. After dinner he took up the memoirs of Marshal de Villars, which amused him. He read aloud many passages, which revived former recollections, and gave rise to many anecdotes.

The Emperor's temperament.—Riding.—Notions of Medicine.

25th.—The Emperor still continued unwell: he had passed a bad night. At his desire I dined with him beside the sofa, which he was unable to leave. he was, however, evidently much better. He had a heap of books scattered around him on the sofa. The rapidity of his imagination, the fatigue of dwelling always on the same subject, or of reading what he already knew, caused him to take up and throw down the books one after the other. At length he fixed on Racine's Iphigenia, and amused himself by pointing out the beauties, and discussing the few faults, to be found in that work. He dismissed me at an early hour.

Contrary to the general opinion, in which I myself once participated, the Emperor is far from possessing a strong constitution. His limbs are large, but his fibres are relaxed. With a very expanded chest, he is constantly labouring under the effects of cold. His body is subject to the influence of the slightest accidents. The smell of paint is sufficient to make him ill; certain dishes, or the slightest degree of damp, immediately take a severe effect on him.

His body is far from being a body of iron, as is generally supposed: all his strength is in his mind. His prodigious exertions abroad, and his incessant labours at home, are known to every one. No sovereign ever underwent so much bodily fatigue. The most remarkable instance of the Emperor's activity and exertion was his ride without stirrups from Valladolid to Burgos, (a distance of thirty-five Spanish leagues in five hours and a half; that is to say, upwards of seven leagues an hour.)* The Emperor had set out accompanied by a numerous escort, in case of danger from the Guerillas; but at every yard he left some of his company behind him, and he arrived at Burgos with but few followers. His ride from Vienna to the Simmering, a distance of eighteen or twenty leagues, is also frequently talked of. The Emperor rode to breakfast at the Simmering, and returned to Vienna immediately after. Napoleon often hunted to the distance of thirty-eight leagues, and never less than fifteen. One day a Russian officer, who had come as a courier from Saint-Petersburgh in the space of twelve or thirteen days, arrived at Fontainebleau at the moment when the Emperor was about to set out on a hunt. The officer had the honour to be invited to join the hunting-party. He of course accepted the invitation; but he dropped down in the forest, overcome by fatigue, and was not found until after considerable search had been made for him.

I have known the Emperor to be engaged in business in the Council of State for eight or nine hours successively, and afterwards rise with his ideas as clear as when he sat down. I have seen him at Saint-Helena peruse books for ten or twelve hours in succession, on the most abstruse subjects, without appearing in the least fatigued. He has suffered, unmoved, the greatest shocks that ever man experienced. On his return from Moscow or Leipsic, after he had communicated the disastrous event in the Council of State, he said: "It has been reported in Paris, that this misfortune turned my hair gray; but you see it is not so, (pointing to his head;) and I hope I shall be able to support many other reverses." But these prodigious exertions are made only, as it were, in despite of his physical powers, which never appear less susceptible than when his mind is in full activity.

* This may appear incredible. Indeed I myself feel doubts now when I read over the statement. But I know that when the subject was spoken of one day at dinner at Longwood, it underwent much discussion, and I noted down on paper what was then admitted to be the correct account. Besides, many individuals who accompanied the Emperor are still living: and the fact may be ascertained.

The Emperor eats very irregularly, but generally very little. He often says, that a man may hurt himself by eating too much, but never by eating too little. He will remain four-and-twenty hours without eating, only to get an appetite for the ensuing day. But if he eats little, he drinks still less. A single glass of Madeira or Champaign is sufficient to restore his strength, and to produce cheerfulness of spirits. He sleeps very little and very irregularly, generally rising at day-break to read or write, and afterwards lying down to sleep again.

The Emperor has no faith in medicine, and never takes any. He had adopted a peculiar mode of treatment for himself. Whenever he found himself unwell, his plan was to run into an extreme, the opposite of what happened to be his habit at the time. This he calls restoring the equilibrium of nature. If, for instance, he had been inactive for a length of time, he would suddenly ride about sixty miles, or hunt for a whole day. If, on the contrary, he had been harrassed by great fatigues, he would resign himself to a state of absolute rest for twenty-four hours. These unexpected shocks infallibly brought about an internal crisis, and instantly produced the desired effect: this remedy, he observed, never failed.

The Emperor's lymphatic system is deranged, and his blood circulates with difficulty. Nature, he said, had endowed him with two important advantages: the one was, the power of sleeping whenever he needed repose, at any hour, and in any place; another was, that he was incapable of committing any injurious excess either in eating or drinking. "If," said he, "I go the least beyond my mark, my stomach instantly revolts." He is subject to nausea from very slight causes; a mere tickling cough is sufficient to produce that effect on him.

Our mode of living at Briars.—My first visit to Longwood.—Infernal machine; its history.

26th—28. On the 26th, the Emperor dressed very early: he found himself quite recovered. He wished to walk out, as the weather was very fine; and, besides, his room had not been put in order for three days. We went into the garden, and he chose to breakfast under the arbour. He was in good spirits, and his conversation turned upon many different subjects and persons.

The Emperor's health being now perfectly restored, he resumed his usual occupation, which, indeed, was his only source of amusement. Reading, dictating, and walking in the garden, filled up all his time during the day. He still occasionally resorted to his favourite path, though the turn of the season, and the change of the moon, had nearly put a stop to our evening walks. The numerous visitors who came to Mr. Balcombe's house, attracted by the hope of meeting the Emperor, annoyed him very much, and, indeed, compelled him to withdraw himself altogether. We therefore remained shut up in our little dwelling. We at first understood that we should remain at Briars only a few days; but six weeks had passed away, and we had yet heard nothing respecting our removal. All this time the Emperor had been as much confined as he had been on board of the vessel. He had taken only one excursion, which was when he visited Major Hudson; and we afterwards learned that this circumstance had occasioned alarm. It had been whispered about at the Admiral's ball, and had reached the ears of our high authorities, who were thrown into great consternation by the event.

The workmen continued their labours at Longwood, which was to be our new residence. The troops who had come with us from England, were encamped in the neighbourhood. The Colonel gave a ball, to which we were invited. The Emperor wished me to go, and that I should, at the same time, take the opportunity of inspecting our future abode. I went with Madame Bertrand, in a carriage drawn by six oxen. In this Merovingian equipage we proceeded to Longwood. This was the first opportunity I had had of seeing any part of the island except the neighbourhood of Briars. The whole road along which we passed presented continued evidences of a great natural convulsion. We saw nothing but huge masses of rock, totally destitute of vegetation. If, at every change of the horizon, we perceived a trace of verdure or a few clusters of trees; yet on a nearer approach, all vanished like the creations of a poet's fancy; we found only a few marine plants and wild shrubs; or what was still worse, some wretched gum-trees. These were the only ornaments of Longwood. I returned on horseback about six o'clock. The Emperor put many questions to me concerning our new residence. Finding that I did not speak of it very enthusiastically, he asked at once whether he should gain or lose by the change. I told what I thought in one sentence. "Sire," said I, "we are here in a cage; there we shall be in a fold."

28th.—The Emperor changed his military uniform, which he had put on to go on board the Bellerophon, for a fancy dress-coat. In the course of conversation this day, the Emperor adverted to the numerous conspiracies which had been formed against him. The infernal machine was mentioned in its turn. This diabolical invention, which gave rise to so many conjectures, and led to the death of so many victims, was the work of the Royalists, who obtained the first idea of it from the Jacobins.

The Emperor stated, that a hundred furious Jacobins, the real authors of the scenes of September, the 10th of August, &c. had resolved to get rid of the First Consul, for which purpose they invented a 15 or 16 pound howitzer, which, on being thrown into the carriage, would explode by its own concussion, and hurl destruction on every side. To make sure of their object, they proposed to lay caltrops along a part of the road, which, by suddenly impeding the horses, would of course render it impossible for the carriage to move on. The man who was employed to lay down the caltrops, entertaining some suspicions of the job which he had been set upon, as well as of the good intentions of his employers, communicated the business to the police. The conspirators were soon traced, and were apprehended near the Jardin des Plantes, in the act of trying the effect of the machine, which made a terrible explosion. The First Consul, whose policy it was not to divulge the numerous conspiracies of which he was the object, did not give publicity to this, but contented himself with imprisoning the criminals. He soon relaxed his orders for keeping them in close confinement, and they were allowed a certain degree of liberty. In the same prison in which these Jacobins were confined, some Royalists were also imprisoned for an attempt to assassinate the First Consul, by means of air-guns. These two parties formed a league together; and the Royalists transmitted to their friends out of prison the idea of the infernal machine, as being preferable to any other plan of destruction.

It is very remarkable, that on the evening of the catastrophe, the Emperor expressed an extreme repugnance to go out. Madame Bonaparte and some intimate friends absosolutely forced him to go to an oratorio. They roused him from a sofa where he was fast asleep; one fetched him his sword, and another his hat. As he drove along in the carriage, he fell asleep again, and awoke suddenly, saying that he had dreamed he was drowning in the Tagliamento. To explain what he alluded to, it is necessary to mention that some years previously, when he was General of the army of Italy, he passed the Tagliamento in his carriage during the night, contrary to the advice of every one about him. In the ardour of youth, and heedless of every obstacle, he crossed the river surrounded by a hundred men armed with poles and torches. His carriage was, however, soon afloat; Napoleon ran the most imminent danger, and for some time gave himself up for lost. At the moment when he now awoke, on his way to the oratorio, he was in the midst of a conflagration, the carriage was lifted up, and the passage of the Tagliamento came fresh upon his mind. The illusion, however, was but momentary; a dreadful explosion immediately ensued. "We are blown up!" exclaimed the First Consul to Lannes and Bessieres, who were in the carriage with him. They proposed immediately to make arrests; but he desired them not to be too hasty. The First Consul arrived safe, and appeared at the opera as though nothing had happened. He was preserved by the desperate driving of his coachman. The machine injured only one or two individuals who closed the escort.

The most trivial circumstances often lead to the most important results. The coachman was intoxicated; no doubt this proved the means of saving the life of the First Consul. The man's intoxication was so great, that it was not until next morning he could be made to comprehend what had happened. He had taken the explosion for the firing of a salute. Immediately after this event, measures were adopted against the Jacobins, who had been convicted of meditating the crime; and a considerable number were banished. They, however, were not the real criminals, whose discovery was brought about by another very singular chance.

Three or four hundred drivers of *fiacres* subscribed a louis or twelve francs each to give a dinner to the First Consul's coachman, who had become the hero of the day and the boast of his profession. During the feast, one of the guests drinking to the health of the First Consul's coachman, observed that he knew who had played him the trick, alluding to the explosion of the machine. He was eagerly questioned, and it appeared that on the very night, or the night preceding the explosion, he had drawn up his *fiacre* beside a gate, whence had issued the little cart that had done all the mischief. The police proceeded to the place, and it was found to be a coach-yard, where all kinds of vehicles were lent on hire. The keepers of the yard did not deny the fact; they pointed out the stall in which the cart stood; it still presented traces of gunpowder. The proprietors declared that they were given to understand the cart had been hired by some Bretons who were concerned in smuggling. The man who had sold the horse, together with every individual who had participated in the affair, were easily traced out; and it was proved that the plot had been formed by the Chouan Royalists. Some active and intelligent men were despatched to their head-quarters in Morbihan. They took no pains to conceal their share in the transaction, and only regretted that it had not succeeded. Some of them were apprehended and brought to punishment. It is said that the chief conspirator afterwards turned Trappist, and sought to expiate his crime by religious austerities.

Conspiracy of Georges, Pichegru, &c.—The Duke d'Enghien.—The Slave Toby.—Characteristic reflections of Napoleon.

29th—30th.—I find in this part of my manuscript some important particulars respecting the conspiracy of Georges, Pichegru, Moreau, and the trial of the Duke d'Enghien; but, as these subjects recur repeatedly in the course of my Journal, I transfer to another part what occurred here, in order to bring all my information on the above points at once under the eyes of the reader.

Mr. Balcombe's little garden, in which we so often walked, was superintended by an old Negro. The first time we saw him, the Emperor, according to his usual custom, desired me to put some questions to him respecting his history; and his answers strongly excited our interest. He was a Malay Indian, and had been forced from his home by the crew of an English vessel, and sold at Saint-Helena, where he had continued ever since in slavery. His story bore every mark of truth. His countenance had a frank and benevolent expression; his eyes were animated and sparkling. In short, his appearance was by no means abject; but, on the contrary, truly prepossessing.

The history of the poor fellow's misfortunes filled us with indignation; and a few days after, the Emperor expressed a wish to purchase him and send him back to his own country. He mentioned the subject to the Admiral. The latter, at first, defended his countrymen, and declared that old Toby (which was the name of the unfortunate slave) must be an impostor; for the thing was impossible. He, however, enquired into the matter, and, finding that the story was but too true, he participated in the indignation which he expressed, and promised to exert his best endeavours for the fulfilment of our design. When we left Briars for Longwood, poor Toby, sharing the common fate of all earthly things, was soon forgotten; and I know not what became of him.

When we were in the garden, the Emperor generally stopped near Toby's hut, and made me question him respecting his country, the days of his youth, his family, his present situation, &c.: one would have supposed that he wished to study the feelings of the old slave. By the Emperor's desire, I invariably closed the conversation by giving him a Napoleon.

Toby was very much attached to us; our presence always seemed to fill him with joy. When we entered the garden, he immediately suspended his work, and, resting on his spade, gazed on us with an air of satisfaction. He understood not a word of the conversation that passed between the Emperor and myself; but he always seemed to anticipate, with a smile, the first words I translated to him. He called the Emperor the *Good Gentleman*: this was the only name he ever applied to him, and he knew him by no other.

I have mentioned the above particulars, because our meetings with Toby were always followed by novel, spirited, and characteristic reflections on the part of the Emperor. The versatility of his mind is well known. Whenever he adverted to the poor slave's misfortunes, he always took a new view of the subject. I shall content myself with noting down the following remarks:—

"Poor Toby," said he one day, "has been torn from his family, from his native land, and sold to slavery: could any thing be more miserable to himself, or more criminal in others? If this crime be the act of the English captain alone, he is doubtless one of the vilest of men: but if it be that of the whole crew, it may have been committed by men, perhaps, not so base as might be imagined; for vice is always individual, and scarcely ever collective. Joseph's brethren could not bring themselves to slay him; while Judas, a cool, hypocritical, calculating villain, betrayed his master. A philosopher has affirmed that men are born wicked: it would be both difficult and idle to attempt to discover whether the assertion be true. This, at least, is certain, that the great mass of society is not wicked; for if the majority were determined to be criminal and to violate the laws, who would have the power to restrain or prevent them? This is the triumph of civilization; for this happy result springs from its bosom, and arises out of its nature. Sentiments are for the most part traditionary; we feel them because they were felt by those who preceded us: thus we must look to the development of human reason and faculties for the only key to social order, the only secret of the legislator. Only those who wish to deceive the people and rule them for their own personal advantage would desire to keep them in ignorance; for the more they are enlightened, the more will they be convinced of the utility of laws, and of the necessity of defending them; and the more steady, happy, and prosperous will society become. If, however, knowledge should ever be dangerous in the multitude, it can only be when the Government, in opposition to the interests of the people, drives them into an unnatural situation, or dooms the lower classes to perish for want. In such a case, knowledge would inspire them with spirit to defend themselves, or to become criminal.

"My Code alone, from its simplicity, has been more beneficial to France than the whole mass of laws which preceded it. My schools and my system of mutual instruction are preparing generations yet unknown. Thus, during my reign, crimes were rapidly diminishing; while, on the contrary, with our neighbours in England, they have been increasing to a frightful degree. This alone is sufficient to enable any one to form a decisive judgment of the respective governments?*

"Look at the United States, where, without any apparent force or effort, every thing goes on prosperously; every one is happy and contented: and this is because the public wishes and interests are in fact the ruling power. Place the same government at variance with the will and interests of its inhabitants, and you would soon see what disturbance, trouble, and confusion, and above all, what an increase of crimes would ensue.

"When I acquired the supreme direction of affairs, it was wished that I might become a Washington. Words cost nothing; and no doubt those who were so ready to express the wish, did so without any knowledge of times, places, persons, or things. Had I been in America, I would willingly have been a Washington, and I should have had little merit in so being; for I do not see how I could reasonably have acted otherwise. But had Washington been in France, exposed to discord within, and invasion from without, I would have defied him to have been what he was in Ameri-

* This fact is corroborated by authentic documents, which exhibit proofs more positive than might be expected. (See *Situation de l'Angleterre, par M. de Monveran.*)

FRANCE.			ENGLAND.	
Inhabitants.	Condemned to death.	Years.	Inhabitants.	Condemned to death.
34,000,000	882	1801	16,000,000	3,400
42,000,000	392	1811	17,000,000	6,400

It is obvious from this statement, that in the year 1801, in France, twenty-six out of a million of inhabitants were condemned to death; and that in 1811, ten years after, the number condemned had diminished two-thirds, leaving the proportion of only nine to a million.

In England, on the contrary, where, in 1801, the number of criminals condemned to death was 212 out of a million of inhabitants, the amount increased by more than one half; there being in 1811, 376 out of a million.

It is worthy of observation, that the condemnations in England, compared with those in France, were as 376 to 9 or as 42 to 1.

The report of the state of mendicity in France, compared with that of the parish poor in England, also presents a prodigious difference: the French list in 1812 exhibiting only 30,000 individuals out of 43 millions of inhabitants; while in England, in the same year, a fourth of the population, or 4,250,000 poor, were thrown upon the parishes.—(*Monveran.*)

was at least, he would have been a fool to attempt it, and would only have prolonged the existence of evil. For my own part, I could only have been a *crowned Washington*. It was only in a congress of kings, in the midst of kings yielding or subdued, that I could become so. Then and there alone, I could successfully display Washington's moderation, disinterestedness, and wisdom. I could not reasonably attain to this but by means of the *universal Dictatorship*. To this I aspired; can that be thought a crime? Can it be believed, that to resign this authority would have been beyond the power of human nature? Sylla, glutted with crimes, dared to abdicate, pursued by public execration! What motive could have checked me, who would have been followed only by blessings?——But it remained for me to conquer at Moscow!—How many will hereafter regret my disasters and my fall!—But to require prematurely of me that sacrifice, for which the time had not arrived, was a vulgar absurdity; and for me to have proclaimed or promised it, would have been taken for hypocrisy and quackery: that was not my way.——I repeat, it remained for me to conquer at Moscow!——"

On another occasion, pausing before Toby, he said:—"What, after all, is this poor human machine? There is not one whose exterior form is like another, or whose internal organization resembles the rest! And it is by disregarding this truth that we are led to the commission of so many errors! Had Toby been a Brutus, he would have put himself to death; if an Æsop, he would now, perhaps, have been the Governor's adviser; if an ardent and zealous Christian, he would have borne his chains in the sight of God, and blessed them. As for poor Toby, he endures his misfortunes very quietly; he stoops to his work, and spends his days in innocent tranquillity." Then, after looking at him for a few moments in silence, he turned away and said: "Certainly there is a wide step from poor Toby to a King Richard!——And yet," continued he, as he walked along, "the crime is not the less atrocious; for this man, after all, had his family, his happiness, and his liberty; and it was a horrible act of cruelty to bring him here to languish in the fetters of his slavery." Then, suddenly stopping short, he added:—"But I read in your eyes, that you think he is not the only example of the sort at Saint-Helena!" And whether he felt offended at being placed on a parallel with Toby, whether he thought it necessary to raise my spirits, or whatever else might be his reason, he went on with dignity and animation: "My dear Las Cases, there is not the least resemblance here: if the outrage is of a higher class, the victims also furnish very different resources. We have not been exposed to corporeal sufferings; or if that had been attempted, we have souls to disappoint our tyrants! Our situation may even have its charms! The eyes of the universe are fixed upon us! We are martyrs in an immortal cause! Millions of human beings are weeping for us: our country sighs, and glory mourns our fate! We here struggle against the oppression of the gods, and the prayers of nations are for us!"—After a pause of a few seconds, he continued:—"Besides, this is not the source of my real sufferings! If I considered only myself, perhaps I should have reason to rejoice! Misfortunes are not without their heroism and their glory! Adversity was wanting to my career! Had I died on the throne, enveloped in the dense atmosphere of my power, I should to many have remained a problem; but now misfortune will enable all to judge of me without disguise."

Origin of Guides.—Another Danger incurred by Napoleon.—The German Officer.

December 1st—3rd. Many incidents fill up this interval; some I reject as unnecessary, some it is proper I should withhold. I here note down only a few anecdotes of the General-in-chief of the army of Italy.

After the passage of the Mincio, Napoleon, having concerted all his plans, and pursued the enemy in every direction, entered a castle on the left bank of the river. He was troubled with the head-ache, and he used a foot-bath. A large detachment of the enemy, in great confusion, arrived, having ascended the river as far as the castle. Napoleon was there, and only a few persons were with him; the sentinel on duty at the gate had just time to close it, exclaiming, To arms! and the General of the Army of Italy, in the arms of victory, was compelled to escape through the back gates of the garden, with but one boot on. Had he been made prisoner, before his reputation was established, the acts of genius which had marked the commencement of his career, would, perhaps, by the common run of mankind, have been considered merely as fortunate and blameable enterprises. The danger which the French General had just escaped (a circumstance which through his plan of operations was likely often to recur) was the origin of the guides appointed to guard his person. These guides have since been introduced in other armies.

In the same campaign, Napoleon incurred another imminent risk: Wurmser, who had been compelled to throw himself into Mantua, and who was debouching suddenly on an open plain, learned from an old woman, that only a few moments before his arrival, the French General, with but a few followers, had stopped at her door, and that he had fled at the sight of the Austrians. Wurmser immediately despatched parties of cavalry in every direction, calculating with certainty on the precious capture. "But," said the Emperor, "I must do him this justice, he gave particu-"lar orders that I should not be killed or harmed in any "way." Fortunately for the young General, his happy star and the swiftness of his horse combined to save him.

The new system of military operations practised by Napoleon disconcerted every one. The campaign was scarcely opened, when Lombardy was inundated with troops in every direction, and the French approached Mantua *pêle mêle* with the enemy. The General-in-chief, when in the neighbourhood of Pizzighitone, saw a tall German Colonel, who had been made prisoner. Napoleon took a fancy to question him, without being known, and enquired how affairs were going on. "Very badly," replied the officer, "I know not how it will end; but no one seems to under-"stand what they are about: we have been sent to fight a "young blockhead, who attacks us on the right and the left, "in front and in the rear, so that we know not how to pro-"ceed. This mode of carrying on war is intolerable; and "for my part, I am very glad to have done with it. . . ."

Napoleon used to relate that, after one of his great actions in Italy, he passed over the field of battle before the dead bodies had been interred: "In the deep silence of a "beautiful moon-light night," said the Emperor, "a dog, "leaped suddenly from beneath the clothes of his dead mas-"ter, rushed upon us, and then immediately returned to his "hiding-place, howling piteously. He alternately licked "his master's hand, and ran towards us: thus, at once soli-"citing aid and seeking revenge. Whether owing to my "own particular turn of mind at the moment," continued the Emperor, "the time, the place, or the action itself, I "know not; but certainly, no incident on any field of bat-"tle ever produced so deep an impression on me. I invol-"untarily stopped to contemplate the scene. This man, "thought I, perhaps, has friends in the camp or in his com-"pany; and here he lies forsaken by all except his dog! "What a lesson Nature here presents through the medi-"um of an animal! What a strange being is man! and "how mysterious are his impressions! I had, without emo-"tion, ordered battles which were to decide the fate of the "army; I had beheld, with fearless eyes, the execution of "those operations, by which numbers of my countrymen "were sacrificed; and here my feelings were roused by the "mournful howling of a dog! Certainly at that moment

"I should have been easily moved by a suppliant enemy:
"I could very well imagine Achilles surrendering up the
"body of Hector at the sight of Priam's tears."

War.—Principles.—Application.—Opinions on several Generals.

4th.—5th. My eyes had become so bad that I was obliged to suspend my occupation: I had nearly lost my sight on the campaign of Italy.

For some time past a sensible change had taken place in the weather. We knew nothing about the order of the seasons. As the sun passed twice over our heads in the course of the year, we said we ought, at least, to have two summers. Every thing was totally different from what we had been accustomed to; and, to complete our embarrassments, we were obliged, being now in the southern hemisphere, to make all our calculations in a manner quite the reverse of that which we had practised in Europe. It rained frequently, the air was very damp, and it grew colder than before. The Emperor could no longer go out in the evening; he was continually catching cold, and did not sleep well. He was obliged to give up taking his meals beneath the tent, and he had them served up in his own chamber. Here he found himself better; but he could not stir from his seat.

Our conversation continued after the dinner was removed from table. To-day the Emperor attacked General Gourgaud on the elements and first exercises of artillery. The General had belonged to that department of the service, and had recently been engaged in the requisite course of study. The discussion was very curious, and was maintained with great spirit. Napoleon never proved himself to be the weaker party: one might have been tempted to believe that he had just passed his examination at the academy.

The conversation then turned on war and great commanders. "The fate of a battle," observed the Emperor, "is "the result of a moment, of a thought: the hostile forces "advance with various combinations, they attack each oth-"er and fight for a certain time; the critical moment ar-"rives, a mental flash decides, and the least reserve accom-"plishes the object." He spoke of Lutzen, Bautzen, &c.; and afterwards, alluded to Waterloo, he said, that had he followed up the idea of turning the enemy's right, he should easily have succeeded; he, however, preferred piercing the centre, and separating the two armies. But all was fatal in that engagement; it even assumed the appearance of absurdity: yet, nevertheless, he ought to have gained the victory. Never had any of his battles presented less doubt to his mind; and he was still at a loss to account for what had happened. Grouchi, he said, had lost himself; Ney appeared bewildered, and his countenance sufficiently expressed the remorse he felt for Fontainbleau and Lons-le-Saunier; Derlon was useless; in short, the generals were no longer themselves. If, in the evening, he had been aware of Grouchi's position, and could have thrown himself upon it, he might, in the morning, with the help of that fine reserve, have repaired his ill success, and, perhaps, even have destroyed the allied forces by one of those miracles, those turns of fortune which were familiar to him, and which would have surprised no one. But he knew nothing of Grouchi; and besides, it was not easy to act with decision amongst the wrecks of the army. It would be difficult to imagine the condition of the French army on that disastrous night; it was a torrent dislodged from its bed, hurling away every thing in its course.

Turning to another subject, he said that the dangers incurred by the military commanders of ancient times were not to be compared to those which attended the generals of modern times. There was, he observed, no positions in which a general might not now be reached by artillery; but anciently a general ran no risk, except when he himself charged, which Cæsar did only twice or thrice.

"We rarely," said he, "find, combined together, all the qualities necessary to constitute a great general. The object most desirable is, that a man's judgment should be in equilibrium with his physical character or courage." This is what the Emperor termed being *well squared*, both by the base and perpendicular.

"If," continued he, "courage be a general's predominating quality, he will rashly undertake what he cannot execute; and, on the other hand, he will not venture to carry any measure into effect, if his character or courage be inferior to his judgment."

He then cited the example of the Vice-Roy, whose sole merit consisted in this equilibrium of character, which, however, sufficed to render him a very distinguished man.

Physical and moral courage then became the subject of discourse. "With respect to physical courage," the Emror said, "that it was impossible for Murat and Ney not to be brave, but no men ever possessed less judgment; the former in particular." "As to moral courage," observed he, "I have rarely met with *the two o'clock in the morning kind*. I mean, unprepared courage, that which is necessary on an unexpected occasion, and which, in spite of the most unforeseen events, leaves full freedom of judgment and decision?" He did not hesitate to declare that he was himself eminently gifted with this *two o'clock in the morning* courage, and that in this respect, he had met with but few persons who were at all equal to him. He remarked that an incorrect idea was generally formed of the strength of mind necessary to engage in one of those great battles on which depends the fate of an army or nation, or the possession of a throne. "Generals," added he, "are rarely found eager to give battle; they choose their positions; establish themselves; consider their combinations; but then commences their indecision: nothing is so difficult, and at the same time so important, as to know when to decide."

He next proceeded to notice several generals, and condescended to reply to some questions that were asked him. "Kleber," said he, "was endowed with the highest talent; but he was merely the man of the moment: he pursued glory as the only road to happiness; but he had no national sentiment, and he could, without any sacrifice, have devoted himself to foreign service." Kleber had commenced his youthful career among the Prussians, to whom he continued much attached. Dessaix possessed, in a very superior degree, the important equilibrium above described. Moreau scarcely deserved to be placed in the first rank of generals; in him nature had left her work unfinished; he possessed more instinct than genius. In Lannes, courage at first predominated over judgment; but the latter was every day gaining ground, and approaching equilibrium. He had become a very able commander at the period of his death. "I found him a dwarf," said the Emperor, "but I lost him a giant." In another general, whom he named, judgment was, on the contrary, superior to courage; it could not be denied that he was a brave man, but he calculated the chance of the cannon-ball, like many others.

Speaking of military ardour and courage, the Emperor said: "I know the depth, or what I call the *draught of water* of all my generals. Some," added he, joining action to his words, "will sink to the waist, some to the chin, others over the head; but the number of the latter is very small, I assure you." Suchet, he said, was one whose courage and judgment had been surprisingly improved. Massena was a very superior man, and, by a strange peculiarity of temperament, he possessed the desired equilibrium only in the heat of battle; it was created in the midst of danger. "The generals," finally observed the Emperor, "who seemed destined to rise to future distinction were Gerard, Clausel, Foy, Lamarque, &c. These were my new marshals."

Situation of the Spanish Princes at Valencey.—The Pope at Fontainbleau.—Reflections, &c.

6th.—The Emperor, after dictating to me this morning, was successively engaged with some gentlemen, with whom he prolonged his walk for sometime. When they withdrew, I followed him into the lower path: he was dull and silent, and his countenance appeared somewhat harsh and ruffled. "Well," said he, as we were returning to dinner, "we shall have sentinels under our windows at Longwood. They wished to force me to have a foreign officer at my table and in my drawing-room. I cannot mount my horse without being accompanied by an officer; in short, we cannot stir a step under pain of being insulted! . . . ." I replied, that this was another drop of sorrow added to the bitter cup which we were doomed to drink to his past glory and power; but that his philosophy was sufficient to defy the malice of his enemies, and to make them blush for their brutality in the face of the whole world. I ventured to remark, that the Spanish Princes at Valencey, and the Pope at Fontainbleau had never experienced such treatment. "Certainly not," resumed he, "the Princes hunted and gave balls at Valencey, without being physically aware of their chains; they experienced respect and courtesy at all hands. Old King Charles IV removed from Compiegne to Marseilles, and from Marseilles to Rome, whenever he wished. And yet how different are those places from this! The Pope at Fontainbleau, whatever may have been the reports circulated in the world, was treated in the same manner. And yet how many persons, in spite of all the indulgences he enjoyed, refused to be appointed to guard him; a circumstance which gave me no offence, for I thought it perfectly natural. Such employments are subject to the influence of delicacy of feeling; and our European manners require that power should be limited by honour." He observed that, for his own part, as a private man and an officer, he should without hesitation have refused to guard the Pope, whose removal to France, he added, had never been ordered by him.—I manifested great surprise.—"You are astonished," said he: "you did not know this? But it is nevertheless true, as well as many other similar facts, which you will learn in course of time. But with reference to the subject on which we have just been speaking, it is necessary to distinguish the conduct of the sovereign, who acts collectively, from that of the private man, whose sentiments are without constraint. Policy, permits, nay, frequently demands, from the one, what would be unpardonable in the other." The hour of dinner, by introducing various subjects of conversation, diverted his melancholy, and cheerfulness finally prevailed.

Meanwhile the Emperor seriously determined to quit his present wretched abode, whatever inconvenience his new residence might present. On going to pass the remainder of the evening with our host, the Emperor directed me to present him a box bearing his cypher, and to tell him he was sorry for all the trouble he had occasioned to him.

On the Nouvelle Heloïse, and on Love.

7th.—The Emperor summoned me to attend him at an early hour. He began to read the Nouvelle Heloïse, frequently remarking on the ingenuity and force of the arguments, the elegance of the style and expressions: he read for upwards of two hours. This reading made a powerful impression on me; it produced a deep melancholy—a mingled feeling of tenderness and sorrow. I had always been fond of the work: and it now awakened happy recollections, and excited deep regret: the Emperor frequently smiled at me. During breakfast the Nouvelle Heloïse was the topic of conversation.

"Jean-Jacques has overcharged his subject," said the Emperor; "he has painted madness: love should be a source of pleasure, not of misery." I alleged that Jean-Jacques had described nothing which a man might not feel, and that even the misery to which the Emperor alluded, was in reality, happiness.—"I see," said he, "you have a little touch of the romantic: has Love's misery rendered you happy?"—"I do not complain of my fate, Sire," replied I; "were I to begin life again, I should wish to retrace the course I have already pursued."

The Emperor resumed his reading after breakfast; but he paused occasionally: the enchantment seemed to seize him in his turn. He at length laid down the book, and we went out to the garden. "Really," said he, as he walked along, "this work is not without fire; it moves, "it rouses the feelings." We discussed the subject deeply: we were very prolix in our remarks, and we at length agreed that perfect love is like ideal happiness; that both are equally airy, fugitive, mysterious, and inexplicable; and that, finally, love is the business of the idle man, the recreation of the warrior, and the ruin of the sovereign.

We were joined by the Grand Marshal and M. Gourgaud, who had just come from Longwood. The Admiral had for some days past been urgent for our removal thither; and the Emperor was no less anxious to go, being so very ill at Briars. However, before he removed, it was necessary that the smell of the paint should be entirely gone, for, owing to his peculiar organization, he could not possibly endure it. In the Imperial palaces, he had never been suffered to go near fresh paint. In his different journeys, the slightest smell of paint frequently rendered it necessary to change the apartments that had been prepared for him; and on board of the Northumberland the paint of the ship made him very ill. He had been informed on the preceding evening that all was ready at Longwood, and that the disagreeable effect of the paint was entirely gone. He accordingly determined to remove on the Saturday following, as he would thus be rid of the annoyance of the workmen on Sunday; but the Grand Marshal and M. Gourgaud now came to say, that they had visited the place, and that it was not habitable. The Emperor expressed much vexation at the first account he had received, and the resolution it had led him to adopt. The two gentlemen withdrew, and we entered the lower walk. The Emperor was much out of humour. M. de Montholon now arrived, very *mal-á-propos*, from Longwood, declaring that all was ready, and that the Emperor might remove as soon as he wished. These two accounts, so contradictory, and so close upon each other, powerfully excited his displeasure. Fortunately, dinner was announced, which diverted his attention from the subject. The cloth was laid in the Emperor's chamber; for he had so severe a cold that he could not endure the tent. After dinner he resumed his reading; and ended the day, as he had begun it, with the Nouvelle Heloise.

The English Lieutenant.—A singular circumstance.—Departure for Longwood determined on.—State of France.—Memorial in justification of Ney.

8th—9th.—Owing to the doubt which had yesterday arisen respecting the paint, I determined to go myself to ascertain the real state of the case, and to acquaint the Emperor with it at breakfast-time. I accordingly set out very early walking three parts of the way, because nobody was up who could prepare a horse for me. I returned before nine o'clock. The smell of the paint was certainly very slight; but it was too much for the Emperor.

On the 9th the Captain of the Minden 74 gun ship was introduced to the Emperor in the garden. The captain had arrived from the Cape of Good Hope, and was on the eve of sailing for Europe. He had had the honour of being presented to Napoleon at Paris, under the Consulate, about twelve years before. He requested permission to introduce one of his Lieutenants to the Emperor, on account of some personal circumstances, which we thought very singular. The young man was born at Bologna, precisely at the period when the French army entered that city. The French General, Napoleon, had by some accident been present at the christening of the child, to whom he gave a tricoloured cockade, which has since been carefully preserved in the family.

After the departure of these gentlemen, the Grand Marshal arrived from Longwood. He thought the paint was by no means offensive: the Emperor was very unwell, and a portion of his property had already been removed; he therefore resolved to proceed to Longwood on the day following, of which I was heartily glad. I had for some days past had an opportunity of observing that a determination had been adopted to compel the Emperor to quit his present abode. I had kept to myself all the communications, public or private, that had been made to me on the subject. I made it a rule to spare him every cause of vexation that I possibly could, and merely contented myself with acting in the way I thought most advisable. Two days before, an officer was sent to carry away the tent, though we had expressed no wish to that effect. The officer had also been directed to remove the outside shutters from the Emperor's windows; but this I opposed, telling him it could not be done, as the Emperor had not yet risen, and I sent him away. On another occasion, with the view of alarming me, I was told as a great secret that if the Emperor did not immediately remove, it was intended to station a hundred soldiers at the gates of the enclosure. "Very well," I replied, and took no further notice. What could be the occasion of all this hurry? I suspect that the caprice of our jailors, and the desire of pushing their authority to the utmost, had more concern in the business than any thing else.

We received newspapers down to the 15th of September; and they became the subject of conversation. The Emperor analyzed them. The future appeared enveloped in cloud. "However," said the Emperor, "three great events present themselves to the imagination;—the division of France, the reign of the Bourbons, or a new dynasty.—Louis XVIII," observed he, "might easily have reigned in 1814, by rendering himself a national monarch. Now he has only the odious and uncertain chance, arising out of excessive severity;—a reign of terror. His dynasty may be permanently established, or that which is to succeed him, may still be in the secret of futurity." Some one present observed, "that the Duke of Orleans might be called to the throne;" and the Emperor, by a string of very forcible and eloquent reasoning, proved that the Duke of Orleans would, at least, never wear the crown in the course of succession: and that it was the well-understood interest of all the sovereigns of Europe, to prefer him (Napoleon) to the Duke of Orleans, coming to the throne by the career of crime. "For," said he, "what is the doctrine of Kings against the events of the present day? Is it to prevent a renewal of the example which I furnished, against what they call legitimacy? Now the example which I have set, cannot be renewed above once in the course of many ages; but that of the Duke of Orleans, the near relative of the monarch on the throne, may be renewed daily, hourly, and in every country. There is no sovereign, who has not, in his own palace, and about his person, cousins, nephews, brothers, and other relations, ready to pursue a course which, one day or other, may cause them to be deposed."

We read, in the same papers, an abstract of the memorial, in justification of Marshal Ney.—The Emperor thought it most pitiable. It was not calculated to save his life, and by no means to maintain his honour. The arguments in his defence were, to say the least of them, feeble, and destitute of point. After all he had done, he still protested his devotedness to the King, and his aversion of the Emperor. "An absurd plan," said Napoleon, "but one which has been generally adopted by those who have figured in the present memorable times, and who seem not to have considered that I am so entirely identified with our prodigies, our monuments, our institutions, and all our national acts, that to separate me from them is to do violence to France. The glory of France is to acknowledge me! And, in spite of all the subtlety, evasion, and falsehood, that may be employed to prove the contrary, my character will still be fairly estimated by the French nation. Ney's defence," continued he, "was plainly traced out. He was led on by a general impulse which he thought calculated to ensure the welfare of his country; he had obeyed without premeditation, and without any treasonable design. A change of fortune had ensued, and he was cited before a tribunal; this was all he had to say with respect to the great events that had taken place. As to the defence of his life, there was nothing to be said on that point, except, indeed, that he was protected by a solemn capitulation, which guaranteed to every individual silence and oblivion with regard to all political acts and opinions. Had he pursued that line of defence, and were his life, nevertheless, to be sacrificed, it would be, in the face of the whole world, a violation of the most sacred laws. He would leave behind him the recollection of a glorious character; carrying to the grave the sympathy of every generous mind, and heaping disgrace and reprobation on his murderers. But this enthusiasm is probably beyond his moral strength," said the Emperor. "Ney is the bravest of men; and every other faculty is subordinate to his courage."

It is certain that when Ney quitted Paris, he was wholly devoted to the King; and that he did not turn until he saw that all was lost. If he then proved himself enthusiastic in the opposite course, it was because he felt he had much to atone for. After his famous order of the day, he wrote to inform Napoleon that what he had done was principally with a view to the welfare of the country; and that as he could not henceforth be agreeable to the Emperor, he begged that he would grant him permission to retire. The Emperor desired him to come, and said he would receive him as he did on the day after the battle of Moscow. Ney presented himself to Napoleon, and said, that after what had occurred, he must of necessity entertain doubts of his attachment and fidelity; and that therefore he solicited no other rank than that of a grenadier in the Imperial Guard. The Emperor replied by stretching forth his hand to him, and calling him the bravest of the brave, as he was accustomed to do. Ney subsequently told the Emperor, ...

. . . .

The Emperor compared the situation of Ney to that of Turenne. Ney might be defended; but Turenne was unjustifiable. And yet Turenne was pardoned and loaded with honours, while Ney was probably doomed to die.

"In 1649," said he, "Turenne commanded the royal army, which command had been conferred on him by Anne of Austria, the Regent of the kingdom. Though he had taken the oath of fidelity, yet he bribed his troops, and declared himself for the Fronde, and marched on Paris. But when he was declared guilty of high treason, his repentant army forsook him; and Turenne took refuge with the Prince of Hesse, to avoid the pursuit of justice. Ney, on the contrary, was urged by the unanimous wish and outcry of his army. Only nine months had elapsed since he had acknowledged a monarch, who had been preceded by six hundred thousand foreign bayonets; a monarch who had not accepted the constitution presented to him by the Senate, as the formal and necessary condition of his return, and who, by declaring that he had reigned nineteen years, proved that he regarded all preceding governments as usurpations. Ney, whose education had taught him to respect the national sovereignty, had fought for five-and-twenty years to support that cause; and, from a private soldier, had raised himself to the rank of marshal. If his conduct on the 20th of March was not honourable, it is at least explicable, and in some respects pardonable; but Turenne was absolutely criminal, because the Fronde was the ally of Spain, which was then at war with his sovereign, and because he had been prompted by his own interest and that of his family, in the hope of abtaining a sovereignty at the expense of France, and consequently to the prejudice of his country."

ESTABLISHMENT AT LONGWOOD.

Removal to Longwood.—Description of the road.—Taking possession.—The Emperor's First Bath, &c.

10th.—The Emperor ordered me to be called about nine o'clock, to accompany him into the garden. He was obliged to leave his chamber very early, as all the furniture was to be removed that morning to Longwood. On entering the garden, the Emperor sent for Mr. Balcombe our host. He then ordered his breakfast, and invited Mr. Balcombe to breakfast with him. He was in charming spirits, and his conversation was very lively.

About two o'clock the Admiral was announced: he advanced with an air of embarrasssment. The manner in which the Emperor had been treated at Briars, and the restraints which had been imposed upon the members of his suite risiding in the town, had occasioned a coolness between them. The Emperor had discontinued receiving the visits of the Admiral; yet on the present occasion he behaved to him as though they had met but yesterday.

At length we left Briars, and set out for Longwood. The Emperor rode the horse which had been brought to him from the Cape. He had not seen him before; he was a small, sprightly, and tolerably handsome animal. The Emperor wore his uniform of the chasseurs of the guard: his graceful figure and handsome countenance were particularly remarkable. His appearance attracted general notice, and I was gratified to hear the observations it called forth. The Admiral was very attentive to him. Many persons had collected on the road to see him pass. Several English officers, together with ourselves, formed his escort.

The road from Briars to Longwood runs for some distance in the direction of the town. It then turns off suddenly to the right, and, after three or four windings, clears the chain of hills forming one side of the valley. The road next opens upon a level height of gentle acclivity, and a new horizon and new scenes present themselves. We now left behind us the chain of barren mountains and rocks which distinguish the landing-side of the island, and saw before us a transverse group of hills, of which Diana's Peak is the highest, and appears like the key-stone, or the nucleus of the surrounding scene. On the left or eastern side, where

Longwood is situated, the horizon is bounded by the broken chain of rocks forming the outline and barrier or the island. There the soil exhibits an uncultivated desert; but on the right the eye rests on an extensive tract of country, which, though rugged, at least presents traces of vegetation: it is covered with numerous residences, and upon the whole, is tolerably well cultivated. On this side, it must be confessed, the picture is romantic and pleasing.

Here a deep valley opens on the left of the road, which is in very good condition; and two miles farther on, where the road turns in an angular direction, stands Hut's gate, a wretched little house, which was selected as the residence of the Grand Marshal and his family. At a short distance from this point, the valley on the left, having gradually increased in depth, forms a circular gulf, which from its vast depth and extent, has received the name of the Devil's Punch bowl. The road is here contracted by an eminence on the right, and it runs along by the side of this precipice, until it turns off in the direction of Longwood, which is close at hand.

At the entrance of Longwood, we found a guard under arms, who rendered the prescribed honours to the august captive. The Emperor's horse, which was spirited and untractable, being unused to this kind of parade, was startled at the sound of the drum; he refused to pass the gate, and it was only by the help of the spur, that his rider succeeded in forcing him to advance. At this moment, I observed very expressive looks exchanged among the persons composing the Emperor's escort. We entered our new residence about four o'clock.

The Admiral took great pains to point out to us even the minutest details at Longwood. He had superintended all the arrangements, and some things were even the work of his own hands. The Emperor was satisfied with every thing, and the Admiral seemed highly pleased. He had evidently anticipated petulance and disdain; but the Emperor manifested perfect good-humour.

He retired at six o'clock, and beckoned me to follow him to his chamber. Here he examined various articles of furniture, and inquired whether I was similarly provided. On my replying in the negative, he insisted on my accepting of them; saying in the most engaging manner, "Take them, I shall want for nothing: I shall be taken better care of than you." He felt much fatigued, and he asked whether he did not look so. This was the consequence of having passed five months in perfect inactivity. He had walked a good deal in the morning, besides riding some miles on horseback.

Our new residence was provided with a bathing machine, which the Admiral had ordered the carpenters to fit up in the best way they could. The Emperor, who, since he quitted Malmaison, had been obliged to dispense with the use of the bath, which to him had become one of the necessaries of life, expressed a wish to bathe immediately, and directed me to remain with him. The most trivial details of our new establishment came once more under consideration; and as the apartment which had been assigned to me was very bad, the Emperor expressed a wish, that during the day, I should occupy what he called his topographic cabinet, which adjoined his own private closet, in order, as he said, that I might be near him. I was much affected by the kind manner in which all this was spoken. He even went so far as to tell me that I must come next morning and take a bath in his machine; and when I excused myself on the ground of the respect and the distance which it was indispensable should be observed betwixt us, "My dear Las Cases," said he, "fellow prisoners should accommodate each other. I do not want the bath all day, and it is no less necessary to you than to me." One would have supposed that he wished to indemnify me for the loss I was about to sustain, in being no longer the only individual about his person. This kindness delighted me, it is true; but it also produced a feeling of regret. The kindness of the Emperor was doubtless the reward of my assiduous attentions at Briars; but it also gave me cause to anticipate the close of that constant intercourse with him, for which I had been indebted to our profound solitude. The Emperor, not wishing to dress again, dined in his own chamber, and desired me to remain with him. We were alone, and our conversation turned on a subject of a peculiar nature, the result of which may be exceedingly important. He asked my opinion and told me to communicate it to him the next morning.

Description of Longwood.

11th—14th. We now found unfolded to us a new portion of our existence on the wretched rock of Saint-Helena. We were settled in our new abode, and the limits of our prison were marked out.

Longwood, which was originally merely a farm belonging to the East India Company, and which was afterwards given as a country residence to the Deputy Governor, is situated on one of the highest parts of the Island. The difference of the temperature between this place and the valley where we landed, is marked by a variation of at least ten degrees of the English thermometer. Longwood stands on a level height, which is tolerably extensive on the eastern side, and pretty near the coast. Continual and frequently violent gales, always blowing in the same quarter, sweep the surface of the ground. The sun, though it rarely appears, nevertheless exercises its influence on the atmosphere, which is apt to produce disorders of the liver, if due precaution be not observed. Heavy and sudden falls of rain, complete the impossibility of distinguishing any regular season. But there is no regular course of seasons at Longwood. The whole year presents a continuance of wind, clouds, and rain; and the temperature is of that mild and monotonous kind, which, perhaps, after all, is rather conducive to *ennui* than disease. Notwithstanding the abundant rains, the grass rapidly disappears, being either nipped by the wind, or withered by the heat. The water, which is conveyed hither by a conduit, is so unwholesome that the Deputy Governor, when he lived at Longwood never suffered it to be used in his family until it had been boiled; and we are obliged to do the same. The trees, which, at a distance, impart a smiling aspect to the scene, are merely gum trees—a wretched kind of shrub, affording no shade. On one hand, the horizon is bounded by the vast ocean: but the rest of the scene presents only a mass of huge barren rocks, deep gulfs, and desolate valleys; and in the distance, appear the green and misty chain of mountains, above which towers Diana's Peak. In short, Longwood can be pleasing only to the traveller, after the fatigues of a long voyage, for whom the sight of any land is a cheering prospect. Arriving at Saint-Helena on a fine day, he may, perhaps, be struck with the singularity of the objects which suddenly present themselves, and may, perhaps exclaim "How beautiful!" but his visit is momentary; and what pain does not his hasty admiration cause to the unhappy captives who are doomed to pass their lives at Saint-Helena.

Workmen had been constantly employed for two months in preparing Longwood for our reception; the result of their labours, however, amounted to little. The entrance to the house was through a room which had just been built, and which was intended to answer the double purpose of an antichamber and a dining-room. This apartment led to another, which was made the drawing-room; beyond this was a third room running in a cross direction and very dark. This was intended to be the depository of the Emperor's maps and books; but it was afterwards converted into the dining-room. The Emperor's chamber opened into this apartment on the right-hand side. This chamber was divided into two equal parts, forming the Emperor's cabinet and sleeping-room; a little external gallery served for a bathing-room. Opposite the Emperor's chamber, at the other extremity of the building, were the apartments of Madame de Montholon, her husband, and her son, which have since been used as the Emperor's library. Detached from this part of the house, was a little square room on the ground-floor contiguous to the kitchen, which was assigned to me. My son was obliged to enter his room through a trap-door and by the help of a ladder; it was nothing but a loft and scarcely afforded room for his bed. Our windows and beds were without curtains. The few articles of furniture which were in our apartments had evidently been obtained from the inhabitants of the island, who doubtless readily seized the opportunity of disposing of them to advantage for the sake of supplying themselves with better.

The Grand Marshal with his wife and children had been left at the distance of two miles behind us, in a place which even here is denominated a *hut*, (Hut's-gate.) General Gourgaud slept under a tent, as did also the Doctor,* and the officer commanding our guard, till such time as their apartments should be ready, which the crew of the Northumberland were rapidly preparing.

We were surrounded by a kind of garden; but, owing to the little attention which we had it in our power to bestow on its cultivation, joined to the want of water and the nature of the climate, it was a garden only by name. In front, and separated from us by a tolerably deep ravine, was encamped the fifty-third regiment, different parties of which were posted on the neighbouring heights.—Such was our new abode.

On the 12th I communicated to the Emperor my opinion on the subject, respecting which we had conversed two days before. He came to no decision, conceiving the affair to be useless. I ventured to maintain that even doubtful as the case might be there was nothing either to lose or to risk, and that it was merely taking a chance in the lottery without the expense of a share. Time, however, has proved that the Emperor judged correctly. The thing would have been perfectly useless; it could have led to no result. . .

. . . .

. . . .

The same day Colonel Wilks, (formerly governor for the East India Company,) who had been succeeded by the Admiral, came to visit the Emperor. I acted as interpreter on the occasion. On the 13th or 14th the Minden sailed for Europe, and I availed myself of the opportunity thus afforded to send letters to London and Paris.

* Dr. O'Meara of the Northumberland.

Arrangement of the Emperor's establishment.—Feelings of the captives with respect to each other.—Traits of the Emperor's character.—Portrait of Napoleon by M. de Pradt, translated from an English newspaper.—Its refutation.

15th—16th.—The domestic establishment of the Emperor, on his departure from Plymouth, consisted of twelve persons. I feel pleasure in recording their names here; it is a testimony due to their devotedness.* . . . .

. . . .

However numerous this establishment may appear, it may be truly said that after our departure from England, during the voyage, and from the time of our landing at Saint-Helena, it had ceased to be serviceable to the Emperor. Our dispersion, the uncertainty of our establishment, our wants, and the irregular way in which they were supplied, necessarily created disorder.

As soon as we were all assembled at Longwood, the Emperor determined to arrange his establishment and to assign to each of us an employment suited to our respective capacities. Reserving to the Grand Marshal the general control and superintendance of the whole household; he consigned to M. de Montholon all the domestic details. To M. Gourgaud he intrusted the direction of the stables; and I was appointed to take care of the property and furniture, and to superintend the management of our supplies. The latter part of my duty appeared to interfere too much with the regulation of domestic details. I conceived it would be conducive to the general advantage, that these two departments should be under the control of one individual, and I soon succeeded in accomplishing this object.

Every thing now proceeded tolerably well, and we were certainly more comfortable than before. But, however reasonable might be the regulations made by the Emperor, they, nevertheless, sowed the seeds of discontent, which

*** Individuals composing the Emperor's household.**

Servants of the Chamber.

Marchand, ...	native of Paris, ...	1st valet de chambre.
St. Denis, called Aly,	native of Versailles, ...	valet de chambre.
Noverraz, ...	Swiss, ...	ditto.
Santini, ...	Corsican, ...	usher.

Servants in Livery.

Archambault, sen. .	native of Fontainebleau, . .	groom.
Archambault, jun. .	ditto, ...	ditto.
Gentilini, ...	native of Elba, ...	footman.

Servants for the Table.

Cypriani, ...	Corsican, died at St. Helena, .	maitre d'hotel.
Pierron, ...	native of Paris, ...	butler.
Lepage, ...	. . . .	cook.
Rousseau, ...	native of Fontainebleau, . . .	steward.

took root, and occasionally developed themselves. One thought himself a loser by the change; another sought to attach too high an importance to his office; and a third conceived that he had been wronged in the general division of duties. We were no longer the members of one family, each exerting his best endeavours to secure the advantage of the whole. We were far from putting into practice that which necessity seemed to dictate to us; and a wreck of luxury, or a remnant of ambition, frequently became an object of dispute.

Though attachment to the person of the Emperor had united us around him, yet chance, and not sympathy, had brought us together. Our connexion was purely fortuitous, and not the result of any natural affinity. Thus, at Longwood, we were encircled round a centre, but without any cohesion with each other. How could it be otherwise? We were almost all strangers to one another, and, unfortunately, our different conditions, ages, and characters, were calculated to make us continue so.

These circumstances, though in themselves trfling, had the vexatious effect of depriving us of our most agreeable resources. It banished that confidence, interchange of sentiment, and intimate union, which might have proved a source of happiness even amidst our cruel misfortunes. But, on the other hand, these very circumstances served to develope many excellent traits in the Emperor's character. They were apparent in his endeavours to produce among us unity and conformity of sentiment; his constant care to remove every just cause of jealousy: the voluntary abstraction by which he averted his attention from that which he wished not to observe; and finally, the paternal expressions of displeasure, of which we were occasionally the objects, and which (to the honour of all be it said) were avoided as cautiously, and received as respectfully, as though they had emanated from the throne of the Thuilleries.

Who can pretend to know the Emperor in his character of a private man better than myself?—I who was with him during two months of solitude in the desert of Briars;—I who accompanied him in his long walks by moonlight, and who enjoyed so many hours in his society? Who like me had the opportunity of choosing the moment, the place, the subject of his conversation? Who besides myself heard him recall to mind the charms of his boyhood, or describe the pleasures of his youth, and the bitterness of his recent sorrow? I am convinced that I know his character thoroughly, and that I can now explain many circumstances which, at the time of their occurrence, seemed difficult to be understood. I can now very well comprehend that which struck us so forcibly, and which particularly characterized him in the days of his power; namely,—that no individual ever permanently incurred the displeasure of Napoleon: however marked might be his disgrace, however deep the gulf into which he was plunged, he might still confidently hope to be restored to favour. Those who had once enjoyed intimacy, whatever cause of offence they might give him, never totally forfeited his regard. The Emperor is eminently gifted with two excellent qualities; a vast fund of justice, and a disposition naturally open to attachment. Amidst all his fits of petulence or anger, a sentiment of justice still predominates. He is sure to turn an attentive ear to good arguments, and, if left to himself, candidly brings them forward whenever they occur to his mind. He never forgets services performed to him, nor habits he has contracted. Sooner or later he invariably casts a thought on those who may have incurred his displeasure; he reflects on what they have suffered, and regards their punishment as sufficient. He recalls them, when they are perhaps forgotten by the world; and they again enjoy his good graces, to the astonishment of themselves as well as of others. Of this there have been many instances. The Emperor is sincere in his attachments, without making a show of what he feels. When once he becomes used to a person, he can not easily bear separation. He observes and condemns his faults, blames his own choice, expressing his displeasure in the most unreserved way; but still there is nothing to fear: these are but so many new ties of regard.

It will probably be a matter of surprise, that I should sketch the Emperor's character in so humble a style. All that is usually written about him is so far-fetched; it has been thought necessary to employ antithesis, and brilliant colouring; to seek for effect, and to rack the imagination for high-flown phrases. For my own part, I merely describe what I see, and express what I feel. This reflection, by the by, comes *àpropos.*

The Emperor was to-day reading with me, in the English papers, a portrait of himself, drawn by the Archbishop of Malines, and worked up with affected antitheses, and contrasts. He desired the Grand Marshal to transcribe it word for word. The following are the principal points: "The mind of Napoleon," says the Abbé de Pradt, in his *Embassy to Warsaw in* 1812, "was vast; but after the manner of the Orientals, and through a contradictory disposition, it descended, as it were, by the effect of its own weight, into the lowest details. His first idea was always grand, and his second petty. His mind was like his purse; munificence and meanness held each a string. His genius, which was at once adapted to the stage of the world, and the mountebank's show, represented the royal robe, joined to the harlequin's jacket. He was the man of extremes; one, who having commanded the Alps to bow down, the Simplon to level its head, and the sea to advance and recede from its shores, ended by surrendering himself to an English cruiser. Endowed with wonderful and infinite shrewdness; seizing, creating, in every question, new and unperceived relations; abounding in lively and picturesque images, animated and pointed expressions, the more forcible from the very incorrectness of his language, which always bore a sort of foreign impress; sophistical, subtle, and changeable, to excess; he adopted different rules of optics from those by which other men are guided. Add to this the delirium of success, the habit of drinking from the enchanted cup, and intoxicating himself with the incense of the world; and you may be enabled to form an idea of the man, who, uniting in his caprices all that is lofty and mean in human character, majestic in the splendour of sovereignty, and peremptory in command, with all that is ignoble and base—joining the eve's-dropper to the subverter of thrones—presents altogether such a Jupiter Scapin, as never before figured on the scene of life."

Certainly here is abundance of fancy, and far-fetched ideas. I pass over the indecorous and disgraceful fact, that a reverend prelate, an Archbishop, overwhelmed with the bounty of his Sovereign, to whom, during his prosperity, he paid the most assiduous court, and offered the most abject flattery, should, in the adversity of that sovereign, indulge in language, so trivial, grotesque, and insulting, as that above quoted. I shall merely dwell on the merit of the Abbé de Pradt's judgment, when he says that the Emperor's "first idea is always grand, and his second petty; that he is the man of extremes; one who having commanded the Alps to bow down, the Simplon to level its head, and the sea to advance and recede from its shores, ended by surrendering himself to an English cruiser." The Abbé de Pradt formed but a faint idea of the sublimity, grandeur, and magnanimity of that noble step. To withdraw himself from the people who were misled by faithless promises, in order to remove every obstacle to their welfare: to sacrifice his own personal interests, for the sake of averting the evils of civil war without national results: to disdain honourable and secure, but dependent asylums: to prefer taking refuge among a people to whom he had, for the space of twenty years, been an inveterate foe: to suppose their magnanimity equal to his own: to honour their laws so far as to believe they would protect him from the ostracism of Europe:—certainly such ideas and sentiments are not the reverse of sublime, noble, and great.

N. B. At this part of my journal were inserted several pages, full of details very discreditable to the Archbishop of Malines, which were received from the Emperor's own mouth, or collected from the different individuals about him. I however strike them out, in consideration of the satisfaction which I was informed the Emperor subsequently experienced in perusing M. de Pradt's *Concordats*. For my own part, I am perfectly satisfied with numerous other testimonies of the same nature, and derived from the same source. An honourable and voluntary acknowledgment is a thousand times better than all the retorts that can be heaped upon an offender. There are persons to whom atonement is not without its due weight; I am one of these.

Just as I had written the above, I happened to read some lines from the pen of the Abbé de Pradt, which are certainly very fine with respect to diction; but which are still finer on account of their justice and truth. I cannot refrain from transcribing them here; as they make ample amends for those already quoted. A declaration of the Allied Sovereigns at Laybach, in which Napoleon was, in terms of reprobation, pronounced to be the representative of the Revolution, called forth the following observations from the Archbishop of Malines :—

"It is too late to insult Napoleon, now that he is defenceless, after having for so many years crouched at his feet, while he had the power to punish..... Those who are armed should respect a disarmed enemy, and the glory of the conqueror in a great measure depends on the just consideration shewn towards the captive, particularly when he yields to superior force, not to superior genius. It is too late to call Napoleon a revolutionist, after having for such a length of time pronounced him to be the restorer of order in France, and consequently in Europe. It is odious to see the shaft of insult aimed at him by those who once stretched forth their hands to him as a friend, pledged their faith to him as an ally, sought to prop a tottering throne by mingling their blood with his." Farther on he says : "*He the representative of the Revolution!* The revolution broke the bonds of union between France and Rome: he renewed them. The revolution overthrew the temples of the Almighty: he restored them. The revolution created two classes of clergy hostile to each other: he united them. The revolution profaned Saint-Denis: he purified it, and offered expiation to the ashes of Kings. The revolution subverted the throne: he raised it up. The revolution banished from their country the nobility of France: he opened to them the gates of his palace, though he knew them to be his irreconcilable enemies, and for the most part the enemies of the public good; he re-incorporated them with the society from which they had been separated. This *representative of a revolution* (which is distinguished by the epithet anti-social) brought from Rome the head of the Catholic Church, to anoint his brow with the oil that consecrates diadems! This *representative of a revolution* (which has been declared hostile to sovereignty) filled Germany with kings, advanced the rank of princes, restored superior royalty, and re-constructed a defaced model. This *representative of a revolution* (which is condemned as a principle of anarchy,) like another Justinian, drew up, amidst the din of war and the snares of foreign policy, those codes which are the least defective portion of human legislature, and constructed the most vigorous machine of government in the whole world. This *representative of a revolution* (which is vulgarly accused of having subverted all institutions) restored universities and public schools, filled his empire with the master pieces of art, and accomplished those amazing and stupendous works, which reflect honour on human genius: and yet, in the face of the Alps, which bowed down at his command; of the ocean, subdued at Cherbourgh, at Flushing, at the Helder, and at Antwerp; of rivers, smoothly flowing beneath the bridges of Jena, Serres, Bordeaux, and Turin; of canals, uniting seas together in a course beyond the control of Neptune; finally, in the face of Paris, metamorphosed as it is by Napoleon,—he is pronounced to be the agent of general annihilation! He who restored all, is said to be the *representative* of that which destroyed all! To what undiscerning men is this language supposed to be addressed, &c."

My situation materially improved.—My bed-chamber changed, &c.

17th.—The Emperor summoned me at two o'clock, when he began to dress. On entering, he observed I looked pale: I replied, that it might be owing to the atmosphere of my chamber, which, from its proximity to the kitchen, was an absolute oven, being frequently filled with smoke. He then expressed a wish that I should constantly occupy the topographic cabinet, in which I might write during the day, and sleep at night, in a bed which the Admiral had fitted up for the Emperor himself, but which he did not make use of, as he preferred his own camp-bed. When he had finished dressing, and was choosing between two or three snuff-boxes which lay before him, he abruptly gave one to his valet-de-chambre (Marchand:) Keep it," said he, "it is always meeting my eye, and it vexes me." I know not what was on this snuff-box; but I imagine it was a portrait of the King of Rome.

The Emperor left his apartment, and I followed him: he went over the house, and entered my chamber. Seeing a dressing-glass, he enquired whether it was the one he had given me. Then putting his hand to the wall, which was heated by the kitchen, he again observed that I could not possibly remain in that room, and absolutely insisted on my occupying his bed in the topographic cabinet; adding in a tone of captivating kindness, that it was "the bed of a friend." We walked out, and proceeded in the direction of a wretched farm which was within sight. On our way we saw the barracks of the Chinese. These Chinese are men who enlist on board English ships at Macao, and who continue at Saint-Helena in the service of the East India Company for a certain number of years, when they return to their homes, after collecting a little store of money, as the people of Auvergne do in France. The Emperor wished to ask them some questions; but we could not make ourselves understood by them. We next visited what is called Longwood Farm. The Emperor was seduced by the name; he expected to find one of the delightful farms of Flanders or England; but this was merely on a level with our lowest *metairies*. We afterwards went down to the Company's garden, which is formed in the hollow where the two opposite ravines meet. The Emperor called the gardener, and the man who attends to the Company's cattle and superintends the Chinese, of whom he asked many questions. He returned home very much fatigued, though we had scarcely walked a mile: this was his first excursion.

Before dinner the Emperor summoned me and my son to our accustomed task. He said, I had been idle, and called my attention to my son who was laughing behind my back. He asked why he laughed; and I replied, that it was probably because his Majesty was taking revenge for him: "Ah!" said he, smiling, "I see I am here acting the part of the grandfather."

Habits and hours of the Emperor.—His style to the two Empresses.—Details.—The Emperor's maxims on the subject of the police.—Secret police for the Examination of letters.—Curious particulars.—The Emperor favourable to a fixed and moderate system of government.

18th—19th. By degrees our hours and habits began to be fixed and regular. About ten o'clock the Emperor breakfasted in his own chamber, and one of us occasionally attended him. At the table of the household we breakfasted at nearly the same hour. The Emperor granted us permission to do the honours of this table as we pleased, and to invite to it whomsoever we might think fit.

No hours were yet fixed for the Emperor's walks. The heat was very great during the day, and the damp came on speedily, and in great excess, towards evening. We were informed, some time before, that coach and saddle horses were coming from the Cape; but they never arrived. During the day the Emperor was engaged in dictating to different individuals of his suite; and he usually reserved me for the interval preceding dinner, which was not served until eight or nine o'clock. He required my attendance about five or six o'clock, together with my son. I could neither write nor read, owing to the state of my eyes; but my son was enabled to supply my place. He wrote to the Emperor's dictation, and I was present only to help him afterwards to correct his hasty scrawl; for, by dint of habit, I could repeat, almost literally and entirely, all that had fallen from the Emperor.

The Campaign of Italy being now finished, we began to revise it, and the Emperor corrected, and dictated anew. We dined, as I have before observed, between eight and nine o'clock. The table was laid out in the room nearest the entrance of the house. Madame de Montholon sat on the right of the Emperor; I on his left; and M. M. de Montholon, Gourgaud, and my son, sat in the opposite places. The room still smelled of paint, particularly when the weather was damp; and though not very offensive, it was sufficiently annoying to the Emperor: we, therefore, sat no longer than ten minutes at table, The dessert was prepared in the adjoining apartment, which was the drawing-room, and we again seated ourselves round the table. Coffee was then served up, and conversation commenced. We read a few scenes from Moliere, Racine, and Voltaire, and always regretted not having a copy of Corneille. We then played at *reversis*, which had been the Emperor's favourite game in his youth. The recollection was pleasing to him, and he at first thought he could amuse himself for a length of time at it; but he was soon undeceived. We played at the game and all its varieties; so that I have seen from fifteen to eighteen thousand counters in use at once. The Emperor's aim was always to make the reversis; that is to say, to make every trick, which is no easy matter. However, he frequently succeeded :—character developes itself every where and in every thing! We retired about ten or eleven o'clock.

To-day, the 19th, when I paid my respects to the Emperor, he shewed me a libel upon himself which had fallen into his hands, and asked me to translate it. Amidst a mass of other nonsense, some private letters were mentioned, which were said to have been addressed by Napoleon to the,

Empress Josephine, under the solemn form of *Madame et chère Epouse.* Allusion was next made to a combination of spies and agents, by whose aid the Emperor peeped into the private affairs of every family in France, and penetrated the secrets of all the cabinets in Europe. The Emperor wished to proceed no further, and made me lay aside the book, saying:—"It is too absurd!" The fact is, that, in his private correspondence, Napoleon always addressed the Empress Josephine very unceremoniously, by the pronoun "thou" (*tu;*) and "my good little Louisa" (*ma bonne petite Louise*) was the form by which he addressed Maria Louisa.

The first time I ever saw the Emperor's running hand, was at Saint-Cloud, after the battle of Friedland, when the Empress Josephine amused herself, by making us try to decypher a note which she held in her hand, and which seemed to be written in hieroglyphics. It was to the following effect:—"My sons have once more shed a lustre over my career: the victory of Friedland will be inscribed in history, beside those of Marengo, Austerlitz, and Jena. You will cause the cannon to be fired (*tu feras tirer le canon;*) Cambacérès will publish the bulletin."

I was again favoured with the sight of a note in the Emperor's hand-writing, at the time of the treaty of Tilsit. It contained the following. "The Queen of Prussia is really a charming woman. She is fond of coquetting with me; but do not be jealous: I am like a cerecloth, along which every thing of this sort slides, without penetrating. It would cost me too dear to play the gallant."

On this subject, an anecdote was related in the saloon of Josephine. It was said that the Queen of Prussia one day had a beautiful rose in her hand, which the Emperor asked her to give him. The Queen hesitated a few moments, and then presented it to him, saying: "Why should I so readily grant what you request, while you remain deaf to all my entreaties?" She alluded to the fortress of Magdeburg, which she had earnestly solicited. Such was the nature of the intimacy, and such the conversations, that were so unblushingly misrepresented in English works of a certain character, where the Emperor was described as an insolent and brutal tyrant, seeking, with the aid of his ferocious Mamelukes, to violate the honour of the lovely Queen, under the very eyes of her unfortunate husband.

As to the grand machinery of espionage and police, which has been so much talked of, what State on the Continent could boast of having less of such evils than France: and yet what country stood more in need of them! What circumstances more imperiously called for them? Every pamphlet published in Europe, was directed against France, with a view of rendering odious in another country, that which it was thought advisable to conceal at home. Still, however, these measures so necessary in principle, though doubtless hateful in their details, were looked at merely in a general way by the Emperor, and always with a strict observance of his constant maxim, that nothing should be done that is not absolutely indispensable. In the Council of State, I have frequently heard him make enquiries into these subjects; investigate them with peculiar solicitude; correct abuses and seek to obviate evils, and appoint committees of his Council to visit the prisons, and make reports to him. Having been myself employed in a mission of this nature, I had an opportunity of observing the misconduct and abuses of subaltern agents; and at the same time of knowing the ardent wishes of the sovereign to repress them.

The Emperor found that this branch of the administration in a certain degree clashed with established prejudices and opinions; and he therefore wished to elevate it in the eyes of the people, by placing it under the controul of a man whose character was beyond the reach of censure. In the year 1810, he summoned the counsellor of State, Baron ———, to Fontainbleau. The Baron had been an emigrant, or what nearly amounted to the same thing. His family, his early education, his former opinions,—all were calculated to render him an object of suspicion to one more distrustful than Napoleon. In the course of conversation, the Emperor said:—"If the Count de Lille were now to discover himself in Paris, and you were intrusted with the superintendence of the police, would you arrest him?" "Yes, certainly," answered the Counsellor of State, "because he would thereby have broken his ban, and because his appearance would be in opposition to every existing law." "If you were one of a committee appointed to try him, would you condemn him?" "Yes, doubtless; for the laws which I have sworn to obey would require that I should condemn him." "Very well!" said the Emperor, "return to Paris; I make you my prefect of police."—[See the Letters from the Cape.]

With regard to the inspection of letters under the government of Napoleon, whatever may have been publicly said on that subject, the Emperor declared, that certainly very few letters were read at the post-offices. Those which were delivered either open or sealed, to private persons, had, for the most part, not been read: to read all would have been an endless task. The system of examining letters was adopted with the view of preventing, rather than discovering, dangerous correspondence. The letters that were really read, exhibited no trace of having been opened, so effectual were the precautions employed. "Since the reign of Louis XIV," said the Emperor, there had existed an office of political police for discovering foreign correspondence; and since that period the same family had managed the business of the office, though the individuals and their functions were alike unknown. It was in all respects an official post. The persons superintending this department were educated at great expense in the different capitals of Europe. They had their own peculiar notions of propriety, and always manifested reluctance to examine French domestic correspondence: this matter, however, remained entirely at their own discretion. As soon as the name of any individual was entered upon the lists of this important department, his arms and seals were immediately engraved at the office; and with such a degree of accuracy, that the letters, after being read, were closed up and delivered without any mark of suspicion. These circumstances, joined to the serious evils they might create, and the important results they were capable of producing, constituted the vast responsibility of the office of postmaster-general, and required that it should be filled by a man of prudence, judgment, and intelligence." The Emperor bestowed great praise on M. de Lavalette, for the way in which he had discharged his duties.

The Emperor was by no means favourable to the system of inspecting correspondence. With regard to the diplomatic information thereby obtained, he did not consider it of sufficient value to counterbalance the expenses incurred; for the establishment cost 600,000 francs. As to the examination of the letters of citizens, he regarded that as a measure calculated to do more harm than good. "It is rarely," said he, "that a conspiracy is carried on through such channels; and with respect to the individual opinions obtained from epistolary correspondence, they may be more dangerous than useful to a sovereign, particularly among such a people as the French. Of whom will not our national volatility and fickleness lead us to complain? The man whom I may have offended at my levee, will write to-day that I am a tyrant, though but yesterday he overwhelmed me with praises, and perhaps to-morrow will be ready to lay down his life to serve me. The violation of the privacy of correspondence may, therefore, cause a prince to loose his best friends, by wrongfully inspiring him with distrust and prejudice towards all; particularly as enemies capable of mischief are always sufficiently artful to avoid exposing themselves to that kind of danger. Some of my ministers were so cautious in this respect, that I could never succeed in detecting one of their letters."

I think I have already mentioned that on the Emperor's return from Elba, there were found in M. de Blacas' apartments in the Thuilleries, numerous petitions and letters, in which Napoleon was spoken of most indecorously. "They would have formed a most odious collection," said the Emperor. "For a moment I entertained the idea of inserting some of them in the Moniteur. They would have disgraced certain individuals: but they would have afforded no new lesson on the human heart: men are always the same!"

The Emperor was far from knowing all the measures taken by the police, in his name, with respect to writings and individuals; he had neither time nor opportunity to inquire into them. Thus he daily learned from his ministers, or from the pamphlets that happened to fall in his way, the arrests of individuals, or the suppression of works, of which he had never before heard.

In alluding to the works that had been suppressed by the police during his reign, the Emperor observed, that having plenty of leisure time during his stay at Elba, he amused himself with glancing over some of these works, and that he was frequently unable to conceive the motives that had induced the police to suppress them.

He then proceeded to converse on the subject of the liberty and restriction of the press. This, he said, was an interminable question, and admitted of no medium. The grand difficulty, he observed, did not lie in the principle itself, but in the treatment of the accused party, or the circumstances under which it might be necessary to apply the principle taken in an abstract sense. The Emperor would have been favourable to unlimited liberty. In all our conversations at Saint-Helena, he constantly treated every great question in the same point of view and with the same arguments. Thus Napoleon truly was, and must remain in the eyes of posterity, the type, the standard, and the prince of liberal opinions; they belonged to his heart, to his principles, and to his mind. If his actions sometimes seemed at variance with these ideas, it was when he was imperiously swayed by circumstances. This is proved by the following fact, to which I now attach more importance than I did when it first came to my knowledge.

In one of the evening-parties at the Thuilleries, Napoleon conversing aside with three or four individuals of the court, who were grouped around him, closed a discussion on a great political question with the following remarable words:—"For my part, I am fundamentally and naturally favourable to a fixed and moderate government." And observing that the countenance of one of the interlocutors expressed surprise, "You don't believe me!" continued he:

"why not? It is because my deeds do not seem to accord with my words? My dear Sir, how little you know of men and things! Is the necessity of the moment nothing in your eyes? Were I to slacken the reins only for a moment, we should have fine disorder; neither you nor I would probably sleep another night at the Thuilleries."

The Emperor's first Ride on Horseback.—Severity of the Ministerial Instructions.—Our vexations and complaints.—The Emperor's Remarks.—Rude replies.

20th—23d. The Emperor mounted his horse after breakfast. We directed our course towards the farm: we found the farmer in the Company's garden, and he attended us over the whole of the grounds. The Emperor asked him a number of questions respecting his farm, as he used to do during his hunting excursions in the neighbourhood of Versailles, where he discussed with the farmers the opinions of the Council of State, in order to bring forward to the Council in their turn the objections of the farmers. We advanced through the grounds of Longwood, in a line parallel with the valley, until finding no farther road for the horses we were compelled to turn back. We then crossed the little valley, gained the height where the troops were encamped, advanced to the Alarm hill, and passing over its summit we arrived beyond the camp, near the Alarm house, on the road leading from Longwood to Madame Bertrand's residence. The Emperor at first proposed calling on her; but, when about half way thither, he changed his mind, and we returned to Longwood.

The instructions of the English Ministers with regard to the Emperor at Saint-Helena, were dictated in that disgraceful spirit of harshness, which in Europe had urged the solemn violation of the law of nations. An English officer was to be constantly at the Emperor's table; this cruel measnre was of course calculated to deprive us of the comfort of familiar conversation. The order was not carried into effect, only because the Emperor took his meals in his own chamber. I have very good reason to believe, that he regretted not having adopted the same resolution on board the Northumberland. An English officer was to accompany the Emperor in his rides on horseback: this was a severe annoyance, which rendered it impossible that his mind could for a moment be diverted from his unfortunate situation. This order was not, however, enforced within certain limits which were prescribed to us, because the Emperor had declared that he would not ride on horseback at all on such conditions.

In our melancholy situation, every day brought with it some new cause of uneasiness: we were constantly receiving some new sting, which seemed the more cruel, as we were destined to endure it for a long futurity. Yet, lacerated as our feelings undoubtedly were, each fresh wound was not the less sensibly felt. The motives that were assigned for our vexations frequently assumed the appearance of irony. Thus, sentinels were posted beneath the Emperor's windows, and before our doors; and this we were informed was for our own safety. We were cut off from all free communication with the inhabitants of the island; we were put under a kind of close confinement; and were told that this was done to free the Emperor from all annoyance. The pass words and orders were incessantly changed; we lived in the continual perplexity and apprehension of being exposed to some unforeseen insult. The Emperor whose feelings were keenly alive to all these things, resolved to write to the Admiral, through the medium of M. de Montholon. He spoke with warmth, and made some observations worthy of remark. "Let not the Admiral suppose," said he, "that I treat with him on any of these subjects. Were he to present himself to me to-morrow, in spite of my just resentment, he would find my countenance as serene, and my temper as composed, as usual. This would not be the effect of dissimulation on my part, but merely the fruit of experience. I recollect that Lord Whitworth once filled Europe with the report of a long conversation that he had had with me, scarcely a word of which was true. But that was my fault; and it taught me to be more cautious in future. The Emperor has governed too long not to know that he must not commit himself to the discretion of any one who may have it in his power to say falsely; *The Emperor told me so and so*; while the Emperor may not have the means of either affirming or contradicting the statement. One witness is as good as another. It is, therefore, necessary to employ some one, who may be enabled to tell the narrator that he speaks false, and that he is ready to set him right; which the Emperor himself cannot do."

M. de Montholon's letter was couched in sharp terms; the reply was insulting and coarse: *No such thing as an Emperor was known at St. Helena; the justice and moderation of the English government towards us, would be the admiration of future ages, &c.* Dr. O'Meara was instructed to accompany this written reply with verbal additions of the most offensive nature: to inquire, for example, whether the Emperor wished that the Admiral should send him sundry atrocious libels and anonymous letters, which had been received, addressed to him, &c.

I was engaged with the Emperor at the time this answer was communicated to him. I could not conceal my astonishment and indignation at certain expressions that were employed. But we could only let philosophy take place of resentment; it was sufficient to reflect that all satisfaction was beyond our reach. To address a direct complaint to the Prince Regent, would perhaps have been to furnish a gratification to that Prince; as well as a recommendation to him who had offended us. Besides, the Emperor could not address complaints to any individual on earth: he could appeal only to the tribunals of heaven, nations, and posterity.

On the 23d the Doris frigate arrived from the Cape, bringing seven horses that had been purchased there for the Emperor.

The Emperor's disdain of popularity, his reasons, arguments, &c.—Conversation respecting my Wife.—On General Gourgaud's Mother and Sister.

24th.—The Emperor had been reading some publication in which he was made to speak in too amiable a strain; and he could not help exclaiming against the mistake of the writer. "How could they put these words into my mouth?" said he, "This is too tender, too sentimental for me; every one knows that I do not express myself in that way." "Sire," I replied, "it was done with a good intention; the thing is innocent in itself, and may have produced a good effect. That reputation for amiability, which you seem to despise, might have exercised great influence over public opinion; it might at least have counteracted the effect of the colouring in which a European system has falsely exhibited your Majesty to the world. Your heart, with which I am now acquainted, is certainly as good as that of Henri IV, which I did not know. Now, his amiableness of character is still proverbial: he is still held up as an idol; yet I suspect Henri IV was a bit of a quack. And why should your Majesty have disdained to be so? You have too great an aversion to that system. After all, quackery rules the world: and it is fortunate when it happens to be only innocent."

The Emperor laughed at what he termed my prosing. "What," said he, "is the advantage of popularity and amiability of character? Who possessed those qualities in a more eminent degree than the unfortunate Louis XVI? Yet what was his fate? His life was sacrificed!—No! a sovereign must serve his people with dignity, and not make it his chief study to please them. The best mode of winning their love, is to secure their welfare. Nothing is more dangerous than for a sovereign to flatter his subjects: if they do not afterwards obtain every thing they want, they become irritated, and fancy that promises have been broken; and if they are then resisted, their hatred increases in proportion as they consider themselves deceived. A sovereign's first duty is doubtless to conform with the wishes of the people; but what the people say is scarcely ever what they wish: their desires and their wants cannot be learned from their own mouths so well as they are to be read in the heart of their prince.

"Each system may, no doubt, be maintained; that of mildness as well as that of severity. Each has its advantages and its disadvantages; for every thing is mutually balanced in this world. If you ask me what was the use of my severe forms and expressions, I shall answer, to spare me the pain of inflicting the punishment I threatened. What harm have I done, after all? What blood have I shed? Who can boast that, had he been placed in my situation, he could have done better? What period of history, exhibiting any thing like the difficulties with which I was surrounded, presents such harmless results? What am I reproached with? My government archives and my private papers were seized; yet what has there been found to publish to the world? All sovereigns, situated as I was, amidst factions, disorders, and conspiracies, are surrounded by murderers and executions. Yet, during my reign, what sudden tranquillity pervaded France!—You are, no doubt, astonished at this chain of reflection," continued he, smiling, "you, who frequently display the mildness and simplicity of a child."

I could not but admit the force of his arguments, and now, in my turn, maintained that both systems might have their peculiar advantages. "Every individual," said I, "should form for himself a character by means of education; but he should be careful, at the same time, to lay its foundation on the character he has received from Nature; otherwise he runs a risk of losing the advantages of the latter, without obtaining those of the character which he wishes to acquire; and his education may prove an instrument to mislead him. After all, the course of a man's life is the true result of his character, and the proper test by which it should be judged. Of what, then, can I have to complain? From the lowest degree of misery, I raised myself by my own efforts to tolerable independence; and from the streets of London, I penetrated to the steps of your throne, and to the benches of your Council-chamber; all this, too, without having cause to blush in the presence of any individual for any thing that I have ever spoken, written, or done. Have I not, then, also performed my little wonders in my own little way? What could I have done better had another turn been given to my character?"

The conversation was here interrupted by some one entering, to announce that the Admiral and some ladies, who had arrived by the Doris, solicited the favour of being presented to the Emperor; but he answered drily, that he would see no one, and that he did not wish to be disturbed.

Under our present circumstances, the personal politeness of the Admiral was felt only as an additional insult; and with regard to those who accompanied him, as no one could approach us but with the Admiral's permission, the Emperor did not choose that the honours of his person should be thus performed. If it were intended that he should remain in close confinement, he ought to be told so; but if not, he should be allowed to see whom he pleased without the interference of any person. Above all, it was not fair that they should pretend in Europe to surround him with every sort of attention and respect, while on the contrary they were annoying him with every kind of indecorum and caprice.

The Emperor walked out in the garden at five o'clock. The colonel of the 53d regiment waited on him there, and begged permission to present to him, next day, the officers of his regiment. The Emperor granted his request, and appointed three o'clock as the hour to receive them. The Colonel took his leave, and we prolonged our walk. The Emperor stopped awhile to look at a flower in one of the beds, and asked me whether it was not a lilly. It was, indeed, a magnificent one.

After dinner, while we were playing our usual game of reversis, of which, by the by, the Emperor began to grow weary, he suddenly turned to me and said, "Where do you suppose Madame Las Cases is at this moment?" "Alas, Sire," I replied, "Heaven knows!" "She is in Paris," continued he; "to-day is Tuesday; it is nine o'clock; she is now at the Opera." "No, Sire, she is too good a wife to go to a theatre while I am here." "Spoken like a true husband," said the Emperor, laughing, "ever confident and credulous!" Then turning to General Gourgaud, he joked him in the same style on his mother and sister. Gourgaud seemed very much downcast, and his eyes were suffused with tears, which the Emperor perceiving, cast a side-glance towards him, and said, in the most interesting manner, "How wicked, barbarous, and tyrannical I am, thus to trifle with feelings so tender!"

The Emperor then asked me how many children I had, and when and how I had become acquainted with Madame

Las Cases. I replied that my wife had been the first acquaintance of my life; that our marriage was a tie which we had ourselves formed in early youth, though it was not finally knit until the greater part of the events of the Revolution had passed away.

The Emperor frequently wounded in his campaigns.—Cossacks.—Jerusalem Delivered.

25th.—The Emperor, who had not been well the preceding evening, was still indisposed this morning, and sent word that it would be impossible for him to receive the officers of the 53d, as he had appointed. He sent for me about the middle of the day, and we again perused some chapters of the Campaign of Italy. I compared that which treats of the battle of Arcola, to a book of the Iliad.

Sometime before the dinner hour, he assembled us all around him in his chamber. A servant entered to announce that dinner was ready; he sent us away, but, as I was going out last, he called me back. "Stay here," said he, "we will dine together. Let the young people go; we old folks will keep one another company." He then expressed a desire to dress, intending, as he said, to go into the drawing-room after dinner.

While he was dressing, he put his hand on his left thigh, where there was a deep scar. He called my attention to it by laying his finger in it; and, finding that I did not understand what it was, he told me that it was the mark of a bayonet wound by which he had nearly lost his limb, at the siege of Toulon. Marchand, who was dressing him, here took the liberty of remarking, that the circumstance was well known on board the Northumberland; that one of the crew had told him, on going on board, that it was an Englishman who first wounded our Emperor.

The Emperor, on this, observed that people had in general wondered and talked a great deal of the singular good fortune which had preserved him, as it were, invulnerable in so many battles. "They were mistaken," added he; "the only reason was, that I made a secret of all my dangers." He then related that he had had thee horses killed under him at the siege of Toulon; that he had several killed and wounded in his campaigns of Italy; and three or four at the siege of Saint-Jean d'Acre. He added, that he had been wounded several times; that at the battle of Ratisbonne, a ball had struck his heel; and at the battle of Esling or Wagram, I cannot say which, a ball had torn his boot and stocking, grazed the skin of his left leg. In 1814, he lost a horse and his hat at Acris-sur-Aube, or its neighbourhood,

After the battle of Brienne, as he was returning to head-quarters in the evening, in a melancholy and pensive mood, he was suddenly attacked by some Cossacks, who had passed over the rear of the army. He thrust one of them away, and was obliged to draw his sword in his own defence; several of the Cossacks were killed at his side. "But what renders this circumstance very extraordinary," said he, "is, that it took place near a tree which at that moment caught my eye, and which I recognised as the very one under which, when I was but twelve years old, I used to sit during play-hours and read Jerusalem Delivered." . . . . Doubtless on that spot Napoleon had been first fired by emotions of glory!

The Emperor repeated that he had been frequently exposed to danger in his different battles, but it was carefully kept secret. He had enjoined, once for all, the most absolute silence on all circumstances of that nature. He said, it would be impossible to calculate the confusion and disorder which might have resulted from the slightest report or the smallest doubt relative to his existence. On his life depended the fate of the great Empire, and the whole policy and destinies of Europe. He added, that this habit of keeping circumstances of that kind secret, had prevented him from relating them in his campaigns; and indeed they were now almost forgotten. It was only, he said, by mere accident, and in the course of conversation, that they could recur to him.

My conversation with an Englishman.

26th.—The Emperor continued indisposed.

One of the English gentlemen, whose wife had yesterday been refused admittance, in company with the Admiral, paid me a visit this morning, with the view of making another and a final attempt to get presented to Napoleon. This gentleman spoke French very well, having resided in France during the whole of the war. He was one of those individuals who were known at the time by the title of *detenus:* who, having visited France as travellers, were arrested there by the First Consul, on the rupture of the treaty of Amiens, as a reprisal for the English Government having, according to custom, seized our merchant-ships before the declaration of war. This event gave rise to a long and animated discussion between the two Governments; and even prevented, during the whole of the war, a cartel for the exchange of prisoners. The English ministers persisted in refusing to consider their detained countrymen as prisoners, lest they should, in so doing, make an implicit renunciation of their sort of *right of piracy*. However, their obstinacy cost their countrymen a long captivity. They were detained in France more than ten years; their absence was as long and as irksome, though not so glorious, as the siege of Troy.

This English gentleman was a brother-in-law of Admiral Burton, the commander on the Indian station, who lately died. This circumstance might very possibly procure for him an immediate communication with ministers on his arrival in England. He might perhaps have been appointed by the Admiral to be the bearer of intelligence respecting us. Instead, therefore, of abridging our conversation, I prolonged it. It lasted more than two hours, and was all calculated on my part with a view to what he might repeat to the Admiral, or communicate to the Government or private circles in England. I am glad I did so. All I said was a recapitulation of our reproaches and griefs; a repetition of our complaints and vexations; a continued exposure of the violation of those laws that are esteemed most sacred; of the outrage on our good faith; of the arrogance, impertinence, and petty insolence of power. I dwelt particularly on the ill treatment to which we were here exposed; and on the caprices of the individual who was appointed as our keeper: "His glory," said I, "should consist, not in oppressing, but in relieving us. He should endeavour to make us forget, by his attentions, all the rigour and injustice of his country's policy. Could he have to fear the reprobation of mankind, while his good fortune enabled him gloriously to connect his name with that of the man of the age, the hero of history? Could he pretend that his instructions would prevent him?—Or European manners enabled him to interpret them suitably without detriment to his honour?"

The Englishman listened to me with great attention. He seemed occasionally to take particular interest in what I said; and expressed his approbation of several of my remarks. But was he sincere, and will he not express very different sentiments in London?

Whenever a ship arrives in England from Saint-Helena, the public papers immediately give insertion to various stories relative to the captives at Longwood of so false and absurd a nature, as must necessarily render them ridiculous to the great mass of the public. When we expressed our indignation at these idle reports in the presence of honourable and distinguished Englishmen here, they replied: "Do not deceive yourselves, these false accounts proceed not from our countrymen who visit you; but from our ministers in London; for, to the excess and violence of power, the administration by which we are now ruled joins all the meanness of the lowest and vilest intrigue."

On the French Emigrants.—Kindness shown by the English.—Resources of the Emigrants.

27th.—The Emperor felt himself better, and rode out on horseback about one o'clock. On his return he received the Officers of the 53d, and treated them in the most amiable and condescending manner.

After this visit, the Emperor, who had desired me to remain with him, walked in the garden. I there gave him an account of the conversation I had had the day before with the Englishman. He then asked me some questions relative to the French emigrants, London, and the English. I told him that though the emigrants in a body did not like the English, yet there were few who did not become attached to some Englishman or other: that though the English were not fond of the emigrants, yet there were few English families who did not show themselves friendly to some of the French. This is the real key of those sentiments and reports, so often contradictory, that are met with on the subject. With regard to the kindness we received from the English, particularly the middle class, from whom the character of a nation is always to be learned, it is beyond all expression, and has entailed a heavy debt of gratitude upon us. It would be difficult to enumerate the private benefactions, the benevolent institutions, and the charitable measures by which our distresses were relieved. The example of individuals induced the Government to assist us by regular allowances; and even when these were granted, private benevolence did not cease.

The Emperor here asked me whether I had been a sharer in the grants supplied by the English Government: I told him that I felt more pleasure in being indebted for support solely to my own exertions; and that the state of society in England was such, that with this feeling a man was sure to succeed. On two occasions I had had an opportunity of making my fortune? Colbert, Bishop of Rhodez, a native of Scotland, who was very fond of me, proposed that I should accompany his brother to Jamaica, where he was appointed to the executive power, and where he was one of the most considerable planters. He would have intrusted to me the direction of his property, and would have obtained for me other employment of the same kind. The Bishop assured me that I should make a fortune in three years. I could not, however, prevail on myself to go; I preferred continuing a life of poverty, to removing to a greater distance from the French shore.

"On another occasion," continued I, "some friends wished to persuade me to go to India, where I should have obtained employment and patronage, and where I was assured that in a short time I should realize a considerable fortune. But this I declined. I thought myself too old to travel so far. This was twenty years ago; and I am now at Saint-Helena.

"However, there were few who had suffered greater hardships than I did at the commencement of my emigration, and who enjoyed greater comforts towards its close. I have often, at night, found myself in want of the means of subsistence for the following day; still I was never discouraged or dejected. I consoled myself with the treasure of philosophy, and compared my own condition with that of numbers around me, who were more wretched than myself: to old men and women, for example, to those who were destitute of education, and who wanting the faculties requisite for acquiring a foreign language, were thus cut off from all resources. I was young, full of hope, and capable of exertion. I taught what I did not well know myself, and I learned overnight what I might have to teach on the succeeding day. My Historical Atlas was a fortunate idea, which opened to me a mine of gold. At that period, however, I had executed only an outline of my plan; but in London every thing is encouraged, every thing sells; and, moreover, Heaven blessed my exertions. I landed at the mouth of the Thames, and reached London on foot with only seven louis in my pocket, without a friend, without an introduction in a foreign land; but I left England in a post-chaise, possessed of 2500 guineas, having gained many dear friends, to serve whom I would gladly have sacrificed my life.

"But supposing I had been an emigrant," said the Emperor, "what would have been my lot?" He took a view of various professions, but decided in favour of a soldier's life. "I should have fulfilled my career after all," said he. "That is not quite certain," I observed. "Sire, you would have been smothered in the crowd. On arriving at Coblentz in any French corps, you would have been placed according to your rank on the list, without any possibility of getting beyond it; for we were rigid observers of forms," &c.

The Emperor then inquired when and how I had returned to France. "After the peace of Amiens," said I, "availing myself of the benefit of your amnesty; yet I joined an English family, and slipped in in a sort of contraband way, in order to reach Paris earlier than I otherwise could have done. Immediately on my arrival thither, fearing lest I should compromise that family, I went in person to make my declaration to the police, and received a paper which I was to present for inspection once a week or once a month. I paid no attention to it; but nothing occurred to me through my neglect. I had determined on conducting myself with prudence, and therefore felt satisfied that I had nothing to fear. At one time, however, I saw that my intention might have cost me dear: it was during the most violent crisis of the affair of Georges and Pichegru. I usually passed my evenings in the society of intimate friends in my own house; I scarcely ever went out. On this occasion, however, impelled by fate, or perhaps by the strong interest which I took in passing events, I strolled about in the Faubourg Saint-Germain till rather a late hour in the evening. I missed the way to the Pont de Louis XIV, which I knew so well, and came out upon the Boulevard des Invalids, without knowing where I was. The posts were every where increased in number, and each consisted of a double guard. I inquired my way of one of the sentinels, and I distinctly heard his comrade, who was a few yards off, ask him why he had not stopped me; he answered that I was doing no harm. I hastened home as fast as I could, terrified at the danger I had so narrowly escaped. I was in formal contravention with regard to the police: the circumstances of my emigration, my name, my habits, and my opinions, all tended to identify me with the malcontents. Every inquiry that could have been instituted respecting me would have been to my prejudice. I could not have referred to any one; and what alarmed me still more was, that they would have found five guineas in my pocket. I had, it is true, been in France two years; but these guineas were the last fruits of my industry; I always carried them about me; and I have them with me still. I used to take a pleasure in seeing them; they reminded me of a period of misfortune which had gone by. It is easy to conceive the conclusions which might have been drawn from so many concurring circumstances. In vain would have been my denials and assertions; no credit would have been given to me. I should, no doubt, have suffered considerably; and yet I was not in the least to blame: such is the justice of men! I never took the trouble to arrange my business with the police, and yet I never got into any trouble.

"When I was presented at your Majesty's court, the emigrants, who like myself had been placed under the superintendence of the police for ten years, applied for their emancipation, which they procured; for my part, I made no application of any sort. Being invited, in your Majesty's name, to a fête at Fontainebleau, I thought it would be a good joke to apply to the police for a passport. They agreed that it was, strictly speaking, necessary, but declined giving it, on the ground that the thing would be ridiculous. At a subsequent period, having become your Majesty's Chamberlain, I had occasion to go on a private journey; and they then exempted me from all future formality.

"On your Majesty's return in 1815, being desirous of serving some emigrants who had returned with the King, I went in their name to the police. Being a Counsellor of State, all the registers were open to me. After having inspected the article relating to my friends, I felt a curiosity to refer to my own. I found myself noted down as a distinguished courtier of the Comte d'Artois, in London. I could not help reflecting on the differences of times, and the changes produced by revolution. However, my register was altogether incorrect. I certainly visited the Comte d'Artois; but not oftener than once a month. As to my being a courtier, if I had been ever so much inclined to be one, the thing was out of my power. I had to provide for my daily subsistence, and I had pride enough to wish to live by my own industry; my time was therefore valuable." The Emperor was very much pleased with my story, and I was happy to have afforded him some amusement.

The frigate Doris sailed this day for Europe.

28th.—Mr. Balcombe's family called, in the hope of seeing the Emperor, but he was again indisposed. His health declines: this place is evidently unfavourable to him. He sent for me at three o'clock: he was slightly feverish, but felt himself better. He complained a good deal of the noise occasioned by the domestic arrangements of the house, which frequently annoyed him. He then dressed, with the intention of going out. I persuaded him to resume his flannel under-waistcoat, which he had laid aside very imprudently in this damp and variable climate. We took a walk in the garden, and the conversation continued to turn on the same subject as before. The Emperor strolled about at random, and we came to the gum-trees which run along the park, conversing on our local situation, and our relations with the authorities, and speculating on the political events of Europe. We were overtaken by a shower of rain, and were forced to take shelter under a tree. The Grand Marshal and M. de Montholon soon joined us. The Emperor made me return with him; and when we got home, he played a game at piquet in the drawing-room with Madame de Montholon. As it was very damp, the Emperor ordered a fire; but as soon as it was lighted, we were driven away by the smoke, and were compelled to take refuge in the Emperor's chamber. Here the game was resumed; but it was very soon suspended by the Emperor's conversation, which became most interesting. He entertained us with anecdotes and minute details of his domestic life, and confirmed, corrected, or contradicted those which Madame de Montholon and myself related to him, as having been publicly circulated. Nothing could be more gratifying: the conversation was quite confidential, and we sincerely regretted its interruption by the announcement of dinner.

Difficult Excursion.—Ride to the valley.—The Marsh.—Characteristic traits.—English undeceived.—Poison of Mithridates.

29th.—There is a spot in the grounds about Longwood, which commands a distant view of that part of the sea where the ships are first seen on their arrival: here, too, there is a tree, the foot of which affords a comfortable seat for the spectator. I had been in the habit, for some days past, of spending a few idle moments here, amusing myself, in idea, with looking out for the ship that was to conclude our exile. The celebrated Munich lingered out twenty years in the heart of Siberia, drinking every day to his return to Saint-Petersburgh: and was at length blessed with the accomplishment of his wish. I shall possess his courage; but I trust I shall not have occasion for his patience.

Ships have successively appeared for several days. Three came in sight very early this morning, two of which I judged to be ships of war. On my return home, I was informed that the Emperor had already risen: I went to the garden to meet him, and to acquaint him with my discovery. He ordered breakfast to be brought to him under a tree, and desired me to keep him company. After breakfast, he directed me to ride out with him on horseback. We rode along by the side of the gum-trees, beyond the confines of Longwood, and then attempted to descend into a very steep and deeply-furrowed valley, whose sides were covered with sand and loose stones, interspersed with brambles. We were obliged to dismount. The Emperor desired General Gourgaud to turn off to one side with the horses and the two grooms who accompanied us, and insisted on continuing his journey on foot, amidst the difficulties which surrounded us. I gave him my arm, and, with a great deal of trouble, we succeeded in climbing over the ridges. The Emperor lamented the loss of his youthful agility, and accused me of being more active than himself. He thought there was a greater difference in this respect than the trifling disproportion of our ages would justify. I told him that the pleasure of serving him made me forget my age. As we were going along, he observed, that any one who could have seen us at that time would recognise without difficulty the restlessness and impatience of the French character, "In fact," said he, "none but Frenchmen would ever think of doing what we are about." At length we arrived, breathless, at the bottom of the valley. What we had at a distance mistaken for a beaten road; proved to be nothing but a little streamlet, a foot and a half wide. We proposed to step across it and wait for our horses; but the banks of this little streamlet were very deceptive. They appeared to consist of dry ground, which at first supported us, but we soon found ourselves suddely sinking as though we had been breaking through ice. I had already sunk above my knees, when by a sudden effort I disengaged myself, and turned to assist the Emperor, who had both legs in the mud, and had got his hands on the ground, endeavouring to extricate himself. With a great deal of trouble and a great deal of dirt, we regained the *terra firma;* and I could not help thinking of the marshes of Arcola, which we had been engaged in describing a few days before, and in which Napoleon was very near being lost. The Emperor looked at his clothes and said, "Las Cases, this is a dirty adventure." "If we had been lost in the mud," added he, "what would have been said in Europe? The canting hypocrites would have proved beyond a doubt, that we had been swallowed up for our crimes."

The horses being at length brought to us, we continued our journey, breaking through hedges, and leaping over ridges; and with a great deal of difficulty we rode up the whole length of the valley, which separates Longwood from Diana's Peak. We returned back by the way of Madame Bertrand's residence; it was three o'clock when we reached home. We then learned that the vessels which had been seen in the morning were a brig and a transport from England, and an American ship.

The Emperor sent for me about seven o'clock; he was with the Grand Marshal, who was reading to him the newspapers from the 9th to the 16th of October. He had not done reading at nine o'clock. The Emperor, astonished to find it so late, hastily rose and went up to the table, complaining of being kept waiting for his dinner. They were stupid enough to give a very ridiculous reason for the delay. This domestic irregularity irritated him very much; and then he was angry with himself for feeling offended; so the dinner passed off in dulness and silence.

However on returning to the drawing-room for the dessert, the Emperor began to converse on the news which the papers had brought us: the conditions of peace, the fortresses ceded to foreign powers, and the fermentation of the great cities of Europe. He treated these subjects in a masterly style. He retired early; and had evidently not forgotten the circumstance which annoyed him at dinner.

He soon sent for me, being desirous to continue the perusal of the papers. As I was preparing to read, he recollected the state of my eyes, and would not allow me. I begged to be permitted to continue, telling him that I read quickly, and should soon have finished them; but he took them away from me, saying, "Nature will not obey our commands. I forbid it; I will wait till to-morrow." He then began to walk about a little, and soon gave utterance to the feelings which had oppressed his spirits. How amiable he appeared in his reproaches and complaints! How just and true was every observation that escaped him! These were a few of the precious moments when Nature, taken by surprise, exposes the inmost recesses of the human heart and character. I left him, saying within myself, as I have so often had occasion to say; "Good God, how little has the character of the Emperor been known to the world!"

They are beginning here to form a more just opinion of him, however. Those Englishmen whose violent prejudices against him were in a great degree excusable from the false accounts they had received, begin now to entertain a more correct idea of his character. They allow that they are strangely undeceived every day, and that the Emperor is a very different being from that Napoleon whose image had been traced to them through the medium of falsehood and political interests. All those who have had opportunities of seeing and hearing him converse, have but one opinion on the subject. The Admiral has more than once, in the midst of our disputes with him, hastily exclaimed that the Emperor was decidedly the most good-natured, just, and reasonable of the whole set. And here the Admiral was in the right.

On another occasion, an Englishman, whom we frequently saw, confessed to Napoleon, with the utmost humility of heart, and as it were by way of expiation, that he had to reproach his conscience with having once firmly believed all the abominable falsehoods related of him. He had given credit to all the accounts of stranglings, massacres, and brutal ferocity; in short, he even believed in the deformities of his person, and the hideous features of his countenance. "And," said he candidly, "how could I help crediting all this? Our English publications were filled with these statements; they were in every mouth; not a single voice was raised to contradict them." "Yes," said Napoleon smiling, "it is to your Ministers that I am indebted for these favours: they inundated Europe with pamphlets and libels against me. Perhaps they might say in excuse, that they did but reply to those which they received from France; and it must in justice be confessed that those

Frenchmen who have since been seen to exult over the ruins of their country, felt no hesitation in furnishing them with such articles in abundant supplies.

"Be this as it may, I was repeatedly urged during the period of my power, to adopt measures for counteracting this underhand work; but I always declined it. What advantage should I have gained by such a defence? It would have been said that I had paid for it, and that would only have discredited me still more. Another victory, another monument,—these, I said, are the best, the only answers I can make. Falsehood passes away, and truth remains! The sensible portion of the present age, and posterity in particular, will form their judgment only from facts. Is it not so? Already the cloud is breaking; the light is piercing through and my character grows clearer every day. It will soon become the fashion in Europe to do me justice. Those who have succeeded me, possess the archives of my administration and police, and the records of my tribunals: they hold in their pay, and at their disposal, those who must have been the executors, and the accomplices of my atrocities and crimes; yet, what proofs have they brought forward? What have they made known?

"The first moments of fury being passed away, all honest and sensible men will render justice to my character; none but rogues or fools will be my enemies. I may rest at ease; the succession of events, the disputes of opposing parties, their hostile productions, will daily clear the way for the correct and glorious materials of my history. And what advantage has been reaped from the immense sums that have been paid for libels against me? Soon every trace of them will be obliterated; while my institutions and monuments will recommend me to the remotest posterity.

"Now, however, it is too late to heap abuse upon me. The venom of calumny," said he, repeating an idea which he had before expressed, "has been exhausted on me; it can no longer injure me; it operates *like the poison on Mithridates.*"

The Emperor ploughing.—The widow's mite.—Interview with the Admiral.—New arrangements.—The Polish Captain Piontkowsky.

30th.—The Emperor desired me to be called before eight o'clock. While he dressed, I finished reading to him the newspapers which I had begun to examine the day before. When dressed, he himself went to the stables, asked for his horse, and rode out with me alone: his attendants not being yet quite ready. We rode on at random, and soon arrived in a field where some labourers were engaged in ploughing. The Emperor alighted from his horse, seized the plough, and, to the great astonishment of the man who was holding it, he himself traced a furrow of considerable length. He again mounted and continued his ride through various parts of the neighbourhood; and was joined successively by General Gourgaud and the grooms.

On his return, the Emperor expressed a wish to breakfast under a tree in the garden; and desired us to remain with him. During the ride he had mentioned a little present that he had intended for us. "It is a trifle to be sure," observed he; "but every thing must be proportioned to circumstances, and to me this is truly *the widow's mite*." He alluded to a monthly stipend which he had determined to settle on each of us. It was to be deducted from an inconsiderable sum, which we had contrived to secrete in spite of the vigilance of the English; and this sum was henceforth Napoleon's sole resource. It may well be imagined how precious this trifle had become. I seized the first moment, on finding myself alone with him, to express my opinion on this subject, and to declare my own personal determination to decline his intended bounty. He laughed at this, and as I persisted in my resolution, he said, pinching my ear, "Well, if you don't want it now, keep it for me; I shall know where to find it when I stand in need of it."

After breakfast the Emperor went in-doors, and desired me to finish reading the newspapers. I had been sometime engaged in reading when M. de Montholon requested to be introduced. He had just had a long conversation with the Admiral, who was very anxious to see the Emperor. I was directed to suspend my translations from the newspapers, and the Emperor walked about for some time as though hesitating how to proceed; but at length taking up his hat, he went into the drawing-room to receive the Admiral. This circumstance afforded me the highest satisfaction; for I knew that it was calculated to put a period to our state of hostility. I was well assured that two minutes conversation with the Emperor would smooth more difficulties than two days correspondence with any one else. Accordingly I was soon informed, that his convincing arguments, and amiable manners, had produced the wished-for effect. I was assured, that on his departure the Admiral appeared enchanted; as for the Emperor, he was very well pleased at what had taken place; he is far from disliking the Admiral, he is even somewhat prepossessed in his favour. "You may be a very good seaman," said the Emperor to him, "but you know nothing at all about our situation. We ask you for nothing. We can maintain ourselves without all those annoyances and privations; we can provide for ourselves; but still our esteem is worth the obtaining." The Admiral referred to his instructions. "But," replied the Emperor, "you do not consider the vast distance that intervenes between the dictation and the execution of those instructions! The very individual who issues them in a remote part of the world, would oppose them if he saw them carried into execution. Besides," continued he, "it is certain that on the least difference, the least opposition, the slightest expression of public opinion, the Ministers would disavow their instructions, or severely blame those who had not given them a more favourable interpretation."

The Admiral conducted himself wonderfully well; the Emperor passed high praises on him; all asperities were softened down, and good understanding prevailed. It was agreed that the Emperor should henceforth freely ride about the Island; that the officer who had been instructed to attend him, should merely watch him from a distance, so that the Emperor might not be offended with the sight of a guard; that visiters should be admitted to the Emperor, not with the permission of the Admiral, as the inspector of Longwood, but with that of the Grand Marshal who did the honours of the establishment.

To-day, our little colony was increased by the arrival of Captain Piontkowsky, a native of Poland. He was one of those individuals whom we had left behind us at Plymouth. His devotedness to the Emperor, and his grief at being separated from him, had subdued the severity of the English ministers, and he received permission to proceed to Saint-Helena.

Lieutenant-governor Skelton.

31st.—Lieutenant-governor Skelton and his lady, who had always shown us great attentions, came to present their respects to the Emperor, who, after an hour's conversation, desired me to translate to the Colonel an invitation to ride out with him on horse-back. The invitation was joyfully accepted, and we set out. We passed through the valley which separates us from Diana's Peak, to the great astonishment of the Colonel, to whom this course was perfectly new. He found the ride fatiguing, and in many parts dangerous. The Emperor detained Colonel and Mrs. Skelton to dinner, and entertained them in the most agreeable way.

New-year's-day—Fowling-pieces, &c.—Colonel Wilks's family.

January 1st—3d, 1816. On new-year's-day we all assembled about ten o'clock in the morning, to present the compliments of the season to the Emperor. He received us in a few moments. We had more need to offer him wishes than congratulations. The Emperor wished that we should breakfast and spend the whole day together. He observed that we were but a handful in one corner of the world, and that all our consolation must be our regard for each other. We all accompanied the Emperor into the garden, where he walked about until breakfast was ready. At this moment, his fowling-pieces, which had hitherto been detained by the Admiral, were sent back to him. This measure, on the part of the Admiral, was only another proof of the new disposition which he had assumed towards us. The guns could be of no use to the Emperor; for the nature of the ground, and the total want of game, rendered it impossible that he could enjoy even a shadow of diversion in shooting. There were no birds except a few pigeons among the gum-trees, and these had already been killed, or forced to migrate, by the few shots that Gen. Gourgaud and my son had amused themselves in firing.

We observed that measures which seemed to be dictated by the best and kindest intentions on the part of the Admiral, always bore an appearance of restriction and colouring of caprice, which destroyed their effect. Along with the Emperor's fowling-pieces, were two or three guns belonging to individuals of his suite. These were delivered to their owners; but on condition that they should be sent every evening to the tent of the officer on duty. It may well be supposed that this proposition induced us, without hesitation, to decline the favour altogether; and the guns were not surrendered to us unconditionally, until after a little parleying. And after all what were the important subjects under discussion? A few fowling pieces; and the owners of them were unfortunate men banished from the rest of the world, surrounded by sentinels, and guarded by a whole camp. I mention this circumstance, because, though trifling in itself, it proves better than many others our real situation, and the mode in which we were treated.

On the 3d I breakfasted with Madame Bertrand, whom I was to accompany to dine at the Governor's. From Madame Bertrand's abode to Plantation House (the Governor's residence), is an hour and a half's journey in a carriage drawn by six oxen, for the use of horses on this road would be dangerous. We crossed or turned five or six passes flanked with precipices several hundred feet high. Four of the oxen were taken from the carriage in the rapid descents, and yoked again in ascending the hills. We stopped when we had got about three parts of the way, to pay a visit to a good old lady of eighty-three years of age, who is very fond of Madame Bertrand's children. Her house is very pleasantly situated: she had not been out of it for sixteen years, when, hearing of the Emperor's arrival, she set out for the town, declaring that if it cost her her life, she was resolved to see him:—She was happy enough to gain her object.

Plantation House is the best situated, and most agreeable residence in the whole island. The mansion, the garden, the out-offices, all call to mind the residence of a family possessing an income of 25 or 30,000 livres in one of the French provinces. The grounds are cultivated with the greatest attention and taste. A resident at Plantation House might imagine himself in Europe, without ever suspecting the desolation that prevails over every part of the Island. Plantation House is occupied by Colonel Wilks, the Governor, whose authority is now superceded by the Admiral. He is a man of most polished manners: his wife is an amiable woman, and his daughter a charming young lady.

The Governor had invited a party of about thirty. The manners and ceremonies of the company were entirely European. We spent several hours at Plantation House; and this, we may truly say, has been the only interval of oblivion and abstraction that we have enjoyed since we quitted France. Colonel Wilks evinced particular partiality and kindness to me. We mutually expressed the compliments and sympathy of two authors, pleased with each other's merits. We exchanged our works. The Colonel overwhelmed me with flattering compliments; and those which I returned to him were of the sincerest kind; for his work contains a novel and interesting account of Hindostan, where he resided for a considerable time in a diplomatic capacity. A spirit of philosophy, a fund of information, joined to singular purity of style, concur to render it a production of first rate merit. In his political opinions, Colonel Wilks is cool and impartial; he judges calmly and dispassionately of passing events, and is imbued with the sound ideas and liberal opinions of an intelligent and independent Englishman.

As we were on the point of sitting down to dinner, we were, to our surprise, informed that the Emperor, in company with the Admiral, had just passed very near the gate of Plantation House; one of the guests (Mr. Doveton, of Sandy Bay) observed, that Napoleon had, in the morning, honoured him with a visit, and spent three-quarters of an hour at his house.

Life at Longwood.—The Emperor's ride on horse back.—Our nymph.—Nicknames.—On islands, and the defence of them.—Great fortresses; Gibraltar.—Cultivation and laws of the island.—Enthusiasm, &c.

4th—8th. When I entered the Emperor's apartments to give him an account of our excursion on the preceding day, he took hold of my ear, saying: "Well, you deserted me yesterday; I got through the evening very well, notwithstanding. Do not suppose that I could not do without you." Delightful words! rendered most touching by the tone which accompanied them, and by the knowledge I now possess of him by whom they were uttered.

The weather has every day been fine, the temperature dry; the heat intense, but abating suddenly, as usual, towards five or six o'clock.

The Emperor, since his arrival at Longwood, had left off his usual dictations: he passed his time in reading in his cabinet, dressed himself between three and four o'clock, and afterwards went out on horseback, accompanied by two or three of us. The mornings must have appeared to him longer; but his health was the better for it. Our rides were always directed towards the neighbouring valley, of which I have already spoken; we either passed up it, taking the lower part of it first, and returning by the Grand Marshal's house; or, on the contrary, went up that side first, in order to descend it in returning: we even went beyond it once or twice, and crossed other similar valleys. We thus explored the neighbourhood, and visited the few habitations which it contained; the whole of which were poor and wretched. The roads were sometimes impassable; we were even occasionally obliged to get off our horses. We had to clear hedges, to scale stone-walls, which we met with very frequently; but we suffered nothing to stop us.

In these our customary rides we had for some days fixed on a regular resting place in the middle of the valley. There, surrounded by desert rocks, an unexpected flower displayed itself: under an humble roof we discovered a charming young girl, of fifteen or sixteen years of age. We had surprised her the first day in her usual costume: it announced any thing but affluence. The following morning we found she had bestowed the greatest pains on her toilette; but our pretty blossom of the fields now appeared to us nothing more than a very ordinary garden flower. Nevertheless, we henceforth stopped at her dwelling a few minutes every day; she always approached a few paces to catch the two or three sentences which the Emperor either addressed, or caused to be translated to her as he passed by, and we continued our route, discoursing on her charms. From that time she formed an addition to the particular nomenclature of Longwood: she became *our nymph.* Among those who were intimate with him, the Emperor used, without premeditation, to invent new names for every person and object that attracted his notice. Thus the pass through which we were proceeding at the moment of which I am now writing, received the name of the *Valley of Silence;* our host at Briars was our *Amphitryon;* his neighbour, the Major, who was five feet high, was our *Hercules;* Sir George Cockburn was my *Lord Admiral,* as long as he were in good spirits, but, when ill-humour prevailed, there was no title for him but such as the *shark,* &c.

Our nymph is the identical heroine of the little pastoral with which Doctor Warden has been pleased to embellish his Letters; although I corrected his error, when he gave me the manuscript to read before his departure for Europe, by telling him; "If it is your intention to form a tale, it is well; but if you wish to depict the truth, you must alter this entirely." It should seem that he thought his tale possessed far more interest; and he has preserved it accordingly. But to return to our *nymph:* I have been informed, that Napoleon brought her great good fortune. The celebrity which she acquired through him, attracted the curiosity of travellers, and her own charms effected the rest: she is become the wife of a very rich merchant, or captain, in the service of the East India Company.

On returning from our rides, we used to find assembled the persons whom the Emperor had invited to dine with him. He had, successively, the Colonel of the 53d, several of the officers and their ladies, the Admiral, the beautiful and amiable Mrs. Hodson, the wife of our Hercules, whom the Emperor went one day to visit in the valley of Briars, and whose children he had taken so much notice of, &c. &c.

After dinner, the Emperor joined our party at cards, and the rest of the company formed another.

The day the Admiral dined at Longwood, the Emperor, whilst taking his coffee, discoursed for a few minutes upon the affairs of the Island. The Admiral said that the 66th regiment was coming to reinforce the 53d. The Emperor laughed at this; and asked him, if he did not think himself already strong enough. Then continuing his general observations, he said that an additional seventy-four would be of more use than a regiment; that ships of war were the security of an Island: that fortifications produced nothing but delay; that the landing of a superior force was a complete success, although its effects might be deferred for a time; provided, however, the distance did not admit of succour arriving.

The Admiral having asked him which, in his opinion, was the strongest place in the world, the Emperor answered, it was impossible to point it out, because the strength of a place arises partly from its own means of defence, and partly from extraneous and indeterminate circumstances. He, however, mentioned Strasburg, Lille, Metz, Mantua, Antwerp, Malta, and Gibraltar. The Admiral having told him that he had been suspected in England, for some time, of entertaining a design to attack Gibraltar: "We knew better than that," replied the Emperor; "it was our interest to leave Gibraltar in your possession. It is of no advantage to you; it neither protects nor intercepts any thing; it is only an object of national pride, which costs England very dear, and gives great umbrage to Spain. It would have been very injudicious in us to destroy such arrangements."

On the 6th I was invited, with Madame Bertrand and my son, to dine at Briars, where our old host had assembled much company. We returned very late, and not without having been exposed to danger, from the difficulties of the road, and the darkness of the night, which obliged us to perform part of the journey on foot, from consideration for Madame Bertrand.

On the 7th the Emperor received a visit from the Secretary of the Government and one of the members of the Council. He asked them a great many questions, as usual, concerning the cultivation, the prosperity, and the improvements of which the Island might be capable. In 1772 a system had been adopted for furnishing meat at half price to the inhabitants from the magazines of the Company: the consequence of which was, great idleness and neglect of agriculture. This system was altered five years ago; which, added to other circumstances, has revived emulation, and carried the prosperity of the Island to a pitch far beyond what it ever enjoyed before. It is to be feared that our arrival may prove a mortal blow to this growing prosperity.

Saint-Helena, which is seven or eight leagues in circumference (about the size of Paris,) is subject to the general laws of England and the local ones of the Island: these local laws are drawn up by a Council, and are sanctioned in England by the Court of Directors of the East India Company. The Council is composed of a Governor, of two civil members, and a Secretary, who keeps the registers; they are all appointed by the Company, and are subject to be removed at pleasure. The members of the Council are legislators, administrators, and magistrates; they decide without appeal, with the aid of a jury, upon civil and criminal matters. There is neither advocate nor attorney in the Island; the Secretary of the Council legalizes all acts, and is a kind of uniqûe notary. The population of the Island amounts at this moment to about five or six thousand souls, including the blacks and the garrison.

I was walking one afternoon in the garden with the Emperor, when a sailor, about twenty-two or twenty-three years of age, with a frank and open countenance, approached us with gestures expressive of eagerness and joy, mingled with apprehension of being perceived from without. He spoke nothing but English, and told me in a hurried manner, that he had twice braved the obstacle of sentinels and all the dangers of severe prohibition, to get a close view of the Emperor. He had obtained this good fortune, he said, looking steadfastly at the Emperor, and should die content; that he offered up his prayers to Heaven that Napoleon might enjoy good health, and be one day more happy. I dismissed him; and on quitting us, he hid himself again behind the trees and hedges, in order to have a longer view of us. We frequently met with such unequivocal proofs of the good-will of these sailors. Those of the Northumberland, above all, considered themselves as having formed a connexion with the Emperor. While we were residing at Briars, where our seclusion was not so close, they often hovered on a Sunday around us, saying they came to take another look at their ship-mate. The day on which we quitted Briars, I was with the Emperor in the garden, when one of the sailors presented himself at the gate, asking me if he might step in without giving offence. I asked him of what country he was, and what religion he professed. He answered by making various signs of the cross, in token of his having understood me, and of fraternity. Then looking steadfastly upon the Emperor, before whom he stood, and raising his eyes to Heaven, he began to hold a conversation with himself, by gestures, which his stout jovial figure rendered partly grotesque, and partly sentimental. Nevertheless it would have been difficult to express more naturally, admiration, respect, kind wishes, and sympathy; whilst big tears started in his eyes. "Tell that dear man," said he to me, "that I wish him no harm, but all possible happiness. So do most of us. Long life and health to him!" He had a nosegay of wild flowers in his hand, which he seemed to wish to offer to us; but either his attention was taken up, or he felt restrained by the Emperor's presence, or his own feelings, and he stood wavering, as if contending with himself for sometime; then suddenly made us a bow, and disappeared.

The Emperor could not refrain from evincing some emotion at these two circumstances; so strongly did the countenances, accents, and gestures of these two men bear the stamp of truth. He then said, "See the effect of imagination! How powerful is its influence! Here are people who do not know me—who have never seen me; they have only heard me spoken of; and what do they not feel! what would they not do to serve me! And the same caprice is to be found in all countries, in all ages, and in both sexes! This is fanaticism! Yes, imagination rules the world!"

Vexatious treatment of the Emperor.—Fresh misunderstandings with the Admiral.

9th.—The grounds round Longwood, within which we have the liberty of taking the air, admit of only half an hour's ride on horseback; which has induced the Emperor, in order to extend his ride, or to occupy more time, to descend into the ravines by very bad, and indeed dangerous ways.

The Island not being thirty miles in circumference, it would have been desirable to have the circuit extended to within a mile of the sea-coast; then we might have had our rides, and even varied them, within a space of fifteen or eighteen miles. The watching of our movements would neither have been more troublesome nor less effectual, had sentinels been placed upon the sea-shore and at the openings of the valleys; or even had they traced all the Emperor's steps by signals. It is true it had been observed to us, that the Emperor was at liberty to go over the whole of the Island under the escort of an English officer; but the Emperor had decided that he would never go out, if deprived of the pleasure of being either entirely by himself, or in the society of his friends only. The Admiral, in his last interview with the Emperor, had with great delicacy settled, that whenever he (the Emperor) wished to go beyond the prescribed limits, he was to inform the English Captain on duty at Longwood of the circumstance; that the latter should go to his post to open the passage for the Emperor; and that the observation, if any, should thenceforth be continued in such a manner that the Emperor, during the remainder of his excursion, whether he entered any house or took advantage of any fine situation for proceeding with his works, might perceive nothing that could for a moment distract his mind from meditation. According to this arrangement, the Emperor proposed this morning to mount his horse at seven o'clock: he had ordered a slight breakfast to be prepared, and intended to go in the direction of Sandy

Bay, to see a spring of water, and to pass the morning amongst some fine vegetation, (an advantage which we did not possess at Longwood ;) and in this spot he proposed to dictate for a few hours.

Our horses were ready; at the moment when we were about to mount them, I went to acquaint the Captain with our intention, who, to my great astonishment, declared his determination of riding beside us; saying that the Emperor could not take it ill, after all, that an officer would not act the part of a servant by remaining behind alone. I replied that the Emperor doubtless would approve this sentiment; but that he would immediately give up his party of pleasure. "You must," said I, "think it very natural, and by no means a ground of offence, that he feels a repugnance to the company of a person who is guarding him." The officer evinced much concern, and told me that his situation was extremely embarrassing. "Not at all so," I observed to him, "if you only execute your orders. We ask nothing of you; you have nothing to justify or explain to us. It must be as desirable to you as to us to get the limits extended towards the sea-shore: you would thereby be freed from a troublesome duty, and one which can do you no honour.—The end proposed would not be the less effectually accomplished by such an arrangement. I will venture to say, it would be more so: whenever we wish to watch a person, we must guard the door of his room, or the gates of the enclosure which surrounds him; the intermediate doors are only sources of unavailing trouble. You lose sight of the Emperor every day when he descends into the deep hollows within the circuit, and you ascertain his existence only by his return. Well, then, make a merit of a concession which the nature of things demands. Extend the limits to within a mile of the sea-shore; you may then also trace the Emperor constantly by means of your signals, from your heights."

To all this the officer replied only by repeating that he wanted neither look nor word from the Emperor; that he would be with us, as if he were not present. He seemed, and indeed he was, unable to comprehend that the mere sight of him could be offensive to the Emperor. I told him that there was a scale for the degrees of feeling, and that the same measure did not apply to all the world. He appeared to think that we were putting our own interpretations on the Emperor's sentiments, and that, if the reasons which he gave me were explained to him (the Emperor), the latter would accede to them. He was inclined to write to him. I assured him that as far as related personally to himself, he would not be able to say so much to the Emperor as I myself should: but that I would go and repeat to the Emperor, word for word, the conversation which had passed between us. I went: I soon returned, and confirmed to him what I had before advanced. The Emperor from that moment gave up his intended jaunt.

Wishing, however, on my own account, to avoid every misunderstanding which might add to discussions at all times disagreeable, I asked him whether he had any objection to show me the account he intended to give the Admiral. He told me he had none; but that he should only give a verbal one. Then resuming our long conversation, I reduced it in a few words, to two very positive points: on his part, that he had told me he wished to join the party of the Emperor; and on mine, that I had replied that the Emperor from that moment gave up his party, and would not go beyond the limits assigned to him. This statement was perfectly agreed upon by both of us. The Emperor ordered me to be called into his room. Brooding in profound silence over the vexation he had just experienced, he had undressed again, and was in his morning-gown. He detained me to breakfast, and observed that the sky seemed to threaten rain; that we should have had a bad day for our excursion. But this was a poor consolation for the cruel restraint which had just deprived him of an innocent pleasure.

The fact is, that the officer had received fresh orders; but the Emperor had only grounded the project of his little excursion upon the anterior promises of the Admiral, at which the Emperor had felt a pleasure in expressing his satisfaction to him. The present alteration, of which nothing had been said to the Emperor, must necessarily have been extremely unpleasant to him. Either the word given him was broken, or an attempt had been made to impose on him.—This affront which he experienced from the Admiral, is one of those which have considerably hurt the feelings of the Emperor.

The Emperor taking a bath, and did not dine with us.—At nine o'clock he ordered me to be called into his room: he was reading Don Quixote, which turned our conversation upon Spanish literature, the translation of Le Sage, &c. He was very melancholy, and said little; he sent me away in about three quarters of an hour.

Marchand's room.—Linen, Garments, &c. of the Emperor.—Spurs of Champaubert, &c.

10th.—About four o'clock the Emperor desired me to be called into his room: he was dressed, and had his boots on; his intention was either to get on horseback, or to take a walk in the garden; but a gentle shower of rain was falling.

We walked about in conversation, waiting for the weather to clear up. He opened the door of his room leading to the topographical cabinet, in order that we might extend our walk the whole length of this cabinet. As we approached the bed, he asked me if I always slept in it. I answered, that I had ceased to do so from the moment that I became acquainted with his wish of going out early in the morning. "What has that to do with it?" said he: "return to it; I shall go out when I please, by the back-door." The drawing-room door stood half open, and he entered it; Montholon and Gourgaud were there. They were endeavouring to fix a very pretty lustre, and a small glass over the chimney-piece: the Emperor desired the latter might be set straight, as it inclined a little on one side. He was much pleased at this improvement in the drawing-room furniture; a proof that every thing is relative! What could these objects have been in the eyes of a man, who, some years ago, had furniture to the value of forty millions in his palaces?

We returned to the topographical cabinet: the rain continued to fall, he gave up his promenade; but he regretted that the Grand Marshal had not arrived; he felt himself this day inclined for work, which he had discontinued for fifteen days. He endeavoured to kill time, whilst waiting for Bertrand. "Let us go and see Madame de Montholon," said he to me. I announced him; he sat down, made me do the same; and we talked about furniture and housekeeping. He then began to form an inventory of the articles in the apartment, piece by piece; and we all agreed that the furniture was not worth more than thirty Napoleons. Leaving Madame de Montholon's, he ran from room to room, and stopped in front of the staircase in the corridor which leads to the servants' room above; it is a kind of very steep ship-stair. "Let us look at Marchand's apartment," said he; "they say that he keeps it like that of a "*petite maitresse*." We climbed up; Marchand was there; his little room is clean; he has pasted paper upon it, which he has painted himself. His bed was without curtains: Marchand does not sleep so far from his master's door; at Briars, he and the two other valets de chambre constantly slept upon the ground, across the Emperor's doorway, so close, that whenever I came away late, I was obliged to step over them. The Emperor ordered the presses to be opened; they contained nothing but his linen and his clothes: the whole was not considerable, and he, nevertheless, was astonished to find himself still so rich. "How many pair of spurs have I?" said he, taking up a pair. "Four pair," answered Marchand. "Are any of them more remarkable than the rest?" "No Sire." "Well, I will give a pair of them to Las Cases. Are these old?" "Yes, Sire, they are almost worn out; your Majesty wore them in the campaign of Dresden, and in that of Paris."—"Here," said he, "giving them to me; these are for you." I could have wished that he would have permitted me to receive them on my knees. I felt that I was really receiving something connected with the glorious days of Champaubert, Montmirail, Nangis, Montereau! Was there ever a more appropriate memorial of chivalry, in the times of Amadis? "Your Majesty is making me a knight," said I; "but how am I to win these spurs? I cannot pretend to achieve any feat of arms; and as to love and devotion, Sire, all I have to bestow, have long since been disposed of."

Still the Grand Marshal did not arrive, and the Emperor wished to set to work. "You cannot write any longer then!" he said to me. "Your eye-sight is quite gone."—Ever since we had been here I had given up work entirely; my eye-sight failed me, which made me extremely melancholy. "Yes, Sire," I replied, "it is entirely gone, and I am grieved that I lost it in the Campaign of Italy, without enjoying the happiness and glory of having served in it."—He endeavoured to console me, by telling me, that I should recover my eye-sight beyond a doubt by repose, adding, "Oh why did they not leave us Planat? that good young man would now be of great service to me." And he desired General Gourgaud to come, that he might dictate to him.

Admiral Taylor, &c.

11th.—As I was walking after breakfast, about half-past twelve, before the gate, I saw a numerous cavalcade approaching, preceded by the Colonel of the 53d: it was Admiral Taylor, who had arrived the evening before with his squadron from the Cape, and was to leave us the next day but one for Europe. Among his captains was his son, who had lost his arm at the battle of Trafalgar, where his father commanded the Tonnant.

Admiral Taylor said, he was come to pay his respects to the Emperor; but he had just received for answer that he was unwell: at which the Admiral was much disappointed. I observed to him, that the climate of Longwood was very unfavourable to Napoleon. I chose an unlucky time for making this observation, as the sky was beautiful, and the place displayed at this moment all the illusion which it is capable of producing: the Admiral did not fail to remark that the situation was charming. I replied in a tone of genuine sorrow. "*Yes, admiral, to-day, and for you, who only remain a quarter of an hour in it."* At this he seemed quite disconcerted, began to make excuses, and begged me to pardon him for having made use of what he called an impertinent expression. I must render justice to the peculiar urbanity of manner which he evinced on this occasion.

The Emperor aimed at by a Soldier.—Our Evening Amusements.—Novels.—Political sally.

12th—14th.—The Emperor had now for several days left off his excursions on horseback. The result of his attempt to resume them, on the 12th, was neither calculated to revive his partiality for this amusement, nor to render it once more habitual to him. We had cleared our valley as usual, and were re-ascending it at the back part opposite Longwood, when a soldier from one of the heights, where there had hitherto been no post, called out several times, and made various signs to us. As we were in the very centre of our circuit, we paid no attention to him. He then came running down towards us, out of breath, charging his piece as he ran. General Gourgaud remained behind, to see what he wanted, while we continued our route. I could see the general, after dodging the fellow many times, collar and secure him: he made him follow him as far as the neighbouring post of the Grand Marshal, which the General endeavoured to make him enter, but he escaped from him. He found that he was a drunken corporal, who had not rightly understood his countersign. He had frequently levelled his piece at us. This circumstance, which might have been very easily repeated, made us tremble for the Emperor's life: the latter looked upon it only as an affront, and a fresh obstacle to the continuance of his exercises on horseback.

Napoleon had left off giving invitations to dinner: the hours, the distance, the dressing, were inconvenient to the guests: to us these parties produced only trouble and constraint, without any pleasure.

The Emperor had unconsciously resumed his regular work. He now dictated daily to the Grand Marshal upon the expedition to Egypt; some time before dinner he ordered me and my son to be called to him, in order to read the different chapters of the Campaigns of Italy over again, and separate them into paragraphs. Cards had gone out of fashion; the Emperor had given them up. The time after dinner was henceforth devoted to the reading of some work: the Emperor himself read aloud; when he was tired, he handed the book over to some other person; but then he never could bear their reading more than a quarter of an hour. We were now reading novels, and we began many which we never finished. *Manon l' Escaut* we soon rejected as fit only for the anti-chamber; then followed the *Memoirs of Grammont*, which are so full of wit, but so little honourable to the morals of the great of that period: the *Chevalier de Faublas*, which is only to be endured at the age of twenty years, &c. Whenever these readings could be protracted to eleven o'clock, or midnight, the Emperor seemed truly rejoiced. He called this making conquests over time; and he found such victories not the most easy to gain.

Politics had also their turn. Every three or four weeks or thereabouts, we received a large packet of journals from Europe; this, like the cut of a whip, set us going again for some days, during which we discussed, analyzed, and re-discussed the news; and afterwards fell again insensibly into our usual melancholy. The last journals had reached us by the corvette La Levrette, which had arrived some days before. They occupied one of the evenings, and gave rise to one of those moments, wherein that ardour and inspiration burst forth from the Emperor, which I have sometimes witnessed in the Council of State, and which escape him from time to time even here.

He took large strides as he walked amongst us, becoming more animated, and only interrupting his discourse by a few moments of meditation.

"Poor France," said he, "what will be thy lot! Above all, what is become of thy glory! . . . .
. . . ."

I suppress the rest, which is of very great length: I *must* suppress it.

The papers seeming to say that England desired the dismemberment of France, but that Russia had opposed it, the Emperor said that he expected this; that it was the natural system that Russia must be dissatisfied at seeing France divided; whilst, on the other hand, the English aristocracy must be desirous of reducing France to the extreme of weakness, and of establishing despotism upon her ruins. "I know," said he, "that this is not your opinion," addressing himself to me; "you are an Englishman." I replied, that it was very difficult to dispute with him; but that it appeared to me that in this same English aristocracy, it must be allowed, that there might possibly exist, sufficiently clear heads, as well as hearts just enough to understand that, after having overthrown that which threatened their existence, it might prove advantageous to raise up that which was no longer to be dreaded. That circumstances were now singularly favourable for establishing a new system, which might for ever unite the two nations in their dearest interests; might render them necessary to each other; instead of keeping them in perpetual enmity, &c. The Emperor concluded the conversation by saying, that he must be very perverse without doubt; but that, with every consideration he could give the subject, he could foresee nothing but catastrophes, massacres, and bloodshed.

On the Secret History of the Cabinet of Bonaparte, by Goldsmith.—Details, &c.

15th.—When I was on board the Northumberland, I had heard the *Secret History of the Cabinet of Bonaparte, by Goldsmith*, spoken of, and; in my first leisure moments here, I felt an inclination to skim it over; but I met with great difficulty in obtaining it, as the English excused themselves from putting it into my hands for a considerable time, saying, it was such an abominable libel that they were afraid to let me have it; and were themselves ashamed of it. I was for a long time under the necessity of urging them incessantly, repeating that we were all proof against such civilities; that he who was the object of them only used to laugh at such things, when chance brought them before his eyes; and moreover, that if this work was so bad as it was said to be, it must have failed in its end, and ceased to be hurtful at all. I asked who this Goldsmith, the author, was. I was told he was an Englishman who . . . .

. . . .

at Paris, and who, upon his return to England, had endeavoured to avoid . . . . and at the same time to gain more money, by loading with insults and imprecations that idol to whom he had so long offered incense. I at last obtained the work. It must be confessed that it would be difficult to collect together more horrible and ridiculous abominations than are presented to us in the first pages of this book: rapes, poison, incest, assassination, and all that belongs to them, are heaped by the author upon his hero, and that from his earliest childhood. It is true, that the author appears to have given himself little concern about bestowing on these calumnies any air of probability; and that he himself sometimes demonstates their impossibility, and sometimes refutes them by anachronisms, alibis, and contradictions of every kind; mistakes in the names, persons, and the most authentic facts, &c. Thus, for example, when Napoleon was only about ten or twelve years of age, and was confined within the bounds of the Military School, he caused him to commit outrages which would require as least the age of manhood, and a certain degree of liberty, &c. The author makes him undertake what he calls the robberies of Italy, at the head of eight thousand galley-slaves, who had escaped from the bagnio at Toulon. Afterwards, he makes twenty thousand Poles abandon the Austrian ranks to join the standard of the French General, &c. The same author makes Napoleon arrive at Paris in Fructidor, when all the world knows that he never quitted his army. He makes him treat with the Prince of Condé, and ask the hand of the Princess Royal as the price of his treachery. I omit a number of things equally absurd and impudent. It is evident that, with respect to the loose and ridiculous anecdotes particularly, he only collected all he could hear; but from what source has he drawn his information? The greater part of the anecdotes have certainly had their rise in certain defamatory and malevolent circles of Paris: but, as long as they were on that ground, they still preserved the appearance of some wit, salt, point, colour, some grace in the relation; whilst the stories in this book have evidently descended from the drawing-rooms into the streets, and have only been picked up after rolling in the kennel. The English allowed it was so coarse, that, with the exception of the most vulgar classes of society, the work was a poison which carried its own antidote along with it.

It may probably excite astonishment that I did not lay aside such a production upon reading the first page of it; but its coarseness and vulgarity are so gross that it cannot excite anger: on the other hand, there is no disgust which may not be got over in order to amuse the heavy hours at Saint-Helena. We consider ourselves fortunate in having any thing to run over. "Time," said the Emperor, a few days ago, "is the only thing of which we have too much here." I therefore continue the work. And besides, I may perhaps be allowed to say, that it is not without some pleasure that I now read the absurd tales, the lies, and calumnies, which an author pretends to derive, as usual, from the best authority, relating to objects which I am now so perfectly well acquainted with, and which have become as familiar to me as the details of my own life; and it is likewise gratifying to lay down pages filled with the falsest representations, and exhibiting a portrait purely fantastical, to go and study truth by the side of the real personage, in his own conversation ever full of novelties and grand ideas.

The Emperor having desired me to come to him this morning after breakfast, I found him in his morning-gown extended upon his sofa. The conversation led him to ask me what I was reading at this moment. I replied, that it was one of the most notorious and scurrilous libels published against him, and I quoted to him upon the spot some of its most abominable stories. He laughed greatly at them, and desired to see the work. I sent for it, and we went over it together. In passing from one horrid calumny to another, he exclaimed, "*Jesus!*" crossing himself repeatedly, a custom which I have perceived is familiar with him, in his little friendly circle, whenever he meets with monstrous, impudent, or obscene assertions; or such as excite his indignation and surprise without stirring up his anger. As we were going on, the Emperor analyzed certain facts, and corrected points of which the author might have known something. Sometimes he shrugged up his shoulders out of compassion; at others, laughed heartily; but he never betrayed the least sign of anger. When he read the article which speaks of his great debaucheries and excesses, the violences and the outrages which he is made to commit, he observed that the author, doubtless wished to make a hero of him in every respect; that he willingly left him to those who had charged him with impotency; that it was for these gentlemen to agree among themselves; adding, merely, "that every man was not so unlucky as the pleader of Toulouse." They were in the wrong, however, he continued, to attack him upon the score of morals; him, who, as all the world knew, had so singularly improved them. They could not be ignorant that he was not at all inclined, by nature, to debauchery; and that, moreover, the multiplicity of his affairs would never have allowed him time to indulge in it. When we came to the pages where his mother was described as acting the most disgusting and abject part at Marseilles, he stopped, and repeated several lines with an accent of indignation, and something approaching to grief, "Ah! Madame! — Poor Madame!—with her lofty character! if she were to read this!—Great God!"

We thus passed more than two hours, at the end of which he began to dress. Doctor O'Meara was introduced to him: it was the usual hour of his being admitted. "*Dottore*," said the Emperor to him in Italian, whilst he was shaving himself, "I have just read one of your fine London productions against me." The Doctor's countenance indicated a wish to know what it was. I showed him the book at a distance; it was himself who had lent it to me: he was disconcerted. "It is a very just remark," continued the Emperor, "that it is the truth only which gives offence. I have not been angry for a moment; but I have frequently laughed at it. The Doctor endeavoured to reply, and puzzled himself with high-flown sentences: it was, he said, an infamous, disgusting libel; every-body knew it to be such; nobody paid any attention to it: nevertheless, persons might be found who would believe it, from its not having been replied to. "But how can that be helped?" said the Emperor. "If it should enter any one's head to put in print that I have grown hairy, and walked on four paws, there are people who would believe it, and would say that God had punished me as he did Nebuchhadnezzar. And what could I do? There is no remedy in such cases." The Doctor came away, hardly able to believe the gaity, the indifference, the good-nature of which he had just been witness: with regard to ourselves, we were now accustomed to it.

The Emperor resolves to learn English, &c.

16th.—About three o'clock the Emperor desired me to come and converse with him whilst he was dressing himself; we afterwards took a few turns in the garden. He observed, accidentally, that it was a shame he could not yet read English. I assured him that, if he had continued his lessons after the two that I had given when we were off Madeira, he would now have been able to read every description of English books. He was perfectly persuaded of this, and ordered me to oblige him henceforth to take a lesson every day. The conversation then led me to observe, that I had just given my son his first lesson in mathematics. It is a branch of knowledge which the Emperor is very fond of, and in which he is particularly skilled. He was astonished that I could teach my son so much without the help of any work, and without any copy-book; he said, he did not know I was so learned in this way, and threatened me with examining, when I did not expect it, both the master and the scholar. At dinner he undertook what he called the Professor of Mathematics, who was very near being posed by him: one question did not wait for another, and they were frequently very keen. He never ceased to regret that mathematics were not taught at a very early age in the Lyceums. He said that all the intentions he had formed respecting the Universities had been frustrated, complained greatly of De Fontanes, lamenting, that whilst he was obliged to be at a distance, carrying on the war, they spoiled all he had done at home, &c. This led the Emperor back to the first years of his life, to father Patrault his Professor of Mathematics, whose history he gave us: I have already introduced it; and it will have been read in the foregoing pages.

First English Lesson, &c.

17th.—The Emperor took his first lesson in the English language to-day. And as it was my intention to put him at once in a situation to read the papers with readiness, this first lesson consisted of nothing more than getting acquainted with an English newspaper; in studying the form and plan of it; in learning the placing, which is always uniform, of the different subjects which it contains; in separating the notices and gossip of the town from politics; and, in the latter, in learning to distinguish what is authentic from what is mere report or conjecture.

I have engaged, that, if the Emperor could endure being annoyed every day with such lessons, he would be able to read the papers in a month without the assistance of any of us. The Emperor wished afterwards to do some exercise; he wrote some sentences which were dictated to him, and translated them into English, with the assistance of a little table, which I made for him, of the auxiliary verbs and articles, and aided by the dictionary for other words, which I made him look out himself. I explained to him the rules of syntax and grammar according as they came before us; in this manner he formed various sentences, which amused him more than the versions which we also attempted. After the lesson, at two o'clock, we went and took a walk in the garden.

Several musquet-shots were fired: they were so near us, that they appeared to have been fired in the garden itself. The Emperor observed to me, that my son (we thought it was he) seemed to have good sport: I replied, that it was the last time he should enjoy it so near the Emperor. "Really," said he, "you may as well go and tell him that he is only to come within cannon-shot of us." I ran: we had accused him wrongfully, for the guns were fired by the people who were training the Emperor's horses.

After dinner, during coffee, the Emperor, taking me to the corner of the chimney-piece, put his hand upon my head to measure my height, and said, "I am a giant to you."—"Your Majesty is that to so many others," I observed to him, "that I am not at all affected by it." He spoke immediately of something else; for he does not like to dwell on expressions of this description.

Our daily habits.—Conversation with Governor Wilks.—Armies.—Chemistry.—Politics.—Remarks on India.—Delphine, by Mad, de Stael.—Necker, Calonne.

18th—20th.—We led a life of great uniformity. The Emperor did not go out in the mornings. The English lesson was very regularly taken about two o'clock; then followed either a walk in the garden, or some presentations, but which were very rare; afterwards a little excursion in the calash, as the horses were at last arrived. Before dinner, we proceeded with the revision of the Campaigns of Italy or Egypt: after dinner we read romances.

On the 20th, the Emperor received Governor Wilks, with whom he had a profound discussion on the army, the sciences, government, and the Indies. Speaking of the organization of the English army, he dwelt much on the principles of promotion therein, expressing his suprise, that, in a country in which equality of rights is maintained, the soldiers so seldom become officers.

Colonel Wilks admitted that the English soldiers were not formed to become so; and said, that the English were equally astonished at the great difference they had remarked in the French army, where almost every soldier showed the nascent talents of an officer. "That," observed the Emperor, is one of the great results of the Conscription; it had rendered the French army the best constituted that ever existed. It was an institution," he continued, "eminently national, and already strongly interwoven with our habits; it had ceased to be a cause of grief, except to mothers; and the time was at hand, when a girl would not have listened to a young man who had not acquitted himself of this debt to his country. And it would have been only when arrived at this point," added he, "that the conscription would have manifested the full extent of its advantages. When the service no longer bears the appearance of punishment or compulsory duty, but is become a point of honour, on which all are jealous, then only is the nation great, glorious, and powerful; it is then that its existence is proof against reverses, invasions—even the hand of time!

"Besides," continued he, "it may be truly said, that there is nothing that may not be obtained from Frenchmen by the excitement of danger; it seems to animate them; it is an inheritance they derive from their Gallic predecessors. . . . Courage, the love of glory, are, with the French, an instinct, a kind of sixth sense. How often in the heat of battle has my attention been fixed on my young conscripts rushing, for the first time, into the thickest of the fight; honour and valour bursting forth at every pore."

After this, the Emperor knowing that Governor Wilks was well informed in Chemistry, attacked him on that subject. He spoke of the immense progress in all our manufactures occasioned by this science. He said, that both England and France, undoubtedly, possessed great chemists; but that chemistry was more generally diffused in France, and more particularly directed to useful results; that in England it remained a science, while in France it was becoming entirely practical. The Governor admitted that these observations were perfectly correct, and, with a liberality of sentiment, added, that it was to him, the Emperor, that all these advantages were owing, and that wherever science was led by the hand of power, it would produce great and happy effects upon the well being of society. The Emperor observed, that of late France had obtained sugar from the beet-root, as good and cheap as that extracted from the sugar-cane. The Governor was astonished; he had not even suspected it. The Emperor assured him that it was an established fact, opposed, as it was, to the rooted prejudices of all Europe, France itself not excepted. He added, that it was the same with woad, the substitute for indigo, and with almost all the colonial produce, except the dye-woods. This led him to conclude, that if the invention of the compass had produced a revolution in commerce, the progress of chemistry bade fair to produce a counter-revolution.

The conversation then turned to the present numerous emigrations of the artisans of France and England to America. The Emperor observed, that this favoured country grew rich by our follies. The Governor smiled, and replied, that those of England would occupy the first place in the list, from the numerous errors of administration, which had led to the revolt and subsequent emancipation of the Colonies. The Emperor said that their emancipation was inevitable; that when children had come to the size of their fathers, it was difficult to retain them long in a state of obedience.

They then spoke of India; the Governor had resided there many years, and had filled high situations; he had made important researches; he was enabled to reply to a multitude of questions proposed to him by the Emperor, respecting the laws, the manners, the usages of the Hindoos, the administration of the English, the nature and construction of the existing laws, &c.

The English are governed according to the laws of England; the natives by local acts made by the several Councils in the service of the Company, with whom it is a fundamental principle to render them as nearly similar as possible to the laws of the people themselves.

Hyder Aly was a man of genius; Tippoo, his son, was arrogant, ignorant, and rash. The former had upwards of 400,000 men; the latter scarcely ever more than 50,000.—These people are not deficient in courage, but they do not possess our physical strength, and have neither discipline nor any knowledge of tactics. Forty-seven thousand men in the English service, of whom only 4,000 were Europeans, were sufficient to destroy the empire of Mysore. It was, however, to be presumed, that sooner or later the national spirit would rescue these regions from the dominion of the Europeans. The intermixture of European blood with that of the natives, was producing a mixed race, whose numbers and disposition certainly prepared the way for a great revolution. Nevertheless, in their actual condition, the people were happier than they had been previously to the dominion of the English: an impartial administration of justice, and the mildness of the government were, for the present, the strongest supports of the power of the parent state. It was also considered expedient to prohibit the English and other Europeans from buying lands there, or forming hereditary establishments, &c.

Madame de Staël's *Delphine* was at this time a subject of conversation at our evening parties. The Emperor analyzed it: few things in it escaped his censure. The irregularity of mind and imagination which pervades it, excited his criticism: there were throughout, said he, the same faults which had formerly made him keep the author at a distance, notwithstanding the most pointed advances and the most unremitting flattery on her part. No sooner had victory immortalized the young General of the Army of Italy, than Madame de Staël, unacquainted with him, from the mere sympathy of glory, instantly professed for him sentiments of enthusiasm worthy of her own *Corinne*; she wrote him long and numerous epistles, full of wit, imagination, and metaphysical erudition: it was an error, she observed, arising only from human institutions, that could have united him with the meek, the tranquil Madame Bonaparte; it was a soul of fire like her's (Madame de Staël's) that nature had undoubtedly destined to be the companion of a hero like him.

I refer to the Campaigns in Italy, to show that this forwardness on the part of Madame de Staël was not checked by the circumstance of meeting with no return. With a perseverance never to be disheartened, she succeeded, at a later period, in forming some degree of acquaintance, so far even as to be allowed to visit; and she used this privilege, said the Emperor, to a disagreeable extent. It is unquestionably true, as has been reported, that the General, wishing to make her sensible of it, one day caused her to be told, by way of excuse, that he was scarcely dressed; and that she replied promptly and earnestly, that it was unimportant, for that genius was of no sex.

From Madame de Staël we were naturally led to her father, M. Necker. The Emperor related, that at Geneva, in his way to Marengo, he received a visit from him, wherein he made known, in an awkward manner enough, his desire to be admitted again to the Administration—a desire, by the by, which M. Calonne, his rival, subsequently came to Paris to express with a degree of levity beyond conception. M. Necker afterwards wrote a dangerous work upon the policy of France, which he attempted to prove could no longer exist either as a monarchy or a republic, and in which he called the First Consul *l'homme nécessaire.*

The First Consul proscribed the work, which, at that time, might have been highly prejudicial to him, and committed the task of refuting it to the Consul Lebrun, "who in his elegant prose," said the Emperor, executed prompt and ample justice upon it. The Necker *coterie* was irritated, and Madame de Staël, engaging in some intrigues, received an order to quit France: thenceforth she became an ardent and strenuous enemy. Nevertheless, on the return from the Island of Elba, she wrote or sent to the Emperor, to express, in her peculiar way, the entusiasm which this wonderful event had excited in her; that she was overcome; that this last act was not that of a mortal; that it had at once raised its author to the skies. Then, returning to herself, she concluded by hinting, that if the Emperor would condescend to allow the payment of the two millions, for which an order in her favour had already been signed by the King, her pen and her principles should be devoted for ever after to his interest. The Emperor desired she might be informed, in answer, that nothing could flatter him more highly than her approbation, because he fully appreciated her talents; but that he really was not rich enough to purchase it at that price.

My new lodging described.—Morning visit, &c.

21st.—I had at length taken possession of the new lodging built for me instead of my former stoving-room. Upon a soil constantly damp had been placed a floor eighteen feet long by eleven wide; this was surrounded by a wall of a foot and a half in thickness, composed of a sort of loam, and which might have been destroyed with a kick of the foot: at the height of seven feet was covered with a roof of boards, defended by a coating of paper and tar. Such were the construction and the outline of my new palace, divided into two apartments, one of which contained two beds separated by a chest of drawers, and would only afford room for a single chair; the other, at once my saloon and my library, had a single window strongly fastened up on account of the violence of the winds and rain; on the right and left of it two writing-tables, for me and my son; on the opposite side a couch and two chairs: this was the whole of the furniture and accommodations: add to this, that the aspect of the two windows is towards a wind constantly blowing from the same quarter, and gradually accompanied with rain, often very heavy, and which, previous to our taking possession, already forced its way through the cracks, or soaked through the walls and the roof. I was to pass the first night in these new quarters; I was indisposed, and my change of bed prevented me from sleeping. I was informed about seven o'clock, that the Emperor was going out on horseback; I replied, that not feeling myself well, I should endeavour to take some rest; but only a few minutes had elapsed when a person hastily entered my apartment, opened my curtains with an air of authority, found fault with me for being so idle, and pronounced that this ailment must be shaken off; then, struck with the smell of the paint, the extreme smallness of the room, and the closeness of the two beds, decided that we could no longer be suffered to sleep huddled together in that way; that it was far too unwholesome; and that I must return to the bed in the topographical cabinet, which I ought not to abandon through false delicacy; and that, if I occasioned any inconvenience there, I should be told of it. It will have been guessed, that this person was the Emperor. I was, of course, soon out of bed, dressed, and well. The Emperor was, however, already far off: I had to seek him in the park. After I had overtaken him, our conversation turned on the long audience he had given to Governor Wilks the day before. He dwelt, with much good humour, on the great importance which my work seemed to have given me in the Governor's eyes, and the extreme good-will towards me with which it seemed to have inspired him. "Of course," continued he, "it is understood that these sentiments are to be mutual; the usual regard and fraternity of authors, as long as they do not criticize each other. And is he aware of your relationship to the venerable Las Cases?" I answered that I knew nothing of the matter; but General Gourgaud, who was on the other side of the Emperor, replied in the affirmative. "And how do you know it yourself?" said the Emperor to me; "Are you not romancing with us?" "The following, sire, are my proofs. Our family had been two hundred years in France, when Barthelemi de Las Cases flourished in Spain; but the Spanish historians all describe him as a native of the same city from which we ourselves came, that is to say, Seville. They all mention him as of an ancient family of French origin, and state his ancestors to have passed into Spain precisely at the time when our family went there."—"What, then, you are not Spanish? He was French, as well as you!"—"Yes, Sire."—"Let us hear all about it; come, Sir Castellan, Sir Knight-errant, Sir Paladin,—let us see you in your glory; unroll your old parchments; come, enjoy yourself."—"Sire, one of my ancestors followed Henry Count of Burgundy, who, at the head of a few crusaders, achieved the conquest of Portugal, about the year 1100. He was his standard-bearer at the famous battle of Ourique, which founded the Portuguese monarchy. Afterwards we returned to France with Queen Blanche, when she came to be married to the father of Saint-Louis. Sire, this is the whole."

The Emperor's readings.—Madame de Sevigné.—Charles XII.—Paul and Virginia.—Vértot.—Rollin.—Velly.—Garnier.

22d.—26th.—These days were rendered unpleasant by almost incessant rain. The Emperor was only twice able to ride out—in the park one morning, and once in the afternoon through our usual valley, which the weather had rendered almost impassable. Nor was it more practicable to make use of the calash; we were therefore compelled to confine ourselves to a few turns in the garden, and to share in the gloom of the weather. We worked, however, the more on this account. The Emperor regularly took excellent and long lessons in English. It is his custom to pass all the morning in reading: he reads whole works of very considerable extent regularly throughout, without feeling in the least fatigued; he always read some part of them to me before he began his English lessons.

One of them was the Letters of Madame de Sevigné, the style of which is so easy, and depicts so faithfully the manners of the time. Reading the death of Turenne, and trial of Fouquet, he observed with respect to the latter, that Madame de Sevigné seemed to evince too much warmth, too much earnestness and tenderness, for mere friendship.

Another was *Charles XII;* in reading whose defence of his house, at Bender, against the Turks, he could not help laughing, and repeating, as they did, "*Iron-head! Iron-head!*" He asked me whether the nature of this monarch's death was a settled point. I told him I had it from the mouth of Gustavus III himself, that he had been assassinated by his followers. Gustavus had examined his body in the vault; the ball was a pistol-bullet; it had been fired very near, and behind him, &c.

At the beginning of the Revolution, I was well acquainted with Gustavus III at the waters of Aix-la-Chapelle; and though I was then very young, I had more than once the honour of conversing with him: he even promised me a place in the navy, if our affairs in France should turn out unfavourably.

Another day the Emperor was reading *Paul and Virginia*; he gave full effect to the touching passages, which were always the most simple and natural; those which abounded with the phatos, the abstract and false ideas so much in fashion when the work was published, were all, in the Emperor's opinon, cold, bad, spoiled. He said he had been infatuated with this book in his youth; but he had little personal regard for its author: he could never forgive him for having imposed on his generosity on his return from the Army of Italy. "Bernardin de Saint-Pierre's sensibility and delicacy," said he, "were little in harmony with his charming picture of Paul and Virginia. He was a bad man; he used his wife, Didot the printer's daughter, very ill; he was always ready to ask charity, without the least shame. On my return from the Army of Italy, Bernardin came to see me, and almost immediately began to tell me of his wants. I, who in my early youth had dreamed of nothing but Paul and Virginia, and felt flattered by a confidence which I imagined was reposed in me alone, and which I attributed to my great celebrity, hastened to return his visit, and, unperceived by any one, left on the corner of his chimney-piece a little rouleau of five-and twenty louis. But how was I mortified on seeing every one laugh at the delicacy of my proceedings; and on learning that such ceremony was entirely superfluous with M. Bernardin, who made it his trade to beg all comers, and to receive from every body. I always retained some little resentment towards him, for having thus imposed upon me. It was otherwise with my family. Joseph allowed him a large pension, and Louis was constantly making him presents."

But though the Emperor liked Paul and Virginia, he laughed, for very pity, at the *Studies of Nature*, by the same author. "Bernardin," said he, "though versed in *Belles Lettres*, was very little a geometrician; this last work was so bad, that scientific men disdained to answer it; Bernardin complained loudly of their not noticing him. The celebrated mathematician Legrange, when speaking on this subject, always said, alluding to the Institute, 'If Bernardin were one of our class—if he spake our language, we would call him to order; but he belongs to the Academy, and his style is out of our line." Bernardin was complaining as usual, one day, to the First Consul of the silence of the learned with respect to his works; Napoleon asked, "Do you understand the differential method, M. Bernardin?"—"No."—"Well, go and learn it, and then you will be able to answer yourself." Afterwards, when Emperor, every time he perceived Saint-Pierre, he used to say to him, "M. Bernardin, when are we to have any more Paul and

Virginias, or Indian Cottages? You ought to supply us every six months."

In reading Vertot's Roman Revolutions, of which in other respects the Emperor thinks highly, he found the declamations much too diffuse. This was his constant complaint against every work he took up; he had in his youth, he said, been much to blame in this respect himself. He may justly be said to have thoroughly reformed afterwards. He amused himself with striking out the superfluous phrases in Vertot; and the result was that after these erasures, the work appeared much more energetic and animated. "It would certainly be a most valuable and successful labour," said he, "if any man of taste and discernment would devote his time to reducing the principal works in our language in this manner. I know no nobody but Montesquiou who would escape these curtailments." He often looked into Rollin, whom he thought diffuse, and too credulous. Crevier, his continuator, seemed to Napoleon detestable. He complained of our classical works, and of the time which our young people are compelled to lose in reading such bad books. They were composed by rhetoricians, and mere professors, he said; whereas such immortal subjects, the basis of all our knowledge throughout life, ought to have been written and edited by statesmen and men of the world. The Emperor had excellent ideas on this subject: the want of time alone prevented him from carrying them into execution.

The Emperor was still more dissatisfied with our French historians; he could not bear to read any of them. "Velly is rich in words, and poor in meaning: his continuators are still worse. Our history," said the Emperor, "should either be in four or five volumes, or in a hundred." He had been acquainted with Garnier, who continued Velly and Villaret; he lived in the basement of Malmaison. He was an old man of eighty, and lodged in a small set of apartments on the ground-floor, with a little gallery. Struck with the officious attention which this good old man always evinced whenever the First Consul was passing, the latter inquired who he was. On learning that it was Garnier, he comprehended his motives. "He, no doubt, imagined," said the Emperor pleasantly, "that a First Consul was his property, as historian. I dare say, however, he was astonished to find Consuls where he had been accustomed to see Kings." Napoleon told him so himself, laughing, when he called him one day, and settled a good pension on him. "From that time," said the Emperor, "the poor man, in the warmth of his gratitude, would gladly have written any thing I pleased with all his heart."

A difficulty overcome.—The Emperor's personal danger at Eylau, Jena, &c.—Russian, Austrian, and Prussian troops. Young Guilbert.—Corbineau.—Marshal Lannes.—Bessieres.—Duroc.

27th.—About five o'clock the Emperor went out in his calash; the evening was very fine; we drove rapidly, and the distance to be traversed is very short. The Emperor made the servants slacken their pace, in order to prolong the ride. As we returned, the Emperor, casting his eyes on the camp, from which we were only separated by the ravine, asked why we could not pass that way, which would double the length of our ride. He was told it was impossible; and we continued our way homeward. But on a sudden, as if roused by this word *impossible*, which he had so often said was not French, he ordered the ground to be reconnoitred. We all got out of the carriage, which proceeded empty towards the difficult points; we saw it clear every obstacle, and returned home in triumph, as if we had just doubled our possessions.

During dinner, and afterwards, the conversation turned on various deeds of arms. The Grand Marshal said, that what had most struck him in the life of the Emperor, happened at Eylau, when, attended only by some officers of his staff, a column of four or five thousand Russians came almost in contact with him. The Emperor was on foot; the Prince of Neufchatel instantly ordered up the horses: the Emperor gave him a reproachful look; then sent orders to a battalion of his guard to advance, which was a good way behind, and standing still. As the Russians advanced, he repeated several times, "What audacity! what audacity!" At the sight of the grenadiers of the guard, the Russians stopped short. It was high time they should, as Bertrand said. The Emperor had never stirred; all who surrounded him had been much alarmed.

The Emperor had heard this account without making any observation; but, when it was finished, he said that one of the finest manœuvres he remembered was that which he executed at Eckmuhl. Unfortunately he did not proceed, or give any particulars. "Success in war," said he, "depends so much on quicksightedness, and on seizing the right moment, that the battle of Austerlitz, which was so completely won, would have been lost if I had attacked six hours sooner. The Russians showed themselves on that occasion such excellent troops as they have never appeared since; the Russian army of Austerlitz would not have lost the battle of the Moscowa."

"Marengo," said the Emperor, "was the battle in which the Austrians fought best. Their troops behaved admirably there; but that was the grave of their valour. It has never since been seen.

"The Prussians, at Jena, did not make such a resistance as was expected from their reputation. As to the multitudes of 1814 and 1815, they were mere rabble compared to the real soldiers of Marengo, Austerlitz, and Jena."

The night before the battle of Jena, the Emperor said, he had run the greatest risk. He might then have disappeared without his fate being clearly known. He had approached the bivouacs of the enemy, in the dark, to reconnoitre them; he had only a few officers with him. The opinion which was then entertained of the Prussian army kept every one on the alert: it was that the Prussians were particularly given to nocturnal attacks. As the Emperor returned, he was fired at by the first sentinel of his camp; this was a signal for the whole line; he had no resource but to throw himself flat on his face until the mistake was discovered. But his principal apprehension was that the Prussian line, which was very near him, would act in the same manner.

At Marengo the Austrian soldiers had not forgotten the conqueror of Castiglione, Arcole, and Rivoli; his name had much influence over them; but they were far from thinking he was present; they believed he was dead; care had been taken to persuade them that he had perished in Egypt; that the First Consul, of whom they heard talk, was only his brother. This report had gained so much credit every where, that Napoleon was under the necessity of appearing in public at Milan, in order to refute it.

After these anecdotes, the Emperor proceeded to mention a great number of his officers and aids-de-camp, distributing praise and censure amongst them as he went on; he knew them all thoroughly. Two of the circumstances which had most affected him on the field of battle, he said, were the deaths of young Guilbert and General Corbineau. At Aboukir, a bullet went quite through the breast of the former, without killing him instantly: the Emperor, after saying a few words to him, was obliged, by the violence of his feelings, to leave him. The other was carried away, crushed, annihilated by a cannon-ball, at Eylau, before the Emperor's face, whilst he was giving him some orders. The Emperor spoke also of the last moments of Marshal Lannes, the valiant Duke of Montebello, so justly called the Orlando of the army, who when visited by the Emperor on his death-bed, seemed to forget his own situation, and to care only for him, whom he loved above every thing. The Emperor had the highest esteem for him. "He was for a long time a mere fighting man," said he, "but he afterwards became an officer of the first talents." Some one then said, he should like to know what line of conduct Lannes would have pursued in these latter times, if he had lived. "We have learned," said the Emperor, "not to swear to any thing. Yet I cannot conceive that it could have been possible for him to deviate from the path of duty and honour. Besides, it is hard to imagine that he could have existed. With all his bravery, he would unquestionably have got killed in some of the last affairs, or at least sufficiently wounded to be laid up out of the centre and influence of events. And if he had remained disposable, he was a man capable of changing the whole face of affairs by his own weight and influence."

The Emperor next mentioned Duroc, on whose character and private life he dwelt some time. "Duroc," concluded he, "had lively, tender, and concealed passions, little corresponding with the coldness of his manner. It was long before I knew this, so exact and regular was his service. It was not until my day was entirely closed and finished, and I was enjoying repose, that Duroc's work began.—Chance, or some accident, could alone have made me acquainted with his character. He was a pure and virtuous man, utterly disinterested, and extremely generous."

The Emperor said, that on the opening of the campaign at Dresden, he lost two men who were extremely valuable to him, and in the most foolish manner in the world: these were Bessieres and Duroc. When we went to see Duroc, after he had received his mortal wound, he attempted to hold out some hopes to him; but Duroc, who did not deceive himself, only replied by begging him to make them give him opium. The Emperor, excessively affected, could not venture to remain long with him, and tore himself from this distressing spectacle.

One of the company then reminded the Emperor, that on leaving Duroc, he went and walked up and down by himself before his tent: no one durst accost him. But, some essential measures being requisite against the following day, some one at length ventured to go and ask him where the battery of the guard was to be placed. "Ask me nothing till to-morrow," was the Emperor's answer.

At this recollection, the Emperor, with an apparent effort, began abruptly to talk of something else.

Duroc was one of those persons whose value is never known till they are lost: this was, after his death, the common expression of the court and city, and the unanimous sentiment every where.

He was a native of Nancy, in the department of La Meurthe. The origin of his fortune has been related above. Napoleon found him in the train at the siege of Toulon, and immediately interested himself for him. His attachment to him increased every day, and it might be said that they never more separated. I have elsewhere mentioned that I have heard the Emperor say, that throughout his career, Duroc was the only person who had possessed his unreserved confidence, and to whom he could freely unburden his mind.—Duroc was not a brilliant character; but he possessed an excellent judgment, and he rendered essential services, which owing to their nature as well as to his reserve, were little heard of.

Duroc loved the Emperor for himself: it was rather to the individual, personally, that his devotion was attached, than to the monarch. In being made the confidant of his prince's feelings, he had acquired the art, and perhaps the right, of mitigating and directing them. How often has he whispered to people struck with consternation by the anger of the Emperor:—"Let him have his way: he speaks from his feelings, not according to his judgment; nor as he will act to-morrow." What a servant! what a friend! what a treasure! How many storms he has soothed; how many rash orders, given in the moment of irritation, has he omitted to execute, knowing that his master would thank him the next day for the omission. The Emperor had accommodated himself to this sort of tacit arrangement; and on that account gave way the more readily to those violent bursts of temper, which relieve by the vent they afford to passions.

Duroc died in the most deplorable manner, at a very critical moment; his death was another of the fatalities of Napoleon's career.

The day after the battle of Wurchen, towards evening the skirmish of Reichenbach had just ended, the firing had ceased. Duroc was on the top of an eminence, apart from the troops, conversing with General Kirchener, and observing the retreat of the last ranks of the enemy. A piece was levelled at this glittering group, and the fatal ball killed both the generals.

Duroc had more influence over the Emperor's resolutions than is imagined. His death was probably, in this respect, a national calamity. There is reason to think, that if he had survived, the armistice of Dresden, which ruined us, would not have taken place; we should have pushed on to the Oder, and beyond it. The enemy would then have instantly acceded to peace, and we should have escaped their machinations, their intrigues, and, above all, the tedious, base, and atrocious perfidy of the Austrian Cabinet, which has ended in our destruction.

At a subsequent period Duroc might still have exerted an influence over other great events, and probably changed the face of affairs. Finally, even at a later conjuncture, at the time of Napoleon's fall, he would never have separated his destiny from that of the Emperor: he would have been with us at Saint-Helena; and this aid alone would have sufficed to counterbalance all the horrible vexations with which Napoleon was studiously oppressed.

Bessieres, of the department of the Lot, was thrown by the Revolution into the career of arms. He commenced as a private soldier in the constitutional guard of Louis XVI. Afterwards having attained the rank of captain of chasseurs, he attracted the Commander-in-chief of the army of Italy by acts of extraordinary personal bravery; and, when the general formed his corps of guides, he chose Bessieres to take the command of them. Such was the beginning of Bessieres, and the origin of his fortunes. From that instant we find him always at the head of the Consular or Imperial guard, in charges of the reserve, deciding the battle, or profiting by the victory. His name is gloriously connected with all our great battles.

Bessieres rose with the man who had distinguished him, and shared abundantly in the favours which the Emperor distributed. He was made a marshal of the Empire, Duke of Istria, colonel of the cavalry of the guard, &c.

His qualities developing themselves as he rose, proved him always equal to his fortune. Bessieres always continued good, humane, and generous; of antique loyalty and integrity; and, whether considered as a citizen or as a soldier, an honest worthy man. He often made use of the high favour in which he stood, to do extraordinary services, and acts of kindness even to people of very different ways of think to his. I know people, who, if they have a spark of gratitude in them, will confirm my assertion, and can bear testimony to his noble elevated sentiments.

Bessieres was adored by the Guards, in the midst of whom he passed his life. At the battle of Wagram a ball struck him off his horse, without doing him any farther injury. A mournful cry arose from the whole battalion; upon which Napoleon remarked, the next time he saw him: "Bessieres, the ball which struck you drew tears from all my Guard. Return thanks to it; it ought to be very dear to you."

He was less fortunate at the opening of the campaign of Saxony. On the very eve of the battle of Lutzen, a trifling engagement occurred, in which having advanced into the very midst of the skirmishers, he was shot dead on the spot by a musket ball in the breast. Thus, after living like Bayard, he died like Turenne.

I had conversed with him a little before this fatal event. Chance had brought us together by ourselves in a private box at the theatre. After talking of public affairs which deeply interested him, for he idolized his country, his last words, as he left me, were, that he was to set out for the army that night, and hoped we should meet again. "But at the present crisis," said he, "with our young soldiers, we leaders must not spare ourselves." Alas! he was never to return.

Bessieres was sincerely attached to the Emperor; he almost worshipped him; he, like Duroc, would certainly never have abandoned his person or his fortunes. And one would really think that Fate, which proved so decidedly hostile to Napoleon in his latter days, had resolved to deprive him of the sweetest consolation by thus removing two such valuable friends; and at the same time to prevent these faithful servants from acquiring the very highest claim to glory, that of gratitude to the unfortunate.

The Emperor caused the remains of these two men whom he much esteemed, and by whom he knew himself to be beloved in return, to be carried to the *Invalides* at Paris. He intended extraordinary honours for them, of which subsequent events deprived them. But History, whose pages are far more imperishable than marble or bronze, has consecrated them, and secured them for ever from oblivion.*

Study of English.—Reflections.—Ride.—Mired Horse.

21st.—Our days passed, as may be supposed, in an excessive stupid monotony. *Ennui*, reflection, and melancholy, were our formidable enemies; occupation our great and only refuge. The Emperor followed his pursuits with great regularity. English was become an affair of importance to him. It was now near a fortnight since he took his first lesson, and from that moment he had devoted some hours, every day, beginning at noon, to that study; sometimes with truly admirable ardour, sometimes with visible

* The following is extracted from the Campaign of Saxony in 1813, by Baron Odeleben, an eye-witness of the circumstance; under the date of the 10th of August at the time of the resumption of hostilities, two or three months after the death of Duroc.

"During the march from Reichenbach to Gorlitz, Napoleon stopped at Makersdorf, and showed the King of Naples the place where Duroc fell. He summoned to his presence the proprietor of the little farm on which the Grand Marshal died, and made over to him the sum of 20,000 francs; 4000 of which were for a monument in honour of the deceased, and 16,000 for the proprietor of the house and his wife. The donation was consummated in the evening, in the presence of the rector and the judge of Makersdorf; the money was counted out before them, and they were charged to get the monument erected."

disgust; an alternative which kept me in the greatest anxiety. I considered success as of the greatest importance, and I every day dreaded to see him abandon the ground gained on the day preceding; and consequently that I should be regarded as having wearied him with the most tedious labour, without having produced the fortunate result I had promised myself. On the other hand, I was also spurred on by the consciousness that I was approaching the goal at which I aimed. The attainment of the English language was a real and serious conquest to the Emperor. Formerly, he said, it had cost him a hundred thousand crowns a year, merely for translations; and how did he know wether he had them exact—whether they were faithful? Now that we were imprisoned, as it were, in the midst of this language, surrounded by its productions, all the great changes and questions which the Emperor had given rise to on the Continent, had been taken up by the English on the opposite side; and in their works presented so many new faces to him, to which he had hitherto been a stranger.

It may be added, that French books were scarce with us; that the Emperor knew them all, and had read them even to satiety; whilst we could easily procure a multitude of English ones altogether new to him. Besides, to learn the language of a foreigner, always prepossesses him in our favour; it is a satisfaction to one's self; it facilitates intercourse, and forms in a certain degree the commencement of a sort of connexion between the parties. However this may be, I began to perceive the limits of our difficulties; I anticipated the moment when the Emperor would have got through all the inevitable disagreeables incident to beginners. But let any one form an idea, if possible, of what the scholastic study of conjugations, declensions, and articles must have been to him. It could never have been accomplished, without great courage on the scholar's side, and some degree of artifice on the part of the master. He often asked me whether he did not deserve the ferula, of which he now comprehended the vast utility in schools; he declared, jestingly, that he should have made much greater progress himself, had he stood in fear of correction. He complained of not having improved, but, in reality, the progress he had made would have been extraordinary in any one.

The more grand, rapid, and comprehensive the mind is, the less it is capable of dwelling on regular minute details. The Emperor, who discovered wonderful facility in apprehending all that regarded the philosophy of the language, evinced very little capacity for retaining its material mechanism. He had a quick understanding and a very bad memory: this vexed him much; he conceived that he did not get on. Whenever I could subject the matters in question to any regular law or analogy, they were classed and comprehended in an instant; the scholar even preceded the master in his applications and deductions; but as to learning by heart, and retaining the gross elements of the language, it was a most difficult affair. He was constantly confounding one thing with another; and it would have been thought too fastidious to require too scrupulous a regularity at first. Another difficulty was, that with the same letters, the same vowels as ours, a totally different pronunciation is required: the scholar would allow of none but ours; and the master would have rendered the difficulties and disagreeables tenfold, had he required any better. Besides the scholar, even in his own language, was incorrigibly addicted to maiming proper names and foreign words; he pronounced them quite at his own discretion, and when once they had passed his lips, they always remained the same, in spite of every thing, because he had thus got them, once for all, lodged, as it were, in his head. The same thing happened with respect to most of our English words; and the master found it best to have the prudence and patience to let it pass; leaving it to time to rectify by degrees, if it should ever be possible, all these defects. From these concurring circumstances actually sprang a new language. It was understood by me alone, it is true; but it procured the Emperor the pleasure of reading English, and he could, in the strictest sense, make himself understood by writing in that language. This was a great deal; it was every thing.

In the meantime, the Emperor regularly continued his Campaigns of Egypt with the Grand Marshal. My Campaign of Italy had long been finished; we were always touching and retouching it, with respect to its topographical form, the arrangement of the chapters, the division of the paragraphs, &c. The small part of it that remained in my hands will be seen in the course of this work.

From time to time he also dictated separate parts to Messrs. Gourgaud and Montholon. To all this work he added very little exercise: a walk now and then, sometimes a ride in the calash, scarcely ever on horseback. On the 30th, however, he chose to return to our valley of Silence which we had long deserted. We were near the middle of the vale; the passage was stopped up with dead bushes, and a kind of bar to restrain cattle. The servant (the faithful Aly) dismounted, as usual, to clear the way for us. We passed on; but, whilst the servant was engaged in assisting us, his horse had strayed from him, and, when he attempted to catch him, ran away. A great quantity of rain had fallen, and the horse sank into a quagmire similar to that in which the Emperor, a few days after our arrival at Longwood, had stuck so tenaciously as to make it doubtful whether he would not remain in it. The servant ran after us to say, that he must remain for the purpose of disengaging his horse. We were in a very difficult narrow road, riding one by one. It was not until sometime after, that the Emperor heard us mention to one another the accident of the servant. He found great fault because we had not waited for him, and desired the Grand Marshal and General Gourgaud to return for him. The Emperor dismounted to wait for them, and ascended a little elevation, on which he looked like a figure on a pedestal in the midst of ruins. He had the bridle of his horse passed round his arm, and began to whistle an air; mute nature echoed the strains, but only to the barren desert. "Yet," thought I, "a short time ago, how many sceptres he wielded! how many crowns belonged to him! how many kings were at his feet! It is true," said I, "that in the eyes of those who approach him, who daily see and hear him, he is still greater than ever! This is the sentiment, the opinion of all about him. We serve him with no less ardour; we love him with greater affection than ever."

But now the Grand Marshal and Gourgaud arrived; they assisted the Emperor to mount again, and we went on.—These gentlemen acknowledged that without their assistance the horse could never have been saved; the united efforts of all three had barely sufficed to disengage him. A considerable time afterwards, turning an elbow of the road, the Emperor observed that the servant had not followed, and said they ought to have remained till they had found he was in a condition to come on. They thought he had staid behind to clean his horse a little. In the course of our ride, at several other turnings, the Emperor repeated the same observation. We arrived at the Grand Marshal's, went in, and rested there a few minutes: as we came out, the Emperor asked whether the servant had passed on; no one had seen him. When we arrived at Longwood, his first question was whether the man had returned. He had been at home sometime, having returned by a different road.

I may perhaps have dwelt somewhat too much on this trifling circumstance; but I did so because it appeared to me perfectly characteristic. In this domestic solicitude, the reader will find it difficult to recognise the insensible, obdurate, wicked, cruel monster, the tyrant, of whom he has so often and so long been told.

N. B. I have mentioned, above, that I should introduce the fragments of the Campaign of Italy which have remained in my hands. Having now arrived at the end of a month, I will insert a few chapters of them.

On my return to France, through that fatal event which placed me at my own disposal, my motives for retaining to myself alone the fragments of the Campaign of Italy, which I had preserved by the Emperor's consent, no longer existing, and the detention of my papers by the English ministry leaving me no means of publishing any thing on Saint-Helena, I distributed some of these fragments, attaching no other condition to their being made public than that of distinctly declaring that they were mere rough drafts, first dictations, which have, no doubt, subsequently undergone great alterations. Now that the restoration of my papers has enabled me to publish the Journal of Saint-Helena, I have thought of collecting all these fragments of the Campaign of Italy, conceiving that they will not be uninteresting to those who like to compare the first sketch with the more deliberate ideas; and particularly as I learn from the depositaries of the manuscript of these Campaigns, that it was the Emperor's will that the whole should be splendidly published, with maps, plans, &c. and dedicated to his Son, and have every reason to believe that it will still be a long time before society can be gratified with this publication. I shall therefore insert the little I possess, which is seven chapters out of twenty-two, either at the conclusion of the months, or in the course of the Journal itself, if I find it flag.

I now present the first of these fragments: Vendemiaire, the Battle of Montenotte, and part of the third chapter, on the Topography of Italy.

THE THIRTEENTH OF VENDEMIAIRE.

N. B. All the words in Italics are corrections made in the original manuscript by Napoleon's own hand.

I. *Constitution of the Year III.*—The fall of the municipality of the 31st of May, of the party of Danton, and of Robespierre, produced, eventually, the fall of the Jacobins, and the end of the revolutionary government. *Afterwards*, the Convention was successively governed by factions, which were never able to acquire any preponderance; its principles varied every month. The interior of the Republic was *afflicted* by a horrible system of re-action; the national domains ceased to find purchasers, and the credit of the assignats sinking daily lower, the armies were unpaid; requisitions and the maximum had alone kept them supplied; the magazines were empty; the soldier was no longer sure even of bread. The recruiting of the army, the laws respecting which had been enforced with the greatest rigour under the revolutionary government, had ceased. The armies continued to obtain great advantages, because they were more numerous than ever; but they were suffering daily losses, which there *were* no means of repairing. The foreign party, supported by the pretext of the restoration of the Bourbons, gained strength every day. The saloons were open, people discoursed there fearlessly; the communications with foreign parts were become more easy: the destruction of the Republic was undisguisedly preparing. The Revolution had lost its novelty; it had alienated many interests; an iron hand had severely oppressed individuals. Many crimes had been committed; they were now most vindictively recalled to memory, and the public indignation was daily more violently excited against all those who had been members of the government, filled official situations, or participated, in any manner whatsoever, in the triumphs of the Revolution.

Pichegru, the first general of the Republic, had been gained over. He was the son of a labourer of Franche-compté, and had been a Minim friar in his youth, at the college of Brienne: he sold himself to the royal party, to whom he surrendered the successes of the operations of his army.

The enemies of the Republic had not many proselytes in the army; it remained faithful to the principles of the Revolution, for which it had shed so much blood, and gained so many victories.

All parties were tired of the Convention; nay, it was tired of itself. Its mission had been the establishment of a Constitution; it perceived, at length, that the safety of the nation and its own required it, without delay, *to fulfil its principal object*. On the 25th of June, 1795, it adopted the Constitution, known under the title of the Constitution of the Year III. The government was entrusted to five persons, under the name of the Directory; the legislature to two councils, called the Council of the Five Hundred, and the Council of the Ancients. This Constitution was submitted to the acceptance of the people called together in primary assembly.

II. *Additional Laws to the Constitution.*—It was a prevalent opinion, that the fall of the Constitution of 1794, was to be attributed to that law of the Constituent Assembly *which excluded its members from the legislature*. The Convention did not *fall into* the same error; it annexed two additional laws to the Constitution, by which it prescribed that two-thirds of the new legislature should be composed of members of the Convention, and that the electoral assemblies of departments should, on this occasion, only have to elect one-third of the two councils. The Convention farther prescribed, that these two additional laws should be submitted to the acceptance of the people, as inseparable parts of the Constitution.

The discontent was thenceforth general. The foreign party, in particular, found all its schemes baffled by these arrangements. It had flattered itself that the two councils would have been entirely composed of new men, strangers to the Revolution, or even, partly, of those who had suffered by it; and thence it hoped to effect a counter-revolution through the influence of the legislature itself.

This party did not want for plausible reasons to conceal the true grounds of its discontent; they alleged, that the rights of the people were disregarded, since the Convention, which had been appointed only to establish a Constitution, now usurped the powers of an electoral body, by giving to its members, of its own accord, the powers of a legislative body; that it was plain that the Convention knew that it was acting contrary to the intention of the people, because it imposed on the primary assemblies the *arbitrary* condition of voting at once on the aggregrate of the Constitution, and its additional laws. The Convention ought only to will that which was the will of the people. Why did it not allow them to vote separately on the Constitution and the additional laws? Because it knew that the additional laws would be unanimously rejected. As to the Constitution, in itself, it was preferable, no doubt, to what existed; and all parties were agreed on that point. Some, indeed, wanted to have a President, instead of five directors; others would have desired a more popular council: but in general this new Constitution was favourably regarded. As to the foreign faction, which was managed by secret committees, it concerned itself but little about forms of government which it did not intend to support; it only studied, in this Constitution, how to avail itself thereof, for the purpose of operating a counter-revolution; and whatever tended to wrest authority out of the hands of the Convention and its partisans, was agreeable to this party.

III. *The additional Laws are rejected by the Sections of Paris.*—The forty-eight Sections of Paris assembled, forming as many tribunes, to which the most violent orators immediately hastened: Laharpe, Serizi, Lacretelle the younger, Vaublanc, Regnault, &c. *It required* little ability to excite all minds against the Convention; but several of these orators developed great talents.

The capital was thus thrown into a ferment.—*After the 9th of Thermidor, the* National Guard *had been organized.* It had been made an object to keep the Jacobins out of it; but this had led to the opposite extreme, and a considerable number of counter-revolutionists were accordingly found in its ranks.

This National Guard consisted of upwards of forty thousand men armed and clothed. It shared fully in the exasperation of the Sections against the Convention; and the additional laws were rejected throughout Paris. The Sections appeared, one after another, at the bar of the Convention, and there warmly declared their sentiments. The Convention, however, still believed that all this agitation would subside, as soon as the provinces should have manifested their opinion, by accepting the Constitution and the additional laws. It thought this commotion in the capital was like those riots so common in London, and of which instances often happened at Rome, at the time of the Comitia. It proclaimed, on the 28th of September, the acceptance of the Constitution and additional laws by the majority of the primary assemblies; but on the following day the Sections of Paris appointed deputies to form a central assembly of electors, which met at the Odeon.

IV. *Armed resistance of the Sections of Paris.*—The Sections had calculated their own strength, and appreciated the weakness of the Convention: this assembly of electors was an assembly of insurgents.

The *Convention* annulled the assembly of the Odeon, declared it illegal, and ordered its committees to dissolve it by force. On the tenth of Vendemiaire the armed power proceeded to the Odeon, and executed this order. The people collected in the Place de l'Odeon, uttered some murmurs, and indulged in some railing, but offered no resistance.

The decree of the Convention, for shutting up the Odeon excited the indignation of all the Sections. That of Lepelletier, of which the central place was the Convent of the Filles-Saint-Thomas, appeared to take the lead in this movement. By a decree of the Convention it was ordered that the place of its sittings should be closed, the assembly dissolved, and the Section disarmed.

On the 12th of Vendemiaire (3d October,) at seven or eight in the evening, General Menou, accompanied by the representatives of the people, who were Commissioners to the Army of the interior, proceeded with a numerous body of troops to the place of meeting of the Section Lepelletier, to carry into execution the decree of the Convention. The infantry, cavalry, and artillery were all crowded together in the rue Vivienne, at the extremity of which is the Convent of the Filles-Saint-Thomas. The sectionaries occupied *the windows of* the houses of this street; several of their battalions drew up in order of battle in the court of the convent, and the military force, which General Menou commanded, *found itself compromised.*

The committee of the Section had declared itself a representation of the Sovereign people, in the exercise of its functions: it refused to obey the orders of the Convention; and, after spending an hour in useless negotiations, General Menou and the Commissioners of the Convention withdrew, by a species of capitulation, without having dispersed or disarmed the meeting.

V. *Menou is deprived of the command of the Army of the Interior.*—The Section, thus victorious, declared itself permanent; sent deputations to all the other Sections; boasted its success, and hastened the organization necessary for securing the success of its resistance. Preparations commenced for the 13th of Vendemiaire.

General Bonaparte, who had been for some months attached to the directors of the movements of the French armies, was in a box at the theatre Feydeau, when some of his friends informed him of the singular events that were passing. He was curious to witness the particulars of so grand a spectacle. Seeing the Conventional troops repulsed, he hastened to the Assembly to observe the effect of this intelligence, and to trace the developements and character which would there be given to it.

The Convention was in the greatest agitation. The representatives with the army, in order to exculpate themselves, loudly accused Menou. The consequences of his want of skill were ascribed to treason. He was placed under arrest.

Various representatives then appeared at the tribune; they described the extent of the danger. The news which every moment arrived from the Sections, showed but too plainly, how great the peril actually was. Every member recommended the general who possessed his confidence. Those who had been at Toulon, and with the army of Italy, and the members of the committee of Public Safety, who were in daily communication with Napoleon, proposed him as more capable than any other person, from the promptness of his *coup-d'œil*, and the energy of his character, of bringing them safely through the present danger. Messengers were sent into the city to seek him.

Napoleon who had heard all that had been said, and knew what was in agitation, deliberated with himself more than half an hour on the course most eligible for him to pursue. A deadly war was breaking out between the Convention and Paris. *Would it be prudent to declare himself*—to speak in the name of all France? Who would dare to enter the lists alone as the champion of the Convention? Victory itself would be attended with a degree of odium, whilst defeat would devote the unsuccessful combatant to the eternal execration of future generations.

Why thus devote himself to be the scapegoat of crimes to which he had been a stranger? Why voluntarily expose himself to add, in a few hours, one more to the list of those names which men shudder to pronounce.

But, on the other hand, if the Convention should sink, what would become of the great truths of our Revolution? Our numerous victories, our blood so often shed, would then be only disgraceful actions. The foreigner, whom we had often vanquished, would triumph, and load us with his contempt; an insolent unnatural crew would re-appear triumphant; would reproach us with our crimes; would indulge their revenge, and rule us like helots, by foreign force.

Thus the defeat of the Convention would place a victorious crown on the brows of the foreigner, and seal the disgrace and slavery of the nation.

This sentiment—the ardour of five-and-twenty—confident in his own powers and his destiny, prevailed. *He made up his mind, and went to the Committee*, to which he represented with energy the impossibility of directing so important an operation, whilst subject to the interference of three representatives, who, in fact, exercised all power, and impeded all the operations of the general. He added, that he had witnessed all the proceedings of the rue Vivienne; that the Commissioners had been chiefly to blame, and had, nevertheless, acted the part of accusers in the assembly with triumphant success.

Struck with these arguments, but unable to deprive the Commissioners of their functions without a long discussion in the assembly, the committee, to conciliate matters, *for they had no time to lose*, resolved to select the General from the assembly itself. With this view, it proposed Barras to the Convention, as General-in-chief, and gave the command to Napoleon, who thus found himself relieved from the three Commissioners, without their having any thing to complain of.

As soon as Napoleon found himself invested with the command of the forces destined to protect the Assembly, he went to one of the cabinets of the Thuilleries, where Menou remained, to obtain from him the necessary information as to the force and position of the troops and artillery.—The army consisted of only five thousand soldiers of all descriptions, with forty pieces of cannon, then at the Sablons, guarded by fifteen men: it was an hour after mid-night.—Napoleon instantly despatched a major of the 21st light horse (Murat) with three hundred cavalry, to proceed, with all possible expedition, to the Sablons, and bring off the artillery to the garden of the Thuilleries. One moment more would have been too late. This officer, on arriving at the Sablons at two o'clock, fell in with the head of a column of the Section Lepelletier, come for the purpose of carrying off the artillery; but his troops being cavalry, and the ground a plain, the Section retreated; and at six in the morning the forty guns entered the Thuilleries.

VI. *Dispositions for the attack and defence of the Thuilleries.*—From six o'clock to nine Napoleon visited all the posts, and placed this artillery at the head of the Pont Louis XVI, of the Pont Royal, of the rue de Rohan, at the Cul-de-sac Dauphin, in the rue St. Honoré, at the Pont Tournant, &c. He intrusted the custody of the guns to officers worthy of confidence. All the matches were lighted, and the whole of the little army was distributed at the different posts, or in reserve at the garden, and the *Place Carrousel*. The generale beat throughout Paris, and the National Guards formed at all the debouches; thus surrounding the palace and gardens. Their drums carried their insolence so far as to come and beat the generale on the Carrousel, and the Place Louis XV.

The danger was imminent. Forty thousand National Guards well armed and trained, presented themselves as the enemies of the Convention: the troops of the line intrusted with its defence were few in number, and might easily be brought over by the sentiments of the population which surrounded them. The Convention, in order to increase its forces, armed 1500 individuals called the Patriots of 1789. They were men, who, after the 9th of Thermidor, had lost their employments and quitted their departments, where they were persecuted by public opinion. Three battalions were formed of them, which were placed under the command of General Berruyer. These men fought with the greatest valour. Their example influenced the troops of the line, and they were of the greatest importance to the success of this day.

A Committee of forty members, composed of the Committees of Public Safety and General Security, directed all affairs. Cambacérès was president: they discussed much, and decided nothing; while the pressure of the danger increased every moment.

Some were desirous to lay down their arms, and receive the sectionaries as the Roman Senators received the Gauls. Others were desirous that the Assembly should retire to Cæsar's camp at the heights of Saint-Cloud, there to be joined by the Army of the coasts of the ocean. Others wished deputations to be sent to all the Forty-eight Sections, *to make various propositions to them.* During these vain discussions, at two in the afternoon, a man named Lafond debouched on the Pont Neuf, coming from the Section Lepelletier at the head of three or four battalions; whilst another column of the same force advanced from the Odeon to meet them. *They joined* in the Place Dauphine.

General Carteaux, who had been stationed at Pont Neuf with 400 men and four pieces of cannon, with orders to defend the two sides of the bridge, abandoned his post, and fell back under the wickets. At the same time a battalion of the National Guard occupied the garden of the Infanta: they professed to be well affected towards the Convention, and nevertheless seized on this post without orders. On another side Saint-Roch, the Theatre Francais, and the hotel Noailles, were occupied in force by the National Guard. The opposite posts were not more than from twelve to fifteen yards asunder. The sectionaries every moment sent women, or advanced themselves, unarmed, and waving their hats over their heads, to fraternize with the troops of the line.

VII. *Action of the 13th of Vendemiaire.*—Matters grew worse every moment. At three o'clock, Danican, general of the Sections, sent a flag of truce to summon the Convention to dismiss the troops which threatened the people, and to disarm the Terrorists. This messenger traversed the posts blind-folded, with all the forms of war. He was thus introduced into the midst of the Committee of the Forty, in which he caused a great sensation by his threats. He was sent back towards four o'clock. The night was coming on, and there could be no doubt that darkness must be favourable to the Sections, considering their great number. They might creep from house to house into all the avenues of the Thuilleries, already strictly blockaded. About the same time seven hundred muskets, belts and catridge-boxes were brought into the hall of the Convention to arm the members themselves as a corps-de-reserve, which alarmed many of them who had not till then comprehended the *magnitude* of the danger in which they stood.

At length, at a quarter after four, some muskets were discharged from the hotel de Noailles, into which the sectionaries had introduced themselves; the balls reached the steps of the Thuilleries. At the same instant, Lafond's column debouched by the quay Voltaire, marching over the Pont Royal. The batteries were then ordered to fire. An eight-pounder, at the Cul-de-sac Dauphin, commenced the fire, and served as a signal to all the posts. After several discharges, Saint-Roch was carried; Lafond's column, the head and flank of which were both exposed to the cannonade from the quay, at the point of the Louvre wicket, and from the head of Pont Royal, was routed. The rue Saint-Honoré, the rue Saint-Florentin, and the adjacent places, were swept by the guns. About a hundred men attempted to make a stand at the Theatre de la Republique; a few shells from the howitzers dislodged them in an instant. At six o'clock all was over.

If a few cannon were heard at long intervals in *the course of the night*, it was to prevent the barricades which some inhabitants had attempted to form with casks.

There were about two hundred killed and wounded on the part of the sectionaries, and nearly as many on the side of the Convention; the greater part *of the latter*, at the gates of Saint-Roch.

The section of the Quinze-Vingts, Faubourg St. Antonine, was the only one that took part with the Convention; it furnished 250 men: so completely had the late political oscillations of this body *alienated all classes* from it. The Faubours, however, if they did not rise in favour of the Convention, certainly did not act against it. It is untrue, that in the commencement of the action the troops were ordered to fire with powder only; that would only have served to embolden the sectionaries and to endanger the troops; but it is a fact, that when once they were engaged, and success had ceased to be doubtful, they fired without ball.

VIII. *The 14th of Vendemiaire.*—Some assemblages still continued to take place in the Section Lepelletier.

On the 14th in the morning some columns debouched against them by the Boulevards, the rue Richelieu, and the Palais Royal. Some cannon had been placed in the principal avenues. The sectionaries were promptly dislodged, and the rest of the day was employed in going over the city, visiting the chief houses of the Sections, gathering in arms, and reading proclamations. In the evening order was completely restored, and Paris was once more perfectly quiet.

After this great event, when the officers of the Army of the interior were presented in a body to the Convention, the members, by acclamation, appointed Bonaparte General-in-chief of this army; Barras being no longer allowed to unite the title of representative of the people with military functions.

General Menou was delivered over to a counsel of war: his death was required. The General-in-chief saved him by telling the judges that if Menou deserved death, the three representatives who had directed the operations and parleyed with the sectionaries, merited the same punishment: that the Convention ought to bring its three members to trial before it proceeded against Menou. The corporate spirit prevailed over the voices of Menou's enemies.

The same commission condemned several individuals to *death*, in contumacy, *amongst others* Vaublanc. Lafond was the only person executed. This young man had evinced great courage in the action; the head of his column, on the Pont Royal, formed again three times under the fire of grape-shot, before it entirely gave way. He was an emigrant; there was no possibility of saving him, however it might have been wished to do so; his imprudent answers constantly defeated the good intention of his judges.

IX. *Napoleon, commander-in-chief of the Army of the Interior.*—After the 13th of Vendemiaire, Napoleon had to re-organize the National Guard, which was an object of the highest importance, as it then reckoned no less than 104 battalions.

At the same time he formed the guard of the Directory, and re-organized that of the Legislative Body. These very circumstances proved eventually one of the causes of his success on the famous 18th of Brumaire. He had left such impressions on this corps, that on his return from Egypt, although the Directory had recommended its soldiers to pay him no military honours except when he was in full uniform, nothing could hinder them from beating *To the field*, whenever, and in whatever dress they saw him.

The few months that Napoleon commanded the Army of the Interior, were replete with difficulties and embarrassments.

These were the installation of a new government, the members of which were divided amongst themselves, and often in opposition to the councils; a silent ferment amongst the old sectionaries who composed the majority of Paris; the active turbulence of the Jacobins, who assembled anew under the name of the Society of the Pantheon; the foreign agents of Royalism, *who* formed a powerful party; the discredit of the finances and paper-money, which spread extreme discontent amongst the troops; and above all, the horrible famine which, at this period, afflicted the capital.

Ten or twelve times the supply of provisions failed entirely, and the scanty daily distributions which Government had been compelled to establish were interrupted. It required no ordinary degree of activity and address to surmount so many obstacles, and to maintain tranquillity in the capital in spite of such a combination of calamities and difficulties.

The Society of the Pantheon daily gave the Directory new causes of uneasiness. The police durst not venture an open attack on this society. The General-in-chief caused the place of its meetings to be sealed up, and the members never stirred more whilst he was in the way. It was not until after his departure that they appeared again, under the influence of Babeuf, Antonelle, and others, and produced the eruption at the camp of Grenelle.

Napoleon frequently had to harangue at the markets, in the streets, in the sections, and Faubourgs; and here it is worthy of remark that he always found the Faubourg Saint-Antonine the most ready to listen to reason, and the most susceptible of a generous impulse.

It was during his command of Paris, that Napoleon became acquainted with Madame de Beauharnois.

After the general disarming of the Sections had been effected, a youth of ten or twelve years of age presented himself before the staff, entreating the General-in-chief to give orders for restoring to him the sword of his father, who had been a general of the Republic. This youth was Eugene Beauharnois, afterwards Viceroy of Italy. Napoleon, moved by the nature of his request, and by his juvenile grace, granted his petition. Eugene burst into tears on beholding his father's sword. The General was touched at his sensibility, and behaved so kindly to him that Madame de Beauharnois thought it incumbent on her to wait on him the next day to thank him for his attention. Napoleon returned her visit without delay.

Every one knows the extrordinary grace of the Empress Josephine, her sweet and attractive manners. The acquaintance soon became intimate and tender, and it was not long before they married.

X. *Napoleon appointed General-in-chief of the army of Italy.*—Scherer, who commanded the army of Italy, was reproached with not having known how to profit by his victory of Loano; his subsequent conduct had not given great satisfaction. Many more official than military characters were seen at his head quarters at Nice. This general asked for money to pay his troops and re-organize the various branches of the service; and for horses, to replace those of his cavalry which had perished for want of food. The Government could give him neither the one nor the other. Evasive answers were given to his demands, and empty promises were made to amuse him. He then declared, that if any farther delay took place, he should be compelled to evacuate the Genoese country, to return to the Roya, and perhaps even to repass the Var. The Directory resolved to supersede him.

A young general of twenty-five could no longer remain at the head of the Army of the interior. The public opinion of his talents, and the confidence which the Army of Italy had in him, designated him as the only man capable of extricating it from the embarrassing situation in which it stood. The conferences which he had with the Directory on this head, and the projects which he submitted to its consideration, left no farther doubt. He set out for Nice, and General Hatri, who was sixty years of age, came from the Army of the Sambre and Meuse, to succeed him in the command of the Army of the interior, which had become of less importance, now that the crisis of scarcity was over, and the government was firmly established.

BATTLE OF MONTENOTTE.

From the arrival of the General-in-chief at Nice, on the 28th of March, 1796, to the Armistice of Cherasco, the 28th of April following, being one month.

I. *Plan of Campaign for entering Italy by turning the Alps.* The King of Sardinia, who from his military and geographical position, had acquired the title of Porter of the Alps, had in 1796 fortresses at the openings of all the passes leading into Piedmont. If it had been wished to penetrate into Italy by forcing the Alps, it would have been necessary to gain possession of these fortresses. Now the roads did not allow the carriage of a battering-train; besides, the mountains are covered with snow during three quarters of the year, which leaves but little time for besieging these places. A plan was, therefore, formed for turning all the Alps, and for entering Italy precisely at the point where these high mountains terminate, and where the Appennines begin.

The Saint-Gothard is the most elevated pass of the Alps. From thence all the others gradually decrease in height. Thus the Saint-Gothard is higher than the Brenner; the latter higher than the mountains of Cadore; the mountains of Cadore than the Col de Travis and the mountains of Carniola. On the other side, the Saint-Gothard is higher than the Simplon; the Simplon higher than the Saint-Bernard, which is higher than Mount Cenis; and Mount Cenis higher than the Col di Tende. From the latter point the Alps continually decrease in height, and at length terminate at the mountains of St. Jaques, near Savona, where the Appennines begin. Then the chain of the Appennines rise again, and proceeds constantly increasing in an inverse direction; so that the Bocchetta, the neighbouring hills, those which separate Liguria from the states of Parma, Tuscany, the Modenese, and the Bolognese, keep always rising. The valley of Madonna, of Savona, and the hills of Saint-Jaques and Montenotte, are therefore, the lowest points both of the Alps and Appennines; the spot at which the former finish, and the latter commence.

Savona, a seaport and fortified town, was placed in such a manner, as to serve both for a magazine and point of appui. From that town to Madonna there is a firm hard road, three miles long; and from Madonna to Carcari, it is four or five miles more. The latter space might be rendered practicable for artillery in a few days. At Carcari are carriage roads, which lead into the interior of Piedmont and Montferrat.

This was the only point by which Italy could be entered without passing mountains: the elevations of the ground are there so inconsiderable, that at a subsequent period, during the Imperial reign, a canal was projected, which was to have connected the Adriatic with the Mediterranean, by the assistance of the Po, and of a branch of the Bormida, which has its source in the heights near Savona.

In penetrating into Italy by the sources of the Bormida, some hopes might be entertained of separating and intersecting the Sardinian and Austrian armies; because from that position Lombardy and Piedmont were both menaced. It was as practicable to march on Milan as on Turin. The Piedmontese were interested in covering Turin, and the Austrians in defending Milan.

II. *State of the two Armies.*—The enemy's army was commanded by General Beaulieu, a distinguished officer, who had gained reputation in the campaigns of the North. This army was well provided with all that was calculated to render it formidable. The French army, on the contrary, was in want of every thing, and its Government was unable to supply it. The army of the Allies was composed of Austrians, Sardinians, and Neapolitans; they already amounted to three times the number of the French army, and were to be increased successively by the forces of the Pope, by re-enforcements from Naples, and by the troops of Modena and Parma.

This army was divided into two grand corps: the effective army of Austria, composed of four divisions, of a strong artillery, and a numerous cavalry, increased by a Neapolitan division, forming a total of 60,000 men under arms. The effective army of Sardinia, composed of three Piedmontese divisions, and an Austrian division of 4000 cavalry, was commanded by the Austrian General Colli, who was himself under the command of General Beaulieu. The rest of the Sardinian forces garrisoned the fortresses, or defended the passes opposite the French army of the Alps; they were commanded by the Duke of Aosta.

The French army was composed of four effective divisions under Generals Massena, Augereau, Laharpe and Serrurier. Each of these divisions could, one with another, muster from 6 to 7000 men under arms. The cavalry, amounting to 3000, was in the most miserable condition, though it had been a long time on the Rhone to recruit itself; but it had wanted for provisions.—The arsenals of Antibes and Nice were well furnished; but means of transport were wanting: all the draught horses had perished for want. The penury of the French finances was so great that all the efforts of the Government could only furnish 2000 louis in specie to the military chest of the army for the opening of the campaign; there was, therefore, nothing to be expected from France. Henceforth no resources were to be hoped for, except from victory. It was only in the plains of Italy that means of conveyance could be organized, the artillery furnished with teams, the soldiers clothed, and the cavalry mounted. All this would be gained by forcing the passage of Italy. The French had indeed at most but 30,000 men, whilst more than 90,000 were opposed to them. If these two armies had had to contend with each other in a general engagement, no doubt the inferiority of the French army in point of numbers, artillery, and cavalry, would have ensured its easy overthrow; but as it was situated, it was enabled to supply the want of numbers by the rapidity of its marches; the deficiency of artillery by the nature of its manœuvres; its inferiority in cavalry by the nature of its positions.—The character of our troops was excellent: all the men had served in the other campaigns of Italy, or in those of the Pyrenees.

III. *Napoleon arrives at Nice.*—Napoleon arrives at Nice between the 26th and 29th of March. The picture of the army which Scherer laid before him, was still worse than he had been able to form any idea of. The supply of bread was very uncertain; distributions of meat had long ceased; for means of conveyance there were only mules, and above 200 of these could not be reckoned upon; it was impossible to think of transporting above twelve pieces of cannon; the position of the army grew worse every day. Not an instant was to be lost: the army could no longer subsist where it was; it was necessary either to advance or recede.

The French General gave orders to put the army in motion. He wished to surprise the enemy in the very opening of the campaign, and dazzle and confound them by brilliant and decisive advantages.

The head-quarters had never quitted Nice since the beginning of the war; they were ordered to be transferred to Albenga. All the civil lists had long considered their posts as fixed, and concerned themselves much more about their own comforts, than the wants of the army. The French General reviewed the troops, and said to them, "Soldiers, you are naked, ill fed; much is due to us, there is nothing to pay us with. The patience and courage you have shown in the midst of these rocks, are admirable; but they win you no glory. I come to lead you into the most fertile plains in the world. Rich provinces, great cities, will be in our power; there you will have wealth, honour, and glory. Soldiers of Italy, can your courage fail!"

Speeches like this, from a young General of twenty-five, in whom great confidence was already placed, on account of the brilliant operations of Toulon, Saorgio, and Savona, directed by him in the course of the preceding years, were received with the most lively acclamations.

For the purpose of turning the Alps, and entering Italy by the Col di Cadibona, it was necessary to assemble the whole army on its extreme right; which would have been a dangerous operation, if the snow had not then covered the debouches of the Alps. The transition from the defensive to the offensive order, is one of the most delicate operations in war. Serrurier was placed at Garezzio with his division, to observe the camps which Colli had at Ceva; Massena and Augereau were placed in reserve at Loano, Finale, and as far as Savona. Laharpe marched to menace Genoa; his van-guard, commanded by Gervoni, occupied Voltri. At the same instant the General-in-chief caused the passage of the Bocchetta and the keys of Gavi to be demanded of the Senate of Genoa. Great apprehensions prevailed in Genoa; the councils placed themselves in permanence.

IV. *Battle of Montenotte*, 11th of April.—Beaulieu, alarmed, hastened with all possible speed from Milan to the succour of Genoa. He removed his head-quarters to Novi, divided his army into three corps; the right, under Colli, composed of Piedmontese, had its head quarters at Ceva; it was intrusted with the defence of the Stura and Tanaro. The centre, under the command of Dargentau, marched on Montenotte, to intersect the French army by falling on its left flank, and cutting it at Savona, on the road of the Cornice. Beaulieu, in person, with his left, covered Genoa, and marched on Voltri. At the first glance these dispositions seemed skilful; but on more profound investigation of the circumstances of the country, it will be seen that Beaulieu divided his force by these means, because all direct communication between his centre and his left became impracticable, except behind the mountains; whilst the French army, on the contrary, was placed in such a manner that it could join in a few hours, and fall in a mass on either of the corps of the enemy; and when one of them should be totally defeated, the other must necessarily retreat.

General Dargentau, commanding the centre of the enemy's army, encamped at Lower Montenotte, on the 9th of April. On the 10th, he marched on Monte-Legino, to debouch by Madonna. Colonel Rampon, who had been ordered to keep the three redoubts of Monte-Legino, having received intelligence of the march of the enemy, pushed forward a strong reconnoitring party to meet him. This party was driven back, from noon till two o'clock, when it entered the redoubts again. Dargentau attempted to carry them by an instantaneous assault; he was repulsed in three successive attacks, and gave up the scheme. As his troops were fatigued, he took up a position, and put off turning these redoubts, in order to reduce them, until the morrow. Beaulieu, on his side, debouched on the 9th, on Genoa.

On the 10th, Laharpe was engaged all day with Beaulieu's van-guard before Voltri, disputing the passes with him, and keeping him in check. But in the evening of the 10th, he fell back on Savona; and on the 11th, at daybreak, he found himself with his whole division in the rear of Rampon, and the redoubts of Monte-Legino. In the same night of the 10th, the General-in-chief marched with the divisions of Massena and Augereau by the Col di Cadibona, and debouched behind Montenotte. At daybreak, Dargentau, surrounded on all sides, was attacked in front by Rampon and Laharpe, and in rear and flank by the General-in-chief. Dargentau was completely routed; his whole corps was cut to pieces; at the same time that Beaulieu arrived before Voltri, where he found no enemy. He did not hear of the defeat at Montenotte, and the entrance of the French into Piedmont, till the 12th. He was then obliged to make his troops fall back, and repass the bad roads into which the dispositions of his plan had thrown him. The consequence was, that three days afterwards, at the battle of Millesimo, only part of his troops could come up in time.

V. *Battle of Millesimo, 14th of April.*—On the 12th, the head-quarters of the French army were at Carcari: the defeated army had retired; the Piedmontese on Millesimo, and the Austrians on Dego. These two positions were connected by a Piedmontese division, which was ordered to occupy the heights of Biestro. At Millessimo, the Piedmontese were on both sides of the road which covers Piedmont; they were joined by Colli with all the force he had been able to bring up from the right. At Dego the Austrians occupied the position which defends the Acqui road, the direct way into the Milanese: they were successively joined by all the troops Beaulieu could bring back from Voltri; they were in a good position for receiving all the reenforcements that might be sent to them from Lombardy. Thus the two great debouches of Piedmont and the Milanese were covered: the enemy flattered themselves that they should have time to establish and intrench themselves there. However advantageous the battle of Montenotte had been for us, the enemy had found means to repair their losses, through the superiority of their numbers: but the next day but one, the 14th, opened to us the two roads of Turin and Milan. Augereau, forming the left of the French army, marched on Millesimo; Massena, with the centre, directed his march on Dego; and Laharpe, commanding the right, took his way by the heights of Cairo. The enemy had formed an appui for their right, by causing the hill of Cosseria, which commands the two branches of the Bormida, to be occupied; but from the 13th, General Augereau, who had not engaged at the battle of Montenotte, pushed the enemy's right with such impetuosity, that he carried the passes of Millesimo, and surrounded the hill of Cosseria. Provera, with his rear-guard, two thousand strong, was cut off. In this desperate situation, General Provera resolved to brave all extremities: he took refuge in an old ruined castle, and there barricadoed himself. From its top he saw the right of the Sardinian army making dispositions for the battle of the following day, by which he hoped to be extricated. All Colli's troops, from the camp of Ceva, were expected to arrive in the course of the night. The French, therefore, felt it of the greatest importance to gain possession of the castle of Cosseria in the course of the day; but this post was very strong, and their attack failed. The next day the two armies engaged. Massena and Laharpe carried Dego, after an obstinate conflict. Menars and Joubert carried the heights of Biestro. All Colli's attacks to extricate Provera were unsuccessful; he was defeated, and hotly pursued; Provera was then compelled to lay down his arms.—The enemy, briskly followed up into the passes of Spigno, left there part of his artillery, with many *colours and prisoners*. The separation of the two armies of Austria and Sardinia was, thenceforward, complete. Beaulieu removed his head-quarters to Acqui, *on the Milanese road*, and Colli returned to Ceva, to prevent the junction of Serrurier, and cover Turin.

VI. *Battle of Dego, August* 15.—In the meantime, a division of Austrian grenadiers, who had been directed from Voltri by Sassello, arrived at three in the morning at Dego. The position was no longer occupied but by advanced posts. These grenadiers, therefore, easily carried the village, and created great alarm at the French head-quarters, where they could not comprehend how the enemy could be at Dego, while we had advanced posts on the Acqui road. After two hours hard fighting, Dego was retaken, and almost the whole of the enemy's division were made prisoners.

In these affairs, we lost General Banel at Millessimo, and General de Causse at Dego. These two officers were distinguished by the most brilliant valour; they both came from the army of the Eastern Pyrenees, and it was remarkable that the officers who came from that army evinced the most extraordinary impetuosity and courage. It was at the village of Dego that Napoleon first distinguished a chief of battalion, whom he made a colonel; this was Lannes, who afterwards was a Marshal of the Empire, and Duke of Montebello, and displayed talents of the first order. He will henceforth be seen to take the principal part in all military events.

The French General now directed his operations against Colli and the King of Sardinia, and contented himself with keeping the Austrians in check. Labarpe was placed in observation near Dego, to secure our rear, and keep Beaulieu in check, who, being greatly weakened, was now chiefly occupied in rallying and re-organizing the wreck of his army. Labarpe's division being compelled to remain several days in this position, suffered greatly from the scarcity of provisions, owing to the want of means of conveyance, and the wasted condition of the country from the presence of so many troops; this circumstance produced some irregularities. Serrurier learning at Garassio the results of the battles of Montenotte and Millesimo, put his troops in motion, occupied the height of San Giovanni, and entered Ceva the same day that Augereau arrived on the heights of Montezemo. On the 17th, after some slight affairs, Colli evacuated the intrenched camp of Ceva, and retired behind the Cursaglia. The same day the General-in-chief removed his head-quarters to Ceva. The enemy had left there all their artillery, which they had not had time to carry off, and had contented themselves with leaving a garrison in the castle. The arrival of the army on the heights of Montezemo too was a sublime spectacle. The immense and fertile plains of Piedmont lay before them. The Po, the Tanaro, and a multitude of other rivers, meandered in the distance; in the horizon, a white girdle of snow and ice, of a stupendous height, surrounded these rich valleys—this promised land. Those gigantic barriers, which seemed the limits of another world, which nature had delighted in rendering thus formidable, and to which art had contributed all its resources, had fallen as if by enchantment. "Hannibal forced the Alps," said the French General, surveying those mountains, "but we have turned them:" a happy expression, which conveyed, in two words, the idea and the results of the campaign. The army passed the Tanaro; for the first time it was now absolutely in the plains, and the cavalry could now be of some utility to us. General Steingel, who commanded it, passed the Cursaglia, at Lezegno, and scoured the plain. The head-quarters were fixed at the castle of Lezegno, on the right of the Cursaglia, near the point at which it falls into the Tanaro.

VII. *Action of Saint Michel; Battle of Mondovi, 20th and 22d April.*—General Serrurier united his forces at Saint Michel. On the 20th he passed the bridge of Saint Michel, at the same time that Massena passed the Tanaro to attack the Piedmontese. But Colli, aware of the danger of his position, abandoned the confluence of the two rivers, and marched in person to take up a position at Montoir. By a fortuitous circumstance, he arrived with his forces exactly before Saint Michel, as General Serrurier was debouching from the bridge. He halted, opposed a superior force to him, and forced him to fall back. Serrurier would nevertheless have maintained himself in Saint Michel, had not one of his light infantry regiments taken to pillage. The French General debouched on the 22d by the bridge of Torre, and directed his march to Mondovi. Colli had already raised some redoubts there, and established a position; his left at Devico, and his centre at La Bicoque. The same day, Serrurier carried the redoubt of La Bicoque, and decided the battle, which took the name of Mondovi. This town and all its magazines fell into the hands of the conqueror. General Steingel, who had advanced too far into the plain, with a thousand horse, was attacked by a body of Piedmontese of twice that number. He made all the dispositions that could be expected from a consummate general, and was effecting his retreat towards the main body when he was mortally wounded by a pike in a charge.—General Murat, at the head of the cavalry, repulsed the Piedmontese, and pursued them during several hours.—General Steingel, a native of Alsace, was an excellent officer of hussars. He had served under Dumourier in the campaigns of the North; and was expert, intelligent, and active: he combined the qualities of youth with those of mature age, and was a true general of advanced posts.—Two or three days before his death, he was the first man that entered Lezegno. The French General arrived there a few hours afterwards, and found that every thing had been provided and attended to. The defiles and fords had all been reconnoitred; guides had been secured; the curate and postmaster had been examined; communications established with several of the inhabitants; spies despatched in various directions; the letters at the post-office seized, and those which could furnish any military information, translated and analyzed; all proper measures taken for forming magazines of provisions for the troops. Unfortunately Steingel was near-sighted, a material defect in his profession, and which contributed to his death. After the battle of Mondovi, the General-in-chief marched on Cherasco; Serrurier advanced on Fossano; and Augereau on Alba.

VIII. *Taking of Cherasco, April 25th.*—These three columns, on the 25th of April, entered at the sametime Cherasco, Fossano, and Alba.—Colli's head-quarters were at Fossano on the very day that Serrurier dislodged him thence.—Cherasco, at the junction of the Tanaro and Stura, was a strong place, but ill defended and unprovided, because it was not a frontier fortress. The French General considered the possession of this place of great importance. He found some artillery in it, and commenced vigorous efforts for putting it in a state of defence. The vanguard passed the Stura, and advanced beyond the little town of Bra. In the meantime the junction of Serrurier had enabled us to communicate with Nice by Ponte-Dinava; we received thence re-inforcements of artillery, and all that could be got ready. We had taken, in the different engagements, many horses and much artillery: in the plain of Mondovi we levied horses on all sides. A few days after its entrance into Cherasco, the army had sixty guns with their stores; the cavalry was remounted. The soldiers who had no distributions during the first eight or ten days of this campaign, began to receive them regularly. Pillage and disorder, the constant attendants of rapid movements, now ceased; discipline was restored, and the appearance of the army improved daily amidst the abundance and resources presented by this fine country. Its losses were repaired. The rapidity of the movements, the impetuosity of the troops, and above all, the art of opposing them to the enemy, at least upon an equality, and often with advantage, in point of numbers, with the constant tide of success, had preserved the men greatly; besides, soldiers arrived by all the debouches, from all the depôts and all the hospitals, at the report of the victorious career and abundant supply of the army. Wines of every kind were found in Piedmont: those of Montferrat resembled the wines in France. Previously to this period the misery of the French had exceeded all description. The officers had for several years received only eight francs per month, and the staff was wholly on foot. Marshal Berthier preserved amongst his papers an order of the day, issued at Albenga, granting to each general a gratification of three louis.

IX. *Armistice of Cherasco, April 28.*—The army was now only ten leagues from Turin.

The Court of Sardinia no longer knew what resolution to adopt; its army was discouraged, and partly destroyed.—The Austrian army, reduced to less than half its original numbers, seemed to think of nothing but covering Milan.—The minds of the people of Piedmont were much agitated, and the Court was far from possessing the confidence of the public. It placed itself at the discretion of the French General, and solicited an armistice; to which the latter acceded. Many people would have preferred that the army should have marched and taken Turin. But Turin is a fortified city; if it had been determined to close the gates against us, they could not have been forced without such a train of artillery as we did not possess. The King had still a great number of fortresses, and notwithstanding the victories which had just been gained, the least check, the slightest caprice of fortune, might overturn every thing.—The two hostile armies, notwithstanding their numerous reverses, were still equal to the French army; they had a considerable artillery, and a cavalry which had not suffered. In the French army, in spite of all its success, a degree of astonishment prevailed; the greatness of the enterprise struck every one; the possibility of success, with such slender means, was a subject of doubt. The least ambiguous occurrence would have been seized on by many persons disposed to exaggeration. Some officers, and even generals, conceived that we ought not to dare to think of conquering Italy with so little artillery, scarcely any cavalry, and so feeble an army, which disease and the distance from home would weaken every day. Some traces of these sentiments of the army may be found in the following proclamation of the General-in-chief, which he addressed to his soldiers at Cherasco.

"Soldiers! You have, in fifteen days, gained six victories, taken twenty-one stand of colours, fifty-five pieces of cannon, and several fortresses; and conquered the richest part of Piedmont. You have made 15,000 prisoners; and killed and wounded more than 10,000 men.

"Hitherto you had fought for barren rocks, ennobled by your courage, but useless to the nation. Your services now equal those of the conquering army of Holland and the Rhine. You were in want of every thing, but you have provided every thing. You have gained battles without cannon, passed rivers without bridges, made forced marches without shoes, bivouacked without brandy, and often without bread. None but republican phalanxes, the soldiers of liberty, could have borne what you have endured. For this you have the thanks of your country. It gratefully acknowledges itself partly indebted to you for its prosperity;

and if, when you took Toulon, you gave an omen of the brilliant campaign of 1793, your present victories forbode one still more glorious.

"The two armies which lately attacked you with confidence, now fly before you with consternation. Those perverse persons who laughed at your wants, and rejoiced in their hearts at the anticipated triumphs of our enemies, are trembling in confusion. But, soldiers! it must not be concealed, you have done nothing, since there remains aught to do. Neither Turin nor Milan are in your power. The ashes of the conquerors of Tarquin are still trodden under foot by the murderers of Basseville. You were in want of every thing at the opening of the campaign; you are now abundantly provided. The magazines taken from the enemy are numerous, the besieging and field artillery have arrived. Soldiers! the country is entitled to expect much from you. Will you fulfil its expectations? The greatest difficulties are, no doubt, surmounted; but you have still battles to fight, towns to take, rivers to cross: *are there any amongst us whose courage is enervated? Are there any who would prefer returning to the summits of the Apennines and Alps, to endure patiently the insults of yon slavish soldiery?* No, there are none such amongst the victors of Montenotte, Millesimo, Dego, and Mondovi. All are burning to extend the glory of the French people. All wish to humble those proud kings who dare to think of enchaining us. All are ambitious to dictate a glorious peace, calculated to indemnify our country for the immense sacrifices she has made. Friends! I promise you this conquest; but there is one condition you must swear to fulfil; this is, to respect the people whom you liberate; to repress the horrible acts of pillage to which the wretches excited by your enemies, abandon themselves; without this you would not be the deliverers of nations, but scourges to them. You would not be the glory of the French people; they would disown you. Your victories, your courage, your success, the blood of our brethren slain in battle, all would be thrown away—even honour and glory. As to me and the other generals in whom you confide, we should blush to command an undisciplined, unrestrained army, acknowledging no law but force. But invested with the national authority, strong in justice and the law, I shall know how to force that handful of dishonourable, cowardly, heartless men to respect the laws of humanity and honour, which they trample under foot. I will not suffer robbers to sully your laurels. I will cause the regulation I have published in orders to be vigorously carried into effect. Pillagers shall be shot without mercy; several have already suffered. I have had occasion to remark the readiness with which the real good soldiers have come forward to enforce the execution of the orders.

"People of Italy! the French army advances to break your chains: the people of France are the friends of all nations; meet her in confidence. Your property, your religion, and your customs shall be respected. We shall make war like generous enemies, and aim only at the tyrants who enslave you."

The conferences for the suspension of hostilities took place at head-quarters, at the house of Sulmatoirs, then maitre-d'hotel to the King, and afterwards the Emperor's prefect of the palace. Latour, the Piedmontese General, and Colonel Lacoste, bearing powers from the King, came to Cherasco. Count Latour, an old soldier, who was lieutenant-general in the service of the King of Sardinia, was extremely hostile to all new ideas, of little information, and a common capacity. Colonel Lacoste, a man in the prime of life, expressed himself with facility, possessed much wit, and made a favourable impression. The conditions were, that the King should abandon the coalition, and send a plenipotiary to Paris to treat for a definitive peace; that in the meantime there should be an armistice; that until the conclusion of peace, or the breaking off of the negotiations, Ceva, Coni, and either Tortona, or Alessandria, should be forthwith surrendered to the French army, with all their artillery and magazines; that the French army should continue to occupy all the ground which was at that moment in its possession; that the military roads in all directions should permit the free communication of the army with France, and of France with the army; that Valenza should immediately be evacuated by the Neapolitans, and placed in the hands of the French General, until he should have effected the passage of the Po. Finally, that the militia of the country should be disbanded, and that the regular troops should be dispersed in the fortresses, in such a manner as to give no umbrage to the French.

Henceforth, the Austrians, left to themselves, could be pursued into the very heart of Lombardy. All the troops of the army of the Alps and the neighbourhood of Lyons, were now become disposable, and would join the army. Our line of communication with Paris would be shortened by one half; finally, we now had points of appui, and grand depôts of artillery, to form our besieging trains, and even to besiege Turin, if the Directory should not conclude peace.

X. *Aide-de-camp Colonel Murat crosses Piedmont, and carries to Paris the news of the successes of the army.*—General Murat, first aide-de-camp to the General-in-chief, was despatched to Paris with twenty-one stand of colours and the copy of the armistice. Napoleon had taken this officer into his service on the 13th of Vendemiaire; he was then a major of the 21st chasseurs. He afterwards married the Emperor's sister, became a Marshal of the Empire, High Admiral, Grand Duke of Berg, and King of Naples. He performed a grand part in all the military operations of the times; he always displayed great courage, and particularly, a singular hardihood, in cavalry movements. The province of Alba, which the French crossed, was of all Piedmont the country most adverse to the royal authority, and that which contained the greatest proportion of revolutionary germs; some troubles had already broken forth there, and others subsequently burst out. If, instead of negotiating, Napoleon had chosen to continue the war with the King of Sardinia, it is in that country that he would have found the greatest assistance, and the greatest disposition to insurrection. Thus, in fifteen days, the principal point of the plan of the campaign was secured; the greatest results were obtained; the Piedmontese fortresses of the Alps were in our power; the coalition was deprived af an ally who had an army of 50,000 men, and who was still more important on account of his situation. The national legislature had five times decreed that the army had deserved well of the country, in the sittings of the 21st, 24th, 25th, and 26th of April.

According to the conditions of the armistice of Cherasco, the King of Sardinia sent Count Revel to Paris to treat for the definitive peace. It was concluded and signed on the 15th of May. By this treaty the fortress of Alessandria remained permanently with the French army. Suza, Labrunette, and the Exilles were demolished. The Alps became open, and the King remained at the disposal of the Republic, having no fortified place but Turin and fort Bard.

Note of the Editor.—We mention here, once for all, that differences will necessarily be found between the official reports and these chapters. They arise from the precipitancy with which the reports were drawn up, from the wish of the General-in-chief to disguise his plans, the necessity of deceiving the enemy with repect to his real strength, &c. For instance, it is said in the report that Beaulieu attacked in person at Montenotte. It was thought so at the time. Farther on it is said, that the attack on Voltri was made by only 10,000 Austrians; but they had in the rear two columns of the same strength, which were to engage on the following day, Beaulieu having judged that on this point he should have to oppose the whole of the French army. It is also said, that Montenotte was attacked by only 15,000 men, because 10,000 men of this corps remained in the rear, and kept up the communication with the right at Ceva. It was against these troops that Massena, debouching at the break of day by Cadibona fired the first cannon.

If there is nothing said respecting the plans of the General-in-chief, or of his negotiations with Genoa, it is because the report published is only an extract from the official correspondence; and because, moreover, as we have already observed, it was part of the General-in-chief's plans to keep the enemy ignorant of his projects, and his mode of warfare.

This may suffice to explain, hereafter, any differences that may be observed. We repeat, that the present observation is to be understood as applying once for all.

FRAGMENTS OF CHAPTER III.

I. *Reasons for remaining on the line of the Ticino.*—The armistice being concluded, and the fortresses of Coni, Tortona, and Ceva, surrendered to us, it was inquired whether we ought now to pass the Ticino. It was well understood that the armistice, which had just placed these fortresses in our power, and separated the Piedmontese army from that of Austria, was useful. But it was asked, whether it would not now be most advantageous to profit by the means already acquired, in order to revolutionize Piedmont and Genoa completely, before advancing any farther. The Directory had the right of rejecting the proposed negotiations, and of declaring its will, by an ultimatum. "Would it not be impolitic," it was said, "to go still farther from France, and pass the Ticino without securing our rear? The Kings of Sardinia, who have been so useful whilst they fought for us, have been the chief contributors to our reverses, as soon as they have changed their policy. At this day, the disposition of that monarch leaves not the smallest room for illusion; the nobles and the priests govern this court, and are the irreconcileable enemies of the Republic. If we were to experience a defeat in advancing, what should we not have to dread from their hatred and vengeance? Even Genoa ought to be a source of great apprehension to us. The oligarchical system still reigns there; and however numerous our partizans in that quarter may be, they have no influence in political decisions. The citizens of Genoa may declaim, indeed; but that is the extent of their power. The oligarchists rule; they command the troops, and can dispose of a or 10,000 peasants, in the valleys of Fontana, Bona, and other places, whom they call to their defence in critical emergencies. Finally, it was asked, where were we to stop? Should we pass the Ticino, the Adda, the Oglio, the Mencio, the Adige, the Brenta, the Piave, and the Tagliamento, in order to reach the Isonzo! Was it prudent to leave behind us such numerous and unfriendly populations! Was not the true way to go fast, that of going wisely; making points of support of every country we should pass, by changing the government, and confiding the affairs of the state to persons of the same opinions and interests as ourselves! If we entered the territories of Venice, should we not oblige the Republic, which could command 50,000 men, to take part with our enemies?"

II. *Reasons for taking the line of the Adige.*—To the foregoing remarks, it was answered: The French army ought to follow up its victory. We ought only to stop on the best line of defence, against the armies which will speedily march against us; that line is the Adige. It covers the valleys of the Po; it intercepts middle and lower Italy; it covers the blockade and siege of Mantua, and probably that place may be taken before the contest can re-commence. By proceeding to the Adige, we gain the means of providing for all the expenses of the army, because the weight of that expense is divided amongst a more numerous population; that of Piedmont, Lombardy, and the Legations. It is feared that Venice may declare against us. The best way of preventing it, is to carry the war, in a few days, into the midst of her states; she is not prepared for such an event; she has not had time to levy troops, and form resolutions; the senate must be prevented from deliberating. Instead of which, if we remain on the Ticino, the Austrians may force Venice to make common cause with them, or she may herself be induced to do so by the spirit of party. The King of Sardinia is no longer formidable, his militia is disbanded, the English will cease their subsidies; internal affairs are in the worst possible condition in his dominions. Whatever step the Court may take, the number of the disaffected will increase; after fever comes debility. 12 or 15,000 is the utmost amount of the forces which this power still retains, and these are disseminated throughout a great number of towns; they are scarcely sufficient to maintain internal tranquillity. Besides, the hatred of Austria towards the King of Sardinia will keep constantly increasing; she will complain, that on the loss of a single battle, she was abandoned by her confederate. She will reproach him with the example of his ancestors, who remained faithful allies even when France was mistress of Turin; whilst in this instance he has deserted the joint cause without even the loss of a fortress. The Court of Sardinia has therefore henceforth much to fear from the Austrians. There is nothing to be apprehended from the oligarchists of Genoa: our best security against them is the immense profit they make by our neutrality. In propagating the principles of liberty in Piedmont and Genoa, in kindling civil war there, we should be raising the people against the nobles and priests: we should become responsible for the excesses which always attend such a contest. On the contrary, we should, when arrived on the Adige, be masters of all the States of the House of Austria in Italy, and of those of the Pope on this side of the Apennines; we should be in a situation to proclaim the principles of liberty, as well as to excite Italian patriotism against foreign domination, and the irritation of the people of Bologna and Ferrara against the Papal government. There would be no occasion to sow division amongst the various classes of citizens: nobles, citizens, and peasants would all be equally called upon to march unanimously for the restoration of the Italian nation. The word *Italia! Italia!* proclaimed from Milan to Bologna would produce a magical effect. Should it be proclaimed on the Ticino, the Italians would say, "Why do you not advance?"

III. *Topography of Italy.*—The great northern plains of Italy, comprised between the Alps which divide them from France, Switzerland, and Germany, the Appennines which divide them from Genoa, Tuscany, and the Adriatic, compose the valley of the Po, the valleys which extend to the Adriatic north of the Po, and the valleys which extend to the Adriatic south of the Po. These valleys are not subdivided by any hills; so that communications might be opened between all the rivers if necessary. They constitute one of the most fertile, grand, and rich plains in the world, covered with opulent cities, and a population of 8 or 10,000,000. This immense plain comprises Piedmont, Lombardy, Parma, Placentia, Modena, Bologna, Ferrara, Romania, and the Venetian countries.

IV. *Valley of the Po.*—The Po rises in Mount Viso, and receives, successively, on its left, at Turin, the Doire, which descends from Mount Genevre; a little lower at Chivasso, the Dorea-Baltea, which comes from the Great Saint Bernard; between Casal and Valenza, the Sesia; at Pavia the Ticino, which descends from Lake Maggiore, and the heights of the Simplon; near Borgo-Forte, the Oglio, from the Lake Iseo; near Governolo, the Mencio, from the Lake of Garda. The Po receives on its right bank all the streams which rise in the Apennines; the Tanaro below

Valenza and Alessandria; the Scrivia, below Tortona and Castel-Nuovo; the Trebbia, above Placentia; the Taro above Casal Maggiore; the Crostollo, near Guastalla; the Seccia, near Saint- Benedetto; the Panaro and the Reno in the vicinity of Ferrara; and finally falls into the Adriatic thirty miles beyond Ferrara, by several mouths. This river may almost be considered as a kind of sea, on account of the great number of streams it receives in all directions: It is raised above the soil, and embanked by dykes, so that the finest countries of Italy are, like Holland, gained by art from the dominion of the waters. There is little or no cause for solicitude respecting the course of the tributary rivers of the left bank; nature there takes its course without causing any inconvenience: thus the Dorea-Baltea, the Ticino, and the Adda, enter the Po without occasioning any damage. It is otherwise with the tributary streams of the right bank. Below the Tanaro all the rivers are subject to great disorders, and give rise to difficult questions in hydraulics. It is necessary to raise the dykes every year, because the countries through which they pass, particularly Parma, Modena, Bologna, and Ferrara, suffer heavy inundations. It is owing to this perpetual recurrence of natural difficulties, that the Italians have become so skilful in hydraulic science. The engineers of that country have carried this branch of our knowledge farther than it has been pursued in any other.

The tributary streams on the opposite side of the Po, also differ in this respect; that those of the left bank are almost always navigable, and scarcely ever fordable; whilst those on the right bank are never navigable, and are almost always fordable. The former are rivers; the latter are only torrents.

N. B. Here finishes this part of the chapter.—I am the more inclined to regret my not having the whole of it, because the remaining part contains a methodical enumeration of all the means of defence which Italy possesses against Austria. This piece the Emperor himself did not hesitate to consider very fine, and entitled to become of classical authority to military men; as long, said he, as the forms and physical details of the Peninsula remain unaltered. It will however, infallibly be found in the complete work of the Campaigns of Italy.

The Emperor speaks in praise of St. Helena,—Scanty resources of the Island.

February 1.—The happiest and wisest philosophy is that which sometimes enables us to view the least unfavourable side of the most disagreeable things. The Emperor, who was doubtless, at the moment, under the influence of this happy feeling, observed as we were walking with him in the garden, that after all, as a place of exile, perhaps Saint-Helena was the best that could be. In high latitudes we should have suffered greatly from cold, and, in any other island of the tropic, we should have dragged out a miserable existence under the scorching rays of the sun. "This rock," continued he, "is wild and barren, no doubt; the climate is monotonous and unwholesome; but the temperature, it must be confessed, is mild and agreeable."

He afterwards asked me, in the course of conversation, which would have been preferable, England or America, in case we had been free to follow our own inclinations? I replied, that had the Emperor wished to spend his days in philosophic retirement, far from the tumult of the world, he should have chosen America; but if he felt any interest, or entertained any after-thought with regard to public affairs, he should have preferred England. And, not willing to be behindhand in giving an additional touch to the flattering picture which the Emperor had drawn of our miserable rock, I even ventured to say, that there might, perhaps, be circumstances under which Saint-Helena would not be found the worst possible asylum. We might here be under shelter, while the tempest was howling in other parts of the world; and we were placed beyond the reach of conflicting passions, circumstances every way favourable to the chance of a happier future. These observations arose out of my wish to represent things on their fairest side; I extended the horizon to the utmost stretch of my imagination.

Meanwhile, in order to afford a correct idea of our place of exile, and the scantiness of its resources, it is only necessary to observe, that we were this day informed it would be necessary to economise various articles of our daily consumption; and perhaps even to make a temporary sacrifice of some. We were told the store of coffee was rapidly diminishing, and that it would soon be entirely exhausted. For a considerable time we have denied ourselves the use of white sugar; there was but very little, and that very bad, which was reserved exclusively for the Emperor's use; and there is now every prospect of this little supply being exhausted before more can be obtained. It is the same with various other necessaries. Our island is like a ship at sea; our stores are speedily exhausted, if the voyage be prolonged, or if we have more mouths to feed than we have the means of supplying. Our arrival has produced a scarcity at Saint-Helena, particularly as trading ships are not now suffered to approach the island; we might be tempted to believe that they avoid it as a fatal rock, were we not aware that the English cruiser carefully keeps them at bay. But of all the privations with which we are threatened, that which most surprises us, and which is most of all vexatious, is the want of writing paper. We are informed that during our three months residence here we have consumed all the paper in the island; which proves either that Saint-Helena is in general, very scantily supplied with that article, or that we have used a most unreasonable quantity. The inmates of Longwood must have consumed six or eight times as much as all the rest of the colony together.

In addition to this, our physical and moral privations must be taken into account; it must be recollected, that we were not in the full enjoyment of even the few resources which the island affords, and of which arbitrary feeling and caprice in part deprive us; for we were not permitted to regale our eyes with the sight of the grass and foliage, in places at a certain distance from Longwood. The Admiral had promised that the Emperor should be free to ride over the whole of the island, and that he would make arrangements with respect to his guard, so as to free him from all annoyance. The Admiral, however, broke his engagement: and by his orders an officer insisted on accompanying the Emperor in his rides. The Emperor consequently renounced the idea of taking any excursion whatever; and we now remained cut off from all communication with the inhabitants.

With respect to physical comforts, our situation was most miserable, either through unavoidable circumstances or mismanagement. Scarcely any of the provisions were eatable. The wine was execrable; the oil was unfit for use; the coffee and sugar were almost at an end; and as I have already observed, we had almost bred a famine in the island. Of course, we could endure all these privations, and might have contrived to exist under many more. But when it is asserted, that we are treated in a style of magnificence, when it is declared that we are very well off, we are induced to unfold our real situation, and to show that we are destitute of every comfort. And lest our silence hereafter should lead to the inference that we are happy, let it be understood that our moral strength may enable us to endure miseries which language would be inadequate to express.

My son's indisposition.—The Emperor gives me a horse.

2d.—My son having been, for some time past, troubled with a pain in his chest, accompanied by violent palpitation of the heart, I called in three surgeons, and they ordered him to be bled.—Bleeding is at present the favourite remedy with the English: it is their universal panacea. They employed it in all disorders, and sometimes where there is no disorder at all. They laughed at the astonishment we evinced at a treatment which was altogether new to us.

About the middle of the day we took a ride in the calash. On our return home, the Emperor wished to see a horse that had just been purchased for him: he thought him very handsome and well made. He tried him; declared that he liked him uncommonly; and then, with the most captivating good-nature, gave him as a present to me. However, I could not ride him: he proved vicious, and he was transferred to General Gourgaud, who is a much better horseman than I am.

The Emperor's progress in learning English.

3d—6th.—The 3d was a terrible day: the rain fell incessantly, and we found it impossible to stir out. The weather has continued wet for several days in succession. I never imagined we could have contrived to stay for such a length of time within doors. The damp is penetrating on every side of our dwelling, and the rain is making its way through the roof. The bad weather without doors had an unpleasant effect upon us within.—I became very dull; and the Emperor was by no means well. "What is the matter with you?" said he to me one morning; "you seem quite altered for these few days past. Is your mind ailing? Are you conjuring up *Dragons*, like Madame de Sevigne?"—"Sire," I replied, "my illness is altogether bodily. The state of my eyes plagues me exceedingly.—As for my mind, I know how to keep that under the bridle. I can even use the bit, if needful; and your Majesty has given me a pair of spurs which will be my last and victorious resource."

The Emperor devoted three, four, and even five hours at a time to the study of English. His progress was really very remarkable; he felt this, and was delighted at it. He frequently says, that he is indebted to me for this conquest, and that he considers it a very important one. For my part, however, I can claim no other merit than the method which I adopted with regard to the other occupations of the Emperor. I first suggested the idea, and then continually reverted to it: and when it was once fairly set on foot, I followed up its execution with a promptitude and daily regularity which stimulated the Emperor to proceed. If any of us happened not to be ready at the moment he wanted us, if it was found necessary to postpone any business till the following day, he was immediately seized with disgust, and his labours were suspended until some circumstances occurred to induce him to renew them. "I stand in need of excitement," said he in one of those transient interruptions, "nothing but the pleasure of advancement can bear me through: for, between you and me, it must needs be confessed that there is nothing very amusing in all this. Indeed there is very little of diversion in the whole routine of our present existence."

The Emperor still continued to play two or three games at chess before dinner; in the afternoons we again resumed *reversis*, which had long been abandoned. Formerly we had not been very regular in paying our debts of honour; and we henceforth agreed to pay the sums that we owed to each other, into a general bank. We began to consider how the money thus accumulated should be disposed of. The Emperor asked our opinions, and some one proposed that the money should be applied to the liberation of the prettiest female slaves in the island. This idea was universally approved; we sat down to play with great spirit, and the first evening produced two Napoleons and a half.

The Emperor learns the death of Murat.

7th—8th.—The frigate Theban arrived from the Cape, and brought us some newspapers. I translated them to the Emperor while we walked in the garden. One of these papers brought intelligence of a great catastrophe. I read that Murat, having landed in Calabria, with a few troops, had been seized and shot. At this unexpected news, the Emperor interrupted me by exclaiming, "The Calabrians were more humane, more generous than those who sent me here." This was all he said; and after a few moments silence, I continued my reading.

Murat, without real judgment, without solid views, without a character proportioned to the circumstances in which he was placed, had perished in an attempt evidently desperate. It is not impossible that the Emperor's return from Elba may have turned his brain, and inspired him with the hope of renewing the prodigy in his own person. Such was the miserable end of him who had been one of the most active causes of our reverses! In 1814 his courage and intrepidity might have saved us from the abyss in which his treachery involved us. He neutralized the Vice-King on the Po, and fought against him; whereas, by uniting together they might have forced the passes of the Tyrol, made a descent into Germany, and arrived on Bale and the banks of the Rhine, to destroy the rear of the allies and cut off their retreat from France.

The Emperor, while he was at Elba, avoided all communication with the King of Naples: but on departing for France, he wrote to inform him, that being about to resume possession of his throne, he felt pleasure in declaring to him that all their past differences were at an end. He pardoned his late conduct, tendered him his friendship, sent some one to sign the guarantee of his states, and recommended him to maintain a good understanding with the Austrians, and to content himself with merely keeping them in check, in case they should attempt to march upon France. Murat, at this moment, inspired with the sentiments of his early youth, would receive neither guarantee nor signature. He declared that the Emperor's promise and friendship were sufficient for him, and that he would prove he had been more unfortunate than guilty. His devotedness and ardour, he added, would obtain for him oblivion of the past.

"Murat," said the Emperor, "was doomed to be our bane. He ruined us by forsaking us, and he ruined us by too warmly espousing our cause. He observed no sort of discretion. He himself attacked the Austrians, without any reasonable plan, and without adequate forces; and he was subdued without striking a blow."

The Austrians, when rid of Murat, cited his conduct either as a reason or as a pretence for attributing ambitious views to Napoleon when he again appeared on the scene. They constantly referred to Murat, whenever the Emperor made protestations of his moderation.

Before these unlucky hostilities of the King of Naples, the Emperor had already concluded with Austria. Other inferior states had signified to him that he might rely on their neutrality. Doubtless the fall of the King of Naples gave another turn to affairs.

Endeavours have been made to represent Napoleon as a man of furious and implacable temper; but the truth is, that he was a stranger to revenge, and he never cherished any vindictive feeling, whatever wrong he might have suffered. His anger was usually vented in violent transports, and was soon at an end. Those who knew him must be convinced of this fact. Murat had scandalously betrayed him; as I have already observed, he had twice ruined his prospects, and yet Murat came to seek an asylum at Toulon. "I should have taken him with me to Waterloo," said Napoleon; "but such was the patriotic and moral feeling of the French army, that it was doubtful whether the troops could surmount the disgust and horror which they felt for the man who had betrayed and lost France. I did not consider myself sufficiently powerful to protect him. Yet he might have enabled us to gain the victory. How useful would he have been at certain periods of the battle? He would have broken three or four English squares. Murat was admirable in such a service as this;—he was precisely the man for it. At the head of a body of cavalry, no man was ever more resolute, more courageous, or more brilliant.

"As to drawing a parallel," said the Emperor, "between the circumstances of Napoleon and Murat—between the landing of the former in France, and the entrance of the latter in the Neapolitan territory; no such parallel exists. Murat had no good argument to support his cause, except success; his enterprise was purely chimerical, both as to the time and the manner of its commencement. Napoleon was the chosen ruler of a people; he was their legitimate sovereign, according to modern doctrines. But Murat was not a Neapolitan; the Neapolitans had not chosen Murat; how, therefore, could it be expected that he would excite any lively interest in his favour? Thus his proclamation was totally false, and void of facts. Ferdinand of Naples could view him in no other light than as a supporter of insurrection; he did so, and he treated him accordingly.

"How different was it with me!" continued the Emperor: "before my arrival, one universal sentiment pervaded France, and my proclamation was imbued with that sentiment:—every one found that it echoed the feelings of his own heart. France was discontented; I was her resource. The evil and its remedy were immediately in unison. This is the whole secret of that electric movement which is unexampled in history. It had its source only in the nature of things. There was no conspiracy, and the impulse was general; not a word was spoken, and a general understanding prevailed throughout the country. Whole towns threw themselves at the feet of their deliverer. The first battalion which my presence gained over to me, immediately placed the whole army in my power. I found myself borne on to Paris. The existing government and its agency disappeared without efforts, like clouds before the sun. And yet," concluded the Emperor, "had I been subdued, had I fallen into the hands of my enemies, I was not a mere insurrectionary chief; I was a Sovereign acknowledged by all Europe. I had my title, my standard, my troops; and I was advancing to wage war upon my enemy."

Porlier.—Ferdinand.—Tables of my Atlas.

9th.—In the papers which I was translating to the Emperor, I found the history of the Spanish General Porlier, one of the most distinguished chiefs of the famous Guerillas. He had made an attempt to excite the Spaniards to rise against the tyranny of Ferdinand; but he failed, was arrested, and hanged.

The Emperor said, "I am not in the least surprised that such an attempt should have been made in Spain. Those very Spaniards who proved themselves my most inveterate enemies when I invaded their country, and who acquired the highest glory by the resistance they opposed to me, immediately appealed to me on my return from Elba. They had, they said fought against me and their tyrant; but they now came to implore my aid as their deliverer. They required only a small sum to emancipate themselves, and to produce in the Peninsula a revolution similar to mine. Had I conquered at Waterloo, it was my intention immediately to have assisted the Spaniards. This circumstance sufficiently explains to me the attempt that has lately been made. There is little doubt but it will be renewed again. Ferdinand, in his madness, may grasp his sceptre as firmly as he will; but one day or other it will slip through his fingers like an eel."

We had now finished our perusal of the newspapers. The Emperor began to turn over the leaves of my Atlas, and I was happy to see him examine the genealogical tables. I had long wished to call his attention to them, but he had always passed them over. I analyzed to him, on the English table, the wars of the Houses of York and Lancaster; which are unintelligible to many readers, without a help of this kind. He was struck with their utility, and examined several of them. With regard to the Russian table, he observed that it is extremely difficult, without such an assistant, to trace the irregular order of succession among the late sovereigns of Russia. On looking over the French table, he was very much surprised at the singular fact, that in spite of seven or eight enforcements of the salic law, Louis XVI should have reigned as though that law had never existed.

The Emperor dwelt much on the accurate and complete agreement of these tables one with another; he frequently adverted to the number of rallying points marked in so small a space; the numerical order of the Sovereign, his degree of succession, the complete list of his ancestry, &c. He repeated what he had before hinted to me, that had he known the value of these tables, he should have engaged me to arrange them in a more convenient and less expensive form, in order to adapt them to the use of the French Lyceums. He added, that he should have liked to see all histories reprinted with similar documents to assist and explain them. I told him that I had entertained the same idea, that it had already been carried into execution, with Hume's History of England, and that, had it not been for the late events in France, it would also have been applied to Pfeffeld's History of Germany, Hainaut's France, and a history of the three Crowns of the North.

About four o'clock I presented to the Emperor the Captain of the Theban, who was to sail next day for Europe, and Colonel Macoy, of the regiment of Ceylon. This brave soldier looked like a mutilated monument; he had not only lost one of his legs, but his face was disfigured by a sabre-cut across his forehead, and several other scars. He had fallen on the field of battle in Calabria, and had been made prisoner by General Panthonaux. The Emperor received him with particular attention; it was easy to see that they felt a mutual sympathy for each other. Colonel Macoy had held the rank of Major in the Corsican regiment, commanded by the new Governor whom we expected. The Colonel remarked to some person, that he thought the Emperor was very ill-treated here; but that he had too high an idea of General Lowe's liberality of mind, not to believe that he would do every thing in his power to ameliorate our condition.

The Emperor afterwards rode out on horseback, when we again went up the valley, and did not return until about seven o'clock. The Emperor then resumed his walk in the garden; the temperature was very mild, and the moon shone delightfully. The fine weather had completely returned.

On Egypt.—Plan for altering the course of the Nile.

10.—The Emperor now begins to make rapid advancement in English; and, with the assistance of his Dictionary, might manage tolerably without me. He was delighted with the decided progress he had made. His lesson for to-day was the task of reading in the Encyclopedia Britannica the article on the Nile, of which he now and then made memoranda, to assist him in his dictations to the Grand Marshal. In this article the Emperor found a fact related which I had formerly mentioned to him, but which he had hitherto considered as an absurd story. The great Albuquerque proposed to the King of Portugal to turn the course of the Nile previous to its entrance into the valley of Egypt, so as to make it fall into the Red Sea, which would have rendered Egypt an impassable desert, and made the Cape of Good Hope the only channel for the great trade of India. Bruce thinks the execution of this gigantic idea not entirely impossible; the Emperor was forcibly struck with it.

About five o'clock the Emperor took an airing in the calash; the drive was extremely pleasant, and the circumstance of some trees having been cut down has, by forming several circuitous roads, made our original space three times as large as before. On our return, we took advantage of the fineness of the evening to walk for a long time in the garden: the conversation was most interesting. It turned on various important subjects, viz. on the variety of religions; on the spirit that had given them birth; the ridiculous absurdities with which they were mingled; the excesses by which they had been degraded; the objections that had been urged against them, &c. The Emperor treated all these subjects with his usual superiority.

Uniformity.—Ennui.—The Emperor's Solitude.—Caricatures.

11.—The Emperor read this morning the article entitled Egypt, in the Encyclopedia, and made some notes from it which cannot fail to be of service to him for his Campaign of Egypt. This circumstance gave him a great deal of pleasure; and he repeated several times in the course of the day how much he was delighted with the progress he had made. He is now sufficiently advanced to read without assistance.

About four o'clock I accompanied the Emperor into the garden: we walked by ourselves for sometime, but were afterwards joined by the rest of the company. The weather was very mild. The Emperor remarked on the calmness of our solitude. It was Sunday, and no workmen were to be seen. He added, that we could not, at least, be accused of dissipation, or of the ardent pursuit of pleasure; in fact, it is difficult to imagine a state of greater uniformity, or a more complete absence of every sort of amusement.

The Emperor endures this mode of life admirably. He surpasses us all in equality and serenity of temper. He says himself, that it would be difficult to be more philosophic and tranquil than he is.—He retires to bed at ten o'clock, and does not rise, that is to say, does not go out, before five or six o'clock, so that he was never more than four hours out of doors; like a prisoner who is led from his cell once a day to breathe the fresh air. But then how intense is the occupation of each day! how various are the thoughts which occupy his mind! With regard to mental exertion, the Emperor said he felt as capable of bearing it as he had ever been; that he did not feel the least ill effect from it in any respect. He was astonished himself at the slight impression that had been made on him by all the late events of which he had been the hero. He said it reminded him of lead which had been passed over marble. Weight may compress a spring, but cannot break it; and it rises again with its own elasticity. He did not think any one in the world knew better than himself how to yield to necessity; this he said was the real triumph of reason and strength of mind.

The hour for our ride had now arrived. As the Emperor was going to meet the calash, he happened to see little Hortense, Madame Bertrand's daughter, with whom he was very much pleased. He called her to him, caressed her two or three times, and took her out in the carriage along with little Tristran de Montholon. During the drive, the Grand Marshal, who had been looking over the papers, gave an account of some bons-mots and caricatures he had found among them. One possessed a good deal of point. The picture consisted of two actions; one represented Napoleon giving to the Princess of Hasfield, with directions to commit to the flames, the letter whose disappearance was to preserve her husband; underneath was written, *tyrannical act of an Usurper*. The pendant was quite another character. We described to the Emperor a great number of the caricatures with which we had been inundated after the restoration. Some of them afforded him great amusement. One in particular made him smile: it had reference to a change of dynasty.

The Emperor observed, that if caricatures sometimes avenge misfortune, they form a continual annoyance to power. "I think I have had my share of them," said he. He then desired us to describe some of those which had been made upon him, and very much approved of one as being in good taste. It was a sketch representing George III, on the coast of England, throwing an enormous beet-root, in a great passion, at the head of Napoleon, who was on the opposite shore, and saying, "*Go and make yourself some sugar.*"

The Emperor's long walk.

12th.—Fine weather had now fairly set in. About four o'clock the Emperor walked in the garden. The temperature was delightful, and we all acknowledged that it was like one of our finest evenings in Europe. We had enjoyed nothing equal to it since we had been on the Island. The Emperor ordered the calash; and by way of a change, instead of driving along by the gum-trees, to get into the road leading to the Grand Marshal's house, he wished to take the road which encircles the upper hollow of our favourite valley, and to gain, if possible, the spot on which is situated the residence of Miss Mason, and which is on the opposite side, facing Longwood. The Emperor invited Madame

Bertrand to take a drive in the calash, in which Madame de Montholon and myself were already seated: the rest of our party followed on horseback, so that we were now all assembled together. At a few paces from Madame Bertrand's, at the military post, which is established near the house, the ground was very rough and uneven; the horses refused to advance, and we were obliged to alight from the calash. The barrier was scarcely wide enough to allow the carriage to pass; but the English soldiers came to our assistance, and in a moment pushed it through by main force.—However, when we had reached the hollow of the valley, we found walking so agreeable, that the Emperor wished to continue it; and after a short time, he ordered the carriage to be driven along the road as far as the gate of Miss Mason's house, while we should proceed with our walk in the valley. The evening was really most delightful; the shades of night were beginning to overspread the sky, but the moon shone brilliantly. Our walk reminded us of those strolls which we had been accustomed to enjoy on fine summer evenings, in the neighbourhood of our country residences, in Europe.

The calash had now returned; but the Emperor declined getting into it. He directed that it should wait at Madame Bertrand's door; but when the Emperor got there he wished to walk on to Longwood, where he arrived very much fatigued. He had walked nearly six miles, which is a great deal for him, who was never a good walker at any period of his life.

Bad temperature of Saint-Helena.—Observation on the spirit of this Journal.

13—16. I have already observed that there is no regular course of seasons at Saint-Helena, but merely irregular successions of good and bad weather. It would be difficult to find four words to express any deviation from our accustomed routine, during these four days. And here I take the opportunity of observing, once for all, that if, in the course of my journal, the events of several days are occasionally found combined in one article, it is because I have cancelled a portion of the notes relating to each day separately. I have been induced to do this from various motives. Sometimes my notes appeared to me too puerile; sometimes, on the other hand, they seemed to be too serious, and required to be accounted for by reference to a more distant period; or occasionally they consisted of personalities, and I make it a rule studiously to avoid every thing of that kind. If in spite of all my care, any offensive personal allusions have escaped me, it can only be when I have been led to them by the essential object of my journal; namely, to describe the character of the Emperor. Even then, I may reflect for my own satisfaction, that these personalities relate only to public characters, and refer to facts already circulated in the world.

I am, however, perfectly well aware that the task I have undertaken, may subject me to many inconveniences; but I consider it as a sacred duty, and shall endeavour to fulfil it to the best of my abilities, happen what will.

The Emperor's views of French politics.

17th.—At six o'clock in the morning the Emperor mounted his horse, and we rode round the park, commencing in the neighbourhood of our valley, and proceeding as far as the road leading from the camp to the Grand Marshal's residence. A party of about 150 or 200 sailors, belonging to the Northumberland, who were daily employed in removing planks of wood, or stones, for the service of Longwood or the camp, ranged themselves in a line fronting Marshal Bertrand's house, while the Emperor passed by. The Emperor spoke to the officers, and smiled complacently on his old ship-mates; he appeared delighted at seeing them.

I have already mentioned that we occasionally received parcels of newspapers from Europe, the contents of which occupied our attention, and occasioned the Emperor to draw some lively and animated pictures. Conversing to-day on the subject of the intelligence we had recently received, the Emperor observed, that the condition of France was by no means improved. "The Bourbons," he repeated, "have now no other resource than severity. Four months have already elapsed, the Allied forces are about to be withdrawn, and none but half measures have been taken. The affair has been badly managed. A government can exist only by its principle. The principle of the French government evidently is to return to old maxims; and it should do this openly. In present circumstances, the Chambers, above all, will be fatal; they will inspire the King with false confidence, and will have no weight with the nation. The King will soon be deprived of all means of communication with them. They will no longer follow the same religion, nor speak the same language. No individual will henceforth have a right to undeceive the people with regard to any absurdities that may be propagated; even if it should be wished to make them believe that all the springs of water are poisoned, and that trains of gunpowder are laid under ground." The Emperor concluded by observing, that there would be some juridical executions, and an extreme desire of re-action, which will be sufficiently strong to irritate, but not to subdue, &c.

As to Europe, the Emperor considered it to be as violently agitated as it had ever been. The powers of Europe had destroyed France, but she might one day revive through commotions arising among the people of different nations, whom the policy of the sovereigns was calculated to alienate; the glory of France might also be restored through a misunderstanding among the Allied powers themselves, which would probably ensue.

As to our own personal affairs, they could only be improved through the medium of England; and she could only be induced to favour us by political interests, a change in her ministers or her sovereign, or the sentiment of national glory excited by the torrent of public opinion. As for political interests, circumstances might bring them about; the change of individuals depends on accidents; finally, with respect to the sentiment of national glory, so easy to be understood, the present ministry had disavowed it, but another might not be insensible to it.

Picture of domestic happiness drawn by the Emperor.—Two young ladies of the Island.

18th.—The Emperor sent for me about ten o'clock; he had just returned home. Some one had informed me that he had been out shooting; but he said he had not. He rode out on horseback as early as six o'clock; but he gave orders that *His Excellency's* slumbers should not be disturbed. We set to work with the English lesson. Breakfast was served up; it was most detestable, and I could not refrain from making the observation. He complained of my eating so little, and added that it was certainly necessary to have a good appetite to make a repast on such fare. We continued our lesson until nearly one o'clock, when the excessive heat obliged us to desist, and take a little repose.

About five o'clock the Emperor went out to walk in the garden. He began to draw a sketch of the happiness of a private man in easy circumstances, peacefully enjoying life in his native province, in the house and surrounded by the lands which he had inherited from his fore-fathers. Certainly nothing could be more philosophic. We could not refrain from smiling at the tranquil domestic picture, and some of us got our ears pinched for our pains. "Felicity of this kind," continued the Emperor, "is now unknown in France except by tradition. The Revolution has destroyed it. The old families have been deprived of this happiness, and the new ones have not yet been long enough established in the enjoyment of it. The picture which I have sketched has now no real existence."—He observed, that to be driven from one's native home, from the fields in which we had roamed in childhood, to possess no paternal abode, was in reality to be deprived of a country. Some one here remarked, that the man who had been robbed of the home which he had created for himself after the storm had blown over; who was driven from the house in which he had dwelt with his wife, and which had been the birth-place of his children, might truly say that he had lost a second country. What a world do we live in! and what vicissitudes has not the present age produced?

We seated ourselves in the calash, and took our accustomed airing. During dinner the conversation turned on two young ladies, residents of the island: the one tall, handsome, and very fascinating; the other not so pretty, but perfectly well bred, and pleasing in her deportment and manners. Opinions were divided respecting them. The Emperor, who knew I was an admirer of the one first described, declared himself in favour of her also. Some one remarked, that if he were to see the second, he would not be induced to change his mind. The Emperor then wished to know the gentleman's own opinion respecting the ladies, and he replied, that he was an admirer of the second. This seemed rather contradictory, and the Emperor requested him to explain himself. "Why," said he, "if I wished to purchase a slave, I should certainly fix on the first; but if I thought I should derive any happiness from becoming a slave myself, I should address myself to the second."—"That is to say," resumed the Emperor, quickly, "that you have no very high opinion of my taste?"—"Not so, Sire, but I suspect your Majesty's views and mine would be different."—The Emperor smiled, and said nothing more on the subject.

19th.—The Emperor rode on horseback very early this morning; it was scarcely six o'clock when he went out. I was quite ready; for I had ordered some one to call me; and the Emperor was astonished to see me so active. We strolled about the park at random, and returned about nine o'clock: the sun was already beginning to be warm.

About four o'clock the Emperor wished to take his English lesson; but he was not very well. He said, every thing had gone wrong with him to-day; and that nothing had been done well. His walk in the garden did not restore him; he was not well at dinner time. He did not play his usual number of games at chess; but retired after the first game.

The Emperor's works in the Island of Elba.—Predilection of the Algerines for the Emperor.

20th.—The weather has been extremely bad. The Emperor had been rather unwell the whole of the night, but felt himself much better in the morning. He did not leave his room before five o'clock. About six we took advantage of a gleam of fine weather to drive round the park in the calash. The horses which have been provided for us are vicious; they shy at the first object that comes in their way, and become restive. They stood still several times during our drive. The rain, indeed, had rendered the roads very heavy, and at one time it required all our efforts to obviate the necessity of returning on foot. The Grand Marshal and General Gourgaud were at one time obliged to alight and put their shoulders to the wheel. At length, after a great deal of trouble, we reached home. The conversation during our drive, turned on the island of Elba. The Emperor spoke of the roads he had made, and the houses he had built, which the best painters of Italy begged, as a favour, to be permitted to adorn with their works.

The Emperor observed, that his flag had become the first in the Mediterranean. It was held sacred, he said, by the Algerines, who usually made presents to the Elba Captains, telling them that they were paying the debt of Moscow.—The Grand Marshal told us, that some Algerine ships, having anchored off the island of Elba, had caused great alarm among the inhabitants, who questioned the pirates with regard to their intentions, and ended by asking them plainly whether they came with any hostile views.—"Against the Great Napoleon!" said the Algerines: "Oh! never . . . . . . we do not wage war on God."

Whenever the flag of the island of Elba entered any of the ports of the Mediterranean, Leghorn excepted, it was received with loud acclamations: all the national feeling seemed to return. The crews of some French ships from Brittany and Flanders, which touched at the island of Elba, testified the same sentiment.

"Every thing is judged by comparison in this world," said the Emperor; "the island of Elba, which, a year ago, was thought so disagreeable, is a paradise compared to Saint-Helena. As for this Island, it may set all future regret at defiance."

Piontkowski.—Caricature.

21st—22d. The Emperor continued to rise early and ride out on horseback, in the park and among the gum-trees.—

He rode only at a walking pace, but this light exercise was of advantage to him, as it enabled him to enjoy the fresh air. He returned with a better appetite, and pursued the occupations of the day with greater spirit. He breakfasted in the garden, under some trees which had been twined together to afford him a shade. One morning, as he was sitting down to breakfast, he perceived at a distance the Polonese Piontkowski, and sent for him to breakfast with him. He always takes pleasure in conversing with him whenever he meets him.

Piontkowski, with whose origin we are not very well acquainted, came to the Island of Elba, and obtained permission to serve as a private in the Guards. On the Emperor's return from Elba, he had gained the rank of lieutenant.— When we departed from Paris, he received permission to follow us; and we left him at Plymouth, among those who were separated from us by order of the English ministers.— Piontkowski, having more fidelity, or more address, than his comrades, obtained leave to come to Saint-Helena.— The Emperor had never known, and never spoken to him, till he came here.

Piontkowski was, indeed, equally unknown to us all.— The English were surprised that we did not give him a warmer greeting on his arrival. Some individuals, who seized all opportunities of saying any thing to our disadvantage, wrote to England that we had received Piontkowski very badly. This story was totally false; but it furnished the English ministerial prints with a subject on which to exercise their usual courtesy and wit. It was asserted that the Emperor had beaten Piontkowski; and I heard of a caricature in which Napoleon was exhibited thrusting his nails into the Polish officer. It was, moreover, alleged that I had fallen upon him like a cannibal, about to devour him; and that it was only by a stick being thrust between my teeth, by the driver of the cattle, that I was prevented from biting a mouthful out of his shoulder. Such were the elegant descriptions that were given of us.

The Emperor's return from Elba.

24th.—After dinner, while we were taking our coffee, the Emperor observed, that about this time last year, he quitted the island of Elba. The Grand Marshal informed him that it was on the 26th of February, and on a Sunday. "Sire," said he, "you directed the mass to be performed at an earlier hour than usual, that you might have the more time for issuing the necessary orders."

They sailed in the afternoon, and next morning at ten o'clock, they were still within sight, to the great anxiety of those who were interested in their success.

The Emperor entered into conversation on this subject, and was, for upwards of an hour, engaged in describing the details of that event, which is single in history, both from the boldness of the enterprise, and the miracle of its execution. I shall insert, in another part of my journal, the details which I collected on this subject.

Campaigns of Italy and Egypt.—The Emperor's opinion on the great French Poets.—Tragedies by late Writers.—Hector.—The Etats de Blois.—Talma.

25th—28th.—Our days were for the most part very much alike; if they seemed long in detail, they were rapidly shortened in a retrospective view. They were without character or interest, and left only imperfect recollections behind. The English went on gradually improving. The Emperor confessed that he had a moment of disgust; his *furia Francese* had he said, at one time, given way; but he added, that I had reanimated him by means of a plan which he considered more certain and infallible than any other—that of reading and analyzing one single page over and over again until it was thoroughly learnt. The grammatical rules were explained by the way. In this manner, there is not a moment lost for study and memory. The progress at first appears slow, the learner seems to advance but little in his studies; but by the time he has come to the fiftieth page, he is astonished to find that he knows the language. We had added a page of Telemachus to the rest of our lesson, and found the benefit of it. By this time however, the Emperor, though he had only had twenty or twenty-five complete lessons, could understand any book; and would have been able to make himself understood in writing. He had not learnt every thing, it is true; but as he said, nothing could be concealed from him for the future, and this was a great thing—this was a decided victory.

The Campaign of Egypt was completed with the assistance of Bertrand, as far as the want of materials would permit. The Emperor now commenced, with another of the gentlemen, a new and very important period; namely: from his departure from Fontainebleau, up to his return to Paris, and his second abdication. He possessed no document relating to these rapid events; but it was that very rapidity, which induced me to entreat him to employ his memory in the establishment of circumstances, which the hurry of events or party spirit might enfeeble or distort.

The Emperor also employed himself very frequently with me, in revising the different chapters of the Campaign of Italy; this was generally done immediately before dinner. He had directed me to arrange each chapter in a regular and uniform manner; to mark out the proper divisions of the paragraphs, and to note down and collect the justificatory articles. This he called the digestive business of an editor. "And your interest is concerned in it," said he to me one day, with an air of kindness which affected me; "henceforward it is your property: the Campaign of Italy shall bear your name, and the Campaign of Egypt that of Bertrand. I intend that it shall add at once to your fortune and to your fame. There will be at least a hundred thousand francs in your pocket, and your name will last as long as the remembrance of my battles."

With regard to our evenings, the reversis had been relinquished a second time; we could not continue it long. After the second or third round, the cards were abandoned for conversation. We resumed our readings; our stock of novels was exhausted, and plays occupied our attention for the future, tragedies in particular. The Emperor is uncommonly fond of analyzing them, which he does in a singular mode of reasoning, and with a great deal of taste. He remembers an immense quantitly of poetry which he learned when he was eighteen years old, at which time, he says, he knew much more than he does at present. The Emperor is delighted with Racine, in whom he finds an abundance of beauties. He greatly admires Corneille, but thinks very little of Voltaire, who, he says, is full of bombast and trick; always incorrect; unacquainted either with men or things, with truth or the sublimity of passion.

At one of the evening levees at Saint-Cloud, the Emperor analyzed a piece which had just been brought out; it was *Hector*, by *Luce de Lancival:* this piece pleased him very much; it possessed warmth and energy of character. He called it a *head-quarter* piece; and said that a soldier would be better prepared to meet the enemy after seeing or reading it. He added, that it would be well if there were a greater number of plays written in the same spirit.—Then adverting to those dramatic productions which he termed *waiting-maids' tragedies*, he said they would not bear more than one representation, after which they suffered a gradual diminution of interest. A good tragedy, on the contrary, gains upon us every day. The higher walk of tragedy, continued he, is the school of great men; it is the duty of sovereigns to encourage and disseminate a taste for it. Nor is it necessary, he said, to be a poet, to be enabled to judge of the merits of a tragedy; it is sufficient to be acquainted with men and things, to possess an elevated mind, and to be a statesman. Then becoming gradually more animated, he added with enthusiasm,—"Tragedy fires the soul, elevates the heart, and is calculated to generate heroes. Considered under this point of view, perhaps, France owes to Corneille a part of her great actions; and, gentlemen, *had he lived in my time, I would have made him a prince.*"

On a similar occasion, he analyzed and condemned the *Etats de Blois*, which had just been presented for the first time at the theatre of the Court; and perceiving, among the company present, the Arch-Treasurer Lebrun, who was distinguished for his literary acquirements, he asked his opinion of it. Lebrun, who was undoubtedly in the author's interest, contented himself with remarking, that the subject was a bad one. "That," replied the Emperor, "was M. Renouard's first fault; he chose it himself, it was not forced upon him. Besides, there is no subject, however bad, which great talent cannot turn to some account, and Corneille would still have been himself even in one like this. As for M. Renouard, he has totally failed. He has shown no other talent but that of versification; every thing else is bad, very bad; his conception, his details, his result, are altogether deficient. He violates the truth of history; his characters are false, and their political tendency is dangerous, and perhaps prejudicial. This is an additional proof of what however, is very well known, that there is a wide difference between the reading and the representation of a play. I thought at first that this piece might have been allowed to pass; it was not until this evening that I perceived its improprieties. Of these, the praises lavished on the Bourbons are the least; the declamations against the Revolutionists are much worse. M. Renouard has made the Chief of the Sixteen, the Capuchin Chabot of the Convention. There is matter in his piece to gratify every party and every passion: were I to allow it to be represented in Paris, I should probably hear of half a hundred people murdering one another in the pit. Besides, the author has made Henrie IV a true Pilinate, and the Duke de Guise a Figaro, which is much too great an outrage on history. The Duke of Guise was one of the most distinguished men of his time; and if he had but ventured, he might at that time, have established the fourth dynasty. Besides, he was related to the Empress; he was a Prince of the house of Austria, with whom we are in friendship, and whose Ambassador was present this evening at the representation. The author has in more than one instance shown a strange disregard of propriety." The Emperor afterwards said, that he felt more than ever fixed in the determination he had formed, not to permit any new tragedy to be played on the public stage before it had undergone a trial at the theatre of the Court. He therefore prohibited the representation of the *Etats de Blois*. It is worthy of remark, that since the restoration of the King, this piece was revived with the greatest pomp, and supported by all the favour which the prohibition of the Emperor would naturally procure for it. But, notwithstanding all this, it failed; so correct was the judgment which Napoleon had passed upon it.

Talma, the celebrated tragedian, had frequent interviews with the Emperor, who greatly admired his talent, and rewarded him magnificently. When the First Consul became Emperor, it was reported all over Paris, that he had Talma to give him lessons in attitude and costume. The Emperor, who always knew every thing that was said against him, rallied Talma one day on the subject, and finding him look quite disconcerted and confounded,—"You are wrong," said he, "I certainly could not have employed myself better, if I had had leisure for it." On the contrary, it was the Emperor who gave Talma lessons in his art: "Racine," said he to him, "has loaded his character of Orestes with imbecilities, and you only add to their extravagance. In the *Mort de Pompée*, you do not play Cæsar like a hero; in Britannicus you do not play Nero like a tyrant." Every one knows the corrections which Talma afterwards made in his performances of these celebrated characters.

Contractors, &c. during the Revolution.—The Emperor's credit on his return from Elba.—His reputation in the public offices as a rigid investigator.—Ministers of Finance and the Treasury.—Cadastre.

29th.—At six o'clock, the Emperor having finished his daily occupations, went out to walk in the garden. We then took a drive in the calash: it was quite dark, and rained very fast when we returned.

After dinner, while coffee was served out, which we took without rising from our seats at the dining-table, the conversation turned on what were termed the Agents during the Revolution, and the great fortunes which they acquired. The Emperor knew the name, the family, the profession, and the character, of every one of these men.

Scarcely had Napoleon attained the Consulship than he became engaged in a dispute with the celebrated Madame Recamier, whose father held a situation in the Post-office department. Napoleon, on first taking the reins of Government, was obliged to sign in confidence a great number of lists; but he soon established the most rigid inspection in every department. He discovered that a correspondence with the Chouans was going on under the connivance of M. Bernard, the father of Madame Recamier. He was immediately dismissed, and narrowly escaped being brought to trial, by which he would doubtless have been condemned to death. His daughter flew to the First Consul, and at her solicitation, Napoleon exempted M. Bernard from taking his trial; but was resolute with respect to his dismissal. Madame Recamier, who had been accustomed to ask for every thing, and to obtain every thing, would be satisfied with nothing less than the reinstatement of her father. The severity of the First Consul excited loud animadversions; it was a thing quite unusual. Madame Recamier and her party, which was very numerous, never forgave him.

The contractors and agents were the class who, above all, excited the uneasiness of the new Supreme Magistrate, who called them the scourge and plague of the nation. The Emperor observed, that all France would not have satisfied the ambition of the individuals of this party who were in Paris; that when he came to the head of affairs, they constituted an absolute power; and that they were most dangerous to the state, whose springs were corrupted by their intrigues, joined to those of their numerous dependants.—In truth, said he, they could never be regarded as any thing but sources of corruption and ruin, like Jews and usurers. They had discredited the Directory, and they wished in like manner to control the Consulate. It may be said, that at that period they enjoyed the highest rank and influence in society.

"One of the principal retrograde steps," said the Emperor, "which I took, with the view of restoring the past state and manners of society, was to throw all this false lustre back into the crowd. I never would raise any of this class to distinction: of all aristocracies, this appeared to me the worst." The Emperor rendered to Lebrun the justice of having specially confirmed him in this principle.—"The party always disliked me for this," said the Emperor; "but they were still less inclined to pardon the rigid inquiry which I instituted into their accounts with the government."

The Emperor said, that in business of this sort he turned the service of his Council of State to the best account. He used to appoint a committee of four or five members of the Council, men of integrity and intelligence. They made their report to him, and if the case required further investigation, they wrote at the bottom of the report: *referred to the Grand Judge to be submitted to his laws.* The individuals implicated generally endeavoured to compromise the affair, when it arrived to this length. They would disgorge one, two, three, or four millions, rather than suffer the business to be legally investigated. The Emperor was well aware, that all these facts were misrepresented in the different circles of the capital, that they produced him many enemies, and drew down upon him the reproach of arbitrariness and tyranny. But he thus acquitted a great duty to the mass of society, who must have been grateful to him for the measures which he adopted towards these blood suckers of the public.

"Men are always the same," said the Emperor: "from the time of Pharamond downwards, contractors have always acted thus, and people have always acted the same with respect to them. But at no period of the monarchy were they ever attacked in so legal a form, or assailed so energetically and openly as by me. Even among the contractors themselves, the few individuals who possessed honesty and integrity, found in this extreme severity a new guarantee for their own conduct. A remarkable instance of this occurred after my return from Elba. Some houses in London and Amsterdam secretly negotiated with me a loan of from 80 to 400,000,000, at a profit of seven or eight per cent. The nett sum, which was deposited in the Treasury of Paris, was paid to them by rentes on the great book at fifty; they were then distributed among the public at fifty-six or fifty-seven."

This resource, so useful in the crisis in which the Emperor was placed, and which must at the same time have been so satisfactory and flattering to himself personally, proves the real opinion that was entertained of Napoleon in Europe, and the confidence which he inspired. This negotiation, which was unknown at the time, explains whence the Emperor derived the financial resources of which he suddenly found himself possessed on his return from Elba; which was a great subject of conjecture at the time.

The Emperor himself said, that he enjoyed singular reputation among the heads of offices and accountants. The examination of accounts was a thing which he very well understood. "The circumstance that first gained me reputation, in this way, was that while balancing a yearly account during the Consulate, I discovered an error of 2,000,000 to the disadvantage of the Republic. M. Dufresne, who was then chief of the treasury, and who was a perfectly honest man, at first would not believe that the error existed. However, it was an affair of figures; the fact could not be denied. At the treasury several months were occupied in endeavouring to discover the error. It was at length found in an account of the contractor Seguin, who immediately acknowledged it on being shown the accounts, and restored the money, saying it was a mistake."

On another occasion, as the Emperor was examining the accounts of the pay of the garrison of Paris, he observed an article of sixty and some odd thousand francs set down to a detachment which had never been in the capital. The minister made a note of the error, merely from complaisance, but was convinced in his own mind that the Emperor was mistaken. Napoleon however proved to be right, and the sum was restored.

The Emperor regarded as a matter of the highest importance, the separation of the departments of finance and the treasury, both for the sake of keeping the business of the two departments distinct, and for enabling them to become mutual checks to each other. The minister of the treasury, under a sovereign like Napoleon, was the most important man in the empire; not merely as minister of the treasury, but as comptroller-general. All the accounts of the empire came under his examination, and he was thus enabled to detect every kind of peculation and abuse, and to make them known to the sovereign; and communications of this nature were daily made. To special appropriations Napoleon also attached the greatest importance, as having been among the happiest springs of his administration.

Speaking of the *cadastre*, he said that according to the plan which he had drawn up, it might be considered as the real constitution of the empire. It was the true guarantee of property, and the security for the independence of each individual; for the tax being once fixed and established by the legislature, each individual might make his own arrangements, and had nothing to fear from the authority or arbitrary conduct of assessors, which is always the point most sensibly felt, and the surest to enforce submission. During this conversation, the Emperor gave his opinion of the talents of MM. Gaudin, Mollien, and Louis, as well as of most of his other ministers and counsellors of state. He concluded by observing that he had succeeded in creating a system of government, doubtless the purest and most energetic in Europe; and that he himself had the details so much at his command, that he was sure he now could, merely with the help of the Moniteurs, trace the complete history of the financial administration of the empire during his reign.

March 1st.—To-day two vessels arrived from the Cape. One the Wellesley, a seventy-four, had another dismounted ship in her hold. They were both Indian-built ships, and were made of teak wood, which in India is three-fourths cheaper than in England. This is an excellent kind of wood; and it is supposed that ships made of it will last much longer than European-built ships; though hitherto it has been complained that they are not such good sailers. However, it is not improbable that this teak wood may produce a revolution in the materials and construction of English ships.

2d.—The Chinese fleet is arrived. Several vessels successively entered the road in the course of the day, and many others are within sight. This is a sort of festival and harvest for the people of Saint-Helena. The money which these transient visitors circulate in the Island constitutes a chief portion of the revenues of the inhabitants.

At five o'clock the Emperor proceeded to the garden, and went on foot as far as an opening between some of the hills, whence we could discern several vessels at full sail, making for the Island. The last ship that arrived from the Cape brought a phæton for the Emperor. He wished to try it this evening, and he got into it, accompanied by the Grand Marshal, and rode round the park. He, however, thinks that this kind of equipage is both useless and ridiculous in present circumstances. After dinner the Emperor complained of being much fatigued, and he retired at an early hour.

The invasion of England.

3d.—The Emperor sent for me at two o'clock; I found him shaving. He told me that I beheld in him a man who was on the point of death, on the brink of the grave. He added that I must have been aware that he was ill, because he must have awoke me often during the night. I had, indeed, heard him cough and sneeze continually: he had a violent cold in his head, which he had caught in consequence of staying out too long in the damp air on the preceding evening. He stated his determination, in future, always to return in doors at six o'clock. After he had dressed, he sat down to his English lesson; but he did not continue at it long, for his head ached severely. He told me to sit down by him, and made me talk for more than two hours about what I had observed in London during my emigration. Among other things he inquired, "Were the English very much afraid of my invasion? What was the general opinion at the time?"—"Sire," I replied, "I cannot inform you: I had then returned to France. But in the saloons of Paris we laughed at the idea of an invasion of England; and the English who were there at the time did so too. It was said that even Brunet laughed at the scheme, and that you had caused him to be imprisoned because he had been insolent enough in one of his parts to set some nut-shells afloat in a tub of water, which he called manœuvring his litlle flotilla." —"Well!" replied the Emperor, "you might laugh in Paris, but Pitt did not laugh in London. He soon calculated the extent of the danger, and therefore threw a coalition on my shoulders at the moment when I raised my arm to strike. Never was the English oligarchy exposed to greater danger.

"I had taken measures to preclude the possibility of failure in my landing. I had the best army in the world; I need only say, it was the army of Austerlitz. In four days I should have been in London; I should have entered the English capital, not as a conqueror, but as a liberator. I should have been another William III; but I would have acted with greater generosity and disinterestedness. The discipline of my army was perfect. My troops would have behaved in London the same as they would in Paris. No sacrifices, not even contributions, would have been exacted from the English. We should have presented ourselves to them, not as conquerors, but as brothers, who came to restore to them their rights and liberties. I would have assembled the citizens, and directed them to labour themselves in the task of their regeneration; because the English had already preceded us in political legislation, I would have declared that our only wish was to be able to rejoice in the happiness and prosperity of the English people; and to these professions I would have strictly adhered. In the course of a few months, the two nations, which had been such determined enemies, would have henceforward composed only one people, identified in principles, maxims, and interests. I should have departed from England, in order to effect, from south to north, under republican colours (for I was then First Consul) the regeneration of Europe, which, at a later period, I was on the point of effecting, from north to south, under monarchical forms. Both systems were equally good, since both would have been attended by the same result, and would have been carried into execution with firmness, moderation, and good faith. How many ills that are now endured, and how many that are yet to be experienced, would not unhappy Europe have escaped! Never was a project so favourable to the interests of civilization conceived with more disinterested intentions, or so near being carried into execution. It is a remarkable fact, that the obstacles which occasioned my failure were not the work of men, but proceeded from the elements. In the south, the sea frustrated my plans; the burning of Moscow, the snow, and the winter, completed my ruin in the north. Thus water, air, and fire, all nature, and nature alone, was hostile to the universal regeneration, which nature herself called for!—The problems of Providence are insoluble!"

After a few moments silence, he reverted to the subject of the English invasion. "It was supposed," said he, "that my scheme was merely a vain threat, because it did not appear that I possessed any reasonable means of attempting its execution. But I had laid my plans deeply, and without being observed. I had dispersed all our French ships; and the English were sailing after them to different parts of the world. Our ships were to return suddenly and at the same time, and to assemble in a mass along the French coasts. I would have had seventy or eighty French or Spanish vessels in the Channel; and I calculated that I should continue master of it for two months. Three or four thousand little boats were to be ready at signal. A hundred thousand men were every day drilled in embarking and landing, as a part of their exercise. They were full of ardour, and eager for the enterprise, which was very popular with the French, and was supported by the wishes of a great number of the English. After landing my troops, I could calculate upon only one pitched battle, the result of which could not be doubtful; and victory would have brought us to London. The nature of the country would not admit of a war of manœuvring. My conduct would have done the rest. The people of England groaned under the yoke of an oligarchy. On feeling that their pride had not been humbled, they would have ranged themselves on our side. We should have been considered only as allies come to effect their deliverance. We should have presented ourselves with the magical words of liberty and equality," &c.

After adverting to a great number of the minor details of the plan, which were all admirable, and remarking how very near it had been to its execution, he suddenly stopped, and said, "Let us go out, and take a turn." We walked for some time; it had been raining for three days, but now the weather was perfectly fine. The Emperor, not forgetting his resolution to be in doors always by six o'clock, immediately ordered the calash; took a drive, and returned home in good time. My son followed on horseback; it was the first time he had enjoyed such an honour. He acquitted himself very well, and the Emperor complimented him on the occasion

The Emperor continued unwell, and retired to rest very early.

The Chinese Fleet.

4th.—To-day the Emperor received some captains of the China fleet. He conversed a long time with two of them, respecting their trade, the facility of their intercourse with the Chinese, the manners of that people, &c. The ships which trade to China are from 14 to 1500 tons burthen, almost equal to sixty-fours; and they draw from twenty-two to twenty-three feet of water: they are laden almost exclusively with tea. One of those just arrived had nearly 1500 tons on board. The cargoes of the six ships which came into the road last night are valued at about sixty millions; and as they will be subject to a duty of 100 per cent. on their arrival in England, 120 millions will thus at once be thrown into circulation in Europe.

Europeans are allowed very little liberty at Canton. Their residence is chiefly limited to the suburbs. They are treated with the greatest contempt by the Chinese, who assume an air of great superiority, and conduct themselves in a very arbitrary manner. The Chinese are very intelligent, industrious, and active; but they are great thieves, and extremely treacherous. They transact all business in the European languages, which they speak with facility.

The arrival of fleets at Saint-Helena is a circumstance equally pleasing to the crews and the inhabitants of the Island. The latter sell their merchandize and purchase provisions; the seamen, on their part are enabled to set foot on land, and to refresh themselves. This state of things usually continues for a fortnight or three weeks; but, on the present occasion, the Admiral, to the great disappointment of every body, limited the period of refreshment to two days only, for the two first ships had anchored off the town.—The others were ordered to remain under sail, and to come up to the town in succession, two by two. It may be supposed that he had received very strict orders, or was under great apprehensions, which we do not doubt.

The Emperor walked for some time in the garden before he got into his calash. Among the trees in the neighbourhood, we perceived some officers newly arrived at the Island, who were endeavouring to get a peep at the Emperor, the sight of whom seemed to be an object of great importance to them.

Etiquette of the Emperor's Court.—Circumstance that took place at Tarare.—Officers of State.—Chamberlains.—Unequalled splendour of the Court of Thuilleries.—Admirable regulations of the Palace.—The Emperor's Levees.—Dining in State.—The Court and the City.

5th.—To-day the Emperor conversed a great deal about his court and the etiquette observed in it. The following is the substance of what fell from him on this subject.

At the period of the Revolution, the Courts of Spain and Naples still imitated the ceremony and Grandeur of Louis XIV, mingled with the pomp and exaggeration of the Castilians and Moors. The Court of Saint-Petersburgh had assumed the tone and forms of the drawing-room; that of Vienna, had become quite citizen-like; and there no longer remained any vestige of the wit, the grace and the good taste of the Court of Versailles.

When, therefore, Napoleon attained the sovereign power, he found a clear road before him, and he had an opportunity of forming a Court according to his own taste. He was desirous of adopting a national medium by accommodating the dignity of the throne to modern customs, and, particularly, by making the creation of a Court contribute to improve the manners of the great, and promote the industry of the mass of the people. It certainly was no easy matter to reconstruct a throne on the very spot where a reigning monarch had been judicially executed, and where the people had constitutionally sworn their hatred of kings. It was not easy to restore dignities, titles and decorations, among a people who for the space of fifteen years had waged a war of proscription against them. Napoleon, however, who seemed always to possess the power of effecting what he wished, perhaps because he had the art of wishing for what was just and proper, after a great struggle surmounted all these difficulties. When he became Emperor, he created a class of nobility, and formed a Court. Victory seemed all on a sudden to do her utmost to consolidate and shed a lustre over this new order of things. All Europe acknowledged the Emperor; and at one period it might have been said, that all the Courts of the Continent had flocked to Paris to add to the splendour of the Thuilleries, which was the most brilliant and numerous Court ever seen. There was a continued series of parties, balls, and entertainments; and the Court was always distinguished for extraordinary magnificence and grandeur. The person of the sovereign was alone remarkable for extreme simplicity, which, indeed, was a characteristic that served to distinguish him amidst the surrounding splendour. He encouraged all this magnificence, he said, from motives of policy, and not because it accorded with his own taste. It was calculated to encourage manufactures and national industry. The ceremonies and fetes which took place on the marriage of the Empress and the birth of the King of Rome, far surpassed any which had preceded them, and probably will never again be equalled.

The Emperor endeavoured to establish, in his foreign relations, every thing that was calculated to place him in harmony with the other Courts of Europe; but at home he constantly tried to adapt old forms to new manners.

He established the morning and evening levees of the old kings of France; but with him these levees were merely nominal, and did not exist in reality, as in former times.—Instead of being occupied in the details of the toilet, and the conversations which might naturally ensue, these levees under the Emperor were, in fact, appropriated to receiving in the morning, and dismissing in the evening, such persons of his household as had to receive orders directly from him, and who were privileged to pay their court to him at those hours. The Emperor also established special presentations to his person and admission to his Court; but instead of making noble birth the only means of securing these honours, the title for obtaining them was founded solely on the combined bases of fortune, influence, and public services.

Napoleon, moreover, created titles, the qualifications for which gave the last blow to the old feudal system. These titles, however, possessed no real value, and were established for an object purely national. Those which were unaccompanied by any prerogatives or privileges might be enjoyed by persons of any rank or profession, and were bestowed as rewards for all kinds of services. The Emperor observed that abroad they had the useful effect, of appearing to be an approximation to the old manners of Europe, while at the same time they served as a toy for amusing the vanities of many individuals at home; "for," said he, "how many really clever men are children oftener than once in their lives!"

The Emperor revived decorations of honour, and distributed crosses and ribbands. But instead of confining them to particular and exclusive classes, he extended them to society in general as rewards for every description of talent and public service. By a happy privilege, perhaps peculiar to Napoleon, it happened that the value of these honours was enhanced in proportion to the number distributed. He estimated that he had conferred about 25,000 decorations of the Legion of Honour; and the desire to obtain the honour, he said, increased until it became a kind of *mania*.

After the battle of Wagram he sent the decoration of the Legion of Honour to the Archduke Charles, and by a refinement in compliment, peculiar to Napoleon, he sent him merely the silver cross, which was worn by the private soldiers.

The Emperor said, that it was only by acting strictly and voluntarily in conformity with these maxims, that he had become the real national monarch; and an adherence to the same course would have rendered the fourth dynasty, the truly constitutional one. Of these facts, said he, the people of the lowest rank frequently evinced an instinctive knowledge.

The Emperor related the following anecdote:—On returning from his coronation in Italy, as he approached the environs of Lyons, he found all the population assembled on the roads to see him pass, and he took a fancy to ascend the mountain of Tarare alone. He gave orders that nobody should follow him, and mingling with the crowd he accosted an old woman, and asked what all the bustle meant. She replied that the Emperor was expected. After some little conversation he said to her:—"My good woman, formerly you had Capet the tyrant; now you have Napoleon the tyrant,—what have you gained by the change?" The force of this argument disconcerted the old woman for a moment; but she immediately recollected herself, and replied, "Pardon me, sir, there is a great difference. We ourselves have chosen Napoleon, but we got Capet by chance."—"The old woman was right," said the Emperor, "and she exhibited more instinctive good sense than many men who are possessed of great information and talent."

The Emperor surrounded himself with great crown officers. He established a numerous household of chamberlains, grooms, &c. He selected persons to fill these offices indiscriminately from among those whom the Revolution had elevated, and from the ancient families which it had ruined. The former considered themselves as standing on an estate which they had acquired; the latter on one which they thought they might recover. The Emperor had in view, by this mixture of persons, the extinction of hatreds and the amalgamation of parties. He observed, however, that he was not displeased at seeing a variety of manners. The individuals belonging to the ancient families performed their duties with the greatest courtesy and assiduity. A Madame de Montmorency would have stooped down to tie the Empress's shoes; a lady of the new school would have hesitated to do this, lest she should be taken for the real waiting-woman; but the Madame de Montmorency had no such apprehension. These posts of honour were for the most part without emolument; they were even attended with expense. But they brought the individuals who filled them, daily under the eye of the Sovereign—of an all-powerful Sovereign, the source of honour and grace; and who declared that he would not have the lowest officer in his household solicit a favour from any one but himself.

At the time of his marriage with the Empress Maria-Louisa, the Emperor made an extensive recruit of chamberlains from among the highest ranks of the old aristocracy; this he did with the view of proving to Europe that there existed but one party in France, and of rallying round the Empress those individuals whose names must have been familiar to her. It is understood that the Emperor even hesitated whether or not to select the lady of honour from that class; but his fear lest the Empress, with whose character he was unacquainted, might be imbued with prejudices respecting birth, that might too much elate the old party, induced him to make another choice.

From this moment until the period of our disasters, the most ancient and illustrious families eagerly solicited places in the household of the Emperor; and how could it be otherwise? The Emperor governed the world: he had raised France and the French people above the level of other nations. Power, glory, constituted his retinue. Happy were they who inhaled the atmosphere of the Imperial Court.—To be immediately connected with the Emperor's person, furnished, both abroad and at home, a title to consideration, homage, and respect.

Upon the Restoration, a royalist, who had preserved himself pure, and in whose sight I had found grace, said to me, in the most serious tone, (for, what a difference in ideas does not difference of party produce!) that with my name, and the openness of conduct I had maintained, I ought not to despair of still obtaining a situation near the King, or in the household of some of the Princes or Princesses. How greatly was he astonished when I replied:—"My friend, I have rendered that impossible: I have served the most powerful master upon earth: I cannot in future, without degradation, stand in the same relation to any other. Know, that when we conveyed the orders of the Emperor to a distance, into foreign courts, wearing his uniform, we considered ourselves, and were every where treated, as upon an equality with princes. He has presented to us the spectacle of no less than seven Kings waiting in his saloons, in the midst of us, and with us. On his marriage, four Queens bore the robe of the Empress, of whom, moreover, one of us was the Gentleman Usher, another the Equery. Trust then, my friend, that a noble ambition may be perfectly satisfied with such honours."

Besides, the magnificence and splendour that composed this unexampled court, rested on a system and a regularity of administration, that has excited the astonishment and admiration of those who have searched amid its wreck: The Emperor himself inspected the accounts several times in the course of the year. All his mansions were found to be repaired and decorated: they contained nearly forty millions in household furniture, besides four millions in plate. If he had enjoyed a few years of peace, imagination can scarcely fix limits, he said, to what he would have accomplished.

The Emperor said, he had conceived an excellent idea, which he was much grieved at not having put in execution: it was to have commissioned some persons to collect the most important petitions: "They should have named every day," said he, "three or four individuals from the provinces, who would have been admitted to my levee, and have explained their business to me in person; I would have discussed it with them immediately, and administered justice to them without delay."

I observed to the Emperor, that the Commission he had created at a very early period, under the name of "Commission of Petitions," came very near the idea in question, and was, in fact, productive of much good. I was president of it on his return from Elba, and the first month I had already done justice to more than four thousand petitions. "It is true," I observed, "that circumstances originally, and custom afterwards had never allowed this establishment to enjoy the most valuable prerogative with which its organization had been endowed, that which would undoubtedly have produced the greatest effect on public opinion; namely, to present to him officially, at his great audience on Sunday, the result of the week's labours." But the nature of things, the constant expeditions of the Emperor, and above all, the jealousy of the Ministers, had concurred to deprive the Commission of this high privilege.

The Emperor said also, he was sorry he had not established it as a part of the etiquette of the Court, that all persons who had been presented, females particularly, who had any claim to obtain an audience of him, should have the unquestioned right of entering the anti-chamber. The Emperor, passing through it several times in the day, might have taken the opportunity to satisfy some of their requests; and might in this manner have spared the refusal of audiences, or the loss of time occasioned by them. The Emperor had hesitated for sometime, he said, about re-establishing the *grand couvert* of the kings of France, that is the dining in public, every Sunday, of the whole Imperial family. He asked our opinion of it. We differed; some approved of it, representing this family spectacle as beneficial to public morals, and fitted to produce the best effects on public spirit; besides, said they, it afforded means for every individual to see his sovereign. Others opposed it, objecting that this ceremony involved something of divine right and feudality, of ignorance and servility, which had no place in our habits or the modern dignity of them. They might go to see the sovereign at the church or the theatre: there, they joined at least in the performance of his religious duties, or took part in his pleasures; but to go to see him eat, was only to confer ridicule on both parties. The sovereignty having now become, as the Emperor had so well said, magistracy, should only be seen in full activity; conferring favours, repairing injuries, transacting business, reviewing armies, and above all, divested of the infirmities and the wants of human nature, &c. . . . . Its utility, its benefits, should form its new charm: the image of the sovereign should be present continually and unlooked-for, like Providence. Such was the new school:—such had been ours.

"Well," said the Emperor, "it may be true that the circumstances of the time should have limited this ceremony to the Imperial heir, and only during his youth; for he was the child of the whole nation; he ought to become thenceforth the object of the sentiments and the sight of all."

On his return from Elba, the Emperor said he had an idea of dining every Sunday in the *Galerie de Dianie*, with four or five hundred guests: this, said he, would undoubtedly have produced a great effect on the public, particularly at the time of the *Champ de Mai*, on the assembling of the Deputies from the departments at Paris; but the rapidity and the importance of business prevented it. Besides, he was apprehensive, perhaps, that there might have been observed in this measure, too great an affectation of popularity, and that his enemies abroad might give it the semblance of fear on his part.

It is the custom, said the Emperor, to talk of the influence of the tone and manners of the Court upon those of a nation; he was far from having brought about any such result; but it was the fault of circumstances and of several unperceived combinations; he had reflected much on the subject, and he thought it would have been accomplished in time.

"The Court," he continued, "taken collectively, does not exert this influence; it is only because its elements, those who compose it, go to communicate, each in his own sphere of action, that which they have collected from the common source; the tone of the Court, then, is not infused into a whole nation, but through intermediate societies.

Now, we had no such societies, nor could we yet have them. Those delightful assemblies, where one enjoys so fully the advantages of civilization, suddenly disappear at the approach of revolutions, and re-established but slowly, when the tempests dissipate. The indispensable bases of company are indolence and luxury; but we were all still in a state of agitation, and great fortunes were not yet firmly established. A great number of theatres, a multitude of public establishments, moreover, presented pleasures more ready, less constrained, and more exciting. The women of the day, taken collectively, were young; they liked better to be out and to show themselves in public, than to remain at home and compose a narrower circle. But they would have grown old, and with a little time and tranquillity, every thing would have fallen into its natural course. And then again," he observed, "it would perhaps be an error to judge of a modern Court by the remembrance of the old ones. The power certainly resided in the old Courts: they said, the Court and the City:—at the present day, if we desired to speak correctly, we were obliged to say the City and the Court. The feudal lords, since they have lost their power, seek to make themselves amends in their enjoyments. Sovereigns themselves, seemed to be, for the future, submitted to this law: the throne, with our liberal ideas, insensibly ceased to be a signiority, and became purely a magistracy: the Prince having only a simple practical character to sustain, always sufficiently dull and tedious in the long-run, must seek to withdraw from it, to come, as a mere citizen, and take his share in the charms of society."

Among a great number of new measures projected by the Emperor for a more tranquil futurity, his favourite idea had been, peace being obtained and repose secured, to devote his life to purifying the administration and to local ameliorations; to be occupied in perpetual tours in the departments: he would have visited, not hurried over; sojourned, not posted through: he would have used his own horses, would have been surrounded by the Empress, the King of Rome, his whole Court. At the same time, he wished this great equipage not to be burdensome to any, but rather a benefit to all: a suit of tapestry hangings and all the other appendages, following in the train, would have furnished and decorated his places of rest. The other persons of the Court, he said, would have been extremely welcome to the citizens, who would have looked upon their guests as a benefit rather than a burden, because they would always have been the sure means of their acquiring some advantage or some favours. "It is thus," he continued, "that I should have been able in the very place to prevent frauds, punish misappropriations, direct edifices, bridges, roads; drain marshes, fertilize lands, &c.—If Heaven had then," he continued, "granted me a few years, I would certainly have made Paris the capital of the world, and all France a real fairy-land." He often repeated these last words: how many people have already said this, or will repeat it after him!

Set of Chessmen from China.—Presentation of the Captains of the China fleet.

6th.—The Emperor mounted his horse at seven o'clock: he told me to call my son to accompany us; this was a great favour. During our ride the Emperor dismounted five or six times to observe, with the help of a glass, some vessels that were in sight: he ascertained one to be a Dutchman; the three colours are always, with us, an object of sentiment and of lively emotion. On one of these occasions, the most mettlesome horse in the company got loose, and occasioned a long pursuit: my son came up with him, brought him back in triumph, and the Emperor observed, that in a tournament this would be a victory.

On our return, the Emperor breakfasted within doors: he detained us all.

Before and after breakfast, the Emperor conversed with me on serious matters, which I cannot trust to paper.

The heat was become excessive: he retired. It was half past four when he sent for me again; he was finishing dressing. The Doctor brought him a set of chessmen, which he had been buying on board the vessels from China; the Emperor had wished to have one. For this he had paid thirty Napoleons: it was an object of great admiration with the worthy Doctor; and, at the same time, nothing seemed more ridiculous to the Emperor. All the pieces, instead of resembling our's, were coarse and clumsy images of the figures indicated by the names; thus, a knight was armed at all points, and the castle rested on an enormous elephant &c. The Emperor could not make use of them, saying, pleasantly, that every piece would require a crane to move it.

In the mean time many officers and others employed in the China fleet were sauntering in the garden. Their curiosity had led them, some hours before, to our dwelling; we had been literally invaded in our chambers. One said, the pride of his life would be to have seen Napoleon; another, that he dared not appear in his wife's presence in England, if he could not tell her that he had been fortunate enough to behold his features; another, that he would willingly forego all the profits of his voyage for a single glance, &c.

The Emperor caused them to be admitted: it would be difficult to describe their satisfaction and joy: they had not ventured to expect or hope for so much. The Emperor, according to custom, proposed many questions to them concerning China, its commerce, its inhabitants; their revenues, their manners; the missionaries, &c. He detained them above half an hour, before he dismissed them. At their departure we described to him the enthusiasm we had witnessed in these officers, and repeated all that had fallen from them relative to him. "I believe it," said he, "you do not perceive that they are our friends. All that you have observed in them, belongs to the Commons of England—the natural enemies, perhaps without giving themselves credit for it, of their old and insolent Aristocracy."

At dinner the Emperor ate little; he was unwell: after coffee, he attempted a game at chess, but he was too much inclined for sleep, and retired almost immediately.

A Trick.

7th.—The Emperor mounted his horse at a very early hour; he told me again to call my son to accompany him. The evening before, the Emperor seeing him on horseback, had asked me if I did not make him learn to groom his horse; that nothing was more useful; that he had given particular orders for it in the military school at Saint-Germain. I was vexed that such an idea had escaped me; I seized it eagerly, and my son still more so. He was at this moment on a horse that no one had touched but himself. The Emperor, whom I informed of it, seemed pleased, and condescended to make him go through a sort of little examination. Our ride lasted nearly two hours and a half, rambling all the time about Longwood.

At our return the Emperor had breakfast in the garden, to which he detained us all.

A short time before dinner, I presented myself as usual in the drawing-room: the Emperor was playing at chess with the Grand Marshal. The valet-de-chambre in waiting at the door of the room brought me a letter, on which was written *very urgent*. Out of respect to the Emperor, I went aside to read it: it was in English; it stated that I had composed an excellent work; that, nevertheless, it was not without faults; that if I would correct them in a new edition, no doubt but the work would be more valuable for it: and then went on to pray that God would keep me in his gracious and holy protection. Such a letter excited my astonishment, and made me rather angry; the colour rushed to my face; I did not, at first, give myself time to consider the writing. In reading it over again I recognised the hand, notwithstanding its being much better written than usual, and I could not help laughing a good deal to myself. But the Emperor, who cast a side-glance at me, asked me from whom the letter came that was given to me. I replied, that it was a paper that had caused a very different feeling in me at first, from that which it would leave permanently. I said this with so much simplicity, the mystification had been so complete, that he laughed till tears came in his eyes. The letter was from him; the pupil had a mind to jest with his master, and try his powers at his expense. I carefully preserve this letter; the gaiety, the style, and the whole circumstance, render it more valuable to me than any diploma the Emperor could have put into my hands when he was in power.

An opportunity for the Emperor to make use of his English.—On medicine.—Corvisart.—Definition.—On the Plague.—Medical practice in Babylon.

8th.—The Emperor had had no sleep during the night: he had, therefore, amused himself with writing me another letter in English; he sent it to me sealed; I corrected the errors in it, and sent him an answer also in English, by the return of the courier. He understood me perfectly; this convinced him of the progress he had made, and satisfied him that for the future he could, strictly speaking, correspond in his new tongue.

For nearly a fortnight past General Gourgaud had been unwell; his indisposition had turned to a very malignant dysentery, which occasioned some alarm. The Admiral now sent him the Surgeon of the Northumberland (Dr. Warden); the Emperor detained this gentleman to dinner. During the repast, and for a long time afterwards, the conversation was exclusively on medicine; sometimes lively, sometimes serious and profound. The Emperor was in good spirits: he talked with great volubility; he overwhelmed the Doctor with questions, and with ingenious and subtle arguments, that perplexed him much: the latter was much dazzled by this brilliancy; so that after dinner, he took me aside to ask me how it happened that the Emperor was so well informed on these matters: he did not doubt but they were his usual topics of conversation. "Not more than any thing else," I said with truth; "but there are few subjects with which the Emperor is unacquainted, and he treats them all in a new and engaging manner."

The Emperor has no faith in medicine, or its remedies, of which he makes no use. "Doctor," said he, "our body is a machine for the purpose of life: it is organized to that end—that is its nature. Leave the life there at its ease, let it take care of itself, it will do better than if you paralyze it by loading it with medicines. It is like a well made watch, destined to go for a certain time; the watch-maker has not the power of opening it, he cannot meddle with it but at random, and with his eyes bandaged. For one who, by dint of racking it with his ill-formed instruments, succeeds in doing it any good, how many blockheads destroy it altogether!" &c.

The Emperor, then, did not admit the utility of medicine but in a few cases, in disorders that were known and distinctly ascertained by time and experience; and he then compared the art of the physician with that of the engineer in regular sieges, where the maxims of Vauban, and the rules of experience, have brought all the chances within the scope of known laws. In accordance, too, with these principles, the Emperor had conceived the idea of a law, which should have allowed to the mass of medical practitioners in France the use of simple medicines only, and forbidden them to employ *heroic* remedies, that is, such as may cause death; unless they made three or four thousand francs, at least, by their profession; which, said he, afforded grounds for supposing them to have education, judgment, and a certain public reputation. "This measure," said he, "was certainly just and beneficent; but in my circumstances it was unseasonable: information was not yet sufficiently diffused. No doubt but the mass of the people would have only seen an act of tyranny in the law, notwithstanding, it would have rescued them from their executioners."

The Emperor had frequently attacked the celebrated Corvisart, his physician, upon the subject of medicine. The latter, waving the honour of the profession, and of his colleagues, confessed that he entertained nearly the same opinions, and even acted upon them. He was a great enemy to medicines, and employed them very sparingly: the Empress Maria Louisa, suffering much during her pregnancy, and teazing him for relief, he artfully gave her some pills composed of crumb of bread, which did not fail to be of great service to her, she observed.

The Emperor, said he, had brought Corvisart to admit that medicine was a resource available only for the few; that it might be of some benefit to the rich, but that it was the scourge of the poor. "Now, do you not believe," said the Emperor, "that seeing the uncertainty of the art itself, and the ignorance of those who practise it, its effects, taken in the aggregate, are more fatal than useful to the people?" Corvisart assented without hesitation. "But have you never killed any body yourself?" continued the Emperor; "that is to say, have not some patients died, evidently in consequence of your prescriptions?"—"Undoubtedly," replied Corvisart; "but I ought no more to let that weigh upon my conscience, than would your Majesty, if you had caused the destruction of some troops, not from having made a bad movement, but because their march was impeded by a ditch or a precipice, which it was impossible for you to be aware of," &c.

Thence the Emperor went on to some problems and definitions, which he proposed to the Doctor. "What is life?" said he to him; "when and how do we receive it? Is that still any thing but mystery?" Then he defined harmless madness to be a vacancy or incoherence of judgment between just perceptions and the application of them: an insane man eats grapes in a vineyard that is not his own; and, in reply to the expostulations of the owner, says:—"Here are two of us; the sun shines upon us; then I have a right to eat grapes." The dangerous madman was he in whom this vacancy or incoherence of judgment occurred between perceptions and actions: it was he who cut off the head of a sleeping man, and concealed himself behind a hedge, to enjoy the perplexity of the dead body when he should awake.

The Emperor next asked the Doctor what was the difference between sleep and death; and answered it himself by saying, that sleep was the momentary suspension of the faculties which are within the power of our volition; and death the lasting suspension, not only of these faculties, but also of those over which our will has no control.

From that, the conversation turned upon the plague. The Emperor maintained that it was taken by inspiration as well as by contact: he said that it was rendered most dangerous, and most extensively propagated, by fear; its principal seat was in the imagination. In Egypt, all those in whom that (the imagination) was affected, perished. The most prudent remedy was moral courage. He had touched with impunity, he said, some infected persons at Jaffa, and had saved many lives by deceiving the soldiers, during two months, as to the nature of the disease: it was not the plague, they were told, but a fever accompanied with ulcers. Moreover, he had observed that the best means to preserve the army from it, were to keep them on the march, and give them plenty of exercise: fatigue, and the occupation of the mind upon other subjects, were found the surest protection, &c.*

* It is mentioned in the Memoirs of M. Larey, as a phenomenon, or at least something remarkable, that the pressure of circumstances during the retreat from

The Emperor also said to the Doctor—"If Hippocrates were on a sudden to enter your hospital, would he not be much astonished? would he adopt your maxims and your methods? would he not find fault with you? On your part, would you understand his language? would you at all comprehend each other?—He concluded by pleasantly extolling the practice of medicine in Babylon, where the patients were exposed at the door, and the relations, sitting near them, stopped the passengers to inquire if they had ever been afflicted in a similar way, and what had cured them. One had at least the certainty, said he, of escaping all those whose remedies had killed them.

9th.—I was breakfasting with the Emperor, after our English lesson, when I received a letter from my wife that filled me with joy and gratitude. She said, that neither fear, fatigue, nor distance, could prevent her joining me; that separated from me she could experience no happiness, and that she was only waiting for the proper season. Admirable devotion! superior to all that we have manifested here, inasmuch as it is exerted with a perfect knowledge of all its consequences. I cannot think that in England they will have the cruelty to refuse her: what does she solicit? favours, interest? No; she begs to share the lot of an exile on a solitary rock; to fulfil a duty, and to testify her affection. How far was I from forming a just estimate of the hearts and minds of those who detained us! Madame de Las Cases found herself constantly repulsed; sometimes under various pretexts; sometimes even without an answer. At last, and as if to rid himself of her importunity, Lord Bathurst caused her to be informed, in the beginning of 1817, that she would be permitted to go to the Cape of Good Hope (500 leagues beyond Saint-Helena), from whence, "if the Governor of Saint-Helena (Sir Hudson Lowe) sees no objection, she will be allowed to join her husband."

I leave without comment this specimen of ill-timed pleasantry, to the consideration of any one who has the feelings of a man. This letter came by the Owen Glendower frigate, which arrived from the Cape, and brought us at the same time the European papers to December 4.

Saint-Jean-d'Acre, having compelled a reduction of the food for the sick to some plain thin biscuits, and their dressings to some brackish water, these invalids traversed sixty leagues of Desert without accidents, and with so much advantage, that the greater part found themselves well when they arrived in Egypt. He attributes this species of prodigy to the exercise, direct or indirect, to the dry heat of the Desert, and above all to the joy of returning to a country which had become for the soldiers a sort of new home.

Trial of Ney.—The Emperor's carriage taken at Waterloo. The interview at Dresden.—On the caprice of women.—The Princess Pauline.—Eloquent effusion of the Emperor.

10th—12th.—The weather had now changed to those miserable pelting rains, which scarcely permitted us to walk in the garden; fortunately we had newspapers to occupy our time. At length I had the satisfaction of seeing the Emperor read them without assistance.

These papers contained many details relating to the trial of Marshal Ney, which was at that time in progress. With reference to this, the Emperor said that the horizon was gloomy; that the unfortunate Marshal was certainly in great danger; but that we must not, however, despair. "The King undoubtedly believes himself quite sure of the Peers," said he; "they are certainly violent enough, firmly resolved, highly incensed; but for all that, suppose the slightest incident, some new rumour, or I know not what; then you would see, in spite of all the efforts of the King, and of what they believe to be the interest of their cause, the chamber of Peers would, all on a sudden, take it into their heads not to find him guilty; and thus Ney may be saved."

This led the Emperor to dilate upon our volatile, fickle, and changeable disposition. "All the French," said he, "are turbulent, and disposed to rail; but they are not addicted to seditious combinations, still less to actual conspiracy. Their levity is so natural to them, their changes so sudden, that it may be said to be a national dishonour. They are mere weathercocks, the sport of the winds, it is true; but this vice is with them free from the calculations of interest, and that is their best excuse. But we must only be understood to speak here of the mass, of that which constitutes public opinion; for individual examples to the contrary have swarmed in our latter times, that exhibit certain classes in the most disgusting state of meanness."

It was this knowledge of the national character, the Emperor continued, that had always prevented his having recourse to the High Court. It was instituted by our Constitution; the Council of State had even decreed its organization; but the Emperor felt all the danger of the bustle and agitation that such spectacles always produce. "Such a proceeding," he said, "was in reality an appeal to the public, and was always highly injurious to authority, when the accused gained the cause. A Ministry in England might sustain, without inconvenience, the effects of a decision against it under such circumstances; but a sovereign like me, and situated as I was, could not have suffered it without the utmost danger to public affairs: for this reason, I preferred having recourse to the ordinary tribunals. Malevolence often started objections to this; but nevertheless, among all those whom it was pleased to call victims, which of them, I ask you, has retained his popularity in our late struggles? They have taken care to justify me: all of them are faded in the national estimation."

The Emperor had reserved one article in the papers, that he might have my assistance in reading it; it referred to the carriage he lost at Waterloo: the great number of technical expressions rendered it too difficut for him. The editor gave a very circumstantial account of this carriage, with a minutely detailed inventory of all its contents; to this he sometimes added the most frivolous reflections. In mentioning a small liquor-case, he observed that the Emperor never forgot *himself*, but took care to want nothing; in noticing certain elegant appendages to his dressing-case, he added that it might be seen he made his toilette *comme il faut* (the expression was in French.) These last words produced a sensation in the Emperor, which certainly would not have been excited by a more important subject.—"How!" said he to me, with a mixture of disgust and pain: "these people of England, then, take me for some wild animal; have they really been led so far as this? or their ——, who is a kind of Ox or Apis, as I am assured, does he not pay that attention to his toilette that is considered proper by every person of any education among us.?"

It is certain that I should have been a good deal puzzled to explain to him the writer's meaning. Besides, it is known that the Emperor, of all people in the world, set the least value on his personal convenience, and studied it the least; but, on the other hand, and he acknowledged it with pleasure, there never was one for whom the devotion and attention of servants had been so diligent in that particular. As he ate at very irregular hours, they contrived, in the course of his journeys and campaigns, to have his dinner, similar to what he was accustomed to at the Thuilleries, always ready within a few paces of him. He had but to speak, and he was instantly served; he himself said it was magic. During fifteen years he constantly drank a particular sort of Burgundy (Chambertin,) which he liked and believed to be wholesome for him: he found this wine provided for him throughout Germany, in the remotest part of Spain, every where, even at Moscow, &c; and it may truly be said that art, luxury, the refinement of elegance and good taste, contended around him, as if without his knowledge, to afford him gratification. The English journalists, therefore, described a multitude of objects that were undoubtedly in the carriage; but of which the Emperor had not the slightest notion: not that he was at all surprised at it, he observed.

The bad weather which continued to confine us within doors, had no influence on the disposition of the Emperor, who at this particular time seemed more unreserved and talked more than usual. He spoke at length, and with the most minute details, of the famous interview at Dresden.—The following are extracts from his conversation:—

This was the epoch when the power of Napoleon was at its height; he there appeared as the *king of kings;* he was actually obliged to observe, that some attention ought to be paid to the Emperor of Austria, his father-in-law. Neither this Sovereign nor the King of Prussia had any household establishment attending them; Alexander had none either at Tilsit or Erfurth. There, as at Dresden, they lived at Napoleon's table.—"These Courts," said the Emperor, "were paltry and vulgar." It was he who regulated the etiquette, and took the lead in them; he made Francis take precedence of him, to his unbounded satisfaction. The luxury and magnificence of Napoleon must have made him appear like an Asiatic prince to them: there, as well as at Tilsit, he loaded with diamonds all that came near him.—We informed him, that at Dresden he had not a single French soldier near him; and that his Court was sometimes not without apprehensions for the safety of his person. He could scarcely believe us;—but we assured him that it was a fact; that the Saxon body-guard was the only one he had. "It is all one," he said; "I was then in so good a family, with such worthy people, that I ran no risk; I was beloved by all; and, at this very time, I am sure the good King of Saxony repeats every day a *Pater* and an *Ave* for me." He added, "I ruined the fortunes of that poor Princess Augusta, and I acted very wrong in so doing. Returning from Tilsit, I received, at Marienwerder, a chamberlain of the King of Saxony, who delivered me a letter from his master; he wrote thus: "I have just received a letter from the Emperor of Austria, who desires my daughter in marriage; I send this to you, that you may inform me what answer I ought to return.'—'I shall be at Dresden in a few days,' was the reply of the Emperor; and, on his arrival, he set his face against the match, and prevented it. "I was very wrong," repeated he; "I was fearful the Emperor Francis would withdraw the King of Saxony from me; on the contrary, the Princess Augusta would have brought over the Emperor Francis to my side; and I should not now have been here."

At Dresden, Napoleon was much occupied in business, and Maria-Louisa, anxious to avail herself of the smallest intervals of leisure to be with her husband, scarcely ever went out, lest she should miss them. The Emperor Francis, who did nothing, and tired himself all day with going about the town, could not at all comprehend this family seclusion; he fancied that it was to affect reserve and importance.—The Empress of Austria endeavoured greatly to get Maria-Louisa to go out; she represented to her that her constant assiduity was ridiculous. She would willingly have given herself the airs of a step-mother with Maria-Louisa, who was not disposed to suffer it, their age being nearly the same.—She came frequently in the morning to her toilette, ransacking among the luxurious and magnificent objects displayed there: she seldom went out empty-handed.

"The reign of Maria-Louisa was very short," said the Emperor; "but it must have been full of enjoyment for her; she had the world at her feet." One of us took the liberty to ask if the Empress of Austria was not the sworn enemy of Maria-Louisa. "Nothing more," said the Emperor, "than a little regular court-hatred; a thorough detestation in the heart, but glossed over by daily letters of four pages, full of coaxing and tenderness."

The Empress of Austria was particularly attentive to Napoleon, and took great pains to make much of him while he was present; but no sooner was his back turned, than she endeavoured to detach Maria Louisa from him by the most mischievous and malicious insinuations; she was vexed that she could not succeed in obtaining some influence over her. "She has, however, address and ability," said the Emperor, "and that sufficient to embarrass her husband, who had acquired a conviction that she entertained a poor opinion of him. Her countenance was agreeable, engaging, and had something very peculiar in it; she was a pretty little nun.

"As to the Emperor Francis, his good nature is well known, and makes him constantly the dupe of the designing. His son will be like him.

"The King of Prussia, as a private character, is an honourable, good, and worthy man; but, in his political capacity, he is naturally disposed to yield to necessity: he is always commanded by whosoever has power on his side, and seems about to strike.

"As to the Emperor of Russia, he is a man infinitely superior to these: he possesses wit, grace, information, is fascinating; but he is not to be trusted; he is devoid of candour; a true *Greek of the Lower Empire*. At the same time he is not without ideology, real or assumed:—after all it may only be a smattering derived from his education and his preceptor. Would you believe," said the Emperor, "what I had to discuss with him? He maintained that inheritance was an abuse in monarchy, and I had to spend more than an hour, and employ all my eloquence and logic, in proving to him that this right constituted the peace and happiness of the people. It may be, too, that he was mystifying; for he is cunning, false, and expert, ... ; he can go a great length. If I die here, he will be my real heir in Europe. I alone was able to stop him with his deluge of Tartars. The crisis is great, and will have lasting effects upon the Continent of Europe, especially upon Constantinople: he was solicitous with me for the possession of it. I have had much coaxing on this subject; but I constantly turned a deaf ear to it. That empire, shattered as it appeared, would constantly have remained a point of separation between us: it was the marsh that prevented my right being turned. As to Greece, it is another matter!" And after talking awhile upon that country, he renewed the subject: "Greece awaits a liberator!—There will be a brilliant crown of glory!—He will inscribe his name forever with those of Homer, Plato, and Epaminondas!—I perhaps was not far from it!—When, during my campaign in Italy, I arrived on the shores of the Adriatic, I wrote to the Directory, that I had before my eyes the kingdom of Alexander!—Still later I entered into engagements with Ali Pacha; and when Corfu was taken from us, they must have found there ammunition and a complete equipment for an army of forty or fifty thousand men. I had caused maps to be made of Macedonia, Servia, Albania, &c.

"Greece, the Peloponnesus at least, must be the lot of that European power, which shall possess Egypt. It should be ours.—And then, an independent kingdom in the North, Constantinople with its provinces, to serve as a barrier to the power of Russia: as they have pretended to do with respect to France, by creating the kingdom of Belgium."

Another of these evenings, the Emperor was holding forth against the caprice of women; "Nothing," said he, "more clearly indicates rank, education, and good breeding among them, than evenness of temper, and the constant desire to please." He added, that they were bound by circumstances to show themselves at all times mistresses of themselves, and to be always attending to their part on the stage. His two wives, he observed, had always been so: they certainly differed greatly in their qualities and dispositions; but they always agreed in this point. Never had he witnessed ill-humour in either the one or the other; to please him had been the constant object with both of them, &c.

Some one ventured to observe, however, that Maria-Louisa had boasted, that whenever she desired any thing, no matter how difficult, she had only to weep. The Emperor laughed at it, and said, this was new to him. He might have suspected it of Josephine, but he had no idea of it in Maria-Louisa. And then, addressing himself to Mesdames Bertrand and Montholon: "Thus it is with you all, ladies," said he: "in some points you all agree."

He continued for a long time to talk about the two Empresses, and repeated as usual, that one was Innocence, and the other the Graces. He passed from them to his sisters, and dwelt particularly on the charms of the Princess Pauline. It was admitted, that she was, without dispute, the handsomest woman in Paris. The Emperor said that the artists were unanimous in considering her a perfect Venus de Medicis. As they were proceeding to analyze her beauty with much elegance and grace, he suddenly asked if a Princess of the time . . . .

A little pleasantry was hazarded on the influence which the Princess Pauline had exercised, at the Island of Elba, over General Drouot, whose assiduous attentions she attracted in spite of the difference of their ages and the harshness of his countenance. The Princess, it was said, had drawn from him the secret of the intended departure, eight days before it took place. He had repeated the fault of Turenne; and upon this the Emperor said, "Such are women, and such is their dangerous power!" Here Madame Bertrand declared that the Grand Marshal, to a certainty, had not done as much. "Madame," retorted the Emperor, with a smile, "he was only your husband." Some one having remarked that the Princess Pauline, when at Nice, had set up a post-wagon on the road, by which dresses and fashions arrived from Paris every day, the Emperor said: "If I had been aware of it, that would not have lasted long, she would have been well scolded. But thus it happens: while one is Emperor one knows nothing of these things."

After this conversation the Emperor inquired what was the day of the month: it was the 11th of March. "Well!" said he, "it is a year ago to-day, it was a brilliant day; I was at Lyons, I reviewed some troops, I had the Mayor to dine with me, who, by the way, has boasted since, that it was the worst dinner he ever made in his life." The Emperor became animated; he paced the chamber quickly. "I was again become a great power," he continued; and a sigh escaped him, which he immediately checked with these words, in an accent and with a warmth which it is difficult to describe: "I had founded the finest empire in the world, and I was so necessary to it, that spite of all the last reverses, here, upon my rock, I seem still to remain the master of France. Look at what is going on there, read the papers, you will find it so in every line. Let me once more set my foot there, they will see what France is, and what I can do!" And then what ideas, what projects he developed for the glory and happiness of the country! He spoke for a long time, with so much interest and so unreservedly, that we could have forgotton time, place, and seasons. A part of what he said follows:—

"What a fatality," he said, "that my return from the Island of Elba was not acquiesced in; that every one did not perceive that my reign was desirable and necessary for the balance and repose of Europe! But Kings and people both feared me; they were wrong and may pay dearly for it. I returned a new man; they could not believe it; they could not imagine that a man might have sufficient strength of mind to alter his character, or to bend to the power of circumstances. I had, however, given proofs of this, and some pledges to the same effect. Who is ignorant that I am not a man for half-measures? I would have been as sincerely the monarch of the constitution and of peace, as I had been of absolute sway and great enterprizes.

"Let us reason a little upon the fear of kings and people on my account. What could the kings apprehend? Did they still dread my ambition, my conquests, my universal monarchy? But my power and my resources were no longer the same; and, besides, I had only defeated and conquered in my own defence: this is a truth which time will more fully develope every day. Europe never ceased to make war upon France, her principles, and me; and we were compelled to destroy, to save ourselves from destruction. The coalition always existed openly or secretly, avowed or denied; it was permanent; it only rested with the Allies to give us peace; for ourselves, we were worn out: the French dreaded making new conquests. As to myself, is it supposed that I am insensible to the charms of repose and security, when glory and honour do not require it otherwise? With our two Chambers, they might have forbidden me in future to pass the Rhine; and why should I have wished it? For my universal monarchy? But I never gave any convincing proof of insanity; and what is its chief characterstic, but a disproportion between our object and the means of attaining it. If I have been on the point of accomplishing this universal monarchy, it was without any original design, and because I was led on to it step by step. The last efforts wanting to arrive at it seemed so trifling, was it very unreasonable to attempt them? But on my return from Elba, could a similar idea, a thought so mad, a purpose so unattainable, enter the head of the most rash man in the world? The Sovereigns, then, had nothing to fear from my arms.

"Did they apprehend that I might overwhelm them with anarchical principles? But they knew by experience, my opinions on that score. They have all seen me occupy their territories; how often have I been urged to revolutionize their states, give municipal functions to their cities, and excite insurrection among their subjects. However I may have been stigmatized, in their names, as *the modern Attila, Robespierre on horseback, &c.* they all know better at the bottom of their hearts—let them look there! Had I been so, I might, perhaps, still have reigned; but they most certainly would have long since ceased to reign. In the great cause of which I saw myself the chief and the arbitor, one of two systems was to be followed: to make kings listen to reason from the people; or to conduct the people to happiness by means of their kings. But it is well known to be no easy matter to check the people when they are once set on: it was more rational to reckon a little upon the wisdom and intelligence of rulers. I had a right always to suppose them possessed of sufficient intellect to see such obvious interests: I was deceived; they never calculated at all, and, in their blind fury, they let loose against me that which I withheld when opposed to them. They will see!

"Lastly, did the sovereigns take umbrage at seeing a mere soldier attain a crown? Did they fear the example? The solemnities, the circumstances that accompanied my elevation, my eagerness to conform to their habits, to identify myself with their existence, to become allied to them by blood and by policy, closed the door sufficiently against new comers. Besides, if there must needs have been the spectacle of an interrupted legitimacy, I maintain that it was much more to their interest that it should take place in my person, one risen from the ranks, than in that of a prince, one of their own family: for thousands of ages will elapse before the circumstances accumulated in my case draw forth another from among the crowd to re-produce the same spectacle; while there is not a sovereign who has not at a few paces distance in his palace, cousins, nephews, brothers, and relations to whom it would be easy to follow such an example if once set.

"On the other side, what was there to alarm the people? Did they fear that I should come to lay waste and to impose chains on them?—But I returned the Messiah of peace and of their rights: this new maxim was my whole strength—to violate it would have been ruin. But even the French mistrusted me; they had the insanity to discuss when there was nothing to do but to fight; to divide when they should have united on any terms. And was it not better to run the risk of having me again for master, than to expose themselves to that of submitting to a foreign yoke? Would it not have been easier to rid themselves of a single despot, of one tyrant, than to shake off the chains of all the nations united? And moreover, whence did they derive this mistrust of me? Because they had already seen me concentrate every effort in myself, and direct them with a vigorous hand? But do they not learn at the present day, to their cost, how necessary that was? Well! the danger was in any case the same: the contest terrible, and the crisis imminent. In this state of things, was not absolute power necessary, indispensable? The welfare of the country obliged me even to declare it openly on my return from Léipsic. I should have done so again on my return from Elba. I was wanting in consistency, or rather in confidence in the French, because many of them no longer placed any in me, and it was doing me a great wrong. If narrow and vulgar minds only saw, in all my efforts, the care of my own power, ought not those of greater scope to have shown, that under the circumstances in which we were placed, my power and the country were but one? Did it require such great and incurable mischiefs to enable them to comprehend me? History will do me more justice: it will signalize me as the man of self-denials and disinterestedness. To what temptations was I not exposed in the army of Italy? England offered me the Crown of France at the time of the treaty of Amiens.—I refused peace at Châtillon: I disdained all personal stipulations at Waterloo;—and why? Because all this had no reference to my country, and I had no ambition distinct from her's—that of her glory, her ascendancy, her majesty. And there is the reason that, in spite of so many calamities, I remain so popular among the French. It is a sort of instinct of after-justice on their part.

"Who in the world ever had greater treasures at his disposal? I have had many hundred millions in my vaults; many other hundreds composed my *domaine de l'extraordinaire:* all these were my own. What is become of them? They were poured out in the distresses of the country. Let them contemplate me here; I remain destitute upon my rock. My fortune was wholly in that of France. In the extraordinary situation to which fate had raised me, my treasures were her's: I had identified myself completely with her destinies. What other calculation was consistent with the height I had risen to? Was I ever seen occupied about my personal interests? I never knew any other enjoyment, any other riches, than those of the public;—so much so, that when Josephine, who had a taste for the Arts, succeeded under the sanction of my name in acquiring some master-pieces, though they were in my palace, under my eyes, in my family apartments, they offended me, I thought myself robbed: *they were not in the Museum.*

"Ah! the French people undoubtedly did much for me! more than was ever done before for man! But, at the same time, who ever did so much for them? who ever identified himself with them in the same manner? But to return.—After all, what could be their fears? Were not the Chambers and the new Constitution sufficient guarantees for the future? Those additional Acts, against which so much indignation was expressed, did they not carry in themselves their own corrective—remedies that were infallible? How could I have violated them? I had not myself millions of arms; I was but a man. Public opinion raised me up once more; public opinion might equally put me down again; and, compared with this risk, what had I to gain?

"But as to surrounding States (I speak particularly as regards England,) what could be her fears, her motives, her jealousies? We inquire in vain. With our new Constitution, our two Chambers, had we not adopted her creed for the future? Was not that the sure means of coming to a mutual understanding, to establish in future a community of interest? The caprice, the passions of their rulers, once fettered, the interests of the people move on, without obstacle, in their natural course: look at the merchants of hostile nations; they continue their intercourse, and pursue their business, however their governments may wage war. The two nations had arrived at that point.—Thanks to their respective parliaments, each was become the guarantee for the other: and who can ever tell to what extent the union of the two nations and of their interests might be carried; what new combinations might be set at work? It is certain that, on the establishment of our two Chambers and our Constitution, the Ministers of England had in their hands the glory and prosperity of their country, the destinies and the welfare of the world. Had I beaten the English army and won my last battle, I would have caused a great and happy astonishment; the following day I would have proposed peace, and, for once, it would have been I who scattered benefits with a prodigal hand. Instead of this, perhaps, the English will one day have to lament that they were victorious at Waterloo!

"I repeat it, the people and the sovereigns were wrong: I had restored thrones and an inoffensive nobility; and thrones and nobility may again find themselves in danger. I had fixed and consecrated the reasonable limits of the people's rights; vague, peremptory, and undefined claims may again arise.

"Had my return, my establishment on the throne, my adoption, been freely acquiesced in by the sovereigns, the cause of kings and the people would have been settled; both would have gained. Now they are again to try it; both may lose. They might have concluded every thing; they may have every thing to begin again: they might have secured a long and certain calm, and already begun to enjoy it; and, instead of that, a spark may now be sufficient to re-produce an universal conflagration! Poor, weak humanity!"

Attached, as I am, to the words and the opinions which I gathered from Napoleon on his rock of exile, and however perfectly persuaded and convinced of their entire sincerity, I do not the less experience an extreme gratification, whenever a testimony from another quarter confirms the truth of them; and I am bound to say, that I have that gratification, as often as opportunity occurs of obtaining other evidence.

The reader has just perused the foregoing remarkable passage, in which Napoleon expresses his ideas, his intentions, his sentiments. What a value do not these expressions collected at Saint-Helena acquire, when we find them re-echoed in Europe, at the distance of 2000 leagues, by a celebrated writer, who, with a shade of difference in his opinions, and at a very different time, had himself received them from the same lips! What a fortunate circumstance for history! I cannot, indeed, forbear bringing forward here this extract of M. Benjamin Constant, as well on account of the intrinsic merit of the expressions, as from the weight they acquire from the distinguished writer who records them; and also from the pleasure I feel in seeing them coincide so exactly with what I have collected myself in another hemisphere. There are the same intentions, the same depth of thought, the same sentiments.

"I went to the Thuilleries," says M. Benjamin Constant in his account; "I found Bonaparte alone. He began the conversation: it was long: I will only give an analysis of it; for I do not propose to make an exhibition of an unfortunate man. I will not amuse my readers at the expense of fallen greatness; I will not give up to malevolent curiosity him whom I have served, whatever might be my motive; and I will not transcribe more of his discourse than is indispensable; but in what I shall transcribe, I will use his own words.

"He did not attempt to deceive me either as to his views, or the state of affairs. He did not present himself as one corrected by the lessons of adversity: he did not desire to take the merit of returning to liberty from inclination: he investigated coolly as regarded his interests, and with an impartiality too nearly allied to indifference, what was possible and what was preferable.

"'The nation,' said he, 'has rested for twelve years from all political agitation, and for a year it has been undisturbed by war: this double repose has begotten a necessity for motion. It desires, or fancies it desires, a public rostrum and assemblies; it has not always desired them. It cast itself at my feet when I came to the government; you must remember, you who made trial of its opinion. Where was your support, your power? No where. I took less authority than I was invited to take.—Now all is changed. A weak government, opposed to the interests of the nation, has given these interests the habit of taking up the defensive, and of cavilling at authority. The taste for constitutions, debates, harangues, seems to return. . . . However, it is only the minority that desires it, do not deceive yourself. The people, or if you like it better, the mob, desire me alone: you have not seen them, this mob, crowding after me, rushing from the tops of the mountains, calling me, seeking me, saluting me. On my return here from Cannes, I did not conquer—I administered. . . . . I am not only, as it has been said, the Emperor of the soldiers; I am that of the peasants, the lower ranks in France. . . . Thus, in spite of all that is past, you see the people return to me—there is a sympathy between us. It is not so with the privileged classes; the nobility have served me, have rushed in crowds into my antechambers; there are no offices that they have not accepted, solicited, pressed for. I have had my *Montmorencies*, my *Noailles*, my *Rohans*, my *Beauveaus*, my *Mortemarts*. But there was no analogy between us. The steed curvetted, he was well trained, but I perceived that he fretted.

"'With the people it is another thing; the popular fibre responds to mine: I am come from the ranks of the people, my voice has influence over them. Observe these conscripts, these sons of peasants, I did not flatter them, I treated them with severity; they did not the less surround me, they did not the less shout '*the Emperor for ever!*' It is because between them and me there is an identity of nature; they look to me as their support, their defender against the nobles. . . I have but to make a sign, or rather to turn away my eyes, and the nobles will be massacred in all the departments. They have carried on such fine intrigues for these six months! . . . . But I will not be the king of a *Facquerie*. If there are any means of governing with a Constitution, well and good. . . . . . I desired the empire of the world; and, to insure it, unlimited power was necessary to me.—To govern France only, a Constitution may be better. . . . . I desired the empire of the world, and who in my situation would not? The world invited me to govern it; sovereigns and subjects vied with each other in hastening beneath my sceptre. I have rarely found any opposition in France; but I have, however, met with more from some obscure unarmed Frenchmen, than from all these kings, so vain at present of no longer having a popular man for their equal. . . . . Consider, then, what seems to you to be possible. Give me your ideas. Free elections, public discussions, responsible ministers, liberty, all this is my wish. . . . . The liberty of the press in particular: to stifle it is absurd—I am satisfied upon this point. . . . . I am the man of the people, if the people sincerely wish for liberty: I owe it them. I have recognized their sovereignty; I am bound to lend an ear to their desires, even to their caprices. I never desired to oppress them for my own gratification. I had great designs, fate has decided them; I am no longer a conqueror, I can no more become so. I know what is possible, and what is not; I have now but one charge: to relieve France, and give her a government suited to her. . . . . I am not inimical to liberty: I set it aside when it obstructed my road: but I comprehend it, I have been educated in its principles. . . . . At the same time, the work of fifteen years is destroyed; it cannot begin again. It would require twenty years, and the sacrifice of two millions of men. . . . . Besides, I am desirous of peace, and I shall obtain it only by dint of victories. I will not hold out false hopes to you; I abstain from telling you there are negotiations in train; there are none. I foresee a difficult contest, a long war. To maintain it, the nation must support me; but, in return, she will require liberty; she shall have it. . . . . The situation is new. I desire no better than to receive information; I grow old; one is no longer at forty-five what one was at thirty. The repose of a constitutional monarch may be well suited to me. It will assuredly be still more suitable to my son.'"—(*Minerve Francais, 94^e liv. tome VIII. 2d Letter on the Hundred Days. By M. B. Constant.*

13th.—The Emperor sent instructions to the Grand Marshal to write to the Admiral to know if a letter which he, Napoleon, should write to the Prince Regent would be sent to him. Towards four o'clock, the Deputy Governor Skelton and his lady desired to pay their respects to the Emperor. He received them, took them to walk in the garden, and afterward out with him in his carriage. The weather had been extremely foggy all day. Upon its clearing up for a short time we saw, on a sudden, a corvette or frigate very near, and coming in with all sails set.

Insult to the Emperor and the Prince of Wales.—Execution of Ney.—Escape of Lavalette.

14th—15th.—We received the Admiral's answer. After beginning, according to his established form, by saying that he knew no person by the title of 'Emperor' at Saint-Helena, he stated, that he would undoubtedly send the Emperor's letter to the Prince Regent; but that he should adhere to the letter of his instructions, which directed him not to allow any paper to be dispatched to England, without having first opened it.

This communication, it must be acknowledged, gave us great astonishment: the part of the instructions cited by the Admiral had two objects in view, both of them foreign to the interpretation put upon them by this officer.

The first was, in the case of our making any complaints, that the local authorities might join their observations, and that the government, in England, might do us justice more speedily, without being obliged to send again to the island for farther information. This precaution, then, was entirely for our interest. The second object of this measure was, that our correspondence might not be prejudicial to the interests of the government, or the policy of England. But we were writing to the Sovereign, to the chief, to the individual in whom these interests, and this government centred; and if there was any conspiracy here, it was not on the part of us, who were writing to him, but rather on his, who intercepted our letter, or resolved to violate the privacy of it. That they should establish jailors about us, with all their equipage, though we did not consider it just still seems possible. But that these jailors should cause their functions to re-act, even upon their Sovereign, was a thing for which we could not find a name! It was to attach to him completely the idea a King without faculties, or of a Sultan buried in the recesses of his Seraglio! It was really a monstrous phenomenon in our European manners!

For a long time, we had little or no intercourse with the Admiral. One thought that ill-humour had perhaps dictated his answer; another supposed that he was fearful the letter might contain some complaints against him. But the Admiral knew the Emperor too well, not to be aware that he would never appeal to any other tribunal, than to that of nations. I, who knew what would have been the subject of the letter, felt the most lively indignation at it! The sole intention of the Emperor had been to employ this method, the only one that seemed compatible with his dignity, to write to his wife, and obtain tidings of his son. However, the Grand Marshal replied to the Admiral, that he either overstepped, or misinterpreted his instructions; that his determination could only be regarded as another instance of flagrant vexation; that the condition imposed, was too much beneath the dignity of the Emperor, as well as of the Prince of Wales, for him to retain any intention of writing.

The frigate that had just arrived was the Spy, bringing the European papers to the 31st of December: they contained the execution of the unfortunate Marshal Ney, and the escape of Lavalette.

"Ney," said the Emperor, "as ill attacked, as he was ill defended, had been condemned by the Chamber of Peers, in the teeth of a formal capitulation. His execution had been allowed to take place; that was another error—from that moment he became a martyr. That Labédoyère should not have been pardoned, because the clemency extended to him would have seemed only a predilection in favour of the old Aristocracy, might be conceived; but the pardon of Ney would only have been a proof of the strength of the government, and the moderation of the Prince. It will be said, perhaps, that an example was necessary? But the Marshal would become so, much more certainly, by a pardon after being degraded by a sentence: it was to him, in fact, a moral death that deprived him of all influence; and nevertheless the object of authority would be obtained, the Sovereign satisfied, the example complete. The refusal of pardon to Lavalette, and his escape, were new subjects of animadverson equally unpopular.

"But the saloons in Paris," he observed, "exhibited the same passions as the clubs; the nobility were a new version of the Jacobins. Europe moreover, was in a state of complete anarchy: the code of political immorality was openly followed; whatever fell under the hands of the sovereigns was turned to the advantage of each of them. At least, in my time, I was the butt of all the accusations of this kind. The Sovereigns then talked of nothing but principles and virtue; but now," added he, "that they were victorious and without control, they practised unblushingly all the wrongs which they themselves then reprobated. What resource and what hope were there then left for nations and for morality? Our countrywomen at least," he observed, "rendered their sentiments conspicuous: Madame Labédoyère was on the point of dying from grief; these papers showed us that Madame Ney exhibited the most courageous and determined devotion. Madame Lavalette was become the heroine of Europe," &c.

Message for the Prince Regent.

16th.—The Emperor had quitted the Encyclopedia Britannica, to take his lessons in English, in the *Annual Register*. He read there the adventure of a Mr. Spencer Smith, arrested at Venice, ordered to be sent to Valenciennes, and who made his escape on the road. This must be a very simple affair, said the Emperor, which the narrator has converted into a statement of importance. The circumstance was totally unknown to him: it was a detail of police of too little consequence, he observed, to have found its way up to him.

About four o'clock the captain of the Spy arrived from Europe, and the captain of the Ceylon about to sail for England, were presented to the Emperor. He was in low spirits—he was unwell: the audience of the first was very short; that of the second would have been the same, had he not roused the Emperor by asking if we had any letters to send to Europe. The Emperor then desired me to ask him if he should see the Prince Regent; on his answering in the affirmative, I was charged to inform him that the Emperor was desirous of writing to the Prince Regent, but that in consequence of the observation of the Admiral, that he would open the letter, he had abstained from it, as being inconsistent with his dignity, and with that of the Prince Regent himself. That he had, indeed, heard the laws of England much boasted of, but that he could not discover their benefits any where; that he had only now to expect, indeed desire, an executioner; that the torture they made him endure was inhuman, savage; that it would have been more open and energetic to put him to death. The Emperor made me request of the captain that he would take upon him to deliver these words, and dismissed him: he looked very red and was much embarrassed.

Spirit of the Inhabitants of the Isle of France.

17th.—An English Colonel, arrived from the Cape on his return from the Isle of France, came in the morning and addressed himself to me, to try to get an introduction to the Emperor. The Admiral had only allowed his vessel to remain two or three hours in the road. Having prevailed on the Emperor to receive him at four o'clock, he assured me that he would rather miss his vessel than lose such an opportunity. The Emperor was not very well, he had passed several hours in his bath; at four he received the Colonel.

The Emperor put many questions to him concerning the

Isle of France, lately ceded to the English: it seems that its prosperity and its commerce suffer from its change of sovereignty.

After the departure of the Colonel, being alone with the Emperor in the garden, I told him that his person seemed to have remained very dear to the inhabitants of the Isle of France; that the Colonel had informed me that the name of Napoleon was never pronounced there but with commiseration. It was precisely on the day of a great festival in the colony, that they learned his departure from France and his arrival at Plymouth; the theatre was to be universally attractive; the news having arrived during the day, in the evening there was not a single colonist, either white or of colour, in the house: there were only some English, who were exceedingly confused and irritated at the circumstance. The Emperor listened to me. "It is quite plain," said he, after some moments of silence: "this proves that the inhabitants of the Isle of France have continued French. I am the country; they love it: it has been wounded in my person, they are grieved at it." I added, that the change of dominion restraining their expressions, they did not dare propose his health publicly; but that the Colonel said they never neglected it notwithstanding; they drank to *him*, this word was become consecrated to Napoleon. These details touched him. "Poor Frenchmen!" he said with expression—"Poor People! Poor Nation! I deserved all that, I loved thee! But thou, thou surely didst not deserve all the ills that press upon thee! Ah! thou didst merit well that one should devote himself to thee! But it must be confessed, what infamy, what baseness, what degradation I had about me!" And addressing himself to me, he added: "I do not speak here of your friends of the Fauxbourg Saint-Germain; for with respect to them it is another matter."

There frequently reached us incidents and expressions which, like those from the Isle of France, were calculated to excite emotion in the heart. The Island of Ascension, in our neighbourhood, had always been desert and abandoned; since we have been here, the English have thought proper to form an establishment there. The Captain who went to take possession of it, told us on his return, that he was much astonished on landing to find upon the beach, *May the great Napoleon live for ever!*

In the last papers that reached us, among many good-natured sallies and *jeux de mots*, it was remarked in several languages, that *Paris* would never be happy till his *Helena* should be restored to him: these were a few drops of honey in our cup of wormwood.

His intentions respecting Rome.—Horrible food.—Britannicus.

18th—19th.—The Emperor was on horseback by eight o'clock. He had abstained from it for a long time: want of space to ride over was the cause. His health suffers visibly in consequence, and it is astonishing that the want of exercise is not still more hurtful to him, who was in the daily habit of taking it to a violent degree. On our return, the Emperor breakfasted out of doors; he detained us all. After breakfast, the conversation fell on Herculaneum and Pompeii; the phenomenon and epoch of their destruction, the time and the accident of their modern discovery, the monuments and the curiosities they have since afforded us. The Emperor said, that if Rome had remained under his dominion, she would have risen again from her ruins: he intended to have cleared away all the rubbish; to have restored as much as possible, &c. He did not doubt that the same spirit extending through all the vicinity, it might have been in some degree the same with Herculaneum and Pompeii.

Breakfast being concluded, the Emperor sent my son to bring the volume of Crevies which contains this event; and he read it to us, as well as the death and character of Pliny. He retired about noon to take some rest. Towards six o'clock we took our usual round in the carriage. The Emperor took with him Mr. and Mrs. Skelton, who were come to visit him. On our return, the Emperor, banished from the garden on account of the damp, went to see Gen. Gourgaud, who was recovering rapidly. After dinner, on leaving the table and returning to the drawing-room, we could not help reverting to the meal we had just made;—literally nothing was fit to eat: the bread bad, the wine not drinkable, the meat disgusting and unwholesome; we are frequently obliged to send it back again; they continue, in spite of our remonstrances, to send it us dead, because by that method they can put upon us such animals as have died naturally.

The Emperor, shocked at this description, could not refrain from saying with warmth: "No doubt there are some individuals whose physical situation is still worse; but that circumstance does not deprive us of the right of giving an opinion on our own condition, or on the infamous manner in which we are treated. The injustice of the English government has not been contented with sending us hither, it has selected the individuals to whom our persons and our supplies are intrusted! For my part, I should suffer less, if I were sure that it would one day be divulged to the whole world in such a way as to brand with infamy those who are guilty of it. But let us talk of something else," said he—"what is the day of the month?" He was told it was the 19th of March: "What!" he exclaimed, "the eve of the 20th of March!" And a few seconds afterwards: "But let us talk of something else." He sent for a volume of Racine, and at first began to read the comedy of the *Plaideurs;* but after a scene or two, he turned to *Britannicus,* which he read to us. When the reading was concluded, and the due tribute of admiration had been paid, he said that Racine was censured for making the *denouement* of this piece too sudden, that the poisoning of Britannicus was not expected so early in the play as it ought to have been. He praised the truth of the character of Narcissus highly, observing, that it was always by wounding the self-love of princes that their determinations were most influenced.

20th of March.—The Accouchement of the Empress.

20th.—After dinner one of us observed to the Emperor, that he had been less solitary, less quiet that day twelvemonth at the same hour. "I was sitting down to table at the Thuilleries," said the Emperor. "I had found it difficult to get there: the dangers I went through in that attempt were at least equal to those of a battle." In fact he had been seized upon, on his arrival, by thousands of officers and citizens; one party had snatched him from another; he had been carried to the palace, and amidst a tumult like that of a mob about to tear a man to pieces, instead of the orderly and respectful attendance of a multitude intent on showing their veneration for an individual. But we ought to look at the sentiment and intention of this case: it was enthusiasm and love carried to a pitch that resembled delirious rage.

The Emperor added, that in all probability more than one person in Europe would talk of him that evening; and that, in spite of all observations, many a bottle would be emptied in his cause.

The conversation then turned on the King of Rome; that day was the anniversary of his birth; the Emperor reckoned that he must be five years old. He then spoke of the accouchement of the Empress, and seemed to take some pleasure in boasting that he had proved himself on that occasion, as good a husband as any in the world: he assisted the Empress to walk about all night; we, who were of the household knew something of the matter; we had all been called together at the palace at ten in the evening; we passed the night there; and the cries of the Empress sometimes reached our ears. Towards the morning the accoucher having told the Emperor that the pains had ceased, and that the labour might yet be tedious, the Emperor went into a bath, and sent us away, desiring us, however, not to go from home. The Emperor had not been long in the bath, when the pains came on again, and the accoucher ran to him, almost out of his wits, saying he was the most unfortunate of men; that out of a thousand labours in Paris there was not one more difficult. The Emperor, dressing himself again as fast as he could, encouraged him, saying that a man who understood his business ought never to lose his presence of mind; that there was nothing in this case that he ought to be uneasy about; that he had only to fancy he was delivering a citizen's wife of the Rue Saint-Denis; that nature had but one law; that he was sure he would act for the best: and, above all, that he need not fear any reproach. It was then represented to the Emperor that there was great danger either for the mother or the child. "If the mother live," said he, without hesitation, "I shall have another child. Act in this case as if you were attending the birth of a cobbler's son."

When he reached the Empress, she really was in danger; the child presented itself in an unfavourable posture, and there was every reason to fear it would be stifled.

The Emperor asked Dubois why he did not deliver her. He excused himself, being unwilling to do it, he said, except in the presence of Corvisart, who had not yet arrived, "But what can he tell you?" said the Emperor. "If it is a witness, or a justification you want to secure, here am I." Then Dubois, taking off his coat, commenced the operation. When the Empress saw the instruments, she cried out in a piteous manner, exclaiming that they were going to kill her. She was strongly held by the Emperor, Madame de Montesquiou, Corvisart, who had just come in, &c. Madame de Montesquiou dexterously took an opportunity to encourage her, by declaring that she herself had more than once been in the same situation.

The Empress, however, still persuaded herself that she was treated differently from other women, and often repeated, "Am I to be sacrificed because I am an Empress!" She declared, afterwards, to the Emperor, that she really had entertained this fear. At length she was delivered. The danger had been so imminent, said the Emperor, that all the etiquette which had been studied and ordered was disregarded, and the child put on one side, on the floor, whilst every one was occupied about the mother only. The infant remained some moments in this situation: it was Corvisart who took him up, chafed him, and brought him to utter a cry, &c.

Catiline's Conspiracy.—The Gracchi.—Historians.—Sleep during a battle.—Cæsar and his Commentaries.—Of different Military Systems.

21st—22d. The Emperor rode out very early; we made the tour of our limits in several directions. It was during these rides that the Emperor now takes his lessons in English. I walk by his side; he speaks a few sentences in English, which I translate, word by word, as he pronounces them; by which method he perceives when he is understood, or is enabled to correct his mistakes. When he has finished a sentence, I repeat it to him, in English, so that he may understand it well himself; this helps to form his ear.

The Emperor was reading to-day, in the Roman History, of Catiline's conspiracy; he could not comprehend it in the way in which it is described. "However great a villain Catiline might be," observed he, "he must have had some object in view: it could not be that of governing in Rome, since he is accused of having intended to set fire to the four quarters of the city." The Emperor conceived it to be much more probable that it was some new faction similar to those of Marius and Sylla, which having failed, all the accusations calculated to excite the horror of patriots, were, as usual in such cases, heaped on the head of its leader. It was then observed to the Emperor, that the same thing would infallibly have happened to himself, had he been overpowered in Vendemiaire, Fructidor, or Brumaire, before he had illumined with such radiant brilliancy an horizon cleared of clouds.

The Gracchi gave rise to doubts and suspicions of a very different sort in his mind, which, he said, became almost certainties to those who had been engaged in the politics of our times. "History," said he, "presents these Gracchi, in the aggregate, as seditious people, revolutionists, criminals; and, nevertheless, allows it to appear in detail, that they had virtues; that they were gentle, disinterested, moral men; and, besides, they were the sons of the illustrious Cornelia, which, to great minds, ought to be a strong primary presumption in their favour. How then can such a contrast be accounted for? It is thus: the Gracchi generously devoted themselves for the rights of the oppressed people, against a tyrannical senate; and their great talents and noble character endangered a ferocious aristocracy, which triumphed, murdered, and calumniated them. The historians of a party have transmitted their characters in the same spirit. Under the Emperors it was necessary to continue in the same manner; the bare mention of the rights of the people, under a despotic master, was a blasphemy, a downright crime. Afterwards the case was the same under the feudal system, which was so fruitful in petty despots.—Such, no doubt, is the fatality which has attended the memory of the Gracchi. Throughout succeeding ages their virtues have never ceased to be considered crimes; but at this day, when possessed of better information, we have thought it expedient to reason, the Gracchi may and ought to find favour in our eyes.

"In that terrible struggle between the aristocracy and democracy, which has been renewed in our times—in that exasperation of ancient territory against modern industry, which still ferments throughout Europe, there is no doubt but that if the aristocracy should triumph by force, it would point out many Gracchi in all directions, and treat them in future as mercifully as its predecessors have done the Gracchi of Rome."

The Emperor added, that it was, moreover, easy to see that there was an hiatus in the ancient authors at this period of history; that all which the moderns now presented to us on this subject was mere gleaning. He then reverted to the charges already made against honest Rollin and his pupil Crevier: they were both devoid of talent, system, or object. It was to be allowed that the ancients were far superior to us in this point: and that because, amongst them, the statesmen were literary men, and the men of letters statesmen; they accumulated professions, whilst we divide them absolutely. This famous division of labour, which in our times produces such a perfection in mechanical arts, is quite fatal to excellence in mental productions; every work of genius is superior in proportion to the universality of the mind whence it emanates. We owe to the Emperor the attempt to establish this principle by frequently employing men on various objects wholly unconnected with each other;—it was his system. He once appointed, of his own accord, one of his chamberlains to go into Illyria to liquidate the Austrian debt: this was a matter of importance, and extremely complicated. The chamberlain, who had previously been a total stranger to public business, was alarmed; and the minister, on hearing of this appointment, being dissatisfied with it, ventured to represent to the Emperor, that his nomination having fallen on a man entirely new to such matters, it might be feared that he would not acquit himself satisfactorily; "I have a lucky hand, Sir," was his answer; "those on whom I lay it are fit for every thing."

The Emperor, proceeding in his criticism, also censured severely what he called historical fooleries, ridiculously exalted by translators and commentators. "Such things prove, in the first place," said he, "that the historians formed erroneous judgments of men and circumstances. For instance," said Napoleon, "when they applaud so highly the *continence of Scipio*, and fall into ecstacies at the calmness of Alexander, Cæsar, and others, for having been able to sleep on the eve of a battle; even a monk, debarred from women, whose face brightens up at the very name—who neighs behind his barrier at their approach, would not give Scipio much credit for forbearing to violate the females whom chance threw into his power, while he had so many others entirely at his disposal. A famished man might as well praise the hero for having quietly passed by a table covered with victuals, without greedily snatching at them."—As to sleeping just before a battle, there was not, he assures us, one of our soldiers or generals who had not twenty times performed that miracle; their chief heroism lay in supporting the fatigue of watching the day before.

Here the Grand Marshal added, that he could safely say he had seen Napoleon sleep, not only on the eve of an engagement, but even during the battle.. "I was obliged to do so," said Napoleon, "when I fought battles that lasted three days. Nature was also to have her due: I took advantage of the smallest intervals, and slept where and when I could." He slept on the field of battle at Wagram, and at Bautzen, even during the action, and completely within the range of the enemy's balls. On this subject, he said, that independently of the necessity of obeying nature, these slumbers afforded a general commanding a very great army, the important advantage of enabling him to await, calmly, the relations and combinations of all his divisions, instead of, perhaps, being hurried away by the only event which he himself could witness.

The Emperor farther said, that he found in Rollin, and even Cæsar, circumstances of the Gallic war which he could not understand. He could not by any means comprehend the invasion of the Helvetii; the road they took; the object ascribed to them; the time they spent in crossing the Rhone; the diligence of Cæsar, who found time to go into Italy, as far as Aquileia, to seek the legions, and overtook the invaders before they had passed the Saone, &c. That it was equally difficult to comprehend what was meant by establishing winter-quarters that extended from Treves to Vannes. And when he also spoke of the immense works which the generals got performed by their soldiers, the ditches, walls, great towers, galleries, &c. the Emperor observed that in those times every exertion was directed to constructions on the spot, whereas in ours they were employed in conveyance. He also thought the ancient soldiers laboured, in fact, more than ours. He had thoughts of dictating something on that subject. "Ancient history, however," said he, "embraces a long period, and the system of war often changed. In our days it is no longer that of the times of Turenne and Vauban: campaign works were growing useless; even the system of our fortresses had become problematical or ineffectual; the enormous quantity of bombs and howitzers changed every thing. It was no longer against the horizontal attack that defence was requisite, but also against the curve and the reflected lines. None of the ancient fortresses thenceforth afforded shelter; they ceased to be tenable; no country was rich enough to maintain them. The revenue of France would be insufficient for her lines of Flanders, for the exterior fortifications were now not above a fourth or fifth of the necessary expense. Casemates, magazines, places of shelter secure from the effects of bombs, were now requisite, and were too expensive."— The Emperor complained particularly of the weakness of modern masonry: the engineer department is radically defective in this point; it had cost him immense sums, wholly thrown away.

Struck with these novel truths, the Emperor had invented a system altogether at variance with the axioms hitherto established; it was to have metal of an extraordinary calibre, to advance beyond the principal line towards the enemy; and to have that principal line itself, on the contrary, defended by a great quantity of small moveable artillery: hence the enemy would be stopped short in his sudden advance; he would have only weak pieces to attack powerful ones with; he would be commanded by this great calibre, round which the resources of the fortress, the small pieces, would form in groups, or even advance to a distance, as skirmishers, and might follow all the movements of the enemy by means of their lightness and mobility. The enemy would then stand in need of battering-cannon; he would be obliged to open trenches: time would be gained, and the true object of fortification accomplished. The Emperor employed this method with great success, and to the great astonishment of the engineers, in the defence of Vienna, and in that of Dresden; he wished to have employed it in that of Paris, which city could not, he thought, be defended by any other means; but of the success of this method he had no doubt.

Days at Longwood.—Trial of Drouot.—Military characters. Soult.—Massena.—The Emperor's comrades in the Artillery.—His name thought by him to be unknown to some people, even in Paris.

23d—26th. The weather was very unfavourable during the greater part of these mornings, on account of the heavy rains, which scarcely allowed us to stir out of doors. The Emperor read a work by a Miss Williams, on the return from the Isle of Elba; it had just reached us from England. He was much disgusted with it, and with good reason: this production is quite calumnious and false; it is the echo and collection of all the reports invented at the time in certain malevolent Parisian societies.

As to our evenings, the weather was almost indifferent to us; whether it rained, or the moon shone brightly, we literally made ourselves prisoners. Towards nine o'clock we were surrounded by sentinels; to meet them would have been painful. It is true that both the Emperor and ourselves might have gone out at a later hour, accompanied by an officer; but this would have been rather a punishment than a pleasure to us, although the officer never could conceive this feeling. He gave us reason to conclude, at first, that he imagined this seclusion to be merely the effect of ill-humour, and thought it would not last long. I know not what he may subsequently have thought of our perseverance.

The Emperor, as I believe I have already mentioned, sat down to table pretty regularly at eight o'clock; he never remained there above half an hour, sometimes scarcely a quarter of an hour. When he returned to the drawing-room, if he happened to be unwell or taciturn, we had the greatest difficulty in the world to get on to half past nine or ten o'clock; indeed, we could not effect it without the assistance of reading. But when he was cheerful, and entered into conversation with spirit, we were presently surprised to find it eleven o'clock, and later: these were our pleasant evenings. He would then retire, with a kind of satisfaction, at having, as he expressed it, conquered time. And it was precisely on those days, when the remark applied with least force, that he used to observe that it must require our utmost courage to endure such a life.

One of these evenings, the conversation ran on the military trials, which are now instituting in France. The Emperor thought that General Drouot could not be condemned for coming in the suite of one acknowledged sovereign to make war upon another. Upon this it was remarked, that what was now mentioned as his justification, would be his greatest danger at the tribunal of legitimacy.

The Emperor acknowledged, in fact, that there was nothing to be said to the doctrines brought forward at this day: but, on the other hand, that in condemning General Drouot, they would condemn emigration, and legitimate the condemnation of the emigrants. Whosoever was found in arms against France, the Republican doctrines punished him with death; it was not so with the royal doctrine. If they should in this instance adopt the Republican doctrine, the emigrant and royal party would condemn themselves.

The case of Drouot, however, in a general point of view, was very different even from that of Ney; and besides, Ney had evinced an unfortunate vacillation of which Drouot had never been guilty. Thus the interest which Ney had excited was wholly founded on opinion; whilst that which was felt for Drouot was personal.

The Emperor dilated on the dangers and difficulties which the tribunals and ministers of justice must experience, throughout the affairs connected with his return from the Isle of Elba. Above all, he was extremely struck by a particular circumstance relating to Soult, who, we were told, was to be brought to trial. He, Napoleon, knew, he said, how innocent Soult was; and yet, were it not for that circumstance, and were he an individual and juror in Soult's case, he had no doubt he should declare him guilty, so strongly were appearances combined against him. Ney, in the course of his defence, through some sentiment which it is difficult to account for, stated, contrary to the truth, that the Emperor had said Soult was in intelligence with him. Now, every circumstance of Soult's conduct during his administration, the confidence which the Emperor placed in him after his return, &c. agreed with that deposition: who, then, would not have condemned him? "Yet Soult is innocent," said the Emperor; "he even acknowledged to me that he had taken a real liking to the King. The authority he enjoyed under him, he said, so different from that of my ministers, was a very agreeable thing, and had quite gained him over."

Massena (whose proscription was also announced to us by the papers) was, the Emperor said, another person whom they would perhaps condemn as guilty of treason. All Marseilles was against him, appearances were overwhelming and yet he had fulfilled his duty up to the very moment of declaring himself openly. On his return to Paris, he had even been far from claiming any credit with the Emperor, when the latter asked him whether he might have reckoned upon him. "The truth is," continued the Emperor, "that all the commanders did their duty; but they could not withstand the torrent of opinion, and no one had sufficiently calculated the sentiments of the mass of the people, and the national impetuosity. Carnot, Fourché, Maret, and Cambacérès, confessed to me at Paris, that they had been greatly deceived on this point. And no one understands it well, even now.

"Had the King remained longer in France," continued he, "he would probably have lost his life in some insurrection; but had he fallen into my hands, I should have thought myself strong enough to have allowed him every enjoyment in some retreat of his own selection; as Ferdinand was treated at Valency."

Immediately before this conversation, the Emperor was playing at chess, and his king having fallen, he cried out—"Ah! my poor king, you are down!" Some one having picked it up, and restored it to him in a mutilated state—"Horrid!" he exclaimed; "I certainly do not accept the omen, and I am far from wishing any such thing: my enmity does not extend so far."

I would not, on any account, have omitted this circumstance, trifling as it may appear, because it is in many respects characteristic. We ourselves, when the Emperor had retired, reverted to the incident. What cheerfulness, what freedom of mind in such dreadful circumstances! we said. What serenity in the heart! what absence of malice, irritation, or hatred! Who could discover in him the man whom enmity and falsehood have depicted as such a monster? Even amongst his own followers, who is there that has well understood him, or taken sufficient pains to make him known?

Another evening, the Emperor was speaking of his early years when he was in the artillery, and of his companions at the mess: he always delighted in reverting to those days. One of his messmates was mentioned, who, having been Prefect of the same department under Napoleon and under the King, had not been able to retain his place on the return of Napoleon. The Emperor, when he recollected him, said that this person had, at a certain period, missed the opportunity of making his fortune through him. When Napoleon obtained the command of the army of the interior, he loaded this person with favours, made him his aid-de-camp, and intended to place great confidence in him; but this favoured aid-de-camp had behaved very ill to him at the time of his departure for the army of Italy; he then abandoned his General for the Directory. "Nevertheless," said the Emperor, "when once I was seated on the throne, he might have done much with me, if he had known how to set about it. He had the claim of early friendship, which never loses its influence! I should certainly never have withstood an unexpected overture in a hunting-party, for instance, or half an hour's conversation on old times at any other opportunity. I should have forgotten his conduct: it was no longer important whether he had been on my side or not: I had united all parties. Those who had an insight into my character were well aware of this: they knew that with me, however I might have felt disposed towards them, it was like the game of prison-bars; when once the point was touched, the game was won. In fact, if I wished to withstand them, I had no resource but that of refusing to see them."

He mentioned another old comrade, who, with wit and the requisite qualifications, might have done any thing with him. He also said that a third would never have been removed from him, had he been less rapacious.

We disputed amongst ourselves whether these people ever suspected the secret, or their own chances; and whether the elevated station, and the Imperial splendour of Napoleon, would have allowed of their availing themselves of his favourable disposition towards them.

With respect to the splendour of the Imperial power, the Grand Marshal said, that however great and magnificent the Emperor had appeared to him on the throne, he had never made on him a superior, perhaps an equal impression, to that which his situation at the head of the Army of Italy had stamped on his memory. He explained and justified this idea very successfully, and the Emperor heard him with some complacency.—But, we observed, what great events took place afterwards! what elevation! what grandeur! what renown throughout the world! The Emperor had listened. "For all that," said he, "Paris is so extensive, and contains so many people of all sorts, and some so eccentric, that I can conceive there may be some who never saw me, and others who never even heard my name mentioned. Do not you think so?" And it was curious to see with what whimsical ingenuity he himself maintained this assertion, which he knew to be untenable. We all insisted loudly, that, as to his name, there was not a town or village in Europe, perhaps even in the world, where it had not been pronounced. One person in company added—"Sire, before I returned to France at the treaty of Amiens, your Majesty being then only First Consul, I determined to make a tour in Wales, as one of the most extraordinary parts of Great Britain. I climbed the wildest mountains, some of which are of prodigious height: I visited cabins that seemed to me to belong to another world. As I entered one of these secluded dwellings, I observed to my fellow-traveller, that in this spot, one would expect to find repose, and escape the din of revolution. The cottager, suspecting us to be French, on account of our accent, immediately enquired the news from France, and what *Bonaparte*, the First Consul, was about."

"Sire," said another, "we had the curiosity to ask the Chinese officers whether our European affairs had been heard of in their Empire. 'Certainly,' they replied; 'in a confused manner, to be sure, because we are totally uninterested in those matters; but the name of your Emperor is famous there, and connected with grand ideas of conquest and revolution:' exactly as those who have changed the face of that part of the world have arrived in ours, such as Gengis Khan, Tamerlane," &c.

Political examination of conscience.—Loyalty and prosperity of the Empire.—Liberal ideas of the Emperor on the indifference of parties.—Marmont.—Murat.—Berthier.

27th.—This day the Emperor was walking in the garden with the Grand Marshal and me. The conversation led us to make our political self-examination.

The Emperor said, he had been very warm and sincere at the commencement of the Revolution; that he had cooled by degrees, in proportion as he acquired more just and solid ideas. His patriotism had sunk under the political absurdities & monstrous domestic excesses of our legislatures. Finally, his republican faith had vanished on the violation of the choice of the people, by the Directory, at the time of the battle of Aboukir.

The Grand Marshal said, that for his part, he had never been a republican; but a very warm constitutional, until the 10th of August, the horrors of which day had cured him of all illusion. He had very nearly been massacred in defending the King at the Thuilleries.

As for me, it was notorious that I had begun my career as a pure and most ardent royalist.—"Why, then, it seems, gentlemen," said the Emperor, with vivacity, "that I am the only one amongst us who has been a republican."—"And something more, Sire," Bertrand and I both replied.—"Yes," repeated the Emperor, "republican and patriot."—"And I have been a patriot, Sire," replied one of us, "notwithstanding my royalism; but what is still more extraordinary, I did not become so till the period of the Imperial reign,"—"How! villain!—are you compelled to own that you did not always love your country?"—"Sire, we are making our political self-examination, are we not? I confess my sins. When I returned to Paris, by virtue of your amnesty, could I at first look upon myself as a Frenchman, when every law, every decree, every ordinance that covered the walls, constantly added the most opprobious epithets to my unlucky denomination of Emigrant.—Nor did I think of remaining, when I first arrived. I had been attracted by curiosity, yielding to the invincible influence of one's native land, and the desire of breathing the air of one's country. I now possessed nothing there: I had been compelled, at the frontier, to swear to the relinquishment of my patrimony, to accede to the laws which decreed its loss; and I looked on myself as a mere traveller in that country once mine. I was a true foreigner, discontented, and even malevolent. The empire came; it was a great event. Now," said I, "my manners, prejudices, and principles triumph; the only difference is in the person of the sovereign. When the campaign of Austerlitz opened, my heart, with surprise, found itself once more French. My situation was painful; I felt as if torn limb from limb; I was divided between blind passion and national sentiment: the triumphs of the French army and their general displeased me; yet their defeat would have humbled me. At length, the prodigies of Ulm, and the splendour of Austerlitz, put an end to my embarrassment. I was vanquished by glory. I admired, I acknowledged, I loved Napoleon; and from that moment I became French to enthusiasm. Henceforth I have had no other thoughts, spoken no other language, felt no other sentiments; and here I am by your side."

The Emperor then asked innumerable questions relative to the Emigrants, their numbers, and disposition. I related many curious facts respecting our princes, the Duke of Brunswick, and the King of Prussia. I made him laugh at the extravagance of our presumption, our unbounded confidence of success, the disorder of our affairs, the incapability of our leaders. "Men," said I, really were not at that time what they have since been. Fortunately, those with whom we had to contend were, at first, only our equals in strength. Above all, we thought, and repeated to one another, that an immense majority of the French nation was on our side; and, for my part, I firmly believed it. I soon had, however, an opportunity of being undeceived; when our assemblages having arrived at Verdun, and beyond it, not a single person came to join us; on the contrary, every one fled at our approach. Nevertheless I still believed it, even after my return from England; so greatly did we deceive ourselves afterwards with the absurdities we related to each other. We said, the government rested in a handful of people; that it was maintained by force alone; that it was detested by the nation; and there must be some who have never ceased to think so. I am persuaded that amongst those who now talk in that manner in the Legislative Body, there are some who speak as they think; so perfectly do I recognise the spirit, the ideas, and the expressions of Coblentz."—"But at what period were you undeceived?" said the Emperor.—"Very late, Sire. Even when I rallied, and came to your Court, I was led much more by admiration and sentiment, than by conviction of your strength and durability. However, when I came into your

Council of State, seeing the freedom with which the most decisive decrees were voted, without a single thought of the slightest resistance; seeing around me nothing but conviction and entire persuasion, it then appeared to me, that your power, and the state of affairs, gained strength with a rapidity I could not account for. By pondering on the cause of this change, I at length made a great and important discovery; namely, that matters had long stood thus, but that I had neither known, nor been willing to perceive it; I had hid my head in the bush, lest the light should reach my eyes. Now that I found myself forced into the midst of its brightness, I was dazzled by it. From the moment, all my prejudices fell to the ground; the film was taken off my eyes.

"Being afterwards sent by your majesty on a mission, and having traversed more than sixty departments, I employed the most scrupulous attention, and the most perfect sincerity, in ascertaining the truth of which I had so long doubted. I interrogated the prefects, the inferior authorities, I caused documents and registers to be produced to me; I questioned private individuals without being known to them, I employed all possible means of trying the truth of my conclusions, and I remained fully convinced that the government was completely national, and founded in the will of the people; that France had, at no period of her history, been more powerful, more flourishing, better governed, or more happy; the roads had never been better maintained; agriculture had increased by a tenth, a ninth, perhaps an eighth in its productions.* A restlessness, a general ardour animated all minds to exertion, and inspired them to aim at a daily personal improvement. Indigo was gained; sugar would inevitable be so. Never, at any period, had internal commerce and industry of every species, been carried to such a pitch; instead of four millions of livres in cotton, which were used at the Revolution, more than thirty millions were now manufactured, although we could obtain none by sea, and received it over land from the distance of Constantinople. Rouen was become quite a prodigy in production. The taxes were every where paid; the Conscription was nationalized; France, instead of being exhausted, contained a more numerous population than before, and was daily increasing.

"When I again appeared amongst my former acquaintance with these data, there was an absolute insurrection against me. They laughed in my face, and almost hooted

*It is a singular fact, that the person from whom I had this information o riculture, in Languedoc, was the identical M. de Villele, who has since b celebrated.

me. Yet there were some sensible people amongst them, and I now possessed strong grounds of argument; I staggered many, and convinced a few: thus, I too have had my victories."

The Emperor said, it must be agreed that our being assembled at Saint-Helena from political causes was certainly a most extraordinary circumstance: that we had come to a common centre by roads originally in very different directions. However, we had travelled through them with sincerity. Nothing more clearly proved the sort of chance, the uncertainty, and the fatality which usually, in the labyrinth of revolutions, direct upright and honest hearts.

Nor can any thing more clearly prove, continued he, how necessary indulgence and intelligent views are to recompose society after long disorders. It was these dispositions, and these principles which had made him, he said, the most fit man for the circumstances of the month of *Brumaire*; and it was those which still rendered him without doubt the fittest in the actual state of France. On this point, he had neither mistrust, nor prejudice, nor passion; he had constantly employed men of all classes, of all parties, without ever looking back, without inquiring what they had done, what they had said, what they had thought, only requiring, he said, that they should pursue in future and with sincerity the common object: the welfare and the glory of all; that they should show themselves true and good Frenchmen. Above all, he had never made overtures to leaders in order to gain over parties; but on the contrary, he had attacked the mass of the parties, that he might be in a situation to despise their leaders. Such had ever been the uniform system of his internal policy; and in spite of the last events, he was far from repenting it; if he had to begin again he should pursue the same course. "It is totally without reason," he said, "that I have been reproached with employing nobles and emigrants—a perfectly trite and vulgar imputation! The fact is that under me there only existed individual opinions and sentiments. It is not the nobles and the emigrants who have brought about the restoration, but rather the restoration that has again raised the nobles and the emigrants. They have not contributed more particularly to our ruin than others: those really in fault are the intriguers of all parties and all opinions. Fouché was not a noble; Talleyrand was not an emigrant; Augereau and Marmont were neither. To conclude, do you desire a final proof of the injustice of blaming whole classes, when a revolution like ours has operated in the midst of them? Reckon yourselves here: among four, you find two nobles, one of whom was even an emigrant. The excellent M. de Ségur, in spite of his age, at my departure, offered to follow me. I could multiply examples without end.—It is with as little reason," he continued, "that I have been blamed for having neglected certain persons of influence; I was too powerful not to despise with impunity the intrigues, and the known immorality of the greater part of them. Neither had that any thing to do with my downfall; but only unforeseen and unheard-of catastrophes; compulsory circumstances; 500,000 men at the gates of the capital; a revolution still recent; a crisis too powerful for French heads; and above all, a dynasty not sufficiently ancient. I would have risen again even from the foot of the Pyrenees, could I but have been my own grandson.

"And, moreover, what a fascination there is respecting past times! It is most certain that I was chosen by the French; their new worship was their own work. Well! immediately upon the return of their old forms, see with what facility they have recurred to idols!

"And, after all, how could another line of policy have prevented that which ruined me? I have been betrayed by M . . . . , whom I might call my son, my offspring, my own work; he to whom I had committed my destinies, by sending him to Paris, at the very moment that he was putting the finishing hand to his treason and my ruin. I have been betrayed by Murat, whom I had raised from a soldier to a king; who was my sister's husband. I have been betrayed by Berthier, a mere goose, whom I had converted into a kind of eagle. I have been betrayed in the senate, by those very men of the national party who owe every thing to me. All that, then, did not in any way depend upon my system of internal policy. Undoubtedly I should have been exposed to the charge of too readily employing old enemies, whether nobles or emigrants, if a Macdonald, a Valence,* a Montesquiou had betrayed me; but they were faithful: let them object to me the stupidity of Murat, I can oppose to it the judgment of Marmont. I have, then, no cause to repent of my interior system of policy," &c. &c.

Chance of danger in battle, &c.—The Bulletins very correct.

28th.—The Emperor during dinner was speaking of the probability of danger in the China vessels, of which one in thirty perished, according to the accounts he had received

* One day at Longwood running over the list of the senators who had signed the deposition, one of us pointed out the name of M. de Valence, signed as secretary. But another explained that this signature was false, that M. de Valence had complained of it, and protested against it: "It is very true," said the Emperor, "I know it; he has behaved well; Valence was true to the Nation."

from some captains. This led him to the chances of danger in battle, which he said were less than that. Wagram was pointed out to him as a destructive battle; he did not estimate the killed at more than 3,000, which was only a fiftieth: we were there 160,000. At Essling they were about 4,000, we were 40,000: this was a tenth; but it was one of the most severe battles. The others were incomparably below.

This brought on a conversation on the bulletins. The Emperor declared them to be very correct; assured us, that, excepting what the proximity of the enemy compelled him to disguise, that when they came into their hands they might not derive any information prejudicial to him from them, all the remainder was very exact. At Vienna and throughout Germany they did them more justice than among us. If they had acquired an ill reputation in our armies—if it was a common saying, *as false as a bulletin*, it was personal rivalships, party spirit, that had established it; it was the wounded self-love of those whom it had been forgotten to mention in them, and who had, or fancied they had, a right to a place there; and still more than all, our ridiculous national defect of having no greater enemies to our successes and our glory, than we ourselves were.

The Emperor after dinner played some games at chess. The day had been very rainy; he was unwell, and retired early.

Unhealthiness of the Island.

29th.—The weather was still bad; it was impossible to set foot out of doors. The rain and the damp invaded our pasteboard apartments. Every one of us suffered in his health in consequence. The temperature here is certainly mild, but the climate is among the most unwholesome. It is a thing ascertained in the island, that few there attain the age of fifty; hardly any that of sixty. Add to this, exclusion from the rest of the world, physical privations, bad moral treatment, it will result, that prisons in Europe are far preferable to liberty in Saint-Helena.

About four o'clock several Captains from China were brought to me, who were to be presented to the Emperor. They had an opportunity of seeing the smallness, the dampness, and bad state of my habitation. They inquired how the Emperor found himself in point of health. It declined visibly, I told them. Never do we hear a complaint from him: his great soul suffered nothing to overcome it, and even contributed to deceive him with respect to his own state; but we could see him decay very perceptibly. I led them shortly after to the Emperor, who was walking in the garden. He seemed to me at that moment more disordered than usual. He dismissed them in half an hour. He went in again, and took a bath.

Before and after dinner he seemed in low spirits and in pain. He began to read to us *Les Femmes Savantes;* but at the second act, he handed the book to the Grand Marshal, and dozed upon the sofa during the reading of the remainder.

Remarks of the Emperor on his expedition in the East.

30th—31st.—This day the weather has continued very bad; we all suffered from it; besides, we are absolutely infested with rats, fleas, and bugs: our sleep is disturbed by them, so that the troubles by night are in perfect harmony with those by day.

The weather changed entirely to fair on the 31st; we went out in the carriage. The Emperor, in the course of conversation, observed, speaking of Egypt and Syria, that if he had taken Saint Jean-d'Acre, as ought to have been the case, he would have wrought a revolution in the East. "The most trivial circumstances," said he, "lead to the greatest events. The weakness of the captain of a frigate, who stood out to sea instead of forcing a passage into the harbour, some trifling impediments with respect to some shallops or light vessels, prevented the face of the world from being changed. Possessed of Saint Jean-d'Acre, the French army would fly to Damascus and Aleppo; in a twinkling it would have been on the Euphrates; the Christians of Syria, the Druses, the Christians of Armenia, would have joined it; nations were on the point of being shaken." One of us having said that they would have presently been reinforced with 400,000 men. "Say 600,000," replied the Emperor; "who can calculate what it might have been? I should have reached Constantinople and the Indies; I should have changed the face of the world."

SUMMARY OF THE LAST NINE MONTHS.

Nine months have already elapsed from the commencement of my Journal; and I fear, that amid the heterogeneous matters that succeed without order in it, I may have often lost sight of my principal, my only object—that which concerns Napoleon, and may serve to characterize him. It is to make up for this, where necessary, that I here attempt a summary in a few words; a summary which I propose moreover, on the same account, to repeat, in future, at intervals of three months.

On quitting France, we remained for a month at the disposal of the brutal and ferocious English Ministry; then our passage to Saint-Helena occupied three months.

On our landing we occupied Briars nearly two months.

Lastly, we have been three months at Longwood.

Now, these nine months would have formed four very distinct epochs, with one who had taken the pains to observe Napoleon.

All the time of our stay at Plymouth, Napoleon remained thoughtful, and merely passive, exerting no power but patience. His misfortunes were so great, and so incapable of remedy, that he suffered events to take their course with a stoical indifference.

During the whole of our passage, he constantly possessed a perfect equanimity, and, above all, the most complete indifference; he expressed no wish, showed no disappointment. It is true, the greatest respect was paid him; he received it without perceiving it; he spoke little, and the subject was always foreign to himself. Any one who, coming suddenly on board, had witnessed his conversation, would undoubtedly have been far from guessing with whom they were in company: it was not the Emperor. I cannot better picture him in this circumstance, than by comparing him to those passengers of high distinction, who are conveyed with great respect to their destination.

Our abode at Briars presented another shade of difference. Napoleon, left almost entirely to himself, receiving nobody, constantly employed, seeming to forget events and men, enjoyed, apparently, the calm and the peace of a profound solitude; either from abstraction or contempt, not condescending to notice the inconveniencies or privations with which he was surrounded; if he now and then dropped an expression relative to them, it was only when roused by the importunity of some Englishman, or excited by the recital of the outrages his attendants suffered. His whole day was occupied in dictation; the rest of the time dedicated to the relaxation of familiar conversation. He never mentioned the affairs of Europe; spoke rarely of the Empire, very little of the Consulate; but much of his situation as General in Italy; still more, and almost constantly, of the minutest details of his childhood and his early youth. The latter subjects, especially, seemed at this time to have a peculiar charm with him. One would have said that they afforded him a perfect oblivion; they excited him even to gaiety. It was almost exclusively with these objects that he employed the many hours of his nightly walks by moonlight.

Finally, our establishment at Longwood was a fourth and last change. All our situations hitherto had been but short and transitory. This was fixed, and threatened to be lasting. There, in reality, were to commence our exile and our new destinies. History will take them up there; there the eyes of the world were to be directed to consider us. The Emperor, seeming to make this calculation, regulates all about him, and takes the attitude of dignity oppressed by power; he traces around him a moral boundary, behind which he defends himself inch by inch against indignity and insult; he no longer compromises any thing with his persecutors; he shows himself sensibly jealous in respect to forms, hostile to all encroachment. The English never doubted that habit would, in the end, produce formality. The Emperor brings them to it from the first day, and the most profound respect is manifested.

It was no small surprise to us, nor a slight satisfaction, to have to observe among ourselves, that, without knowing how or why, it was nevertheless perceptible that the Emperor now stood higher in the opinion and the respect of the English, than he had hitherto done; we could even perceive that this sentiment was every day increasing. With us the Emperor entered fully into an examination of the affairs of Europe. He analyzed the projects and the conduct of the Sovereigns; he compared them with his own; weighed, separated, spoke of his reign, of his deeds; in a word, we once more found the Emperor, and *all* Napoleon. Not that he had ever ceased to be so for an instant, as regarded our devotion and our attentions; nor that we, on our side, had any thing to endure.

Never did we experience a more even temper, a more constant kindness, a more unaltered affection. It was, in fact, among us, and in the most familiar manner, that he concerted his attacks upon the common enemy; and those which appear the most vigorous, and seemed to be dictated by anger, so far from it, were almost always accompanied with some laughter or pleasantry.

The Emperor's health, during the six months preceding our establishment at Longwood, did not seem to undergo any change; notwithstanding his regimen was so completely altered. His hours, his food, were no longer the same; his habits were completely deranged. Though accustomed to so much exercise, he had been confined all this time to a room. Bathing had become a part of his existence, and he was constantly deprived of it, &c. It was not till after his arrival at Longwood, and when he was again supplied with some of these things, when he rode on horseback, and returned to the use of the bath, that we began to perceive a sensible alteration.

It is a singular circumstance, that so long as he was ill situated, he suffered nothing; it was not till he was better, that he was seen to be in pain. May it not be that, in moral as in physical order, there is often a long interval between causes and their effects.

REFERENCE

TO THE NAMES OF

DISTINGUISHED INDIVIDUALS,

MENTIONED IN THE FIRST VOLUME.

REFERENCE &c.

CONTENTS

OF THE

FIRST VOLUME.

RESIDENCE AT BRIARS.

ESTABLISHMENT AT LONGWOOD.

END OF THE FIRST VOLUME.

Spotted something that isn't quite right?

Let us know and we'll fix it for future reprints.
And as a thank you for your diligence, we'll
send you a free Sothis book of your choice.

publisher@sothis.press

This page intentionally left blank

Printed in Great Britain
by Amazon

46266813R00229